THE
NEEDLE-
WATCHER

THE
NEEDLE-
WATCHER

THE NEEDLE-WATCHER

The Will Adams Story
British Samurai

by
RICHARD BLACKER

CHARLES E. TUTTLE COMPANY
Rutland, Vermont & Tokyo, Japan

Representatives

Continental Europe: Boxerbooks, Inc., *Zurich*

British Isles: Prentice-Hall International, Inc., *London*

Australasia: Book Wise (Australia) Pty. Ltd.
104-108 Sussex Street, Sydney 2000

Published by the Charles E. Tuttle Company, Inc.
of Rutland, Vermont & Tokyo, Japan
with editorial offices at
Suido 1-chome, 2-6, Bunkyo-ku, Tokyo, Japan

© *1973 by Charles E. Tuttle Co., Inc.*

Library of Congress Catalog Card No. 72-89743

International Standard Book No. 0-8048-1094-X

First edition, 1932 by
William Heinemann Ltd., London
First Tuttle edition, 1973
Sixth printing, 1983

Tokyo 3/7/85

PRINTED IN JAPAN

To

Roy E. B. Bower

who also lies abroad for his country

TABLE OF CONTENTS

vii

PUBLISHER'S FOREWORD

The Needle-Watcher was first published in 1932 and quickly attracted the attention of discerning critics, who commended it not only for the excellence of its writing but also for its remarkable re-creation of early-seventeenth-century Japan, which was then little known to the West. It seems only fair that this fascinating novel should once again be made available to the general reader, particularly in a time when interest in Japan has become world-wide.

The book reconstructs the story of Will Adams, a native of Gillingham, in Kent, England, who voyaged to Japan at the beginning of the seventeenth century. His knowledge of seafaring vessels at the time causes him to be taken into the favor of the first Tokugawa shogun, Ieyasu, and eventually to become recognized as the founder of the Japanese navy. It is a thoroughly absorbing tale, perhaps sometimes incredible but always true to the known historical facts.

Adams was one of the most picturesque and daring of Britain's maritime traders, and this depiction of him as the first Englishman to settle in what was then a hostile land is written not only with distinction but also with an imaginative grasp that takes it right out of the class of the ordinary historical novel. It is an epic tale of strange adventures, and it creates an atmosphere of rare and haunting quality. In its understanding of the Japanese mind it is hardly less than superb.

Will Adams died in Japan in 1620 and is buried at Yokosuka. Every year a ceremony is still held to commemorate the anniversary of his death. There is also a memorial to him at Ito, in Shizuoka Prefecture, as well as one at his birthplace in England.

It is a pleasure indeed to bring this splendid novel once again to the attention of discriminating readers—especially to readers with an intelligent interest in Japan and its history.

PART I

1600

CHAPTER I

To the fourteen men who beheld it, the scene presented neither beauty nor any other thrill. The eyes of a dozen of them were dulled by habitude, for they were natives—four soldiers and the eight coolies who had carried the visitors over the ten miles of road from Sakai to Osaka.

The two visitors themselves looked upon the sight as they would have looked upon any sight in that world of glare and shadow; or upon no sight at all. Their wits were still astray with fever, their skins broken with sores, their sinews all slack. Rocks of granite hewn into giant ingots and piled into a crag that was a castle meant nothing to them; of no great interest for men so weary were the low battlements encircling the crag, and the glimmer, before the battlements, of the great moat with its rafts of tangled lotus.

A new and peculiar avenue began to flank the road some distance ahead of them. It was of trees that appeared to be not trees at all, but timbers stuck in the ground. They were leafless and branchless, yet with other timbers projecting from them, and upon the projecting cross-timbers were lesser projections and lumps and small festoons. Over them there circled, and upon them squatted, birds.

The visitors took their seats again upon the woven reeds slung to bamboo poles; and the coolies, still chewing morsels of their sudden snack, shouldered them.

A soldier nodded his canopy of straw hat and the procession took the road again.

The stomachs within the visitors still had a sensibility in their haggard emptiness; for it was the movement of their stomachs that led their eyes to discover that the avenue, now on either hand of them, was of squat wooden crosses. Their design was unfamiliar to eyes accustomed to the Holy Pictures of Europe, for they were like the letter H turned on its side and raised a little above the ground on a single stump. Arms and fragments of arms were still held to the upper transverse

3

timbers by lappings of festering cord; upon the lower ones were smears and gobbets of feet once small and shapely.

The Englishman in the hammock on one pole and the Dutchman in the hammock behind him said no word. Their grunts were weary oaths addressed nowhere, produced by the retching of their stomachs as much as by any movement of their brains.

Their bearers, shoulders hunched to the poles whereon their meagre hammocks were slung, spat and trotted on.

A grunt was all that the scene and the stench of it could produce in the throat of Adams, from Gillingham in Kent, on that afternoon of April in the year 1600. For he knew that an end, of one sort or another, was due. He was an old man, spent and infirm; his age was thirty-six.

The Dutchman, as jaded and as broken as himself, was ten years younger.

It was but two years before that they had been young and lusty seamen. For the English seaman of those days—unless he was, happily, the champion-elect of financiers—the only living to be picked up was on coasting-freighters or on privateersmen in the Narrow Seas on the look-out for Hollanders with grain for Lisbon.

For Hollanders the profession was in better sort, since the Flemish seaman in those years had not the Englishman's dearth of sea. As the underling of Spain he had sailed both east and west. Then if he settled down to a quieter life as mariner or master, he came to the Thames with grain cargezoned to London; or as a prisoner with the prize of grain cargezoned to Lisbon. He had, in either event, told his yarns and made his friends in the taverns of Rotherhithe and Deptford. Desertions from his crew would give him room for an Englishman or two on board his carrack for the return, and would leave polyglot loafers to brag or grumble among the loafers of the Thames and Medway.

The Netherlands' revolt from Spain opened the Dutch ports to Englishmen; and it also left the Dutchman's carrack with no safe and sure destination but England. The waterside gossip of Rotterdam became the gossip of the Thames.

In September of 1597 Melchior van Santvoort, purser of a

carrack with grain for Gravesend, was able to tell a tale that won the attention of even so good a sceptic as Timothy Shotten; and Shotten told it to young Will Adams.

Shotten, like Adams, was a pilot and navigator by profession and he had done many things to make a living. He knew the talk of Dutchmen, from campaigning and from captivity among them.

He knew van Santvoort to be a young man of sense; for Shotten had served earlier as master of a fly-boat in Frobisher's meagre patrol of the Straits. Twice, before the Netherlands' revolt, he had cut out a carrack on which Santvoort was purser. Shotten knew, each time, that if he had had the master of the carrack to deal with he could have bluffed and browbeaten out of him the bills of lading on Lisbon that would have made him a prize; but each time the young purser, Santvoort, ambled up and told a tale with a twinkle under one slightly drooped eyelid, of contrary winds and lost bearings, and produced a set of papers in perfect order which showed his carrack to be bound not for Lisbon but for the Thames.

Santvoort was, thereafter, a man to whom Shotten was prepared to listen; and he told in September of 1597 of the return to Rotterdam of ships that had left it two years before for the Spice Islands. They had run the blockade of Spaniards and Portuguese in the Eastern Seas and had rendered a return to the sober merchants who had sent them forth, of two crowns for one.

But Santvoort, the eyelid drooping again as he savoured the liquor in the Gravesend tavern, had more to tell than of things already done. He knew of work that was still ahead for men who were workless; and such men were Shotten himself and his friend Will Adams—trained navigators driven to any shift of gang-supervising or stevedoring for the groats of bare subsistence for themselves and their wives and children.

Santvoort had friends and solid relatives in counting-houses and store-rooms in Rotterdam. A return of two for one was good enough dividend, even if it had been spread over two years. The Zuider Zee was full of ships, the wharves and taverns full of men to sail them. The anxiety of the merchants was not for ships and men, therefore, but for the right ones.

Behind Santvoort was an uncle with a purse to be thrown, with other purses, into a new adventure; and this uncle had a sound opinion of Santvoort himself. They had seamen enough among the swashbucklers from the dismantled garrisons. What they wanted most was pilots.

Santvoort talked of these things even more slowly than was his habit, lest his English friends and hosts over the bottle should miss a word; for both of them were known pilots. With all due allowances made for the liquor, he had reason for his well-wishing towards Shotten; Shotten had dealt with him fairly in the old blockade-running days. In his well-wishing towards the younger man and new acquaintance, Adams, there was no reason at all.

It was simply that he liked him; and five minutes of half-understood conversation were enough to discover that Adams, too, was unemployed—a seaman with a wife and children at Gillingham, but without a sea.

For Adams there followed eight months of some anxiety whether he should get this job through the offices of the friendly young Dutchman. In the end he did get it—after shipping across to Rotterdam and back again in a dozen paltry berths.

In June of 1598 the adventure was ready and five carracks sailed out of the Zuider Zee for the Indies. Shotten and Adams were both aboard—Shotten in the flagship of the Admiral of the fleet and Adams pilot-major of the *Liefde*.

The influence of Santvoort had gone further than giving Adams his post; it had shipped Adams's young brother also on the *Liefde* as a mariner.

Within a year of sailing the brother had been killed in an ambush by islanders off the coast of Peru. Shotten, with the admiral, was lost in "a wondrous storm of wind, with much rain."

The friends left to Adams were the new ones made among a crew of a hundred and twenty men in a vessel eighty to a hundred feet long. Of the five ships only the *Liefde* was still afloat.

When she sighted Japan after two years at sea, only twenty-four men of her crew were still alive; and of the twenty-four only Adams and Santvoort and five others could stand upon their feet.

For five months she had ridden the Pacific with Adams seeking "the Northern Cape of the Island of Japon in a height of thirty degrees." He found it not—"by reason that it lay falce in all charts and globes and maps."

Dismasted; with a jury-rig of whatever spars and rags and tackle the invalids could drag from sodden lockers to splice together and bend and hoist; with a rudder that squeaked and wagged at its gudgeons, she tottered at last into the calm of Bungo-nada, between Shikoku and Kiushiu.

Her timbers still held together. Enough pitch remained in her seams to make of pumping a task possible for a team of scarecrows. She still, in a manner, answered the helm—and so the scarecrows had dragged aside a half-world and flung it behind them and arrived at the "Island of Japon" which Lintschoten's map had shown them, falsely, to lie in the thirtieth degree of latitude.

They were not yet ashore, but they were as near as made no difference.

Adams was in command; for the captain was a skeleton below, moaning and gurgling in a skin of verminous parchment.

It was the pilot himself who went forward with the top-mawl and struck out the wedge that let the anchor fall. It fell fair, symbolical of their victory and their surrender.

The effectives mustered, seven scarecrows about the main-mast's stump, to watch countless specks growing out of the blur of land that lay on the water; but they exchanged no word. A thought of the *Liefde's* armament would have been an ironic jest. The gun-ports had been stoutly battened in the crew's lustier days against lusty seas, and no gunner was among the survivors. A day's work of the whole seven might have found in the powder-magazine a single pistol-charge that was not a damp paste. As for pikes or cutlasses—the single swing of the mawl had left Adams panting for breath.

They watched the specks, and said nothing. When the specks were a mob of peculiar skiffs made fast to the *Liefde's* sides and grappled to one another, they still said nothing. Their old world was dragged aside and flung behind. To criticise the new one they had no wits; to resist it they had no strength.

Little men were aboard, swarming all over the ship; nimble, chattering, and most amiably smiling. Adams and Santvoort and the others stood and watched things go—upon the shoulders and in the hands of the nimble little men. Charts and globes and maps went; instruments, and whatever was left of the carpenter's and sailmaker's tools. The pictures went from the cuddy and the saloon.

Apathetically Adams showed a man how the hawser was wound upon the capstan, to prevent his cutting the cable and losing the newly-dropped anchor.

Oars splashed in the din, and the *Liefde* was atow westward to the harbour. Still the seven said no word, for their destinies had passed from their own hands to the hands of the palely swarthy little men in the boats who chattered and smiled and towed them to the shore and did not—for some reason—kill them.

CHAPTER II

ASHORE it was the same. They were lodged in a house where three died the day after landing. The remainder had "all refreshing that was needful."

Requirements were fulfilled—food and drink and shelter; and sleep.

Three more died; but the wonder was—if there was any wonder at all—that they had not died before.

Then a priest arrived from Nagasaki, a Portuguese. He conversed with the convalescents in Dutch. Adams and van Santvoort commented upon him in English, cursing him and knowing him at once for an enemy. Here some faint impulse towards effort of the old sort might have stirred within them— some fresh glimmer of the old illusion that destiny was still theirs to man-handle in one direction or another. But the glimmer was soon extinguished and the illusion gone. They were not even men any more, but only the husks of men, parched and empty; and they were utterly prisoned. Their only door was the padre from Nagasaki. Through him, and him alone, could thoughts escape from them to the genial little men who smiled; only through him could there be any meaning in the answer of smiling chatter. Through this door the only meaning that came was softly spoken, but it was grim and sinister. . . . Infidels and rebels; pirates, thieves trapped through the merciful justice of Almighty God at their thieving; sorry scavengers of the seas driven by their fever and their sins to seek a haven among just and righteous men baptised in the true faith. (For there were converts with the padre, a small retinue of Japanese brothers with tonsured heads who could understand Portuguese and a little Spanish, but neither Dutch nor English.)

The brothers and the padre sought the conversion of the invalids; and van Santvoort sprawling in his thoughts as he sprawled in his gait told them (in Spanish, that the words might get beyond the padre to his brethren) that they might

9

go seek it in hell. It did not seem to him that an insult or a
rudeness one way or the other could make much difference to
anyone.

Pirates; robbers. . . . In their mute helplessness they had
nought to do but look from under the low eaves of the house to
the water where the battered and stripped *Liefde* was careened,
to the distant mountains of Iyo that stood out of the haze into
the pallor of the dawn, and at the great cliff that flung the bay
into the shadow of the setting sun.

Pressing most upon the mind of Adams, while Santvoort
and the padre bickered, was his quarrel with the maps and
charts and globes; his suspicion, that was now a dead certainty,
of their error. The padre would do nothing to help him in the
getting and setting down of solid evidence. He would make no
move whatever towards salving the pilot's books from the ship
or recovering his instruments from the fishermen who had
filched them. He only mumbled of salvation, of sea-robbers and
spies; and went off, one hand caressing the other in the sleeves
of his cassock.

Adams did what he could with sticks and string and pegs
whittled from a piece of bamboo. With the sticks he fixed
bearings from the moon to the fore- and hind-guards of the
Little Bear. When the shadow of the house's eaves began to
veer outwards again from the steps, his sticks were fixed at the
angle between the sun and the horizon. With his string he
drew a circle on the floor. He divided up its circumference, and
with this protractor he measured the angles recorded by his
sticks.

Good luck and vanity had kept one of his possessions in his
breeches pocket instead of among the instruments in the
cabin—a pocket compass mounted in a case of ebony and
tortoise-shell. His *Regiment of the Pole Star* and his book of
Seaman's Secrets would have saved him immense excogitations
and calculations from half-forgotten formulæ. It would have
saved him, perhaps, from entertaining, with his busy doings,
the men and women who passed through the house, smiling and
always chattering. They were the servants detailed at the
Daimio's orders to take care of the foreigners. They were also
relatives of the servants; friends of the relatives; friends and

relatives of the servants' friends. For them Adams was distinguished from the other hairy convalescents by his sticks, his pegs and his string; by his head bent over his calculations and over the compass set on the balustrade of the porch.

Already he stood out from the indistinguishable others who did nothing but lie, or sit or stand—according to the varying states of their distempers—and stare.

Adams, alone among them, had a name. Already they called him Anjin; Pilot; Contemplator, *savant*—or watcher—of the Needle.

The busyness of Adams had little interest for van Santvoort. For him it made little consequence whether the charts had been right or wrong in showing Japan to lie southward of thirty degrees. He looked only at facts accomplished. There they were, he and Adams and the others. There, also, charts or no charts, was Japan. Survival itself exceeded his expectations and he had done nothing towards its achievement. He had merely held the ship's food in his stomach, in the last weeks of the voyage, better than most of the others and had drawn more nourishment from it to his arms and his legs. He had lounged and stood and lain within earshot and hands' reach of the Englishman, doing and getting done whatever he was told, hoping for nothing in particular when any hope at all would have been a fantasy; expecting whatever came. Now that Adams had no use for the Dutchman's weight on a rope or a pump-handle the Dutchman found himself at an end.

Adams, too, came to an end. He could take his Bible oath that the chart was wrong, but at that he had to leave it. Only his books, his cross-staff and his globes could tell him the full and exact truth; and between his books, his instruments and himself stood the padre. So he, too, began to take van Santvoort's view, and fewer words were spoken as they sat or lay in the shadow of their room looking across the bay at the sharp hills and beyond them to more hills that rose mistily into the sky with the shape of limbs and breasts; and they looked at the women with the stature of children, who came and went about them. They were fragrant with the scent of distant flowers and they moved and looked unhumanly like dolls and strange puppets.

In the old life that they had left behind them it had been possible to take some kind of action about things in general—about, for example, the smiles of playful women. In this new life—if, indeed, it could be considered life at all, so fantastic was all the furniture of it and so problematic its duration—they could do nothing and they were at a dead end.

When an envoy arrived in the Bay with a despatch from the Shogun who ruled Japan, the padre said, "The Emperor has heard of you. You are to go before him." It was to the room in general that he said it; but it was Adams and Santvoort only who went—Adams for the simple reason that he was fit and as ready to go as anyone, and Santvoort because the summons was for two.

"Do you go with us?" Adams asked the priest.

"No," he answered. "I am but a priest of God; I stay here."

Their departure was without omen. The good-byes and God-speeds of the sixteen whom they left behind were little more than monosyllables grunted out of the apathy of their distemper. The sixteen saw, no doubt, that the destinies of Adams and Santvoort were at vague hazard. But they had been at hazard for two years now and the sixteen had immediate hazards of their own—the fever in their limbs and the tremor in their bowels. The *Liefde's* captain was now Admiral of the whole adventure; but he, lying on his mat, gave no formality to the investiture of Adams' with powers plenipotentiary.

"The Portingall?" was all he said, looking at the padre's back. "Does he go with you?"

"No," said Adams, "he stays."

As they went down the steps, the priest said, "—Justice in this land is very straight. Repent——"

"I repent already," snorted the Dutchman, "that my knife was idle at my belt before they took it from me." He spat and they walked on, down the hill.

It was a stiff and rough descent for legs still unsure in sea-boots that had stiffened with the brine dried into them. In less than half a mile they sat down by the roadside and pulled off the boots. Their happy retinue of men and women clustered about them to look and to marvel upon the hair on their calves.

The appearance, out of the crowd, of men with sword-hilts protruding from their girdles set the marvellers back a few yards without causing them to abate their marvelling. Some natural clown from the crowd came forward with straw sandals, and a peal of laughter recognized his jape; for one hairy foot of either sailor could have been laid upon both sandals to conceal them utterly from view.

The soldiers, however, were bent upon business. One of them shouted into the crowd and the bamboo poles were produced with the plaited seats slung upon them. Adams and Santvoort gratefully sat and rested their beards on their arms folded over their poles. Their boots they never saw again.

At a pier in the harbour they found the galleys that carried them over the Inland Sea to Sakai.

With a shrug of his shoulders the soldier in command of the party allowed both prisoners to be taken aboard the same galley; unarmed, unshod, grey-visaged in the shabby tangle of their beards, they presented no great menace to the half-dozen swordsmen who accompanied them.

The casual retinue that had followed them from the house followed them still, till the staves of petty officials and the poles of boatmen knocked them and pushed them into the solidity of a mob that chattered its farewells to the Old Hairy Ones—An-jin and the Other.

The Old Hairy Ones, for their part, removed the great straw hats which hospitality had thrust upon their heads, and sat down under the galley's awning.

Their suspension in the vacuum between two worlds was now complete. Stout and lusty Protestants both, they meditated, no doubt, upon the wrath of God and His Infinite Mercy; for it was all they had on the asset side. It was valuable in that it would serve them in either event; whether, that is to say, they lived or died.

This question, for the twenty days of their passage of the Inland Sea, appeared to them as an open one, save only for the sinister shadow of the padre. He alone, it seemed, in all that country had known not how to smile.

CHAPTER III

At Sakai they landed, and took the road again. After ten miles of it, when their bowels, despite the steadiness of their gazing eyes, faintly shook at the message from the crosses, they thought again of the padre. His talk, they saw, had not been empty when he had talked of death for Pirates and Robbers and Enemies to the Majesty of Japan. Death, which was that whole rotting avenue, was wide enough to embrace more than the malefactors specified by the priest. It was wide enough to embrace just and unjust alike; wide as storm or pestilence. They were nauseated, but not afraid; and this simply because fear was a thing forgotten. They saw the odds and accepted them. Besides this, their minds were static, numbed by the immense fact that of a whole world they had come to the end.

Of the city of Osaka Captain John Saris had a good deal to say thirteen years later; but Saris, so far from being at the dead end of any world, was at the well-omened beginning of a new one. There was a caparisoned horse at his disposal, a halberdier by way of personal body-guard. There was, too, another Englishman with him who made of his journey a great matter, an affair of comfort and of consequence.

"We found Osaka," says this Saris, "to be a very great Towne, as great as London within the walls, with many faire Timber bridges of a great height, serving to passe ower a river there as wide as the Thames at London . . . hauing a castle in it, maruellous large and strong, with very deepe trenches about it, with many drawe bridges, with gates plated with iron. The Castle is built all off Freestone, with Bulwarks and Battlements, with loop-holes for small shot and arrows, and divers passages to cast stones upon the assaylants. The walls are at the least sixe or seven yards thicke . . ."

It was through a postern in the inmost of these same walls that Adams and Santvoort were carried to an outhouse in the castle yard. Within minutes they were at ease, reclining in a great tub of hot water. The bulky pocket-compass that had spent some years in Adams' breeches-pocket was now on a cord around his neck. At a small tub a few yards from them their shirts and breeches were being scrubbed and whacked.

The warm water, the cool shade of afternoon, the fact that nimbly living men again outnumbered corpses and gobbets of flesh adhering to crosses reduced the two to the frame of mind wherein curious ceremonial is accepted as normal routine.

From the bath they went to mats whereon blind men gently pounded and kneaded and massaged their spent muscles. Other men with sharply shining blades in their hands approached them. They did not cut their throats, but clipped their hair and shaved their faces. Others again gave them millet-broth and rice. Thereafter they lay upon the mats, with roughly-woven coverlets, and slept.

At twilight they were roused and before them were their dried shirts and breeches. The scouring at the tub had brought back some of the old lustre to codpieces that had flaunted, in another world, virility. Straw sandals had been plaited for them that were not a jest, but fitted their feet.

Bare-shanked—for hose were things of the past—and bare-headed, for it was now evening, they walked among soldiers towards "the great King of the land."

The court, Adams himself noticed at the time, was "a wonderful costly house, gilded with gold in aboundance." He had learned from the soldiers, the boatmen and the bearers the name by which he was known; so that when someone in the chamber said "An-jin" he stood forward in the Presence.

Before him, in the light of suspended lanterns, on a low cushioned divan, sat Tokugawa Ieyasu. Adams saw him first as a robe of simple magnificence draped upon a lithe body, hands folded upon feet in white socks below two long sword-hilts. The head was shaved, to make of the face a smooth mask that extended from the chin to the extreme top of the cranium. The lips were parted in a faint smile—not the smile of the whole nation that clicked and twinkled upon every passing triviality, but the smile of a sage that hovered, immobile, about the contemplation of a dream. The eyes looked out upon Adams with the nation's alert interest in whatever new thing was brought before them, but behind this bright glint was a shadow also; and the shadow swallowed into its unfathomable depths whatever lively image the glint and sparkle brought to it.

Soldier to the extent of nimble wrestler and swordsman-acrobat; philosopher, statesman, economist and dreamer; man of no fear, no mercy, no hate—Ieyasu, sitting on his low divan in the lantern-light, had troubles enough of his own as he looked out, through the depths of his dream, upon his latest prisoners.

What he saw was a large, cumbersome frame in a newly-patched, newly-washed shirt and coarse, threadbare breeches. It was not poised lightly and easily as the bodies to which his sight was accustomed, but was planted clumsily over slightly splayed, prodigiously hairy shanks and wide feet. Forearms, again prodigiously hairy, were folded across the chest, and above them, between the flaps of the open shirt, in a tangle of brown hair like the pelt of a young fox, hung the execrable workmanship in ebony and tortoise-shell, of Adams' compass-case. Youth had been restored to the pilot's face by the meticulous shaving of it, and by the clipping that had set the hair standing upright on his head. He appeared, in the soft light of the lanterns, instead of a battered and spent seaman of thirty-six, more like a sick young man of twenty-five or thirty.

The eyes of the two met and for a few moments were engaged in scrutiny. Adams looked into eyes that saw more than any other two eyes in that, or perhaps any, country. And they, in their turn, looked upon and recognised—a possibility.

"An-jin . . ." The Shogun mused aloud.

Adams had no thought wherewith to answer the thoughtful summons, if summons it was. Instead of thought he made a gesture. He slipped the cord necklace over his head, stepped forward and held it out with the clumsy pendant compass, to Ieyasu.

The Shogun took it from him.

Adams stepped back, stripped of his last possession—for his shirt and his breeches were no more a worldly possession than the skin on his back or the hair on his chest.

The gesture may have been a happy fluke that counted for

much by virtue of its symbolic value. It was a gift, given with obvious freedom and spontaneity; it was useless enough to Adams now between walls of freestone six or seven yards thick with an avenue of corpses beyond. It was the only articulate answer he had to the speaking of his name—Pilot.

Ieyasu spoke to one who stood beside him. The man left them and returned immediately with a silk coat which he held, for Adams to thrust his arms into the loose sleeves. A second coat was handed by the bearer to Santvoort where he stood behind Adams.

So far none but the Shogun had spoken, so that speech seemed to be a thing of the past and neither Adams nor Santvoort uttered either thanks or comment.

From their dull and despondent apathy this movement and pantomime braced them into a moment of suspense. But the faces about them were impassive as ever. Impassive was Ieyasu with his smile; impassive the guards at the door; impassive the coat-bringer, impassive the man who had sat or stood within sword's thrust of them for every moment that they had been within the walls. Nothing, from the impassivity of them all, was likely to happen. And nothing did happen.

A nod from the Shogun on his divan produced a movement and a beckoning from their attendant. Adams and Santvoort turned, in their new coats, to follow him out. Before they went, however, the eye of Adams again met the eye of Ieyasu.

In their outhouse they sat and talked, while within a yard of them was their attendant, nimble as a leopard and still as an image. His presence was the presence of two swords girded to a power like the power lurking in a cloud that can split the stillness of the sky with a blade of lightning.

They talked though there was still nothing, or next to nothing, that they could say.

Adams mentioned the rich gilding of the audience chamber, the bronze and silver-work of the lanterns. They examined their coats. Adams's was the better one. They agreed that there was a general friendliness in the atmosphere; that the things on and about the crosses had been, probably, only scamps and utter rascals. They had seen no skin that was white in all the festering garbage. They wished to God that they could have spoken in the gibberish of Japan; or they wished again that someone could have come to them through the doorway of their good Dutch or indifferent Portuguese or Spanish—someone other than the sinister padre.

"Perhaps he will come," Santvoort suggested.

"Perhaps," said Adams.

"We might kill him," was the Dutchman's next suggestion.

They looked at their attendant—hands tucked into voluminous sleeves half a dozen inches from sword-hilts.

"Perhaps," said Adams.

A menial brought them food again; broth and rice and shreds of fish. They ate and then slept.

When they awoke in the morning, before they had exchanged a word, a man raised himself from squatting and went out. His place was immediately taken by their regular escort. He accompanied them to the bath and sat beside them afterwards while they sunned themselves. Even their very fair sense of well-being after their weeks of malaise scarcely opened up talk between them. If they had known anything at all they could have talked equally whether their knowledge had been of doom, or of harmlessness, or of a dog's chance between the two. But they knew nothing—except, possibly, that all the others knew something which they could not tell; the Emperor and the silent, wakeful men about him and the inscrutable escort who never left them while they woke.

Speculation could lead them nowhere.

"You would not think," Adams ventured, "that they would give us handsome coats to kill us in."

Santvoort shrugged his Dutch shoulders. "You would not think," he said, "that a man would shake hands with himself in greeting of another. Yet these men do it."

"In a latitude of thirty," Adams said later, "it would be hotter than this."

"In the latitude of hell," said Santvoort, "it would be hotter still."

The thought led no further.

"The coats, Melchior," said Adams. "The coats are a good sign."

When they had eaten breakfast their escort rose and indicated their sandals, and beckoned them towards the courtyard again. His sign towards their coats, lying on their mats, may have been meant to inform them only that they were going again to the presence whence the coats had come. Adams, however, said: "Aye; we'll wear our coats."

They were dizzied for some moments in the soft light of the chamber. They made clumsy obeisance in the direction of the divan before they exclaimed aloud, "God's body!" and "Hell's damnation!" and stopped in their breathing; for beside the divan, with his thumbs stuck in his girdle, his head and shoulders peculiarly contracted in sly humility, was the Nagasaki priest.

He, too, for a moment was shaken. He saw young men shaved and clipped and kempt and natty in silk jackets where he had expected ragged castaways.

The padre's smile was not as the smile of the others. His eyes shifted and shot from Adams to Santvoort and the guards and attendants, and slid, sidelong, to Ieyasu.

The Shogun did not give him so much as a glance.

As though reading the pages of a deep and difficult book he kept the focus of his eyes and of his smile on Adams. When he had read the riddle upon the page, or the answer to the riddle in his mind, he nodded.

The priest's shoulders bowed still more narrowly. His tongue played over his teeth to moisten the lips.

"Englishman and Hollander," he said, speaking slowly and portentously in his excellent Dutch, "the Lord Generalissimo's Majesty charges you with piracy, robbery and murder upon his seas. You are conspirators against his Dominion. You seek to bring war into his peace."

It was still not at the priest that Ieyasu looked. He glanced once at Santvoort, once at their particular escort; and then rested his gaze on Adams.

"Liar!" Santvoort snorted. And then, "Will, for God's love——"

Adams began to speak.

He started in Dutch, laboriously and thoughtfully at first, and fairly calmly.

There was strict piety and no savour at all of profanity when he asserted, by God's Body and His Blood, that the padre lied and that he knew he lied. A copy of the Rotterdam Company's indenture with him, and its Articles, was in the ship's book for any man to see that the intent of the voyage was peaceful trade. The cargezon and the bills of lading would show that there was not an article on board that had not been lawfully bought and peaceably loaded before the anchor had been weighed. If they were murderers and pirates, where were the witnesses to their murder and their piracy?

"Witnesses!" said the priest. "Good." He licked his lips again. "His Majesty has his witnesses."

Bowing, he clicked out some sounds and Ieyasu nodded.

"They have confessed all. Both of them." While the priest said this, two men were brought in, pale and travel-worn, still wide-eyed and a-tremble with their fever, ragged and haggard.

Adams and the Dutchman stared at them aghast; for they had left these same men, restless and scratching and mumbling on their mats, in the house at Oita.

"Master Gilbert de Conning," the priest said, "has made and signed a deposition. He is chief merchant of your ship."

"Chief merchant my——" said Adams. "He is a Huguenot, and a whoreson cook."

"Chief merchant," insisted the priest, "merchant of the goods you bought; receiver of the goods you stole. He has confessed and firmed his confession in writing. Witness thereto is Jan Abelson van Owater." The second man slunk a little forward.

"Bastards both," snorted Adams, and the chamber spun about him.

The Dutch language was shrunk too small and too thin for any further use. His mind flung away from it to the mother language spoken by that other William of his age, more famous than himself. Most of the lively, robustious words that have been cut, from time to time, out of the works of Shakespeare, tumbled over each other upon ears that understood them not but felt only the heat of the explosion that shot them forth. Other words came too, that would probably have been new and vastly interesting to Shakespeare himself—words peculiar to docks and wharves and bawdy-houses of the riverside; and words used only in the fo'c'stle of ships labouring at sea.

Santvoort recognised some of these and they gave him the spirit of the Pilot's discourse. In the specialised remarks of any Dutch seaman who had sailed with Spaniards, he added anything that Adams might have missed in his homely English.

Adams was still convalescent and the outburst left him pumped, and a little exhausted. It left him, too, with a sudden feeling of flat futility. The turbulence of speech in live words had given an illusion of the old, familiar world again wherein effort brought, sometimes, its result; where strife, sometimes, brought victory to the strivers. But the illusion was suddenly gone. Words, here, were meaningless and forceless, like water squirted over statues. Effort was a fantastic memory for naked men among men clad in swords.

The two renegades, de Conning the cook, and Owater whom Santvoort had cuffed a dozen times over the head, grinned in calm discomfort at each other. Thought of strife was thought of suicide. Adams shrugged his shoulders and abandoned it.

Ieyasu himself was seen to have been studying this outburst —for was not the conduct of men but writing on the page of Life?

He straightened a little on his divan and spoke.

Adams and Santvoort were led back to their outhouse, where they lay down upon their mats and found, at their leisure, new words and new combinations of words to apply to the priest and to Conning and van Owater.

Their escort sat by the door, deaf as ever and dumb, filled with his own distant thoughts.

CHAPTER IV

In the afternoon their accustomed escort was replaced by one they had not seen before.

Whereas the old one had regarded them no more than as if they had been pots of crockery or logs of timber, the new one—a younger man—sat nearer to them, regarding them as matters of some interest.

They fell again to speculation between themselves upon the priest. As their thoughts warmed again and the tone of their voices heightened they saw that their guard was squatting eagerly forward, straining towards their meaningless heat. They owed him an explanation. Santvoort gave it, by puffing out his cheeks, thrusting forward his lower lip and indicating, with his hands, a slack paunch. Then he bent his shoulders and chafed his hands together and cringed and rumbled in Portuguese. The escort's eyes disappeared in wrinkles of delight. He doubled up and straightened out and exploded in an abandonment to laughter that seemed, even to Santvoort, the maker of the joke, out of all proportion to the joke's quality. For all the Japanese laughter they had already seen from the visitors over-running their house in Oita, they did not yet realise that a convulsion to an amused Japanese is not much more than a smile to an Anglo-Saxon. It was therefore as new material for portent-reading that they took the outburst. Santvoort tried him again. He stood up to the pantomime; and as he mimicked the priest standing beside the Shogun's divan, bowing and scraping and rumbling at himself and Adams, he saw that another soldier had come to the door, attracted by the first one's laughter. He went through with it, thrusting out his stomach and folding his hands upon it. There were fresh peals of laughter; but this was not what Santvoort wanted. He summarised his sketch when the audience was calm again, cutting it down to a gesture or two, and ended it with what would have been to the blindest and deafest of mutes a string of curses. Baring and grinding his teeth, he shook his fist. The soldier at the door strolled away and the escort shrugged casually at the anger of Santvoort, and waved his hand.

"Gone?" Adams exclaimed, repeating the gesture incredulously.

The escort nodded and again indicated departure, and the priest as being no longer of any import.

Here indeed was food for thought—a portent of proper significance.

But which significance?

The fine reception of Santvoort's mimicry might have meant that the priest was without credit. The laughter could have meant equally that their guard's head was empty of wit and that the padre's departure meant that they were already doomed.

They fell silent again.

The original escort came back towards evening. The cheery deputy rose with some deference and seemed to make a brief report on his tour of duty, and was dismissed. The old one sat down, in the same spot, in the same position and in the same envelope of detachment and disregard that he had sat in through all their waking hours for two days.

The change cast a fresh gloom over the prisoners. Excitement was gone from them and the riddle was once more inscrutable and dead. All had slowly become confused again; points upon which three hours before they had had no doubts became freshly doubtful.

They doubted, by evening, even whether the priest was really gone. Santvoort tried his mimicry on the insensate guard mimicking the padre's bulk; he tried with gestures to indicate travel, and the question whether such travel was taking place. In his eagerness he talked while he moved and mimed.

The escort turned wholly towards him. The smile of his mask became the smile of a listening man. He spoke. In careful Dutch he said, "Speak in Portuguese or Spanish. I understand them better than Hollander, for I was but a short time in the island of Java."

"God!" the other two exclaimed together, with the hair suddenly wriggling on their scalps. "God!"

Santvoort collapsed out of his posturing and sat, hunched up on the mat.

"But you understand some Dutch? . . . Dutch? . . . You?"
The surprise and the shock were still terrific. "You have heard
—understood——"

"Not all," said the man. "But enough."

Again the other two said "God!"

"Listen then," said Adams, "the priest is a liar. A——
Melchior, for God's sake tell him in your glib Portuguese."

"I have heard," said the escort. "I heard your speech in the
chamber; and I have heard you two in speech by yourselves."

"But—listen——" Adams began.

The escort shook his head. "To-morrow," he said, "you will
go again before the General. Or the next to-morrow."

"But the priest?" Santvoort insisted in his question. "He
has gone?"

"Yes," said the other. "He is gone."

"And the others—the traitors? The English-bastard-
Frenchman and the misbegotten Hollander?"

"They," said the escort calmly, "are of little consequence."

"And we?" The question came from Adams.

"You," the escort shrugged his shoulders. "You would seem
to be neither crooked men nor yet enemies."

"Why then are we prisoners?" Adams asked.

"Prisoners?" said the other in some surprise. "Who made
you prisoners? There are no prisoners in this land. There are
some men who await speech with the General . . ."

"Yes," said Adams. "And there are crosses with rotting
flesh upon them."

"But no prisoners," said the other. "The crosses are for
low-born, crooked ones who ply no good among men. Thieves
and informers and mischief-makers of small account—but
that account a bad one."

"We are safe then?" Adams exclaimed; and to Santvoort,
too, the thought pointed towards speculations completely new.

"Safe?" said the soldier thoughtfully. The thought itself was
as alien as the word. "Am *I* safe?"

"You have two very handy swords," said Santvoort. "We
are naked."

"You have hands," said the other. "If I have swords, my enemies also have swords, as yours have hands; so where is safety?"

"For me," said Adams, "I would deem it safe not to be set upon those crosses."

"Crosses," said the soldier, "are for malefactors. I have told you; thieves and house-burners and such."

"And who is to say whether or no we be malefactors?" It was again Adams who spoke; and he asked his question not as an eager, anxious man in present torment but as an old man wearied by a bother.

It was as a mere bother that the soldier, too, considered the question.

"Some say this," said he, "and some that. It is for the Shogun to judge. To-morrow, perhaps. Or to-morrow." He yawned.

The other two turned from him towards each other. Speech which before had been so sparse between them for the emptiness of their thought had now become itself a hazard. Yet they found themselves soon talking about the ship and the trimming of her that would be necessary, and the waiting of many months for the change of wind. They had seen the timber for new masts and spars, on junks and in gateways and bridges. Sections of it they had seen in the crosses. They would do better, Adams was sure, with an altered rig; instead of the square sails on the main and fore with the small lateen mizzen, they would try a fore-and-aft sail at the fore. The loss of charts and instruments was no great matter. He knew that he could make a cross-staff for the reading of his bearings, and with his eyes shut he could plot a course from Japan to Java. The chief question was how many of the fourteen they had left behind at Oita (striking out the dogs de Conning and van Owater) should survive their dysentery and fever, to man the *Liefde* homeward. . . .

So they were back in their old familiar world again where life was an hourly counting of resources and possibilities; a chaffering with Destiny.

Puzzled by the question of the *Liefde's* new rigging, and how far a dozen men could handle her; menaced by the gauntlet of Spaniards and Portingalls that would have to be run off the Philippines and Moluccas, they went at length to sleep.

CHAPTER V

THE next morning they were a little shy of each other, for their ecstasies of speculation had carried them further than the bounds of seemliness as these bounds appeared in the light of day. They were not given time, however, to adjust their relationship to their embarrassment, for they had only bathed and eaten when the escort told them they were to go again before the Shogun.

"We'll be shaved, Will," Santvoort suggested. "We'll show him a cleaner face than the padre's."

He crackled the stubble on his chin and asked the escort for the barber.

When they had been shaved—to the eyelids, ears and inside the nostrils so that only eye-brows remained—they followed across the outer yard and then through inner yards and arrived finally into a room where they had not been before. It was startling at first, because it was the only room they had entered in Japan with all its walls of masonry. Built in the fortification of one of the inner ramparts it had the aspect of a large prison cell with a door of bronze-covered timber, and was lighted only by lanterns.

Ieyasu was seated before a writing-desk studying what turned out to be the pair of brass globes from the *Liefde*. Beside the globes were the ship's log-book, some papers, Adams's dividers and a roll of charts.

"Look, Melchior," said Adams, and the two smiled. Once again in the mellow light that played on the familiar objects that had been blotted from memory by the apathy of sickness and despair, the intimacy of hope was again seemly.

The escort took instructions from the Emperor and then said, "Speak, An-jin. Tell him."

The questions he asked appeared to be mere formality. He had had answers to them all the day before and Ieyasu seemed to pay no attention to the translated replies. He was concentrated upon the brass globes and upon the two pale men. His tongue asked one question—some seeming triviality such as whence or why they had come—and he got a straight answer in words; but his eyes and his knitted brows asked another to which the answers were not so straight or clear.

Adams was given a writing-brush and ink-tablet from the desk, and a sheet of paper. He scribbled a map of all the world as he knew it, starting from Holland and a little cross that was his own country, showing the coasts of the enemies, Portugal and Spain. He plotted the course Southward and Westward, Southward and Westward again, then North and again West, touching in the coasts as they had touched them on that two-year-long journeying till it ended in the Emperor's own Japan and the stone-girt room wherein he now expounded the way.

When he had done and laid down his brush, wiped his brow on his hand and his hand on the worn weft of his breeches, Ieyasu the soldier, the designer and the dreamer had found some answer to the question asked not by words but by his gaze and by the knitting of his brows.

Adams met his gaze and smiled; for there was a nearness in the gaze for a moment that bridged the accidental silence of strange speech.

Santvoort had followed the plotting of the course and the exposition so that when they were done he, too, stood back as though the completed task had been his also. He saw the interchange of glances and saw therein some glint of approval that gave him confidence.

"Ask him, then," he said quickly to the interpreter-escort; "ask his Lordship if we may do our business and go."

Adams, too, in the same moment, had leapt upon the same thought. But Adams, instead of tumbling into speech with the question, had paused.

He did not ask the question.

In his silence his gaze steadied upon Ieyasu, and he continued to smile.

The interpreter put his question and received first a pause and then an answer. He gave it to them, slowly as Ieyasu himself had spoken slowly. The address of it seemed mostly for Adams.

"It is a poor country upon which you have chanced," he

said. "Its hospitality is meagre and shabby. Nevertheless, such as it is, it is yours. You are his Lordship's guests."

He bowed before Ieyasu and they also bowed; for the doorkeeper was swinging open the door and they were being conducted out through it into the twilit passage and the sunlight beyond.

Ieyasu had made his guess; for guessing was his occupation and his sole preoccupation now. His greatest faculty was that of assessing men; of forming a quick opinion that this man was a keeper of faith while the other, possibly, was not. It was for the purpose of exercising this faculty that he was now at Osaka instead of three hundred miles away in his fortress court of Yedo.

For two years he had searched his country from its one horizon to the other for a peer, and found none; and he was now preparing to exterminate a rival.

For a generation and a half of men the Mikado had been confined in the sacred retirement of Kioto which was to last, undisturbed, for three centuries. For those three centuries the ruler of the country was a military dictator, the Shogun—generalissimo. So absolute was he, and so negligible (and revered) the Mikado, that foreigners so intelligent and truth-seeking as Jesuit and Franciscan missionaries, as business men and solid sailors from Portugal and Spain, recognised the Shogun as "Emperor"; and an Englishman, thirteen years later, described the Mikado as "thould Pope of all Japon."

The first of the ruling Shoguns, Nobunaga, cut his belly at the successful treachery of an underling Lord when Ieyasu was a brilliant and courageous soldier of thirty-eight. Eight years later Ieyasu was appointed by Hideyoshi, the second of the Shoguns, as governor of the Eastern Provinces, whose turbulence and hardihood had brought about the death of Nobunaga.

Hideyoshi, the second Shogun, before his death appointed Ieyasu president of a board that was to act as regent for his infant son. The infant son and his mother Ieyasu placed in retirement, for the obvious successor of Hideyoshi was not any possible board or council but the president, Ieyasu. As governor of the Eastern Provinces he had held a court at Yedo, and it was from Yedo that he proposed to rule Japan. It

seemed the lesser of two immediate evils, the better of two
chances. In Yedo and the North he was strong. He knew the
gruffer type of Lord and vassals that he had there subdued.
Already his system was pretty well established, of peopling his
court with hostages and governing the eight wild provinces
through the hostage-givers; either the provincial Daimio himself served at Court while his son governed the province, or
the son was at Court—with a sound spy in the shape of a rival
on his right hand and a possible enemy on his left—while the
Daimio governed the province. So the North and East had
for two years been in the hollow of his hand while the South,
for the same time, had been a growing problem. The memory
of Hideyoshi's regard for him had made his name great enough
in the South; but now the memory of Hideyoshi himself was
being utilised by an enemy to undermine the greatness of the
name. Ieyasu's governor of the South was Ishida Mitsunari,
a man admirable in every respect save that he was Ieyasu's
enemy. No man knew whether, in his heart, it was for himself
that this Ishida Mitsunari wanted a power unshadowed by the
might of Ieyasu, or whether it was in accordance with the
memorable will of Hideyoshi that he was proclaiming to the
Lords of the South how Ieyasu was distorting this will for
his own ends, overshadowing the unlimited power of the
board of Regents with his own usurped power, setting at
nought the edict of their dead Lord Hideyoshi that his infant
son should in fact, as in spirit, be Shogun.

The infant, moreover, and his mother were in the South also,
a focus for the loyalty and enthusiasm of the anti-Ieyasu
party.

It was in the variety of the party that Ieyasu's problem lay.
It was in the South that the words and works of at first Xavier
and his proselytes, and later of the Franciscans, had spread.
Christians had arisen to the number of nearly half a million
souls, to shake the power of the Buddhist monasteries. Men of
business had arisen to trade with the Portuguese and Spanish
traders; and a new strength had arisen to rival the strength of
the loyal sword and the soldier's arm—the strength of the
Spanish piece-of-eight. Yet among the new minds there
existed still some who had been vassals of Ieyasu before they

had been vassals of Hideyoshi; and these were his vassals still.

Assassination would have seemed to some, in Ieyasu's circumstance, a ready way out of the Ishida Mitsunari difficulty; but Ieyasu had little use for the assassin. His mind was balanced, for he was now an ageing man. Buddha, whose image hung at his breast (where Will Adams had carried a compass-needle), gave him his dreams of perfection in the individual soul. Confucius gave him dreams of a nation and a polity built out of what others had seen to be only alert War-Lords. The Bushido—the code of the Samurai—gave him his guide to immediate action wherein the infallible standard of right and wrong was benevolence of conduct only. Buddha and Confucius and the Bushido agreed for the moment that the assassin was not a means to Ieyasu's end.

Thus Ieyasu himself had come to the South. He had come with a retinue sufficient to defend his person and to maintain his dignity; but the work before him was the work which he must do alone. It was to see men and talk with them; to see them singly in quiet speech—out of scores and out of hundreds and out of thousands—and to conclude from a glance, from a word, from a silence or from the mysterious something or nothing that holds men together in friendship or thrusts them apart in enmity, whether this man was a well-wisher, or evil.

In such a mood he was, and tautened to a pitch of particular alertness, when the two sailors were brought before him, bathed and shaved as clean as boys.

The familiar padre standing at his right hand clamoured for their death, seeing in them the enemies of God and Church and the ruinators of a possible Holy Empire in the East, and of the Eastern trade.

Ieyasu saw his very proper vehemence of spirit. Priests were familiar to him. Looking at the strange sailors, he meditated upon the fact that the power of the priests and of their Church was a mighty power indeed in the South—it was the power which Hideyoshi had encouraged to grow so that it extinguished the might of the Buddhist monasteries. Seeing the greatness of this power, and feeling the weight of it that could so easily go into the scales against him, Ieyasu saw nevertheless in the sailors—in their glance or their speech or in their silence —whatever it was that caused him to dismiss the padre with courtesy and benevolence and full hospitality, but without satisfaction; and to have Adams and Santvoort moved to a better lodging.

CHAPTER VI

"So Anjy," Santvoort said as they followed the escort to their new lodging which stood apart from the barrack-like group of houses under the walls. "So . . . we are his Lordship's guests."

It was the escort who answered. "Yes," he said. "I no longer attend you; but I will come from time to time to see that you want for nothing."

"And what are we to do?" asked Santvoort.

"What you will," said the other. "You may not open doors. But all doors already open you may enter, with welcome. And those who wait upon you you may command to do your bidding; for they are not soldiers but servants."

He left them at their new lodging's door.

They inspected their house, seeing the tub of water which would be hot from coals in a cylinder in the middle of it whenever they should be minded to take a bath. They saw a man stooping busy over pots and pans on the kitchen hearth, one who smiled and indicated that whenever they should clap their hands together he would come. In the cupboards of the centre room they found cotton drawers and tunics, straw-hats, paper napkins and sleeping coverlets.

"It looks," said Santvoort, "as though they expect us to stay." From the door they could see a battlemented wall and a postern manned by an armed sentry.

Adams considered the landscape; it was the pale ochre of bare trampled earth in the courtyard, the warm grey of the wall and its shadow, toothed into the sky with tufts of herbage; and above it the empty distance of the sky.

"Yes," said he. "But there are steps up the side of that wall, Melchior."

"Are you minded to run away then?" asked the Dutchman. "For me it is sleep. Hours and hours and nights and days of sleep since we are not to be crossed, as per the padre. Does the thought not make you sleepy, too, instead of looking for ways to climb through or over a wall a mile thick and a league high?"

"Aye, it makes me sleepy. And there is no running away. But I could make an observation from that wall-top these nights while the sky is good. If I had seen the cross-staff with the Emperor I would have asked him for it."

"When he had given us our lives," said Santvoort, "you would have asked him for your cross-staff?"

Adams shrugged his shoulders. "I do not think he ever had a serious mind to kill us. He is no slaughterer of men. He had no cause."

"Cause! He had the padre's word and the evidence of those two bastards that we are thieves and enemies."

"He had our evidence that they are rogues and liars. Yes, I would have asked him for the cross-staff to make my observations. I'll ask him yet. It may come to him as the other things came—God knows how. And I'll ask him if he has my almanac. I'll ask our little talker. He is a fair man."

"Fair!" said Santvoort smiling. "Fair indeed he is. Every man is fair who did not set us upon those crosses."

Adams said, "I was confident all the time that they were not for us."

"Oh, you——" Santvoort snorted. "Confident! It is easy to talk now when you have had the Emperor's word; and set yourself up. Confident—but you were confident that you could sail the world, and bring a ship round it to Japan!"

"And, by God!" Adams exclaimed, staring at the fellow incredulously, "didn't I?"

"Yes—you did indeed——" Santvoort laughed. "Was it you, Will, that brought us? Or was it the sea and the winds and the tides that shook us and drove us and dismasted us and drifted us into an ants' nest of fishermen and gibbering monkeys who towed us into a harbour? It was you, I suppose, who spared us our lives too?"

Adams consigned him to hell and again consigned him to hell. "Aye, to hell! and to sleep!" He strutted off with what dignity he could in the unfamiliar straw sandals, and paced about the courtyard in a fume, cursing the Dutchman for the kind of stupidity that so well suited the squareness of his

cropped head and the way his large ears were adjusted to it—
at an angle of some seventy degrees.

In his fuming and mumbling to himself in his own tongue
it did not occur to him as any particularly worthy or tre-
mendous achievement that he had brought the boat to Japan.
But it was a fact so self-evident that the denial of it by anyone
was enough to make anyone else, who was not a fool, angry.
And Santvoort's impudent questioning of the other fact set him
mumbling with the same indignation; for it, too, was one of
the patently self-evident kind. If Adams had not got them off
with their lives, who—or what—had? Santvoort himself—
perhaps and indeed! Santvoort standing inert and stupid like
a sack of damp powder that might—or might not—blow up!
Then he remembered how the oaf had jibed at him, too, for his
contention that the other Dutchman, Lintschoten, had done
peculiar and fantastic things to the position of Japan on his
charts.

This, at any rate, he knew he would be able to make quite
clear even to Santvoort. An Emperor who had been able to
get globes and charts and some books out of the rabble that
had filched them from the boat would, by the same powerful
and mysterious means, be able to get the other books, the cross-
staff, the astrolabe and ship's compass. Or, given enough time
and a length or two of marlin and some straight laths of wood
and a knife, he himself would make a cross-staff sufficient for
his purpose. . . . And if that would not get facts into the
thick head of the (now, no doubt, snoring) Hollander, nothing
would.

That was the way things went between them for some days,
now that the weight of apprehensiveness was lifted from their
minds, and their bodies were growing sound again.

Adams tried and tried again to draw fire from the drowsy
Dutchman, to rouse him to the point of having the matter
properly out; but Santvoort's fire was not to be drawn. The
fellow merely smiled at Adams with a smile that was an irritating grin, enjoying some joke so private and of such a kind
that Adams was sure he would continue to nurse it to himself
and to enjoy it even when there should be evidence to prove
him a pig-head and a fool.

So he consigned him to hell again, joke and all, in English and in growling Dutch and in Portuguese. He left him behind —excommunicating him from his thoughts even when he persisted in putting on sandals and straw hat and accompanying him—and went about the courtyards of the inner castle and the barracks, looking vaguely about him for the materials out of which he could make the cross-staff. In the end, the volume of conversation he addressed to the boy who attended them resulted in a visit from their interpreter. Adams wanted to see the Emperor again to ask for his books and instruments. The Emperor, said the soldier, had other and pressing affairs at the moment; but he should have his audience as soon as possible. In the meantime he thought he could provide the lengths of wood that Adams sought, with the line and knives he wanted for fashioning his cross-staff.

The boy brought them next morning, and Santvoort thriftily took the two small ends that Adams cut off from the smoothly planed battens. This action, and the Dutchman's apparently aimless whittling at them, were faintly irritating to the more purposeful Adams. He took the one batten through which he was carving a mortice to slide upon the staff, and went out of the room to do his work at peace in the shade outside.

When the boy came to tell him with smiling chatter and gestures of ravenous eating that a meal was ready for them, the mortice was nearly done. Adams licked and sucked the blister made on his thumb by the slender knife-handle, and went in.

Santvoort was very solemnly collecting together the chips and shavings which he had spent the morning in producing on the floor.

Adams, now that a start had been made towards the objective of measuring angles between stars and the moon, was willing to be a little amiable. But it was Santvoort who was now morose.

Adams therefore ignored him. He drank the bowl of broth and set to work on the rice, prodding at it, coping with it as best he could with the chopsticks.

When he saw that the Dutchman was grinning again he would have asked him what tickled him now, but Santvoort held up his hand for silence and then produced from his shirt, with a gesture of magnificence, two pieces of wood carved and scooped into shapes that were easily recognizable as spoons.

"Permit me, Mineheer Anjy," he said.

Adams saw then that he had been wasting choler on him. "Melchior, you fool," he said, but the Dutchman's good humour had caught him. "If I'd known you had the patience and the skill, I'd have set you to cutting out the mortice in the second cross-piece."

"My patience and my skill are both limitless," said Santvoort, "when it is a matter of making tools to convey food more readily from a full and helpless dish to an empty and lively stomach. When it is a matter of conveying information from a distant star to an empty head, the work is yours. And perhaps it *was* you that kept us off the crosses, Will. I am but a stranger to these people, but you they seem to know of old, calling you by your name of Anjy."

"It is An-*jin* they call me," Adams corrected him, "the Japan word for Pilot. Not Anjy. Our old guard told me."

"He shall tell us the Japan word for spoon-maker then," Santvoort grinned. "I, too, must have a name. Now that we have spoons to eat our rice with and Japan to eat it in, all we lack for our complete comfort is—our exact latitude."

"And you'll have that," said Adams, "as soon as you've cut a mortice through the second cross-piece while I, somehow, get the bar marked off."

"Without your proper latitude," the Dutchman said, "you are like a bereaved widow."

The remark moved the thoughts of Adams far away.

"That uncle of yours, Melchior," he said, "—you spoke of me to him so that he will remember?—in a month it will be two years since we sailed, and my wife will be able to claim my wages according to the indenture."

"He will remember," said Santvoort. "He, too, seemed to know you of old, as these Japonians do. As I myself did, now I come to think of it. When old Tim Shotten brought you along in tow that day in your well-named Gravesend, it was as though I was meeting again with some old schoolfellow who had just forgotten me and my language. Why is it, Anjy?"

Adams knew now that huffiness was a silly response to the Dutchman's nonsense. "Probably," he said, "because your brains differ from other men's. But God knows how my wife will get her claim pressed on the company."

The thought, now that he had put it into Dutch words, set up an uneasy stirring in his mind. He had been pondering, till then, the matter of graduating the sticks for his cross-staff; no easy matter since he had neither protractor nor divider but only string and a straight-edge—straight as he could make it with his eye and careful scraping with his knife. The unease made active by Santvoort's casual use of the word "widow" threw the problem into disorder.

His wife was apt, one way or another, to make a mess of that claim. She could not help it; it was no blame to her; but there it was. She could not herself ship to Rotterdam, as he could have shipped, to make her claim on the copy of the indenture he had left with her and explained to her. Nor could he—now that old Timothy Shotten was undoubtedly lost and the bones of Tom Adams his young brother left ashore in Peru —think of any suitable emissary. The kind of vague thought that kept revolving in his mind was the ease with which he himself could have settled the whole matter in a week or within a fortnight . . . and after settling it he would have returned with a free mind to the making of his cross-staff and the reading of his observations.

CHAPTER VII

THERE was more leisure in the atmosphere of his next meeting with Ieyasu. The attitude of the Emperor was more whimsical; his smile had less of meditation and more of geniality than it had had before. Information from his agents and from his own examinings of men and of facts had recently led him to believe that a Southern army opposed to himself would be weak on its right flank, where opinion was stronger for himself. He had seen his genial old friend Matsura Ho-in who could, and assuredly would, strike at the possible enemy's rear with a dauntless company led by other Korean veterans grizzled and scarred as Ho-in himself. . . .

The Pilot, fidgeting and anxious about an armful of books and instruments, amused him. He asked the interpreter why he so urgently wanted them; what was the use of instruments of navigation to a pilot who had no ship?

Adams explained that the charts were wrong; that he wanted to fix upon them the true position of Japan by determining the position of the castle. How, the Emperor asked, could he do that? Adams told the interpreter to mention the instrument he was making out of wood, since the ship's cross-staff was still missing from the collection held by the Emperor. He turned up a page of bearings in the almanac and took the dividers. He tried to make it clear that by using the notches on the disc of the astrolabe he could draw degree-rays that would enable him to graduate his cross-staff; and it was clear that Ieyasu cared not a plum for astrolabes and dividers and globes and compasses; but he cared, peculiarly, for the way Adams conducted himself towards these things and towards himself. He let him talk and gesticulate. He let him draw a circle and divide it into quadrants, showing how an angle of ninety degrees could be accurately arrived at; and in the manner of an elder humouring a child, he pushed the complete heap of things towards Adams.

"Let him climb upon his wall and do his deeds," he said to

the interpreter.

Thus they were dismissed again in friendly sort: for the interpreter told him, after more words from his Lord Ieyasu, that it was well with the ship and his friends, except that two more had died of their sickness. He did not know which two.

For five or six weeks they stayed where they were. The time did not hang unduly heavily upon them, for they were still in need of food and sleep.

Santvoort was the best of companions in convalescence; for he ate as well as he rested, nodding and smiling the slow smile with which he assumed that the morrow should be no worse than yesterday or to-day.

It took the best part of that five or six weeks for them to become fully conscious of their safety. It was not until this consciousness had become established—based, as it was, on nothing but the whimsical smile of a strange, nimble little man— that their minds moved out of their lethargy to speculate upon the future.

Adams could speculate only on the means of adapting the new circumstances to the old plan; for his mind was not of the sort that is easily shaken into a vision of new ideas.

He saw a ship; it was dismasted, battered and sprung—but it remained a ship and the only problem was masts and canvas, pitch and resin and carpenters.

They had brought a cargo of merchandise; and here again the problem was clearly defined—to sell what had not been pilfered and to recover what had; for the Emperor, he kept on telling Santvoort, was fair. Santvoort, however, divined the future more accurately, or else had less interest in it.

The fellow, Adams reflected, had no wife; no children of whom he knew, to place upon him the obligation of proving any bond. It was well enough for him to shuffle about in the sun or snooze in the shade with a heart content. Chance, through no fault of his own, had bereft him of the only responsibility he had ever known—the handful of men he had undertaken to control; and the bereavement made of him a man of leisure and complete ease. Just as responsibility always seemed to slide from the round wide shoulders of Santvoort, so upon the square ones of Adams it always seemed to settle.

Weighted by the wife in Gillingham and the small daughters, he had set out upon this adventure. Now the ship itself and her cargo had become entirely his concern; and upon him also had fallen the onus of all relationship to the Emperor. Santvoort was oblivious of the significance of the stars in their courses and cared nought for the sun's declivity, while Adams cared for both.

He worked at the figures in the *Liefde's* log, at his observations and at the chart he was making; and he brooded upon the condition of the ship and her cargo and upon the house on the hill at Gillingham where he had left a woman and the children with a promise of better days.

They could make a few meanings clear to the serving-boy now as he busied himself about them with food. The soldier-interpreter was generally available to them when they wanted him, but the Emperor was not. He was away, Adams gathered, for an indefinite time. When at last he did have access again to Ieyasu Santvoort stayed at their lodging, contentedly nursing a mild pain in his stomach.

Led into the chamber by the interpreter, Adams was met by the same whimsical smile. Ieyasu spoke directly to him this time, slowly, so that Adams was able to recognize the phrases as greeting. In reply he aired his knowledge of a phrase of thanks, and Ieyasu laughed to the interpreter, who said to Adams, "You will soon have opportunity for learning more."

Adams showed the chart he had made, comparing it with the false one from Lintschoten's book by which he had sailed. Ieyasu, for all that he studied the chart carefully enough, seemed to find a greater interest outside it.

The explanations of Adams drifted from halting Portuguese to Dutch less halting. From Dutch they became English, but it was all one; for the interpreter, at a sign from his Lord, had ceased trying to interpret. Adams was thus undisturbed and uninterrupted in his sketch of the homeward course.

He stopped and asked directly when steps might be taken for the selling of the cargo and for the trimming of the ship.

"Presently," was the answer. "Presently. In good time."

It was now the end of June. War was brewing for Ieyasu

and Ieyasu was brewing the last of it for Ishida Mitsunari. He had disposed his men and had taken their pledges in his enemy's rear.

He spoke again and the interpreter said: "His Lordship now gives you your leave. You will return with the Dutchman to your friends, and to your ship. Let your way be the way of peace."

Even if he had had the tongue, Adams would not have had the words for all his thoughts. Of returning to his friends he could have spoken, for he saw now that they had all come from death to life again. Of the ship also he could have spoken; and of the business before him of unlading her and of trimming her again for the sea. But of the friendship that was already in his heart for the man with whom he had actually exchanged no syllable, there was the realisation which was as yet too dim for any thought that could become a word. He rolled up his charts and shuffled a salute, and went back to Santvoort with the news.

CHAPTER VIII

A DOZEN soldiers escorted them on their return journey, whereas there had been only four in the party that brought them up. They walked, nimble enough and tolerably comfortable, in their linen shifts and sandals.

They were received on the ship at Oita, as Adams himself says, "with weeping eyes; for it was given them to understand that I was executed long since."

The return was another link in the chain of accidents that made of Adams the big man of the castaways, the "Number One." He came back after two months with good news and good hopes and a plan, to men who had spent the time in dingy convalescence and suspense. He had seen the dismissal of the padre, while the others had brooded in the shadow of his hostility.

The Captain, Jacob Quarternak of Rotterdam, for all that survival had made him "Admiral" of the expedition, accepted whatever words came from the vitality and the reasonable hopes of his pilot.

Adams therefore was simply tumbled into command of the survivors; and Santvoort, by the sheer beefiness of his health, was tumbled into his lieutenancy.

The house ashore, for some reason or other, had been given up so that the party had been quartered, for a month, on the ship. That month of pigging it aboard and of listless hospitality to men, women and children in a daily thousand or so had made a garbage-heap of the *Liefde*. The sightseers were guests in the true, full local sense of the word; they brought, each one, their little gift—fruit and fish and drink, or some trifle of raiment, and each gift had shed its wrapping or its rind. (In natural compensation they had taken away, each one, any oddment of fitting, furniture or cargo that had come readily to hand.)

The only survival of discipline that Adams and Santvoort found aboard was that no one but the Captain and the Surgeon, in addition to smiling and prying guests, ever entered the cuddy.

The soldiers were enough, by their very presence, to clear the ship of the general rabble, and to keep it clear. Holding the crew aboard was another matter. It was not till Santvoort had knocked down the sailmaker that the men realised that the ship was still a ship and that there was work ahead of them.

There came an inkling among them that they were presently going home again, and with the inkling they fell to work. A cook was found among them to replace the renegade de Conning, for there had been no cooking while gifts of food in a thousand handfuls had made a surfeit and a litter.

Millet and barley and fish appeared each morning now, not a gift but a ration.

Adams and Santvoort were continually going ashore to retrieve men who had, somehow, gone before them to friends they had made among the ship's visitors. They had no difficulty in finding them; for a very lane seemed to open for them as they stepped ashore, through the crowds that smilingly awaited them; and a hundred guides led them to the house of laughter where their man was gone.

The cleaning of the ship came to an end, and the real difficulties of the position had to be faced.

Lockers had been stripped; every bight of rope, every hank of marlin was gone. There was not a stitch of canvas anywhere. The carpenter had been dealt with more exhaustively than the absent cook—for the galley still held bare utensils enough for boiling millet and fish, and could muster dishes and lids enough for serving a meal to the four officers.

Adams and Santvoort made inventories and lists; and they walked—aboard and ashore—cursing the thieves and seeking frantically for someone to whom they could put their grievance.

Wherever they went at least two of the soldiers, they noticed, sauntered after them.

The soldiers, in reply to anything the Englishman or Dutchman tried to say, had only a smile, a shaken head and shrugged shoulders. Ashore the only replies they had were invitations within houses. Children and young women stroked the hair on their calves, their forearms and their chests. The roughness of their chins was a joke beyond the expression of ordinary laughter. The two of them together were called, in great friendliness, 'The old hairy ones'; and for Adams there was always the name An-jin.

They, for their part, said much in English, in Dutch, in Portuguese and in Spanish—but the words only bounced back upon them from the flat, smiling faces. All they could find in the chatter and clatter of tongues and teeth was greeting and the everlasting joke and curiosity about their hairiness and Adams's name of "Pilot." Till one day they were addressed in Portuguese, and the sound struck them as words from the mouth of his ass had struck Balaam before them.

"Come with me—quietly," was whispered by a man who was, for a moment, nearer to them than the rest of the merry rabble at the waterside. Then, "Shushshush-shush."

They may, or may not, have seen him before; for they had taken little note of individuals in the pattern that always shifted and revolved about their goings and comings. They went with him to a house where they had been before to retrieve missing members of the crew. Women smiled at them and gave them wine, and drew the door across in the face of the other followers. For the women, however, the guests had only the briefest of the thanks they had approximately learned to utter. They had neither eyes nor ears for them just then, but only for the man who had spoken words out of the din of gibberish.

"Take us to the governor," said Adams, "we'll pay. Money. We have goods to sell. You'll be the gainer by it."

The man smiled. "You have seen your only Governor," he said quietly. "The Shogun himself, Ieyasu. You are his; guarded by his soldiers. Even now they are but twenty paces from you; one at the front of the house, one at the back."

"But we have goods to sell," Adams insisted.

"True," said the man. "But none may buy them."

"But, by God, anyone may *steal*, it seems," exclaimed Adams; and he would have discoursed largely upon this point if the man had not quieted him with another "Shushshush-shush" and a headshake.

"That is another matter," he said. "There will be no more stealing now that you are here, and the soldiers. You and your goods also are the property of the Shogun."

"The Shogun is our friend." Adams snorted this at him, for the man was of the sort to be impressed by such a claim.

"True," he said. "And therefore you have about you a score of blades. If any man molest you he will be cleft at a blow from shoulder to navel. In the like manner will he be cleft who lays a hand upon your goods."

"But," Adams repeated, "the Shogun is our friend."

"And soldiers are soldiers," replied the other. "He is their friend also, and they his."

"But the goods are ours." This was Santvoort's first contribution to the talk. "We can do what we please with what is ours."

"True," said the other. "It is yours and you may keep it. Indeed, you must keep it."

"Then how in hell's name can we make any move?" said Adams.

"You would move?" asked the man.

"Move?" said Adams; "how else can we trim the ship for sea and sail her? We've got to go home, haven't we?"

The man thought quietly for a few moments. "You have another friend also," he said at length, "the padre of Nagasaki."

"The padre of Nagasaki!" said Adams, and Santvoort snorted.

"Nevertheless," said the man, "it is he that sent me. He is returning here. Since you are not pirates and enemies, he comes as your friend."

"He can go to hell," was their only retort.

"You will find him your friend," the quiet one insisted. "Receive him and take his counsel if you would move in any such way that the soldiers leave their swords in their girdles. In a day or two—or three—he will be here. And now"— girls were in the outer hall grouped together chattering— "and now if you would have entertainment——"

"Entertainment——" said Adams thoughtfully. "We have had our belly full of entertainment from yourself. If we may not sell our goods, and so buy—Entertainment!" Then he turned suddenly to Santvoort. "Melchior, we will go again to the Emperor, ourselves."

"Three men only," said the Jap, "—or perhaps four—know where the Shogun is at this moment; or where he is likely to be in the next two or three months. And remember the soldiers."

"Are we prisoners then?" asked Santvoort.

"Guests," said the other, and smiled. "Guests. With all those blades to protect you."

"Well, then," said Santvoort, "as guests we would like something, some fruit or vegetable—something green for our cook to serve with that everlasting broth and cake and fish. Or beef. Is there no beef in this country?"

"No. No beef," said the man. "The padre, perhaps, when he comes—but not one so humble as this person. This person could, perhaps, undertake the vegetables."

"Very well," said Santvoort. Then he added, as a diplomatic afterthought, "but we have no money to pay with till we have sold some of our goods."

"Pay?" said the other. "Money——?" He shook his head and abased himself. "There is more than payment in the august honour of doing a trifling service to the Shogun's chosen and protected friends."

They smiled and uttered thanks to the girls grouped in the hall, for it is a hard face in which such smiles will not beget a smile; and they went out cursing.

"He may be lying," said Adams.

"That we can soon see," said the Dutchman. "We'll go back to the boat and I'll come ashore again with something to sell. We'll try a piece of broadcloth from that opened fardel."

The loiterers seemed to realise that they had some purpose before them as they hurried to the boat, followed by their two soldiers. They hung back to let them pass.

They came ashore again, Santvoort carrying the roll of broadcloth under his arm.

Among booths and stalls their pace slacked as they looked about for wares that should indicate a market for their own.

"We'll sell it," said Santvoort, "for anything. And we'll buy some fruit—if we can find anything but radishes."

At a bench whereon there was a display of printed cotton cloths and some silk he greeted the shopkeeper. Among the wares on the bench he laid the roll of broadcloth and then went behind the bench to place himself on the same side of the counter as the little man.

With a friendly pressure on his shoulder Santvoort urged him round the bench till it was obvious to him and the dullest in the crowd that the Hairy One had become the shopkeeper and the toothless old huckster the customer.

Even the soldiers smiled, and Santvoort extended himself to the business and to the joke of it. He rubbed his hands together and nodded and jerked his head and chattered a cease-less whine of gibberish, pushing his moth-eaten and rat-eaten broadcloth towards his customer. He next held up his hands and slowly counted off ten on his fingers and thumbs.

The old man picked up the cloth and fingered it and unrolled the end. He rubbed it, flicked away the fluff from moth incur-sions and examined the edges where rats had been. Then he re-wrapped the end he had unrolled and shook his head and held it out, with thanks, to Santvoort. The Dutchman held up one hand alone and counted off five. Still the old man shook his head, and Santvoort reduced his demands to one. He had not the faintest idea of what it was that he had de-manded at first ten and had now climbed down to one; but even if it was one farthing the old man refused the offer.

Santvoort took the cloth from him and then held it out, with the other hand waving away any suggestion at all of price. Obviously it was a free gift that he was offering. The old man bowed over it and nodded and spoke; but he would not take it.

Santvoort then laid it down on the bench again and said, "Come on, Will; quickly."

As they turned to go, they both saw the old man glance at the soldiers. He stayed the Dutchman with a quick hold on his arm. He thrust the cloth quickly back to him and then, bowing and speaking gently and with great humility, he gave first to Adams and then to Santvoort, a roll of paper napkins.

"That bastard," said Santvoort, as they walked away, "was speaking the truth. But if we may not sell and therefore may not pay, we may still, so it seems—buy. Here!"

Abruptly he stopped at a stall displaying fruit and sea-weed and pickles. A full repetition of his first pantomime was unnecessary; for if the fruiterer himself had not left his fruit to witness it, a report of it had reached him even as it was being enacted. Pointing first at the cloth and then at two melons was all that was required.

Santvoort laid down the cloth. The fruiterer picked it up, examined it, looked at the soldiers and handed it back again. Then with the same expression and tone of humility and gentleness that the old haberdasher had used for his gift-making, he handed them each a melon.

To Adams he made the further gift of a small bunch of radishes.

CHAPTER IX

THEY found themselves that night, Adams and Santvoort, living life on the old terms again—puzzling over means and testing obstacles to an end that was desirable and clear. It was only, they thought, their dumbness that blocked them utterly. To the soldiers roosting on the foredeck while Adams and the Dutchman sat aft, they went and said, "Mitsu, Mitsu." It was the name—or nickname, or title—by which they had heard their interpreter-escort addressed at Osaka. With him they felt they could make some headway against the absurd impotence whereby at present they could gain only paper napkins and melons and radishes.

"Mitsu, Mitsu," they demanded.

From the soldier in apparent command they got what seemed to be some sort of reassurance, some indication that all would be well—if, indeed, it was not well already. (They had not yet discovered that the Japanese soldier had only one tone and one gesture for predicting future events, regardless of whether the event was to be fulfilment of his dearest wish or his immediate death.)

The next day they spent in brooding and chafing and looking idly ashore for their Portuguese-talker of the day before. But his features had dissolved into the similar features of a hundred or a thousand others. A man beckoned them again to the little house where the other had startled them with his talk, but they found nothing there but wine and laughter. The talker of the day before had given an air of secrecy to himself, so they attempted no enquiries. Laughter for its own precious sake had little appeal for them at the moment, so they merely glanced into the house and passed on.

It was at the cargo itself that Adams did most of his grumbling now—bales upon bales of Dutch broadcloth which was, of all the things he could think of, the most unlikely to find buyers. . . . Likelier wares would have been the things that had been stolen from the ship, things which they themselves must now either buy or make. Santvoort said there was small hardware stowed somewhere in the hold, and somewhere, too, with the broadcloth, were rolled sheets of lead. They knew already, however, that the art of theft depended here less on the visibility of objects and the movement of thieves than on some mystery. Things were not *taken* away; they just vanished. And so, without a sheltered and enclosed and locked place wherein to unlade and guard the cargo, they could not start a hunt for the knives and nails and axe-heads and pots and sheets of lead that might produce money for them, where an armful of moth-eaten broadcloth had left the bazaar's hucksters cold and idiotic, and themselves with a brace of melons and a bunch of radishes.

The following morning, when he went up on deck he stopped, as though stunned by his astonishment, and then shouted down the companion:

"Melchior! He's here!"

This sudden information could mean only one thing; and the Dutchman came lumbering up. The two of them in a moment were shaking the hands of Mitsu from Osaka.

"Man! Why didn't you wake us?" Adams burst the question out in English first, and then forced it into Dutch.

"I too had need of sleep, An-jin," Mitsu said; and then, "only the fool would wrestle with time."

"A fool—or anyone with feet as well cooled as ours are," said Melchior.

"Yes," said Adams. "Now, thank God, we can move. We will sell our cargo now and get for it—money."

"You have no need to sell things—for money, An-jin," Mitsu replied. "I myself have brought money for you, and given it in trust to the Lord of this place. Fifty pieces. It is yours whenever you have need of it."

"Need of it!" Adams exclaimed. "Man, the ship is stripped naked. We have need of all the money we can get to fit her for sea again."

"The Shogun's guests have no need of a ship ready for sea," said Mitsu. Then his tone became less formal. "An-jin," he said, "for you there is no use in a ship ready for sea. You are a—guest."

"Guest be damned——" said Adams. "Go on, Melchior—tell him we've a cargo to sell and a ship to make good. Then we're off."

The answer to the Dutchman's statement was, "His Lordship's message is the gold he has sent for your comfort. In his heart is friendship; in his girdle, and mine, and in the girdles of a thousand thousand others—swords. This is the word he sends you, An-jin, with his benevolent greetings."

Adams saw the object vanishing from life again, as though a cable mooring them to its firm solidity had suddenly parted. The parting did not, however, leave them adrift but stuck. They were ringed about by ring within ring of things impenetrable, incomprehensible and intangible.

The outermost ring of all was mountains that chopped the blue lid of sky into a disc with a fanged, jagged edge. The innermost was now, not the amiable smile and meaningless chatter of the foreshore throng, but—closer than this—the score and more of protruding sword hilts.

The flicking of a head from its shoulders by the blade of the Justice of the Peace for some trivial crime in Oita was a sight less unusual than the tipping of rubbish from a barrow; for rubbish was left to rot and stink in the crazy streets. The trial, upon the corpse, of new blades in the hands of young bloods or of old blades repaired or newly edged, made of every lithely decorated hilt a possibility to be recognised among the facts of life.

"Guests——" snorted Adams. "Guests indeed! Here, regard me, Mitsu. We came as we came. And so we will go."

"In this?" asked the Jap. His smile was at the stumps that were left of mast-houndings, at the sagging deck-house and the sprung seams.

A mumble was sufficient to express the thought of Adams.

Mitsu continued, solemnly: "Now you, An-jin, regard me. You have no ship. Any man who would carry you—if any such could be found—would be cut before he had carried you a league. Friendship is offered to you. Take it in good part. More than friendship no man may gain from another."

"Friendship——" snorted Adams. "It's prisoners he's made

of us. Just like the dogs de Conning and Owater. Are they, too, his friends?"

"They were your enemies," said Mitsu. "How could they be his friends?"

"Why does he keep them, then?" asked Adams.

"He does not keep them," said the other. "They were of no worth."

"Has he killed them?"

Adams stared, surprised at the thought now that he had come to consider it so flatly by itself.

"They," said the other, and he shrugged his shoulders at the triviality, "were of no worth. No worth whatever."

"Hear that, Melchior?" said Adams.

"Aye," said Santvoort, "but the padre, Mitsu? He, too, is of no worth."

"Padres," said the Jap, "are a different pair of sandals."

The question of the padre was one which Adams and the Dutchman had often discussed, finding no particular answer.

"What are padres to the Emperor?" Adams asked. "Is he a believer in their teaching? Are you?"

"He is a believer in men," said Mitsu. "As for me, I am his servant. Beliefs of padres and priests are no concern of mine. My sole concern is whether they are his friends or his enemies, for a man may not live under the same sky as his Lord's murderer or in the same town as his enemy."

"So the padre is his friend?" Adams displayed some contempt in his question.

"Between enemies and friends," Mitsu explained, as glibly as though he were quoting from a book of rules, "there is the multitude of all the world. It is of no account. No more than the myriad of dust-grains between two footfalls. It is the ground beneath the foot only that is of consequence."

"All very fine," said Santvoort. "But those two rascals of ours did no worse than the padre with his dirty lies. He started it, Mitsu—and yet they, you say, have been done for."

"In the padre's conduct," said Mitsu, "there was policy. In theirs was nought but fear and greed."

"Call it spite, not policy," said Santvoort. "For why, in God's name, should he have wanted us stuck up and spiked on those crosses of yours?"

"He is a priest, not a soldier," Mitsu spoke now as though merely making a suggestion and not quoting obvious truth, or a rule. "Priests think deviously and not straight. It may have been because, though even whiter and hairier than himself, you do not believe in his God. Priests give great importance to such matters; but he had neither enmity nor greed nor fear."

"And who told you we do not believe in his God?" demanded Adams.

"It is well known," was the answer. "It is given out by him and all of the Portingals. Spaniards, too, say that in your country and the Hollander's you have denied the God, and burnt up his temples and destroyed his images; stealing the gold. So they have declared you pariah; and you, in your turn, have turned to sea-robbery and murder for a living."

"God Almighty!" said Adams. "And you believe any of that? You and the Emperor?"

"How should a man believe or disbelieve what is of no consequence? But remember this, my friends——" He grinned as he remembered the way these two had exploded at the padre in the chamber of Ieyasu. "Remember this. The Law is law for all—even for his Lordship's friends. The penalty for a sword drawn with any purpose but the cleaning or the testing of the blade, is death. His Lordship's guests must have no brawls. If they seek justice against another they must seek it from his Lordship himself, not by means of enmity and personal quarrel."

"Justice!" said Adams. "Is it justice to make prisoners of honest men with letters of friendship to him from their nation?"

"How prisoners?" the Jap demanded a little peevishly. "Have I not said 'guests'—and again 'Guests,' and—'Guests'? You have safety and food; and money now, and entertainment even by women."

"Let his Lordship keep his money and his entertainment and his women," said Adams. "We'd have money of our own—and entertainment—and women—if you had not made prisoners of us—you with your bellyful of sword-hilts and your cant of friendship and justice. If there is any justice, let us see the

Emperor again and have it. Let us tell him our case and make him let us go."

"When his Lordship has leisure again for such matters you shall indeed see him," said the other. "In the meantime let not your necks grow heated."

"In the meantime," said Adams, "if there is any way of going, we will go."

With this defiance he snapped the conversation to an end and stumped off to tell the Captain that they had got no further.

CHAPTER X

AFTERWARDS the Jap could get no more than a mumble or a grunt in answer to his cheery greetings of the Pilot. He shrugged his shoulders; for to him, by his own statement, the incomprehensible was inconsequent. To him a day, a week— or a month or a year—were all one. His possessions were in his girdle. He had little to do, and his chief concern was the temper of his heart. The fuming and freeting of a man over something that was neither here nor there were quite beyond him.

Adams challenged him two or three days later. "Where's all this money of ours?" he said. "I want to buy a sword."

"The money, An-jin, is with the Daimio's clerk," he answered. "We will go to him. But no man but a soldier may carry swords. It is the law."

"Oh, is it?" said Adams. "I did not say I wanted to carry swords. Carrying is another matter. I want to *buy* one."

"If any man sold you a sword," said Mitsu very calmly and very cheerfully, "or gave you one, I would cut him from neck to navel. Even him——" he nodded towards the shore.

Adams could only grunt again before following his gaze; but when he had done so he snorted.

It was the padre at whom Mitsu now grinned.

"It is perhaps as well, An-jin," he said, "that you have no sword. It would go against my stomach in our friendship. I would be constrained to call some other to execute you."

The padre had apparently concluded his bargain with a fisherman; for he was putting off in the little skiff with an attendant who carried a great bundle on his shoulders.

Adams again, scarcely believing his eyes, called down the companion to Santvoort, "Bring the hook, Melchior"; for one boat-hook was among the treasured relics of the ship's smaller loose furniture. "We'll show him who can come aboard!"

They stood at the side, amidships where the freeboard of the *Liefde* was scarcely more than the height of a man, and where a square port was left open for the easier getting into, and out of, the ship's dinghy.

"Aye, we'll show him," said Santvoort, and he spent a moment or two in thoughtful consideration of the rival merits of the pole's steel-shod end, and its butt. The latter seemed to carry the day, for he leaned the butt over the side.

He said, "Half way through the port would leave his great behind sticking well out for a drubbing. You could hold him from below, Will. Then shove him out again—into the boat or the water."

Any criticism from Adams of this simple scheme was postponed by Mitsu, who said quickly from the poop: "An-jin, no bloodshed. No violence . . ." Then he disappeared. They heard him quickly collecting the other two soldiers who had squatted on the afterdeck, and taking them away with him out of sight, behind the wreck of the deck-house.

In this time the skiff had come to within a dozen yards of the ship's side where the fisherman backed with his solitary oar.

"Good-day, my sons," said the padre, and made the sign of the cross. It would have surprised the others less if he had raised an arquebus and emptied it at them.

"Good indeed!" said the Dutchman, caressing his boat-hook; and Adams mumbled, "It will be an awkward hold on the rascal from two foot below the level of him."

"It is as your friend that I come," the priest said quietly. "See!" He indicated the bundle held on the low thwart by his attendant. "A present. Food and wine."

"And d'you think we want for food?" said Adams. "We who are the friends of the Emperor himself?" A swagger came into his attitude.

"I too am your friend, my son," the priest said quietly.

"Friend——" said Adams to Santvoort. "Friend means many things in this country, Melchior. You can clap a man in gaol, and be his friend. You can cut him from neck to navel and be his friend. You can tell the black lies that will bring him to be crossed and stuck like a pig—and be his friend . . ." He was thoughtful as he said this, not simply cantankerous, for he had been thinking deeply upon this very puzzle—the puzzle of Ieyasu's smile, and the ring he had made about them of swords; the puzzle of Mitsu with his cheerful, irrepressible amiability, and his brief gesture and big talk of cleaving one from neck to navel.

"I know it is hard, my sons," the priest went on, and he sat down wearily beside the bundle.

They saw now that he was an old man and tired. "Nevertheless I am your friend. You shall hear me—if you will soften and listen. You shall also see, if you will take this package."

"And what have you got?" said Santvoort, "in the package?"

"A little wine," said the priest. "Not much—but good. Wine and fruit. And beef."

"Beef!" said Santvoort. "Let us see his beef, Will. Fresh beef, padre?"

"Fresh," he answered. "Fresh—but a little salted and already cooked against the journey. The sooner it is eaten, the better."

"And what price do we pay for your salted beef?" asked Adams. "Our heads?—And what price do you pay for giving beef and wine to pirates and robbers and murderers and enemies of his Majesty the Emperor?"

"There is no price," the priest answered humbly and gently. "It is as a friend that I have come so far. It is only as a guest that I may come further. It is for you to decide, for I have wronged you once. The wine and the beef and the fruit are yours in any case. But before you dismiss me, remember that I have lived and laboured for twenty years in this country. I know much and can do much, for these people are strangers to me no longer. I speak their tongue and I comprehend their thoughts—and their thoughts are as different as their tongue from ours."

Santvoort was trying to visualise a piece of fresh beef—a rib perhaps, a sirloin, or a good fillet from the rump. Adams was grappling again with the puzzle of thoughts and of ways of thinking that were as alien as the speech of sudden clicks and snaps and hisses.

To Adams the old and tired man sitting in the boat said he understood them. To Santvoort his quietness said that his parcel held beef that might be a rib, a sirloin or a fillet from the rump. Adams, too, had casually wondered what cold beef would look like, pickled but slightly in brine.

"Use the hook for holding the skiff alongside, Melchior," he said. "Leave his behind to itself." Then he called, "Come aboard, padre."

The old man scrambled through the port and took the bundle from his attendant.

Santvoort helped him up the last three steps of the companion to the deck. He relieved him of the bundle, handing to Adams the precious boat-hook; and the three of them joined the Captain and the Surgeon in the cuddy.

Santvoort unpacked the bundle.

There were three bottles of Spanish wine, oranges from the Philippines, and the beef—a roasted brisket.

"It is only a poor present, my sons," the old man said. "But it is as much as we could carry—four days of hard travelling it is from Nagasaki. It would be the merest trifle among many; but among you four it might serve to show my friendship. I would suggest that you allow your cook to bring in the customary food. Cover this with the wrapping and the Captain's cloak—so. . . . That, too, is why we cooked it for you beforehand; beef is, as it were, contraband in this country. One does not talk much of eating beef; for even believers without the old superstitions are still few."

Santvoort covered up the gift with the wrappings and the Captain's cloak and they sat squeezed round the table.

It was only from hearsay that the Captain and the Surgeon knew of the priest's fine doings before Ieyasu. All they had experienced of him was his persistent commiseration with them over the undoubted execution of Adams and Santvoort. Speech came more easily to them than to the other two.

"So you've got us bottled up here, padre!" the Captain said, not without the faint touch of geniality befitting a man who knows that he is beaten. "Prisoners. For how long?"

The priest slowly crossed himself again. "Your captivity is not my doing," he said. "Far otherwise. Very far otherwise. It is indeed of that that I have come to talk with you."

He paused a moment and leaned closer while the others looked at each other through the light that came from the narrow doorway, and then at him.

"My sons," he said, "in all this country—I am now your only friend."

That word "friend," with its grotesque and ironic implications, was getting a little on the nerves of Adams.

"Have you come to deliver us, then?" he sneered. "To set us free?—take us all home again?"

"Not all," said the priest quietly. "That I cannot do—for your captor is powerful. But I have come to set you free; you four who are the big and important ones. Nor can I myself take you home. But I can put you where there are ships. I can send you as far as the Moluccas. For such as you, the getting home from there would be no great matter. We will talk of it presently. First call for your skilly, my friends, and throw it quietly over the side and eat your beef and drink your wine."

The cook brought in their broth and millet-cakes and knives and mugs and a pitcher of water. Santvoort went out to tip the broth over the side and the priest sat on the locker, smiling and carving slices from the beef.

When they had sat down to it and their mugs of wine the Captain drank to the priest's good health. Then he said, "You have lied before, padre. We know that the thing you speak of is forbidden."

"Do you not know that beef also is forbidden?" was the padre's smiling answer.

They considered this.

"A month ago you would have had us killed out of hand," said Adams. "Now——" suddenly he stopped, a gobbet of the excellent meat poised on his knife-point. "Steady, Captain! Melchior! Doctor! . . . How in God's name do we know what he may not have put in this beef?"

They slowly laid down their knives. "Or in the wine, damnation take him!" Adams added, having already drained half his mug.

The priest set his great pale hand on the pilot's shoulder and laughed. For some reason or other they believed in his laugh and went on eating again even before he had said: "Do not be afraid. If harm came to you from my beef or my wine, I would not reach Nagasaki alive. As for the sheer doing of such a deed, could I not a hundred times have poisoned the lot of you even before you went up to the court? Believe me, the law of this country is a law of iron."

"It beats me," said Adams, and he fell into thought. "But if you are so frightened of the Emperor's wishes, how can you think of getting us out of the country? He has forbidden it, as he has forbidden murder."

"*I* would not get you out of the country, my son," the priest said. "It is well known already that your wish is to go. And so if you went—well—it is you who would be the law-breakers."

He shrugged his round shoulders and smiled upon them. "If you went, the doing of it would be yours—not mine. Any little facilities I might give you would not, in fact, be traced; the Emperor and his emissaries are busy at the moment with greater affairs than the departure of a few unwilling guests."

"And what are these facilities of yours?" asked Adams. It was the curious fact that he again had become the spokesman of the others. His Portuguese was slower and more cumbersome than theirs. His forwardness was again determined by trivial accidents; their mouths, at the moment, were full of beef or wine, or their minds were jumping ahead of the priest's words, or lagging behind them. For no other reason Adams was the one to say, "What can you do?"

"The nights are moonless," said the priest. "Presently we shall part in obvious friendship. To-morrow night I will send a skiff with presents for you. Four men will come aboard carrying them." He paused. "Four men will leave the ship." He bent nearer to them. "They will be bigger men than the four who come aboard—but my boatmen will answer any questions asked by your guard on board. The distance from here to the shore is nothing to swimmers like the four who will bring your parcels."

Among the thoughts of his four listeners there was a quick computation of chances; the computation of chances had for long been the habit of their daily life.

"And then," said Adams, "what happens?"

"Another boat," said the priest, "and other boatmen will take you by water to Nagasaki. In Nagasaki we have craft of our own, and a certain freedom. Here there is a tally of all the boats that can float; but in Nagasaki brothers of mine will see to it that you board a soma for the Moluccas."

"And in the Moluccas," suggested Adams, "the cutting of our throats would be a simple, harmless matter; there is no Emperor to protect us in the Moluccas."

"My son," said the priest, sadly shaking his head. "I am no murderer. I seek only to do the work before me."

"The work before you was once to get us stuck up on crosses."

"My work," said the priest, "was to remove you from blocking the way of the faith."

"Throat-slitting would surely achieve that, as Mr. Adams suggested." It was the Captain who spoke this time. "You cannot get away from that."

"If you would understand," said the priest, "I will explain to you. My sons—if you would only see——" He was the old man again, tired and a little frail for all his bulk, appealing to them so humbly and so earnestly that they listened.

"Here, in this field," he went on, "you are the enemies— not of me, for you also are men and the children of God—but of the faith, for you are blind. I speak plainly that you may believe. For half a century we have laboured in this field; and our labours have been blessed. The seed of truth has prospered and the harvest has been great. But you, in your blindness . . . My sons, if you, too, had the faith——"

"Perhaps," said Adams, "but we have not." He so plainly saw the sly old dog working round again to his conversion-talk that he lost sight of the tired old man with a possibly reasonable argument.

The tired old man came back again with a gesture of resignation and a gently spoken "Exactly. You have said it. And so, what was for me to do? If thine eye offend thee— pluck it out. . . . I was even willing to put you—brothers of mine and children of God—on the crosses of thieves and house-burners. But that way was denied. I am willing now to risk much to set you away from here towards your own country."

"And what is to prevent our coming back?" said Adams. It seemed a good question for purposes of sounding. "Alive we could always come back—with a better ship, better charts and a better cargo."

"Come back?" said the priest, and the smile he now smiled was a very wise one. "Do you think that men who have once broken faith with their Lord in this country ever come back? No, my sons. Such men are called 'ronin' thereafter. Exiles and wanderers with every loyal door and mat and brazier forbidden them. It is only darkly as thieves that such men could return, or openly as enemies. I am not afraid of your coming back."

"And so," Adams said, "you have nothing to fear. Even if we would we could not harm you, while to us you can give no surety. If we should get to the Moluccas and if we were lucky we should find only Portingals. Unlucky we should fall in with Spaniards; throats cut or backsides lashed to galley-thwarts."

"Even Spaniards dare not molest a Japan vessel in the Japan Sea," said the priest.

"But it is a voyage," said Adams. "A mischance could take us to the Philippines instead of the Moluccas." It was the way of Adams to pursue an argument when an argument was offered.

"Of mischances I can say nothing," said the priest. "I can only give you the most that any layman can rely on in the face of mischances. In the boat that comes for you to-morrow night will be four pistols and four knives. They will token my good faith to you. If there should be not knives and pistols you can call your guard who are the trustiest of Ieyasu's men and denounce my men who will have stayed aboard and so—me."

He rose to his feet, the ceiling's lowness compelling him to stoop. Yet there was dignity in him, the dignity of the bargainer who is open in his bargaining.

"And when do we decide?" asked Adams, whose aim now was to be rid of him so that the four might consider.

"By noon to-morrow," he answered. "If at noon to-morrow the Captain's coat is hung at the taffrail with a white shirt on either side of it, at the earliest full darkness of night the boat will be here."

CHAPTER XI

HE cheerily shouted his farewell to them when he had scrambled down from the port into his skiff, smiling and waving his great hat, then making the sign of the cross. They called back from the deck waving their hands in ostentatious friendliness, mindful of the soldiers who stood at the rail above them, watching.

Santvoort went back with the captain and the surgeon to the cuddy; Adams took his straw hat from its peg by the cuddy door and went up on the poop. He looked, casually, for Mitsu, but did not see him.

Wherever he looked he saw a detail of the ship's familiar helplessness. The hole in the deck at his feet had only the bent pin of the pivot sticking out, rusty, from its iron collar; for the steering whip-staff—a comely and handy and detachable piece of timber—had gone the way of other comely, handy and detachable things. He sat on a water-breaker from which one hoop had gone and which, until a cooper had spent half a day upon it, could hold not a pint of water; and he stared at the binnacle.

There was irony in his thoughtful gaze, for he—An-jin as they called him, Contemplator of the Needle—now contemplated only an emptiness where there was no needle. The card had gone, and the binnacle might have been another leaky keg for all the use it was.

The pitch oozed out of seams and wriggled into blisters even as he watched it.

The broad, hunched shoulders of the padre rose and lurched as the skiff was grounded. He stepped out of it, gathering up the skirts of his cassock into the hands that fumbled also with destinies.

He had explained himself. Even Adams believed that he had told the utmost truth; but in believing him he distrusted him the more. The explanation was Popery. . . . And at that point the mind of Adams stuck.

Before going down to the others in the cuddy he looked once more for Mitsu, but still did not see him.

"A pistol and a knife," the captain was saying—"All very well; but it would require more than a pistol and a knife for the sinking of a Spaniard, if matters came to it."

"Nevertheless," said Santvoort, "a pistol and a knife would be more comfortable than no pistol and no knife."

They discussed it all in the sombre, considerate manner of directors of an insolvent company. There was no emotion in their talk, just the consideration of liabilities, speculation as to assets. Assets resolved themselves into the promised knife and pistol. The thought of meat again—regular or even occasional meat—may have played some part in their estimates. Also they may have had thoughts of drink that was not brewed from rice; but whatever thoughts they may have had, their words were of the pistol and the knife.

"And, Will?" said Santvoort, "what does Will say?"

"Yes," said the surgeon. "What does Mr. Adams say?" For Adams had so far said nothing.

"What I say," said Adams, "is that he can fill his pistol with balls and swallow it, and sit on his knife. To hell with him."

They laughed first; and then they stared at Adams.

Adams was, in a sense, staring at himself; for he had not realised, till then, that his decision was so vehement, or indeed that he had come to a decision at all.

"Do you not want a pistol and a knife, then?" asked the captain.

"I want them well enough," said Adams. "And there is nothing I can see to prevent our having them. If they come in the boat we can take them. But as for going with the dog, that is another story."

"Do you think he still lies?" asked Santvoort. Their minds were still open on that point and Adams, after his vehemence, surprised them by saying, quietly, "No."

"Then, if he is honest——" one of them began; but Adams interrupted him; "Even if he is honest he is—he is——" he hesitated and stumbled for some word that would make clear to them the thought that was dim in his own mind. "He is himself."

That was the best he could do with it, for his decision had come from a process too simple for discussions or explanations. He had considered Ieyasu who had called him "An-jin" and the priest who had called him "son." As the result of the two considerations his decision was already made. He could not have explained it any more than certain other men could have explained their choice when they dropped the business of net-mending and followed after the stranger who had said to them, "Follow me."

"You go," he said, "if go you must. I will stay. The odds are against your getting home—but there is a chance that you may do it that way."

"Do you not want to go, then?" It was Santvoort who actually asked the question though something in the manner of Adams's speaking had brought it uppermost into the minds of all three.

"Well enough," said Adams. "I suppose I do want to go, as you do. But——"

"Four would have a better chance than three," the surgeon suggested.

Adams shrugged his shoulders. "That," he said, "no man can say. The contrary may be the truth. It is all a hazard. Perhaps my staying here would make your going safer, since I know the Portingal's share in it, and could perhaps hold him to his bargain. But that is as it may be. Go. I stay."

"Who said we were going?" demanded Santvoort. "If it is not good enough for you, Will, it is not good enough for me. I stay too."

"We have by no means decided," said the captain. "There is still much to be said on both sides. But if Santvoort and you are already resolved—well, it is all one to me."

"And to me," said the surgeon. "For, when in doubt do nothing, is the soundest wisdom that I have ever learned."

"Doubt," said Adams. "I am in no doubt. I will follow no man who lies and schemes counter to the Emperor. He would have crossed us, but the Emperor spared us."

They drank another round of the wine the padre had brought them, and another to empty the second bottle.

They began to see their rejection of the offer in the light of an adventure, and talked of it brightly.

"In doubt do nothing, according to the surgeon," Adams said, "but there is much we can, and will do. We will discover the whole plot to Mitsu and his men." Santvoort opened the third bottle. He filled the mugs, and Adams went on. "Let the boat come; Mitsu and others will board it instead of us. The pistols and knives will prove it—and the carrying of arms is itself a powerful offence."

They grew loud in their talk after their months of perplexed silence.

Adams was as lusty as the best of them. "We'll show them!" he shouted. "The Emperor shall see who are his prowling enemies, and who his friends. Drink to him, lads!" They raised their mugs and stood absurdly ceremonious with their shoulders bent under the cuddy ceiling, steadying themselves with a hand on the table.

"The Emperor!" Adams gave them the toast, pompous enough for a Lord Mayor's banquet. "Ieyasu! our friend!"

The others mumbled after him, "The Emperor," and bent their knees to straighten their throats to the heel-taps in their mugs.

It was the drink that had brought lustiness and final lucidity to the words of Adams. It was assisted, possibly, by his luck.

For at a knot-hole in the planking of the cuddy's dim ceiling was the flat, neat little ear of Mitsu, where it had been for three hours.

For three hours the swordsman who was also acrobat and the trustiest of Ieyasu's secret service men had been stewing in his sweat between the timbers of the poop deck and the planks of the cuddy ceiling. He had not spent ten minutes on the ship before finding that the removal of a small locker-side above the tiller would give him a place where an eye and an ear placed alternately at the knot-hole would tell him much that his Lord would be interested to know.

CHAPTER XII

HE listened with the blandest innocence when Adams and Santvoort disclosed to him next morning the padre's plot.

"It's proof," Adams said hotly at the end of the tale, "proof, man! What more do you want than a promise of firearms and blades?"

"Ieyasu's judgment is his proof," said the other. Then he grinned. "As you have cause to know." His superiority to them both in taking this information as neither a joke nor a disaster exasperated Adams. It seemed that speech itself was no way of communicating with these people. He cursed in English and in Portuguese and then said, "If you won't tell the Emperor, I will."

"Naturally I will tell him," said Mitsu. He grinned again, and this time Adams felt that communication was not so impossible. Mitsu straightened his torso and his throat and held up an imaginary mug and said, pompously, in as good Dutch as he could make of it: "Ieyasu, our friend." He staggered away a pace or two with a seaman's unsteady pace and then collapsed in laughter. It was minutes before they could get anything out of him but explosions, and Adams stood by in profound dismay.

Foreground and background were an enigma as vast as reefs and shoals, as rocks and mountains and stars when a man had neither line nor staff, neither compass nor tables wherewith to sound and plot them. Imperturbability could make a meaningless image of a face perched above the nimbleness of a leopard. Laughter could convulse the face and paralyse the body—the gurgling and giggling as of a tickled two-year-old. The secrets in a man's heart were stifled because other men could not comprehend his talk; and a man could keep no secrets because the very walls had ears. . . .

"An-jin," said Mitsu when his laughter was spent, leaving him weak but very happy. "An-jin, it is lawful for a soldier to punish any man carrying weapons. To-night we will make a game."

The game was a simple one—simple as Mitsu's laughter, and was as simply played.

The boat drew alongside two hours before midnight. The lantern produced by the soldier who answered the boatman's hail suddenly went out. It was in pitchy darkness that the four men with their gifts from the padre climbed up, and still in pitchy darkness that four men lowered themselves from the port into the boat, and the boat shoved off. In darkness and in silence the boatman plied his oars till a thin bamboo whistled in the air and came to sudden rest across his shoulders. His howls were lost in the laughter of Mitsu and his three colleagues as they beat him and then tossed him over the boat side to swim for it, or sink.

They came back to the ship where lights had been lighted and brought aboard four small pistols and powder-horns, four bags of balls and four neat poniards. The fact that the four present-bearers had disappeared, that Adams was recovering from a kick in his stomach and Santvoort was massaging the back of his neck were grounds for fresh laughter; for Adams had scorned Mitsu's idea that he and Santvoort and two or three of the crew could not hold four Japs.

The parcels contained wine and dumplings and oranges and three volumes of religious writings. Adams, who took no unnecessary risks in matters of religion, laid the books away in his locker, and went out again—taking one bottle of the wine—to Mitsu.

He still could not believe that this coup was nothing but a theme for a joke. He found, in time, that Mitsu was able to be a little serious over it, but only because he wanted reassurance that he had not technically interfered with the Jesuits.

The next day this anxiety seemed to grow upon him and he left them.

They saw no more of the padre nor heard from him. They made no further attempt at barter, but walked on the beach. They were followed by a soldier, and the soldier was followed by the crowd of idlers that grew a little smaller every day as the novelty wore off the hairy ones.

In a fortnight Mitsu returned. He came aboard to say that he had despatches for the Daimio; he asked Adams to see to things so that the ship might be moved, and in three days the hulk of the *Liefde* was rolling to the tide again and gently pitching to the pull of the skiffs that towed her weight behind them. Adams stood at the tiller, staring at the binnacle which was still empty and of no use, as he himself was useless. A cripple, an idiot or a child could have done his hand's turn of swinging the bows to the cables that trundled the dead ship after the team of skiffs; southwards first by east, and then east by north they tugged her. The wake they made for her passage was like the troubled ghost of the wake she herself had left when life had still been in her; when there had been spars and stumps of mast and rags of gasping canvas; when there had been compass and astrolabe and tables, and in Adams wit enough and stomach enough to use them; wit enough and stomach enough to fly with skill from the fury of sea and winds which they had no means of facing.

For all its helplessness and needlessness, aboard the hulk that lurched, lifeless and passive, after the skiffs of lusty little oarsmen, the *Liefde's* crew was in good heart. They were all well again from their distemper—all of them that had not died. The underlings had been ragged and penniless; but sailors did not care. The Delight-Valley of the town of Oita had been a small one, but it had been full of laughter. The *Liefde's* men had been jolly freaks as they swaggered ashore in their rags, and they found great hospitality. The girls who were good to them were smaller and daintier than their experience had ever before embraced; but they had not been sharks for money, and so the crew had no great disaffection for Japan.

As for the four who were the masters of these men, they had given themselves the illusion that this sojourn was now an adventure of their own choosing. In the first day they restored sailing-discipline among the ragamuffins who spent their watches in dreams of the glamour they had already known in the lantern-like houses of Oita, of the further ease and splendour that lay beyond the horizon. The crew were sailors still; their preoccupation for the voyage was the luck they should find at the end of it; and they were as nondescript a lot as any brigand could have commanded. Hospitality had led to the exchange of gifts and tokens. There was neither a button nor a buckle left among them. Some were still bearded—shaggy or neatly trimmed—others had been jocularly shaved from throat to crown in the manner of their hosts. Others, again, had a fortnight's stubble over such previous shaving. The Swart from Barbary had gone one better than the rest by instructing a friendly barber to shave the wool from the back of his head as well as the front of it, getting the utmost value from the great ebony knob that had been so obviously admired by certain daughters of happiness in the Oita bazaar. Shirts and woollen caps, hose and belts and breeches had often gone the way of the buckles and buttons of the more thrifty. Some of the crew mustered, therefore, in cotton drawers or loin-cloths; in a tunic tucked, shirtwise, into them or flapping loose; in a short jacket or flowing gown. Some had sandals, and all had straw hats for shade from the sun and shelter from the drizzle.

Santvoort, with no particular thought for the morrow, was wearing out his breeches. Adams, brooding casually upon the future, had folded breeches and his last two shirts into his chest with his books and dividers and protractors, and sat in native drawers by the whip-staff hole and binnacle. For sunless days and hours of rain he wore his leather coat that had somehow survived the thousand visits that had been made upon the ship; for sunshine he had the jacket tokening Ieyasu's first impulse of friendship. The captain and surgeon, whose fevers and weight of responsibility had kept them from adventuring much ashore, clung to their hose and breeches and cloaks, their hats and shirts and doublets. There was a pair of scissors among the four of them; so they trimmed their beards in the manner to which they had grown them. They were obviously officers properly distinguishable from the men, while between them all was the common bond of a promise that they were not doomed; and they had found, so far, that respite in that country was good enough for the simple wants of sailor men.

To port there was no horizon. Behind the low, jagged hills of the coast all was a riddle of mist and shifting cloud, till out of the riddle there arose the shape of Fuji. In the mist that could have been over Thames or Medway it was golden or silver, blue or grey or palely orange in the dawns and noons and evenings, black against the sunset, lost in its own shadow among the shadows of the nearer hills that sprawled out to sea. Only its shape it did not vary, impressing its immutability upon the minds of the *Liefde's* men as it was impressed already upon the minds of the nimble oarsmen who towed them—the shape of rice poured slowly, clean and dry, from a measure.

The voyage ended with the closing in upon them, aport and astern, of the tumbled crag and cliff that is the peninsula of Izu.

First ahead, and then to starboard, came gentle breakers and low rounded hills—sandy-brown and breast-like, or bristling with dark pines—the peninsula that was the home of fishermen; and the flotilla swerved into the landlocked Gulf of Yedo, where it was already twilight while the sun still shone out at sea.

A derelict prize was no uncommon sight in Yedo harbour, atow behind a team of fishing skiffs; a battered junk, Chinese or native Japanese, or the timbers of a carrack from the Portuguese or Spaniards plying from the Moluccas and the Philippines. There was nothing about the *Liefde* to distinguish her from any of these, and the flotilla made no great stir at the waterside. The hawsers slacked and dropped from her sides into the dark water as the rowers rested on their oars; and Adams and Santvoort went forward to look to the anchor, seamen alertly following them, for letting it fall was to be to them the symbol of a voyage's end. But they saw that a skiff was hurrying to them with Mitsu in the stern. He hailed them and stayed them.

Scrambling aboard he explained that they were not to anchor, but to make fast to a mooring; and so the symbol at the voyage's end was not of the freedom of riding at anchor, but of the captivity of a hulk made fast to a disused jetty.

The officers went back to the poop, seamen slouched again into a group, amidships, while hawser-ends were carried to the jetty by skiffs and the ship was warped alongside by fishermen.

"Soldiers will guard the ship, An-jin," Mitsu said cheerfully, but with the crispness of an order. "For you and for the others there is hospitality ashore."

"Soldiers may *eat* the ship," Adams mumbled, "for aught I care. They will eat the rest of the cargo."

"*Soldiers*, An-jin," Mitsu emphasised. "Soldiers, mark you. There will be no more thieving."

CHAPTER XIII

MITSU explained to Adams and Santvoort that the houses to entertain them were but a stone's throw from each other. Santvoort's was the first they came to, about a mile from the jetty; and the Dutchman went cheerfully in with the bundle he had brought from the ship, saying he would visit Adams when he had made himself comfortable. "In the morning, Hollander," Mitsu said. "It is already late, and men may not be abroad by night so near to the palace, unless a soldier accompany them."

"Very well, morning then," Santvoort agreed.

For nearly two and a half years now Adams and Santvoort had scarcely been out of earshot of each other. If this sudden parting of them gave any hint of purpose sinister, the suggestion was denied by the easy, cheery manner of Mitsu. He motioned and spoke to a youth who had stood in the road, idly watching them, and the youth at once came forward and took from Adams the bundle he had made aboard in a piece of sailcloth.

"Your host, An-jin, is a man of some distinction," Mitsu explained as they strolled on. "A soldier. It would embarrass him to see his guest carrying his own luggage."

"And the boy?" Adams asked, indicating the porter.

"Oh—he? One of the City's young." It was as though Adams had asked him the name of some particular pebble in a watercourse, of a grain in a dish of rice. "They fetch and carry. They ply trades of one sort or another."

"And do the bidding of any man who commands them?" asked Adams. "Are they slaves then? Dogs?"

"Slaves?" said Mitsu in surprise. "Certainly they are not slaves and dogs. But I am a soldier."

"And my host also is one who may go out and command men to do things?" Adams asked.

"Certainly," said Mitsu. "If he has justice and reason. It is just and reasonable that a loitering youth should carry dunnage for a soldier or his friend and guest."

"How long, Mitsu, is this to go on?" Adams asked. "I mean this 'guest' business?"

"That," said the other, "is between you and the General."

"But I have work to attend to," Adams said. "We came here for a purpose and can still fulfil it with our cargo."

"As to work, it may be that the General will himself have work for you to do, apart from the cargo. But you will be very well in the house of Magome Sageyu, your host."

"And suppose I will not do the Emperor's work?" asked Adams.

"Then," said the other, shrugging his shoulders, "I suppose you will not do it. It is no great matter. To-morrow, however, I will come to take you to the palace where the General would speak with you."

The door of the house was opened by Magome Sageyu himself. In the brief moment of ceremonial of meeting and greeting, the youth with the bundle was utterly ignored. He put down the bundle on the doorstep and loitered off. Magome clapped his plump hands together and a girl appeared in the narrow hall-way. Magome, without interrupting his speech with Mitsu, indicated the bundle. The girl passed by the three men, a glint of ebony teeth between her smiling lips. She stooped to the bundle, turned with it, and was gone again into the back of the house. Magome chatted on, his hands resting each on a sword hilt, and Mitsu translated his welcome and the extension of the meagre and rough hospitality of a simple old soldier and his daughters to the distinguished Contemplator of the Needle.

Adams felt rather a fool. "Contemplator of the Needle," set him awkwardly on stilts of some sort. The peculiar, faint bombast that had come into the manner of Mitsu as he stood up to Magome and his phrases, sword-hilts to sword-hilts, while Adams stood with his hands in the empty pockets of the breeches he had donned for the occasion, was foolery. Yet a warmth came from the geniality of the little old soldier with a wrinkled forehead that shone from his eyebrows to the top of his head, darkened only by a long scar, and the mouth that flickered with glib phrases and set again into a toothless smile.

This warmth was not foolery; nor was the smile of the little creature—child or woman—whose back, nimbly bent for the picking up of Adams' dunnage, had been a smooth sash and enormous bow; nor was foolery the passing friendliness that had met him in the eyes that glanced up from a dozen or fifteen inches below the level of his own.

He had pushed off his sandals, as Mitsu had discarded his. They followed their host through the small hall and the room at the end of it, to the steaming bath-tub. Already there was a change of clothes there for Adams out of his bundle, native drawers and shirt and tunic and coat.

Adams fussed for a few moments after the bath, over the clothes he had discarded, but Mitsu told him it was no matter, the women would see to them.

Wine and the meal were served by the girl who had carried off the bundle and another almost indistinguishable from her.

There was no harshness in the way old Magome ignored his two daughters. His benevolence seemed to be for their ministrations and to include the girls merely as a part thereof.

The click and rattle of speech that Adams heard was beginning at last to be not mere gibberish. His ear was beginning to detect words and phrases and sentences; questions and answers; sagacities and jests—they were still meaningless, but they had some hint of shape. The friendliness between the two soldiers when the wine had warmed them and the food comforted them out of their first ceremonious stiffness, the inclusion in it of the dumb needle-watcher squatting on his heels, and his inclusion equally in the silent, deft service from the girls gave him an ease which he had seldom known before. For where had there ever been such a general smoothness? Certainly not during the apprenticeship in the shipyard of Nicholas Diggins in Limehouse. Not on the barges and hoys of the coastal trade, nor the nondescript victualling-ships of Elizabeth's Navy; not in the handier vessels of the Barbary Merchants where he had learned his craft of needle-gazing and star-reading.

In the little brick house on the hill at Gillingham he might, perhaps, have known glimpses of such ease; but there, in Gillingham, there had always been an end to them. Mary, the thrifty one, knew only too well that there was a bottom to every purse of a seaman's wages; and in those hard days Mary knew, and Adams knew, that every meal in the house at Gillingham drew the bottom of the purse nearer to the top. In the course of jobs grabbed up because they were better than nothing with intervals of waiting and scrambling for them, Mary became the double responsibility of Mary and a child; then another child; and spaciousness and ease were altogether gone from Gillingham. They had been gone from a dozen years of restless life.

In the eating of that first dinner in the house of Magome Sageyu an opinion was formed in the mind of Will Adams. A dozen years later he committed it thoughtfully to a sheet of rice paper with a reed pen: "the people of this island of Japon are good of nature, courteous above measure . . ."

Ceremonial stiffness came again, from nowhere, into the bearing of the host and Mitsu when Mitsu rose to go. A lantern was brought for him by one of the daughters, since no man might be abroad by night without advertising himself for any to see, by a light. Another call from Magome—some words including the familiar "An-jin" produced another lantern from the back of the hall, in the same hands that had carried away the pilot's bundle.

Adams followed Magome and the girl with the lantern to a little room at the end of the passage. A sleeping-mat was spread for him, and a coverlet. Smiling some gently silent message of goodness of nature, of courtesy above measure, the girl slid aside a papered panel of the room's side and showed the small cupboard where the contents of Adams's bundle had been set out—his breeches and his already washed and dried shirt, his instruments and two books, his woollen cap, a horn spoon and some English pence.

Adams could say "Thank you"; and he said it slowly, twice. The girl withdrew, and her father smilingly begged that the needle-contemplator would deign to sleep in peace and honourable comfort in a place so poor. Adams recognised the good-night phrase and answered with "Sleeping honourably." To Magome, too—excited a little towards a chuckle by the pilot's speech—Adams said "Thank you."

CHAPTER XIV

SANTVOORT appeared at the house in the morning just as Mitsu was taking Adams with him to the palace. Adams introduced him to his host as the "Hollander" and Santvoort, quite glibly discarding his sandals at the door, found the old man's hand in his sleeve and shook it. For the Dutchman was in high spirits, immensely proud of a new jacket that fitted him amply, cut out and stitched overnight in the household of the kite-maker that lodged him. For it he had given the kite-maker some heavy brass buttons.

"There is no need for the Hollander to come," Mitsu said.

"There is need for him to walk," said Santvoort. "After three weeks aboard. He will wait outside if the Emperor does not require him. He will be quite comfortable sitting in the sun."

"We are guests now, right enough, Will," he said as the three of them turned away from the house. "Something will surely come of it. There is no more of that business of watching us with soldiers and saying us 'Nay' at every turn." He told now of the simple transaction that had given him the coat for buttons. "We could not have done that at the last place. This place is better altogether."

"And well it might be," said Adams. "Mitsu says it is the capital of all the land." He turned to Mitsu. "There would be good merchants here," he suggested, "we could readily sell our cargo."

"Not many merchants," said Mitsu. "Osaka is more the merchant's city. This is a city of soldiers. But as for selling, there will be enough. It is of some selling that the General would see you."

"There——" said Santvoort.

In a mile of walking they had passed carpenters at work in their yards; smiths and weavers and dyers.

"Buying, too, will be easy," said Adams. "There is timber, and the workmen seem good."

It was a trick of their minds, Santvoort's no less than Adams's, that they thought coherently along the alternatives of their destiny without any overlapping of the alternatives themselves. They thought of staying; and in such thinking they accepted the staying and considered it apart from the possibility of anything otherwise. So also when they thought of going they thought of the ways and means only of that going.

Till now, Adams reminded the Dutchman, it was only in the great bridges of Osaka that they had seen timbers that would make a mast.

When they came to the crossing of the canals and moats about the castle itself they saw that in Yedo, too, there was good timber.

They passed sentries who might have been drowsing loafers, drowsing loafers who might have been sentries. Most of the straw-hats tilted up, most of the faces under them cracked into a smile for Mitsu and his charges.

Occupied completely with thoughts of the cargo's market, of masts, of planks, of the twisting of reeds or silk into rope if the country had no hemp, of victualling—and of doing it all at some profit—Santvoort sat down on a stone in the courtyard and Adams went in with Mitsu.

Ieyasu, here, was not the mighty Shogun seated in rich state in a gilded chamber as he had been at Osaka. An older man was with him, and a younger and the three sat together on a mat, talking. There were no formalities beyond a nondescript combination of salute and bow from Adams, who also sat down on the spot indicated by Ieyasu in front of the three.

"He trusts you have found some small comfort in the house of his soldier Magome Sageyu," said Mitsu, who remained standing.

"Aye; thank him," said Adams; "quite comfortable. And I hope he is well."

Thereafter Mitsu became a vehicle that scarcely delayed the speech that passed from one to the other.

Adams wished, said Mitsu, to sell the contents of his ship. Very well. Of the eighteen pieces of ordnance on the *Liefde* the General would buy sixteen, of which he had need on his walls.

Adams was staggered. Of what use, without ordnance—or with but two pieces—was a ship in seas verminous with Portingals and Spaniards?

Of what use, asked the others quietly, was ordnance on a ship that could not go to sea?

Could not? retorted Adams. The *Liefde* was a good ship. All he wanted was material, some good workmen and a little time, and he could make her as seaworthy as ever she had been.

There was a pause.

Then words came slowly from Ieyasu, slowly and deliberately from Mitsu. Interpretership was a trust sacred in the hands of any man of honour. It was an art also, whereby the smile and gentleness or the frowning anger of the principal became at once the smile or the frown of his interpreter.

Mitsu smiled and spoke gently. "When the heart of man is torn between two desires, An-jin, his mind is without a friend. It waits only on the issue of a fight between two enemies. Of these, even the victor emerges weakened by the combat—and is a poor friend. A man in doubt is a man in fetters. Therefore be without doubt. Your ship, An-jin, is not to sail. Not yet."

Adams said, "Enough of this nonsense of buying, and guests, and friendship, then. You have got us. Do as you will. Steal the ordnance. Steal the whole damned ship—cargo and all; but don't talk of pirates and robbers again. Or friends."

The answer came, smoothly and gently. "Beware of anger, Pilot. For, as doubt is a shackle upon the limbs of a man, so anger a blindness in his eye."

"And thieving is thieving," said Adams, "whatever else you may call it. You say you will buy our ordnance?—but of what use is money to us if we may not buy the things that will put our ship to sea? It is as though you gave us no money—if we may not buy with it what we want."

"Money can buy much besides fittings for a ship."

"But we want no other things," said Adams.

"The fault then is in you," said Ieyasu. "Not in the money. See how a man in doubt is fettered; he may not even move his hand for the spending of money."

"Oh—take the pieces," said Adams. "But it is by no transaction of buying or selling that you get them from me.

They are not mine. I am the pilot, not the Admiral. If you would deal, honestly, it is with him you must deal—the captain. It is nothing to me. I only take his orders."

"And thus you are rid of doubt!" The words came with laughter—not laughter at a man before company which is an insult equal to a spitting in his face; but the laughter of a friend for a friend. "There is no action freer from doubt than an obedience to orders."

Adams said, "If he will sell them, well and good."

"And you?" said Ieyasu. "Will you tell him to sell them? As you told him not to break faith with me and sail with the priest?"

"All I told him then was that I myself would not go with the padre," said Adams. His anger had, somehow, abated; but he was still ready to disagree upon details.

"Did you not realise that it would have been the only way of going?" This was cajolery, not argument.

"Aye," said Adams. "I suppose I did."

"So there is no doubt in you." Ieyasu went on quietly. "This talk of going is only talk; and you will stay—undoubting, as my guest in this inconsiderable city."

"Aye," said Adams. "It looks mighty like it. For here, I suppose, are not even priests and rascal Spaniards to aid us."

"That is true," said Ieyasu. "There come no other foreigners here. All the men here are mine."

"Like our ordnance," said Adams.

"Of a metal every whit as sound," was the smiling answer.

Adams shrugged his shoulders against the defeat this talk held for him. "If I could speak your tongue," he said; "or if you could understand mine, I would have more to say."

"It will come soon enough, An-jin," said Ieyasu. "Lesser men than you have learned to speak our tongue in a very few moons. We will see then what you have to say. In the meantime see your captain and tell him we would buy his pieces."

"He, too, is responsible to others," said Adams. "We are but the servants of a great company. What we have we only hold for them."

"Very well, then," said Ieyasu. "I will hold it in turn for you. Your pieces—the property of your masters—will be safer on the walls of my fortress here than on your ship. More lives stand between them and destruction on these walls than at the waterside. You yourself shall instruct us in their care; and in their use—if your captain will condescend to lend them to me as a friendliness to a friend. As to the other service of which you spoke—to other masters—that, surely, is dissolved by your disasters. You are all guests now—equally. You have no masters other than your host. Take whatever comfort you may find in his hospitality and learn, meanwhile, to speak his tongue."

"Yes," Adams mumbled. "All very well." He was thinking not so much of himself at the moment as of what he would say to the others. For himself there seemed to be a vague reasonableness about it all. He knew now that he was defeated utterly; but, somehow, in the defeat there was no sting. But the telling to others that they were defeated—captain and crew—was another story altogether.

"Shun doubt, An-jin," said Ieyasu quietly with the voice of Mitsu. "Follow the swing of the needle. Deal with destiny as it is—not as it might be but is not."

Adams replied, mumbling again . . . "All very well to talk . . ."

CHAPTER XV

To Santvoort he said, "We might as well face it, Melchior. Here we are, and here we are likely to stay. He will not let us go, and go we cannot."

"What is it he would do with us?" asked the Dutchman. Adams treated the question as though it had been addressed to Mitsu, who was walking back with them. But since Mitsu treated it as though he himself had been a dozen leagues away, Adams said, "God knows . . . make gunners of us, perhaps—but look——" he pointed at an immense bronze piece mounted at an embrasure in the wall. "Mitsu," he said; "you have ordnance already."

"Yes," said Mitsu, "in abundance. But it is said that pieces from your Europe do not, at times, split in the firing."

"Have you gunners then?" asked Adams.

"Yes," said Mitsu. "Not soldiers, you understand—but artisans from below; makers of crackers and fireworks. They shoot off ordnance when there is need, for a wage. It is not, I think, for the base occupation of working cannons that the General would hold you as his——"

"For God's sake," Santvoort interrupted him, "don't say 'guests' again. It is the best joke we have heard in this country, but it was the first one and it has lost its fun."

Adams was thinking that it was, at any rate, time now for Mary to have lodged her claim in Rotterdam and to have had justice and payment from that good uncle of Santvoort's.

"What is your Japan word for 'guest,' Mitsu?" he asked.

Mitsu very solemnly said, "Okyaku Sama."

Adams repeated it. Then to Santvoort he said, "Swallow that, Melchior. And look——"

They stopped, looking towards the harbour.

Mitsu said, "You see your road now and I will return to the castle. If you lose your way any man but a zany can put you upon it again. I will see you again to-morrow, An-jin, when you have told your captain of his loan to my General. You know the house of his lodging, by the water. If you have need of anything, tell Magome."

"Aye," said Adams, "I'll tell him. I know your language now. 'Okyaku Sama'—honourable guest."

"It is sufficient for the time being," said Mitsu and left them.

They stood still, looking at the harbour.

The sun was at its height and their two shadows were the shadows of their great straw hats; discs that touched, rim to rim, in the soft white dust of the road. Behind them was the castle that Ieyasu had built as a bulwark against the Eastern turbulence in his early days, and now was his bulwark against the treachery of West and South. Its strength was of stone and mortar, of bronze pieces and of powder and shot. The cement of this bulwark was the mortar that held the stones together; it was also the judgment of Ieyasu that picked his men, and the peculiar genius of him that held them. The palace was the symbol, in the sprawl of city, of the city's unity. And the city's unity was the unity of a storm. There were currents in it, and under-currents, and whirls and eddies; there were depths and shallows, raging wildnesses and stillnesses as of death. Stillnesses that were death. The men of it had thoughts that mingled together into the single thought of an army; and thoughts that were solitary, incommunicable by word, but active in every daily shift of each man's matching his poor wits against a hard destiny. Every neighbour, every stranger, every friend was a tool for the hazardous cobbling together of a livelihood, for the fabrication of a scheme, the materialisation of an ideal whose material was nought but the conduct of men.

And it was heedless of this storm and its whirls and eddies that the two strangers stood in the shadow of their straw hats looking over the squat roofs of the crazy city of Yedo that was to become Tokyo.

They raised their eyes to the sky and stood without moving; for they beheld above the roofs a dragon. It was scarlet in the light and black in the creases of its shadows; and it lurched and swooped away from a colossal fish.

The monsters circled and manœuvred while the Englishman and the Dutchman watched them in wonder.

They stood poised in the air. They trembled and shook as they sped abreast, further aloft from the earth, till the dragon suddenly stopped and tottered. It writhed in an agony and then tumbled away, sinking slowly and lifeless to earth again, like a corpse trembling on the tide.

The fish soared magnificently upward. . . .

"God!" said Adams. "They can make kites that will answer the helm of a thumbnail at their thread's end a mile away. . . . And they rig their ships square with shutters of wood instead of sails, and with as much answer in them to wind and helm as a gammon of ham."

"They've made *us* answer to wind and helm right enough," said the Dutchman. Then he shrugged his shoulders. "I'm sorry, Will, for you, with your wife and your home and such like. For me it does not matter. He can't keep us here for ever; and I'd as lief see something of this land. It's been a great way to come, and——"

"Aye," said Adams thoughtfully. "He can't keep us here for ever. I, too, would as soon—as soon——" he glanced, as he hesitated, over roofs and dusty roadways, at the harbour with its rabble of junks and skiffs and rafts of timber. "I'd as soon—I mean, Melchior—if we went home now, we would be going as a failed and tatterdemalion lot; empty-pouched and empty-handed. But when we do go——"

That was all they could say of it; so they walked on.

"The captain will take it in pepper," said Santvoort.

Adams said, "Not he. He's too weary for sneezing. I'll tell him it is good that we stay awhile and fill our pockets; and as good he will take it."

Adams was right. The captain was older than himself by ten or a dozen years, older than Santvoort by twenty-five. His life, ashore and afloat, had been a series of small, successful commands; for a shipmaster was a commander first and a sailor second, since the mere technicalities of sailing were a job for the pilot. Ashore he had commanded details of the coastal garrisons; afloat he had commanded units of a flotilla. His schooling, therefore, was less in the invention of orders than in the taking of them, and handing them on.

Adams and Santvoort found him seated with the surgeon in

the courtyard of their house. It was a larger house than Magome's, brighter in the painting of its pillars and, unlike the kite-maker's that lodged Santvoort, neat and uncluttered in the courtyard.

The two Dutchmen, still snobbish with their buckled breeches and cloaks, their woollen hose and leather shoes, sat on a low bench—strange giants where the oaks and pines of the garden's edge raised their gnarled and ancient shapes no higher than the stranger's heads.

Beyond the garden there was a bright knot of men and women and a scramble of children, smiling and chattering and staring.

Adams and Santvoort saluted, and the antic produced a rattle of comment from the onlookers; the word "An-jin" clicked freely in the talk.

"The Emperor sent for me, Captain," Adams said, wasting no time. "We are to stay here a while. A year perhaps." This last statement was no conscious invention. A year, or a little more or a little less, had occurred in his mind as the reasonable period wherein a naked man might clothe himself, might fill his pockets and find some means of returning to the wife and country that claimed him.

The information did not particularly disturb the captain. It was, in fine, an order.

"There is some business done," Adams went on. "His Majesty would place some of our pieces on his walls. They are skilled in the use of ordnance and already have some good pieces of their own casting. Ours will be as well on the walls as in the ship. Besides, Captain, when we get leave to unlade the ship, and trim her, the ordnance will be well out of her. You are to fix a fee for its hire."

The captain thought a few moments. It was scarcely his affair, this business in its details. He supposed, however, that as he was now Admiral, he could not utterly wash his hands of it.

"That is good," he said. "See to it, Mr. Adams, and tell me. See also to the cargo, you and Santvoort, and make a full inventory. And the crew must be held in hand, Mr. Adams. Find their lodging from your interpreter so that, if there be occasion, there can be a muster."

He had had many a company in billets before this. He knew the difficulties, but his very familiarity with them made of the difficulty a vague comfort. "If the lodgings are scattered they must be changed so that word may pass easily from one to another."

Adams did not argue the point. He was well satisfied, for the moment, with the captain's acceptance of the position, and with the surgeon's silence. Any questioning from them would have aggravated the questions at the back of his own mind, questions which he could only answer by dealing with destiny as it was, and not as it was not but might be.

CHAPTER XVI

DESTINY as it was, within the next hour, contained a pressure from Magome at the door of his house, upon Santvoort to step within and eat a meal with himself and Adams.

The Dutchman noticed and told Adams that between the household of his own host, the kite-maker, and this one there was a difference. He did not define it beyond stating that the old soldier was a Cavalero. "And these girls, Will . . ." he said, "—a man's cap comes off to them by nature."

"They are dainty," said Adams.

"Aye, but they are somewhat else, too, than dainty. The bawdy little dancers and singers in Oita were dainty enough. But it was not his cap that a man hastened to remove——"

"They go about their work," Adams said, smiling at the sisters as they carried their trays, "like the edge of a blade."

"Like moths, Will," said the Dutchman, "or butterflies—with their great wings of the bow folded over their rumps."

This exhausted the poetry in the guests. They looked away from the blade-edges—the moth-butterflies—to the father of them whose skull's toughness had once prevented his brains from falling in two. The old man entertained them by smiling and pointing to every object within sight, slowly telling them the name of it and smiling while the Englishman and the Dutchman repeated the word after him. They ate their meal to the last morsel on every dish. "Please God," said Santvoort, "our guts will shrink in time, or I shall go hungry for a year—if year it is to be."

After the meal they sauntered from the house of the soldier to the house of the kite-maker, and Adams saw in an instant what Santvoort had meant by the difference between the two. Dignity was utterly lost here in geniality. Santvoort was already hail-fellow-well-met. His introduction of Adams to his host was forestalled by the craftsman's smile and quiet hailing of Adams as "An-jin." Children played about him as he worked, crawling in the litter of paper around him, sticking their plump fingers in his pot of paste, bouncing away from the cut he occasionally gave with a slender bamboo on a retreating stern.

He worked as only a genius can work, attending with half his mind to his craft and with the other half to his guests, his children and to every passer-by in the road that bounded his workshop. He split his bamboo and pared the slender wands with a single sweep of his knife. He was making, at the moment, nothing so magnificent as the dragon and great pike that had fought, thread against thread, that morning. Jobs like that were special commissions for some leisurely merchant or soldier who was a master in the handling of a kite. Now he was turning out only the cheap small things that children and hobble-de-hoys would fly at the festival. Splitting a bamboo for spine or ribs, he would run his blade along it, removing shavings fine as silk. Screwing up an eye he would look along its length. He would balance it, in one gesture, on his blade, correcting some hair-wide fault. He defended the heap of finished pieces against the happy children with a flick of the material in his hand.

In the yard behind him poles were set up and woven about with silk drying in the sun; the fine thread had been imperceptibly coated with powdered flint in a paste whose recipe was his own and his darkest secret.

He, too, had seen the tumbled drifting away of the dragon that morning, the swoop and triumphant ascent of the pike. It was he who had supplied the thread to the pike-owner; and he was happy.

Adams examined some of his finished work in a pile, held down by stones upon the corners.

Santvoort improved the hour by selecting a few odd sticks of bamboo from the master's scrap-heap and whittling and shaving them into a supply of tooth-picks.

Old Magome came out of his house next door and walked past the kite-maker's yard. Loiterers made way for him as he stepped along, stilted and portly, on his high sandals, the sword hilts thrust out of his paunch like the antennæ of some great insect.

He had only a short word for the kite-maker who paused in

his work and in his incomprehensible chatter to smile at the old soldier and to greet him. The old soldier, it was clear enough, was in no genial mood at seeing his guest, the pilot, squatting in the rubbish of a kite-maker's yard. The kite-maker's geniality and vivacity were quite undiminished by the snub. He smiled broadly with admiration after the stiff and pompous old man, and he conveyed to Adams and Santvoort that the admiration had a sound foundation: he took an unsplit bamboo lath and whipped it out of his left hand in the manner of a sword being whipped out of a scabbard; he fought an enemy with it, defeating him in half a dozen passes, giving the *coup de grâce* to the bottom of the infant crawling nearest to the paste-pot. He slew another thus and another to show the hairy ones the stuff his august and honourable neighbour was made of; but Adams was more interested in the kites than in the historic exploits of his host. He could not see, with the things lying piled one upon another, how the tackle would be bent to them to give the control which steered them—rising, swooping, curving and diving through the air—as half a score could be seen doing in any patch of sky, for the festival was near. The grace and swiftness of them was a marvel as great as the waddling, lumpish clumsiness of the shutter-rigged junks in the harbour.

He went into the house to see Santvoort's room and then, having seen it and having smiled and mumbled syllables to an old woman, to young women and to children inside the house, he left the Dutchman at peace with himself and the world and went across the road to his own lodging.

The two girls peeped out at him, friendly and shy, from the living-room as he entered the house; so instead of going to his own room he left his sandals and went in to them. They were at work, sewing. The elder one—if it were possible to distinguish as elder, by some subtle air of greater seriousness, the one that had appeared first and carried away his bundle—was a little abashed by his entry. She moved as though to conceal the work she was doing upon Adams's breeches. They had been unpicked at every seam and washed, and were now being sewn together again (just as the younger one was sewing together a jacket of her father's which also had been unpicked for washing). Artist as she was at her work, she would have preferred its owner to have found it finished instead of still, as it were, on the bench or easel. For an instant Adams was as aghast as any man at the shock of any ruin; but after that instant he smiled down at the eyes that looked up at him; he realised that if the old breeches were done for utterly, it was no great matter.

He would outlive more in that country than a pair of threadbare worsted breeches.

"Thank you," he said as he had learned to say it from a people who seemed to use the word more than any other. With his great hand he patted, not the head, which looked too precarious a feat of hair-dressing to be tampered with, but the firm, round little shoulder.

Her eyes sank away from his; the ebony teeth appeared again between her parted lips as she assured him it was nothing; and the other one, having nothing in particular to be shy about, begged him to be seated.

He lowered himself to the vacant mat, still a little cow-like in his movements compared with the nimble grace of theirs.

The younger one said something involving the word "An-jin" and Adams shook his head. "Adams," he said, tapping his chest. "Adams. Will Adams."

They would not have it. "An-jin," they insisted—Contemplator of the Needle. And then said the elder one slowly, "An-jin Sama."

"Very well, then," said he; for that, too, was no particular matter any more than the ruined breeches. He shrugged his shoulders. "'An-jin Sama,' then. And you?" he looked from one to the other.

The younger one answered. The answer sounded very like Magdalena; and it was by the name of Magdalena that he thereafter called her.

The other, inclining her widely-sashed torso a little towards him and bowing her head, recited a name in which the sounds simplest for his ear were "Bikuni."

His ear and his intelligence had been enough in the last few months to have told him that in adding "Sama" to his name of "An-jin" they had shown him a courtesy. "Bikuni," he said,

and smiled at the achievement of his ear and his intelligence—
"Bikuni San."

His reward was a chuckle of laughter and smiling glances
from one girl to the other.

The dissected breeches were not the only work that had been
engaging Bikuni San. From the tools and materials at her side
she handed to him a small bundle—jacket, tunic and drawers
newly washed and neatly folded; ready for him when he should
have bathed. This business of intermittent bathing was also,
like destroyed breeches and the casual substitution of one
name for another, no great matter. He could accept it as he
had accepted the others.

He went out and took his bath and changed into the fresh
garments, leaving the discarded ones by the tub. In the room
he found that the girls had set a tray for him with cakes and
thin biscuits and a draught of water. He sat down before it,
gathering either that they had had theirs or else that they did
not care for any. And it was thus that Magome returned to
find them. The old man was as obviously pleased by the sight
of the Pilot, bathed and combed and at ease, quietly eating
cakes and biscuits while the two girls sewed, as he had been
huffy at finding him squatted with the kite-maker.

In an instant Magdalena was gone from the room and in
moments she was back again with another tray, for her father.
He sat by Adams, adding to his smile the further geniality of
telling the Pilot the names of the cakes and biscuits. Adams
replied as genially by airing the knowledge he had gained
without Magome's teaching.

"Magdalena," he said, and then "Bikuni San."

The old man was delighted. Geniality alone would not have
accounted for the volume of his laughter. Behind it, as well as
geniality, there was a pleasing secret of some small triumph.

CHAPTER XVII

Mitsu arrived from the palace next morning with a troop of soldiers behind him, and behind the soldiers a score of workmen and coolies. From the bosom of his tunic he produced a document which he unrolled and expounded to Adams as a deed whereby the Pilot and the Captain of the Holland ship undertook to rent to the Shogun Ieyasu the ship's ordnance at a fixed rental per month to be paid to Adams and the Captain on the first day of each moon. Adams and the Captain were to supervise the removal of the pieces from the ship, responsibility for their safety to pass from them only when the guns had been landed.

The document was in Japanese.

Adams refused, flatly, to sign it.

If it had been written in Dutch which he could understand or in Portuguese of which he could understand as much as mattered, he would have signed; but as it was, he would not.

Did it matter, Mitsu asked, whether he could understand it or not? Were they not in all possible respects at the complete discretion of the General? Of what consequence was it whether he understood the paper, letter for letter? The word of a master was his only bond. Only the master's word was the reality. Writings, in one language or another, were only poor pictures of that reality.

Adams agreed. The signing of a document at all was foolery; but the signing by him of a picture where he could see neither head nor tail would be a foolery utterly beyond him.

Ruination of the last pair of breeches in the world did not particularly matter to Adams; taking his name from him and giving him another did not matter; smiling him off to a bath-tub at odd moments in the day did not matter. But the signing of a document he could not understand went utterly against his grain.

"No, Mitsu," he said. "God damn me if I do it."

"Perhaps," said Mitsu quietly rolling up the document, "the

Hollander will sign it, with the Captain. Perhaps, too, it would be more fitting. You are only their pilot."

"Perhaps," said Adams, seeing that it was bluff.

"The money would naturally go to them in such a case," said the Jap.

"Naturally," said Adams. "In such a case they would have earned it."

Magome stood watching it all with great interest. He knew that a bargaining was in progress. He was prepared for the process to cover any number of days up to a full week; for he could feel that the Englishman was a stout bargainer.

"I wonder that you have not made it clear to his Majesty that I am no more than the pilot," Adams said next. "Go to him, Mitsu. There is still time; but perhaps he would take it amiss that you have lodged the Captain with a merchant, the Hollander with a toy-maker and I, the mere Pilot, with a Cavalero."

Mitsu sulkily unrolled the document again and laid it on the writing-box. Magome hugged himself with fresh interest.

"Know that a maker of kites is no toy-maker, Pilot," said Mitsu. He said it because it was the only statement he could find at the moment with any dignity in it. "Know also that the choice of your lodging was made by the General himself."

"Thank you," said Adams. "It is my hand he wants, then, to the paper. Write his words in Hollands or in Portingal and I will sign."

"Write?" said Mitsu. "It is not for me to write."

"Let the Hollander write it then, or let the Captain write it in Portingal."

"And of what use is that?" asked Mitsu. "I cannot read it."

Adams shrugged his shoulders. "It is of equal use to that one, which we cannot read." He smiled at the pouting little soldier. "After all, Mitsu, they are only poor pictures of the same reality!—the word."

"I said it is the word of the master that is his sufficient bond," said Mitsu.

"But are we not all masters now?" asked Adams. "The old service that bound us was ended with our being cast away among you. We are masters—and all, equally, guests."

Mitsu swore darkly. Magome saw that the Englishman had done something rather neat; for he had seen few men who could set Mitsu to mumbling curses.

Adams made a concession. "We will sign that writing in your language, Mitsu. But we will sign it written out also in Hollands or Portingal; or both."

"You are talking to a soldier, Pilot," said Mitsu pompously. "Not to a chaffering huckster. I brought you one writing to sign. What sort of a law do you think would permit me to return to my General with three writings?"

"I do not yet know your law," said Adams. "But if that is unlawful, let us sign none of them. Let us go to the General with the three writings and ask him what he himself would have us do."

"He has already told me."

"He has not told me," said Adams.

"I have told you. I am his emissary."

"You are not my emissary," Adams said. "I, too, have words to say."

"Be careful, Pilot," said Mitsu. "You are dealing with the General."

"I am dealing also with a fair man," said Adams.

Magome saw that in this last bout Mitsu had fought well enough and steadily, but only as a man who had a stick or some blunt thing in his hand against a good sword.

Mitsu said, "I will bring the Hollander."

"And the Captain?" asked Adams.

"One extra document will be enough," said the other. "Two hidden writings would have no more use than one."

He stumped out of the room and Magome took the opportunity of reading through the short deed he had left on the box.

The soldiers and the workmen outside took no interest in the going of their leader into the house of the kite-maker, and his returning with the Dutchman. One day was as another for them; whether they trotted from one place to another to do the work, or squatted, waiting to trot, was all one.

Santvoort took a writing brush and a slab of ink and did the best he could with them to set down in Dutch the purport, which Mitsu gave him, of the deed. Adams had shaken his head and laid aside the sheet of paper produced by Magome, and the Dutchman got his writing into half a dozen lines at the bottom of the same sheet with the original.

It was the sum mentioned that had most impressed Magome in the document; and on seeing what could not be anything but an improvement being made in the bargain, he felt that the only safe thing for him to do was to go out of the room.

He hurried off.

When Mitsu told him in the hall-way that they were going, he and Adams, to seek an audience at the palace, he felt again that it was well for him to be alone—or in the company of the amiable Dutchman, who could neither comprehend his words nor read the delight in his features.

The two walked up to the castle, Mitsu showing that he had no urgent need for conversation by moving at a choppy, trotting pace with which it was impossible for Adams to keep step. Adams tried a while—losing a pace or two and grabbing up his distance again. Then, managing to keep his sandals, he discovered a slithering movement for a long stride that kept him abreast of the scurrying Jap.

"Take that, my lad——" he said, when a stretch of a hundred yards had shown him the success of this new method.

Mitsu was ready for jocularity again.

"With legs as long as yours," he said, "and as hairy, it is small wonder that you should keep pace with one who is made in the shape of a man. You do not walk on land, An-jin. You swim."

"And you do not walk," said Adams. "You dance."

"Dancing or swimming," said the other, "it is all one; for we shall both soon get to the General—who neither dances nor swims."

"You're not afraid, are you, Mitsu?" The whole affair seemed a not very difficult matter to Adams now; and he could not, in any case, see that Mitsu was responsible.

"Soldiers are not afraid," was the mildly pompous answer. "They sometimes fail to see—if they try to look so far—the outcome of events."

He was still a little uneasy, however, as Adams followed him into Ieyasu's chamber.

He made a considerable speech and unrolled the document. Ieyasu took it and examined it, peering at the Dutchman's diminutive scrawl. Then he spoke.

"He says that you have reason, An-jin," said Mitsu; but Ieyasu's expression indicated nothing. With a dreamy deliberation he moved his dirk a hand's-breadth out of its scabbard. To Adams, because of Ieyasu's dreaminess, the gesture meant nothing. To Mitsu it was no surprise, because anything at all that the General might do with his dirk in those or any other circumstances would have been no surprise. Ieyasu held the document's edge under the exposed edge of the dirk and slowly pulled it up—the blade cleaving it through. Again, again and once again he did this, smiling and speaking.

"Only the word is good, An-jin," Mitsu translated; "as between soldier and lord, friend and friend. And a full understanding of the word. A writing not understood is a word, even as you said, unspoken. But even as a soldier draws his sword only to use it, so he gives his word only to abide by it. Fairness breeds fairness. For, as his face seen in the mirror of water, so is the face of man to man. Your word is your bond—for yourself and your Captain and your Hollander-friend and the others; and his Lordship's word is his. Is it good?"

"Aye," said Adams. "It is good. But I can't speak for the Captain. He may think otherwise."

Mitsu translated again: "He will not; and if he does it is no matter. For it is with you that his Lordship deals. If you would have the hair shaved from off your face and head a barber will be caused to wait on you—weekly or daily—as you prefer."

"Thank you," said Adams. "But it is no matter. It can grow."

CHAPTER XVIII

MAGOME was pompous no more, nor huffy with his guest the Pilot.

Adams could squat with Santvoort beside the kite-maker or his neighbour, a carpenter, and amuse himself with tools on scrapped pieces of wood, and the old soldier, bristling with his swords, would pause with a hand resting on each hilt and speak to the artisans and again, more cheerily and more slowly, to the Pilot and the Dutchman.

The *Liefde's* guns had been removed and a bag of money paid over to Adams and the Captain. Mitsu had explained the coins; explaining, with a Spanish riall of eight, that a tael was its equivalent; that ten mace were a tael, ten candereen a mace, and a hundred gin a candereen.

In the course of the explanation it became clear, with no allusion to such a triviality, that any man who conveyed money from one man or one place to another received, as by a law of nature, some of the money he had so conveyed. In obedience to this august law—surprised by it, but awed by its majesty into acceptance—Mitsu smilingly tied three tael into the corner of his tunic and went his way.

The captain, the surgeon, Adams and Santvoort set out the balance on the bench in the garden of the lodging and counted it. The amount was duly set down by the Captain in his book, with a brush and ink-block borrowed from the merchant in the house; its value in rialls of eight and in Dutch crowns was duly set against it. It was agreed among the four, and their argument formally recorded in the book, that money was due to them and to the crew, and that this money was distributed among them against such due in proportion that tallied with the proportions of their wages from the Company. The captain, now Grand-Admiral of the fleet, pushed aside his share into a separate heap. Adams, Pilot-major, took his. The surgeon, as Surgeon-General, and Santvoort, boatswain-in-chief, took theirs. The balance was divided into twelve equal piles.

Adams and Santvoort went forth to muster the crew, proclaiming to them the distribution of a prize; and the crew was not long in answering the summons. They turned up, all twelve of them, from the street that lodged them, followed by every available member of their respective households. The Swart waved back the three girls that were his especial escort and they fell into the crowd that stood happily in the road while the captain addressed his men.

He was the good commander again and they listened attentively to him. Those that wore breeches hitched them about their waists and hooked their thumbs into belts. Those that wore drawers and tunics and jackets pulled them and straightened them and stood with folded arms.

They were twelve, the captain pointed out, instead of fourteen because two, being blackguards and rascals, had gone the way of blackguards and rascals—God knew where. From that they could see for themselves that straight behaviour was expected of them and demanded of them. The money he was about to hand to them was on account of wages. He would endeavour, when the time came, to show the Company the fairness of considering it as prize, in addition to wages, but he wanted it to be clear that decision on this point rested, not with him, but with their employers. They must continue to bear their employers in mind. It was only for a short time, as seamen for a little while ashore, that they were scattered thus, and idle. Their indentures still held. Chance, just as it had landed them there, would set them aboard again; for the Emperor was a fair and just man. He urged them to comport themselves peaceably and well, a credit to himself and to their country; for they could best serve their country among these strange people by showing that its men were sound, peaceable and decent. He alluded to the vicissitudes that could well arise from over-whoring, from squandering their prize on debauchery and brawling.

He made each man, as he took his money, put his mark against his name in the book.

The sail-maker, supported by the Swart, raised a cheer. The Swart's three girls were close about him again, clamouring and scrambling and laughing up to his broad white grin. The twelve were immersed breast-deep in the gay tide of their friends; and the tide bore them back again to the bazaar.

The captain and the surgeon had breeches pockets in which to stow their treasure; Adams and Santvoort, in their tight-fitting artisans' drawers draped over with tunics and short summer-robes, adopted Mitsu's simple way of tying the great coins into the corners of their garments. They walked slowly and thoughtfully, holding up the robes to keep the weighted ends from knocking against their shins.

"What are you going to do with it, Will?" Santvoort asked.

"Change one of the smaller pieces and go out to discover something of the worth of it," said Adams. "The rest I shall give to the old man, my host, to keep for me."

"And when he has kept it for you?" asked the Dutchman. "What then?"

"Who can say 'What then?' " Adams answered testily, for it seemed that Santvoort was trying to bait him. "A man need not spend all the money he gets as soon as he gets it. Unless he is a fool."

"Or a cleverer one than we are, Will." Santvoort was serious enough. "It could as well be a bunch of stones for all the good it can do us—and so I am better off than you in having the smaller load to carry. For what is money to men who have food and drink set before them whenever they sit down in a house? Food that is only a bag of wind, it is true, with no ballast; and drink in morsels that warms the belly but leaves the head cold. Still, it's the best they can do; and money could not improve upon it."

"We don't know that, Melchior," said Adams; "when we can speak the language we might find—something."

"Women?" suggested Santvoort. "Nay, there are women in abundance even for the dumb. In my house there are too many. It has but five rooms or three—according to whether they hoist or furl the walls between them. . . . My house is not like yours, Will."

"No. Mine is no bawdy-house," said Adams. "And it were perhaps as well for you to remember the same. That old man, by all accounts, is no loiterer in the matter of drawing his swords; and if those girls are not his daughters, they are his wives. But I think they are his daughters."

"Praise God on their behalf, that it is not from any family likeness that you say that!" the Dutchman chuckled. Then he became thoughtful again. "Will," he said, "the eye becomes adjusted to strange things. If I were to see now what we once would have called a fine girl I think I would laugh, as Mitsu and the others always laugh when they call us 'old hairy ones.' These women here with their black teeth and oiled top-knots, creatures so small as to run two to a good armful—they stay in my mind, even when my eyes are shut, as great possibilities of loveliness."

Adams smiled. He had heard expositions enough before from the Dutchman on the subject of women; but he had never known them take a wistful turn.

"Perhaps," he suggested, "you could buy a house with that money of yours. Your host has paper enough to make you one."

Santvoort ignored the joke. He said, "It is difficult to recollect what we did spend money on—except women."

"You might have spent it on nought but women," said Adams. "I——"

"Pah!" Santvoort interrupted him. "You even more than I. I only hired them while you spent all you had—and all you were likely to have—on paying for the one you had got. So it is all the same. When your belly is full and there is a shirt to your back, the only use for money is women. Not a dozen women filling a house like mine to overflowing. But one——"

"For you, Melchior?" Adams laughed. "One woman? Say one at a time, lad."

Santvoort was puzzled by the Englishman. At times he would be solemn as an owl over nothing, as huffy and as testy as an old great uncle; and at others he would break out in cheery ribaldry.

"One at a time, then," he admitted sulkily. "For that is all that even you can say. And you've had your own already— for eight years or ten, before we sailed, you'd had your house and your wife—so it would not matter if you were now shut in a paper house with a dozen women all as beautiful—when your eye has once got adjusted to them—as a flower or butterflies. You could sleep on a bag of money and dream richly. But you, who do not deserve it——"

"Make no mistake, Melchior," Adams said quietly. "There is no frolicking with the women in my house." He said it only out of kindness. Melchior, for all his austere and able handling of any rabble aboard a ship, had fallen into many a silly scrape ashore. It could well have escaped whatever machinery of perception functioned in his square skull that Magdalena and Bikuni San were a different story altogether from the flowers and butterflies in a kite-maker's jolly household.

"We could buy some presents!" Santvoort exclaimed with sudden inspiration. "Stuffs for the women to make gowns, and some gay combs. Something for the children; and wine and some confections. The men think well of wine and feasting, Will."

"Aye, we could," said Adams. "We could also throw the money into the harbour. For that is what we should be doing —until we have learnt something of the language, and of the money's value. You could easily pay the price of a house for a stoup of wine to-day, and be none the wiser."

"I'll go out with my host," Santvoort said brightly. "I'll let him buy."

"Note down whatever you can, then," said Adams. "I've a point of lead in the house. It takes well on their paper."

Santvoort went with him to the house for the lead and the paper, and then went shopping with his host.

Adams went in, with his weighted skirts, to Magome.

CHAPTER XIX

MAGOME, in the living-room, waved him to a mat. Adams squatted with a thud and clatter of his money.

The old man's forehead, considered as a feature of his face, was a wedge whose one side was the line of his eyebrows, and the other the old deep scar. One eyebrow was complete, and vivaciously cocked; the other was a little tuft that disappeared into the cavity which was the scar's end. The wedge was all wrinkles, and above it, on the scar, rested the shaved dome which curved away to the tight, stiff top-knot.

"Condescend honourably to sit," said he, the tough old hands resting, as ever, on the sword-hilts.

There was much, he knew, that he should have said; but he knew also that it was in him to say much that should not be allowed to escape in words; so he was not sorry at the soldier's luck that for the moment held his tongue or stopped the ears of the Needle-watcher.

Adams, however, had nought but regret for his dumbness. He knew well enough, already, how glib and easy was the process in this country by which anything could become a present; and it came into his mind as he thanked his smiling host for the hospitality in his gesture and smile, that steps must be taken to prevent any misunderstanding in the transaction that was about to take place.

He solemnly untied the first bundle of great coins in his skirt, keeping it sheltered between his knees. He had got some sense of value from the beaming pleasure of Mitsu as he had appropriated and tied up, on his own judgment, three good tael from the leather sack when the Captain had broken the Shogun's seal and held the open mouth towards the soldier. Forty-three tael, half a dozen mace and some candereen were the Pilot's share of the remaining coins, and he had decided that five tael would be a suitable and a handsome gift to his host. He counted the five slowly out from between his knees into his hand. Making a very distinct, ceremonious gesture of it, he held the money out to Magome. The old man snatched his hands away from their perches and tucked them into his sleeves tightly against his paunch. Obviously, as he smiled and chattered, he could not think of any such thing as the Pilot was suggesting. He was shocked and surprised, though touched and delighted, that the Contemplator of the Needle should have had a thought so generous towards his unworthy self. . . . Adams was satisfied that his own point was clear. Further ceremonial in the matter became superfluous and he merely shoved his hand forward, saying, "Come on, man. Take it!"

No. It was too much for the soldier. He still chattered and objected and withdrew himself from the brilliant and magnificent glare of such generosity; but—perhaps—since——

He withdrew one hand from the folds of the sleeve and coyly, very coyly, stayed the pressure of Adams and took just one coin. It was the least he could do in the face of the overbearing and most amiable insistence of his guest.

"Four more," said Adams. "Here they are."

It was too much. Altogether too much for the astonished warrior. Yielding—since the breast-plate of steel that will turn aside the arrow of an enemy is softer than a silken doublet against the kindness of a guest and friend—yielding, he took a second tael as though it were the most delicate blossom from a fragrant garden.

"Come on, man!" said Adams again. "I mean it. Here they are!"

Protesting, Magome took a third; and protesting further, a fourth. Magically they disappeared about his pocketless person; but at the fifth he absolutely stuck. Adams knew, somehow, that this was indeed the end of it, just as he had known that all the rest had been coquetry. His own attempt at impressive gesture and ceremonial faded utterly in the light of Magome's next performance.

Magome stood and spoke.

There was nothing now in the world to curb an eloquence that had made of him, a quarter of a century earlier, an exile hunted from his own province with a cleft scalp and a cracked skull; for his present listener could hear nothing, but could only see the gestures.

And in them he saw the magnificence of a Lord, the swagger of a ruffian, the austerity of a priest, the gaiety of a boy, the tenderness of a mother and the fealty of a friend.

Adams in turn had to do something. Getting up on his knees, to leave his shirt and its burden undisturbed on the floor, he took Magome's hand in his and shook it.

But he had more to do and he set about doing it. He sat, not as Magome sat on his heels, but flat on his buttocks with his legs stretched out in front of him. Between them he untied the second knot of money, adding it to the first one. He counted the tael into three heaps of ten each and one of nine, setting them in a row at his side. Next to them he set four of the six mace. The remaining two of these and the odd candereen he stuffed carefully into his sash. Then he looked about him. Seeing nothing that could be of the service he required, he removed the few coins he had placed in his sash and tied them again in the skirt of his robe and unwound his sash. Spreading it on the floor he wrapped it slowly over and over round the cylinder made by his thirty-nine tael and four mace. By kneeling over them and patting them, and patting his chest, he cleared any vestige of doubt that could have lingered in the mind of a half-wit as to the ownership of that cylinder. Then he went to the writing-box in the corner of the room and took a sheet of paper and the writing-brush. On the paper he made thirty-nine large strokes and four small ones. He went through a performance of impressive failure in an attempt to push the cylinder into the writing-box, which was obviously too small for it. He looked about the room in search of some other possible receptacle; but the room held, at the moment, nothing but mats, the writing-box and a screen. He indicated the possibility of a cupboard in the wall and Magome smiled, and scuttled away from the room. He returned with a small chest—a sheer slab of polished wood that showed neither join nor lock nor hinges. Setting it down upon the floor, obscuring Adams's view of it with his stooping body and hanging sleeves, he did whatever was necessary to release the lid. He turned to Adams for the money. Adams very solemnly handed him the paper and the writing-brushes. The old man counted the marks, large and small. Below them he wrote his initials or his signature—smiling his approval of the astuteness of the depositor—and handed the receipt back to Adams.

They laid the cylinder on the wrappings that covered whatever other treasures the chest already held, and he pressed the lid back into position.

He took Adams with him to replace the chest under the floor-boards in the room where his sleeping-mat was spread.

He called to the girls as they went back to the other room, and Magdalena followed a few moments after them with drinking cups and rice spirit of the kind that had opened the first dinner.

He was in the highest of humours even before they had sat down to drink; and after two cups of the liquor the words in his breast and his throat that it was useless to utter, produced a discomfort that Adams could see.

Adams, sashless now and pocketless, fumbled for some housing for his receipt. He moved, finally, to stuff it between his skin and the waist of the tight drawers he wore. A sudden, surprised clucking of disapproval on the part of Magome ended in a contemptuous guffaw. He leaned forward and thrust his hand against his guest's bare stomach and ripped the flimsy drawers away, splitting first one leg of them and then the other with two neat movements. Swearing or grumbling or praying, he twisted the rags into a ball between his hands and shouted through the door.

Adams stuffed the receipt into his sock and was, he thought, ready for anything.

He was surprised, however, to see Bikuni in the doorway, listening to a dramatic discourse of which the subject was the rags in the old soldier's hand and—as obviously—that section of himself which the rags had recently adorned. Very humbly the girl took her scolding for the outrage that a guest so honourably distinguished as the Needle-watcher should have gone breeched in the vile garment of a workman or coolie. . . .

Bikuni took the rags from her father and bowed and withdrew. While she was gone, Magome struttingly showed Adams that what the man of any distinction wore beneath his jacket and his sash and his robe and his tunic under-robe was, magnificently, nothing.

The girl returned, and Magome took from her a sash and folded hakama—the loose, skirt-like pantaloons with a thin board in their waist at the stern, wherein a gentleman sometimes walked abroad, wearing them over and not under his robes. He gestured Bikuni towards Adams with the large gesture of gift-bestowing.

Adams took the things and thanked her.

The new sash he wound about his waist, deftly, and exactly as he had learned to do from Mitsu.

Magome smiled and nodded and clucked his approval of the Pilot's skill. He stepped forward to pat the sash and straighten a fold in it; and he adjusted the overlappings of robe and tunic. Then he stood back, caressing the sheathed marvellous blades in his own sash, sad at the thought that in the sash of the Needle-watcher there were none.

From some shadow of ceremony and ritual about them as they dined, and from the cool feeling, one against the other, of his dramatically unbreeched hams, the Needle-watcher knew that he had taken a step with regard to his destiny. The geniality of his host told him while they were both still sober as judges that the step was all to the good; but it told him nothing of its direction.

Magome was generous with his meagre store of wine that night; they drank of it again after the meal; and Adams went to his mat and his coverlet in a mist that glowed with the warmth of hospitality—till it was a black, impenetrable fog.

The fog, he realised, was the language. And even a needle-watcher had nought to do in a fog but hold a steady course till he had got through it, or till it lifted.

CHAPTER XX

THIS fact remained clear in his mind the next morning from the general tumble of the night's ideas, clear and solid as Magome's receipt and the folded pantaloons that were added to his possessions.

He advanced towards his fog-watching on his first encounter with Magome. He confronted him with the writing-brush and ink and a paper napkin and tried to make it clear that he wanted to learn to write his name of Needle-watcher, An-jin. The old man shuffled so that Adams thought his meaning was missed. "Magome, then," he said, "Magome Sageyu." He would have explained himself by producing the receipt with the signature, but Magome readily took the brush. He scorned the napkin, however, and produced a small sheet of paper from the writing box, after economically passing over several slightly larger ones. Good paper, Adams perceived, was not to be trifled with to the extent of using a large piece when a small one would do.

Magome wrote his name and Adams tried him again with An-jin; but the old man, admitting no defeat, called Bikuni. She wrote the signs, or drew the pictures that were the signature of Adams—and it was clear that hers was fine writing while her father's was a scrawl. She wrote her own name for Adams next, and then the name of Magdalena.

But it was many days before the fog began to lift.

He had enough Dutch for fluent conversation with Sant-voort; enough Portuguese for a rough understanding, and a little Spanish. These he had acquired from the simple fact that the human ear is permanently open. He had taken no particular steps about the matter. Words had tumbled into his ears and fixed themselves in his brain to fit themselves to a skeleton of idiom and of thought that was the same for all of them.

But the Japanese language was no language at all. Xavier, studying it with the devotion of a scholar and the patience of a saint, gave it as his balanced opinion that the tongue of Japan was Satan's masterpiece of a device for keeping a people in ignorance of the works and the mercy of God. It served, at any rate, to keep the bewildered Adams in ignorance of the thoughts of Magome, the old pensioned soldier, and the thoughts of Bikuni, his daughter.

Magome saw in the Pilot a chance such as he had never seen before; and Bikuni, in the most accurate sense of ballad and romance, was in love with him.

Magome was, first and last and all the time, the phenomenon unique in a unique society for which "gentleman" was a weak and colourless word. An Englishman of leisure appeared in due course in Japan. A man of even his resources in the matter of accurate terms and words nicely chosen (if spelt slap-dash) was stumped by the phenomenon of such as Magome. The word he found for them at last was Cavalero.

Some forty years before the arrival of Adams at the house of Magome, an argument in the street of a Southern village had produced a headless trunk in the gutter, the wound upon the head of Magome and—just as the blood from it was blinding him and his senses were tottering—a second corpse, the younger brother of the first one.

It was then, by the luck of good soldiers, the hour of dusk. A servant carried Magome to a boat; for he who had killed, except an enemy of his Lord in battle, must either cut his belly or fly.

The times, on the whole, were easy ones for a swordsman of any repute. Gentlemen, such as Magome, exiled by an immutable law from their own province, became "Ronin." They were the focus, if they were worth it, of a vow of vengeance; but they found employment enough and a soldier's ration in practically any province that appealed to them, so long as their swords remained good.

Only twice in the course of the forty years had Magome been constrained to move on again from his adopted provinces— when the vendetta (duly and officially registered with the Notary) had developed as far as the crises which Magome faced with his usual skill. It was now twenty-six years since there had been any crisis or any menace; and the vendetta was

probably forgotten. If any members had survived of the
families of the two brothers whose insulting behaviour and
poor swordsmanship had made of Magome a Ronin, and of
the families of the two avengers who had subsequently joined
them, they had probably become hucksters of one sort or
another in the Southern and Western towns. For it was there
that doubloons and rialls of eight were becoming weapons that
blunted the edges and corrupted the metal of the swords of the
Samurai. They had probably forgotten, these kinsmen of the
dead four; they had forgotten Bushido, the code of the
Samurai, and become men of business, chaffering with Portuguese and Spanish pedlars and their half-bred and polyglot
rabble that was said now to overrun the village of Magome's
youth.

The old man still spat when he thought of it—of a soldier
who would trade, and forfeit the status of soldiers.

But even a soldier had to live; and Magome was becoming
old for soldiering. He had, furthermore, his daughters. To
live—and that they should live in seemly style—he had
swallowed pride as much as it was fitting that any cavalero
of the old school should swallow it. Ieyasu in his fortress-city
of Yedo, through his underlings, had given casual work to
Magome as he gave it to any cavalero of the old school—a man
who kept his given word as certainly as he used his drawn
sword; but the ageing man's gorge rose against the indirect
service of a Lord through the agency of underlings as it rose,
more and pitiably more, against hard rations and bare lodging
where other men, younger and less tried, could daily be seen
lording it.

It was lawful and seemly that a swordsman should receive
a fee for teaching his craft to the young, provided that they,
too, were of the right blood. For twenty-five years he had
taught fencing in the yard of his house and thus been able to
buy, honourably, a measure of wine for occasions.

What he wanted, however, as his years increased, was an
estate. The small one to which he had been born had gone
from him, by immutable law, when the head had gone from
the shoulders of the bragging and jeering young man who had
drawn his sword against him; and the miserable fees of a fencing

master were not likely to produce an estate to replace it. The work he did unwinkingly in the secret service of the Shogun was the simple routine duty of a soldier and its fee was no more than his house and rations.

At other times, perhaps some stripling pupil would have cast his eyes upon the master's daughters, or would have been approachable through a marriage-agent—if Magome could have raised the agent's fee; but now—and for the past half-dozen years—noble families had been imported yearly into Yedo as hostages, and there were dowered brides and to spare for any young man whom Magome would have considered decent—a man, that is, who served not underlings of the Shogun but the Shogun himself.

Mitsu, straight from the Shogun, billeting Adams upon the old man, had said "Treat him handsomely. He is a worthy one and approved by the General." He had produced coins to ensure entertainment that befitted a worthy one, approved by the General; and Magome had thought at first, with some hardness and bitterness in his heart, that here would be another underling to lord it over himself.

When he saw that Adams was no dignitary, but a simple, sprawling creature who squatted with a kite-maker and played with the tools and the chips of wood in the yard of a carpenter, he saw that the wind is ill indeed that blows no good. Vaguely, too, he liked the Pilot. When he saw him push his prodigious hairy right hand into his sash instead of using it to firm the document leasing the *Liefde's* guns to the Shogun, he was struck into a state of most acute attentiveness. When he read the figures in the document itself his attentiveness reached a pitch of bewilderment.

On the basis of those figures he had spent a day estimating the Pilot's share of the money at about twenty tael; and the Pilot had lounged in, as though nothing whatever had happened, with forty-three. From rousing the old man's imagination, he had proceeded, still as though nothing had happened, to touch his heart. He had done it with his smile, perhaps; or with the magnificence of five tael held out in his great paw to the threadbare cavalero, and with his simple confidence in handing over to his care all he possessed in the world.

It is small wonder, then, that the cavalero ripped away from the loins of the Needle-watcher the close-fitting linen that was emblematic of meniality, and gave him first the nudity and then the voluminous hakama of the gentleman-at-large.

And Bikuni, whose very humility would have made her speechless if she had not been already dumb to the Pilot, was utterly in love with him.

Magome had been a widower for a dozen years. When he had settled in Yedo after the two old encounters that had seemed to see the end of the vendetta, his wife had joined him. She was an old woman nearing forty when she set out from her brother's house to join the husband she had not seen for twenty years. A son was beyond her; but she bore Bikuni and Magdalena with the least possible delay.

She had done towards their education whatever could be done for genteel children by the time one of them was ten and the other seven. When she died her piety and devotion to the fencing-master with the cleft crown were already a distinguished example of conduct, and a tale that was told to the young. The children of such a mother, and of a father with sword-play that was also a tale told to the young, were companions welcome in the household of any hostage-nobleman.

They thus grew up, with the thoughts and in the practice of the craft of ladyship. They could write so that the elegance of their writing was the envy of greater calligraphists than Magome who had summoned Bikuni to set down the pictures of three or four names. They could answer verse with verse and they could meditate upon fortitude and fidelity and obedience, and other virtues that were of the mystery of love. On the lure of it they could also meditate; upon its warmth and its depth and its sweetness.

It was unseemly (in the writings of the sage) that young women should occupy themselves with the wearing apparel of men-folk in the household; but in a household where there was no matron and where a man was as helpless as the Needle-watcher, seemly conduct itself demanded that Bikuni should execute the duties of matron.

It was she, therefore, who sewed and unpicked and washed

and sewed again the garments of Adams; thinking, as she folded them, of the great chest they would enfold, of the broad back, white and peculiarly smooth, while the chest was rough with hair, of the arms that were prodigious in their girth, but shapely.

CHAPTER XXI

SANTVOORT, set upon the way of it by the sheet of paper and the point of lead that Adams had given him, compiled a price-list. Guided by this, Adams one day brought home some fruit and wine to which Magome replied on the following day with more fruit and more wine. Santvoort dined with them and it passed unnoticed, till the evening was nearly done, that neither he nor Adams nor Magome had been quite dumb. Words strung themselves together in questions and answers and comments till the Englishman and the Dutchman were aware that a great war was tearing at the country and that Mitsu was away with his lord, fighting it. Of the issue Magome seemed to be in very little doubt.

"When?" Adams and Santvoort both asked him; for it had occurred to them both that they were still waiting for something to happen, and the something it now seemed must be the end of this war.

Magome shrugged his shoulders as the girls came in. He did not know.

Santvoort moved to go, but Magome waved him to his heels again. There was no hurry; he, himself, with a lantern, would see him to his home next door.

The girls took no part in the skeleton of conversation which Magome, after laying a finger to his lips, diverted from the subject of the war to the cargo still sealed into the hold of the *Liefde*. He asked if it contained swords or firearms or crockery or clothes or money. He drifted from their answers into a doze.

The girls sat away from them, sewing; and the Dutchman and the Englishman fell into a quiet conversation of their own.

"They are a long way off, Will," Santvoort said. "In my house it is different. I'm married."

"Married?" said Adams, his eyes startled away from their contemplation of Bukuni.

"Aye," said Santvoort. "Three days ago. It must be that

I'm married. The family approves—it's the tallest of them, the one that was trouncing the little boy the other day when you were there. A fine woman, Will. Fine. A daughter, I should think. Anyhow, the old man made a big speech three days ago when they were all present—she, too, very solemn and shy, smiling at me. We'd been talking together about the place, she and I; and I suppose the old man had come to conclusions. He wasn't far wrong. So they made a sort of festival for us, with all the family mustered, and cakes and things set out and special dishes for us two. All very solemn, and the old man asked me something very carefully and I said aye, it would be well. And I suppose it means that I'm married. Don't you? They've given us the room at the end of the place. The old man rigged it up with bits of scantling from next door, and paper."

Adams was puzzled. Marriage had meant more to him than that, and it meant more still. It had meant, in fine, and in the perspective of jobs and domestic interludes, a burden. It had meant other things as well; but those things had, although they had varied the burden as to its content, left it, for all its variations, a burden.

Marriage had, in short, changed him. To Santvoort it appeared to furnish only a topic that was almost casual. Santvoort was not changed, and he was not burdened.

"Why didn't you ask me to come, Melchior?" Adams asked.

"How was I to know what was happening?" asked Santvoort. "When she stepped out and up to me with the dishes and looked up smiling prettily, and the old man talked, I thought it might be a sort of troth-taking. I saw nothing against it. It was only when the room was given to us that I saw it was a marriage. And I still saw nothing against it. But it was too late to make a guest of you. Well, I see nothing against it now."

"If it is a marriage," said Adams doubtfully.

"It's a marriage right enough," said Santvoort. "There have been other things going on. Neighbours have come in and grinned at me and said things. And the old man has put things up on the posts; tickets and flags and signs. And we've all been into town to the notary and I gave him my name. It's a marriage right enough."

"But you saw me yesterday," said Adams. "You could have told me as we went to buy my wine."

"It was on the tip of my tongue, Will. But—somehow—it stayed there. It seemed hard on you; those two there are a long way from you. There's that something about them and your old soldier. A marriage here would have to be a different sort of marriage. A real marriage."

"You forget, lad, that I've had a real marriage already."

"No," said Santvoort. "I was remembering that too when I held my tongue. Much good it does you! But if you had been lodged in the house of the carpenter——"

Adams grunted interruption. He had caught something of the snobbery of his host. "The carpenter indeed!" he said. He looked at the old man nodding under his scar and the black rope's end of his top-knot; at the girls bent to their work. "I am very well where I am, Melchior. Very well indeed."

Santvoort continued, as usual, along the line of his own thought.

"I daresay you could change it easily enough when they come back from their warring, his Majesty and Mitsu. If we are staying here for some length of time, it is as well to be comfortable."

Old Magome's head tumbled forward to a snore. It woke him up and he blinked benignly upon his guests. Santvoort got up to go; and Magome, too, rose. Bikuni lifted the lantern to his hand. Adams offered to take it, and Santvoort and he both tried to assure the old man that he need not stir.

But he made it very clear that he must; only a Samurai, or a man accompanied by a Samurai with a lighted lantern, might be abroad by night.

At the door he put on his sandals, and with the casual gesture of a man buttoning a glove or turning up his collar, he made sure that his sword moved smoothly in its scabbard.

Adams, while he was gone, helped the girls to collect together the materials of their needlework.

He alone, it seemed, could not follow the Dutchman's happy principle of making himself comfortable. He was happy enough, in a general sense. He liked his host and felt that his money was safe with him. He knew that Mary must, somehow or other, have pulled through in Gillingham; her relations were behind her and they would have come forward when they knew that they could not blame him for his disappearance. He had done his best; and he was sure that if he were not now a prisoner he would be hurrying in some way to get home again. . . . And Bikuni laughed a little as she said words to him in the course of their picking up; and came near to him, brushing her hand lightly against the sandy hairs that twinkled on his wrist.

Magdalena said nothing; but smiled so as to make cronies of herself and the Pilot while Bikuni remained alien.

He was happy enough: but he was certainly not, in Santvoort's broad and spacious sense of the word, comfortable.

The surgeon and the captain had settled down to a routine of sitting in the sun when it was fine and sitting in the house when it rained. They walked, at intervals, about the harbour and found always new satisfaction in seeing that an ancient watchman dozed about the *Liefde's* decks and that the great seals of the Shogun were on her hatches. Talking to each other whenever they had need of talk, they adventured little into the syllables of Japan; and whatever they talked about produced in them both the outlook of men with confidence, though no spectacular ambitions, in the future.

The surgeon had spent half a morning in setting the thighbone of one of the ship's men who had been brought to him on a litter by four of the others. The accident had happened in a tavern. He stitched up a wound in the shoulder of the Swart. When this work was done the captain reminded them —patients and attendants—that the law of the land was death to brawlers, and that they must look to these things.

As for the men themselves, so comfortable were they that it was not always easy for Adams or Santvoort to find them. Three or four of them were often at the waterside, cheerful and lusty among the rabble of stevedores. Some pottered about taverns in the manner of employees rather than guests. Two walked slowly and preoccupied, men already diseased; while the Swart, with his amiable grin and his bandaged shoulder, became the established door-keeper of one of the newer houses that had grown to meet the demands of the city as it became a garrison and something of a royal court. Already the house was known by the figure of the Swart. In his cotton drawers and silk jacket he stood a dozen inches higher than any client of his house; he had come by his wound honourably, in the execution of his duty, so that he need never want for employment again.

They were all, then, at moorings of one sort or another. All but Adams; he was not yet comfortable.

CHAPTER XXII

Upon Adams, the Contemplator of the needle, there was some peculiar curse; the curse that lay upon Nostromo. There was a strangeness in the substance of his fibre, as there was strangeness in the fibre and the substance of the needle he contemplated, making it a centre of vibration and unrest. Other metal is lumpish and inert, and the air about it is unheeding and quiet, seeking only to corrupt and weaken it with rust. But about the needle's metal there is no quiet. Itself it quivers and dips and swings; and the very ether about it is rent and shaken with the unseen forces that converge from their distances and meet only in their pull upon the thing for which there is no rest. . . .

Thus: Ieyasu conferred with the foremost of his generals in a commandeered tavern on the hillside of Yoro. He had marched the two hundred miles from Yedo, and the effective strength of the army some leagues behind him was a hundred and fifty thousand men. The issue, he knew, would be fought out at Sekigahara; for Sekigahara was not only a natural stage for battles that were each a hundred-thousand personal combats; it was a mountain pass opening upon the gentler slopes that became the shores of lake Biwa. Sekigahara was also a symbol; it was the last of the great barrier-stations on the royal way to Kioto; and it was between Yedo and Kioto that the present issue lay.

The effective strength of Ieyasu's enemy no man knew—least of all Ishida Mitsunari, its general. He could count only upon a minimum—a hundred-thousand; perhaps a hundred and twenty; for Southward, to the right flank of his loyal minimum, were the fiefs and lordships without number that were as the sea itself to which their small dominions reached; as countless as its sands, as shifting as its currents and its tides.

From the greater lords of these men in council it was Ieyasu who got the most that it was in them to give in honesty; they would man the heights upon his left, and upon the right of his enemy; they would shoot no arrow and draw no sword till they had seen which way the day was going. If it tended towards him, Ieyasu, then they would come down from their mountains to set their bow-strings and draw their swords and work upon the flank of his enemy and upon its rear.

One man alone stood out of this undertaking. From the farthest end of all Japan he came—from so far indeed that many wondered why he came at all. He brought no arguments and stated no reasons. All he stated was a fantastic, reasonless and obstinate fact. This was Matsura Ho-in, Lord of the little island of Hirado—twice as neighbourly to Korea itself as it was, in space, to the tavern where Ieyasu made his final plans. He limped his road and growled his way to declare that he would loiter on no hilltops with bows unstrung and swords undrawn. That had not been his manner or the manners of his islanders when an army had been carried in great ships to fight across the sea in Korea. He and his islanders would again take ship as they had taken it then; they would sail the Inland sea and land somewhere near Osaka, and fall straightway upon the rear of Ieyasu's enemy. Numbers . . . he snorted at numbers, for it is only once that any man can die. He snorted at some remark that was made about his age, and about the infirmity of his thigh that had shrunken, and set with a bend in it after the Korean campaign. He snorted at the suggestion of a day's rest—for he had work to do in the mustering and the manning of his transport ships; and he stumped off towards the hundred odd leagues of his journey home, to see to these things.

He left Ieyasu thinking in such a way that his thoughts fixed themselves upon the hairy needle-watcher.

Even from where he sat among his generals on the hillside of Yoro he could see a speck of white sail in Owari Bay. Himself he knew but little of ships; he knew only of what they carried. They had brought first the strange power of a creed that had undermined and destroyed the leagued powers of the country's ancient monasteries. Bringing this, they had made it possible for his predecessor and for himself to rule the land. After the priests came traders; ships brought gold, and with the gold they brought a strength to men who had had no strength before; so that it was not always now a sword, but a purse with which a man had to reckon in an enemy. Ships had carried a vast army to Korea and they would soon carry the handful of Matsura Ho-in and his men from Hirado to Osaka. So that ships could carry not only the mysteries that had made soldiers strong against priests and weak against merchants but could carry soldiers and weapons themselves; and he, Ieyasu, had no ships.

Looking at the sail in the Bay, and seeing from its whiteness that it must have been the sail of a foreigner from Nagasaki, he thought of the difference that lay between Adams and the other foreign men who had come his way. The difference was simply that in first looking at him with the tattered Dutchman behind him he saw possibility of friendship and, from the friendship, use of some sort. He had not weighed the possibility with any exactness nor considered the ultimate use. He had merely thrown Adams on one side for preservation, instead of throwing him on the other for destruction with his raga-muffin crew. He was again glad that he had saved the fellow.

CHAPTER XXIII

CASUALTIES of the battle of Sekigahara counted in dead alone; and they amounted to a hundred-thousand odd.

While Ieyasu was winning it at this cost the Pilot was remote enough from the General's busy mind. But he was present and active in the minds of others.

At Nagasaki the news of the victory brought many wise heads together in conference, and lambs came together with lions in perturbed council. Portuguese and Spaniards, enemies in the Moluccas and the Philippines, became friends in the taverns and chapels and monasteries of Nagasaki—even in the store godowns and counting-houses. The business men and shippers who now were of the community had come first as the guests of priests and their proselytes. The priests had come as the guests of Hideyoshi; and so priests and business men—Spaniards and Portuguese alike—had swallowed whole the propaganda that described the rivalry of Ishida Mitsunari and Ieyasu as a struggle of the memory of Hideyoshi against a sinister force that would destroy it. Swallowing the propaganda, they had assumed as a matter of course the destruction of Ieyasu.

It was because of his discretion and his zeal that the padre had been sent a few months before to conduct the affair of the castaway Dutchmen. Spaniards and Portuguese had each agreed that the other was nuisance and menace enough, without Dutchmen getting any foothold in the country. The failure of the padre to put a finish to the Dutchmen had lost importance in the confident prospect that Ieyasu himself would not figure greatly on the scene much longer. At his exit his supers—with his last fad of the castaway Dutchmen and the Englishman—would go also. Stories came on coasting junks and along the roads and ferry-ways and were forgotten with other gossip of the day. Yedo itself was remote and its days of significance numbered. What was it to merchants with their business organised and established in the friendly South if, in the dis-

tant Yedo, it was the caprice of the self-styled Shogun to make
of the Englishman the Number One man of the castaway crew,
lodging him in the house of an old soldier of some distinction?
What did it matter if he took apparent pleasure in the speechless society of the Englishman, looking at geometrical figures
drawn with the Pilot's instruments? . . . At his drawings of
the earth's face, and the seas?

Before Sekigahara it mattered nothing.

After Sekigahara it mattered a great deal; it became, from
gossip, serious politics. Individuals sought out the padre to
question him about his failure. Councils summoned him.

Hirado, they reminded him, was but fifty miles away, the
lordship of Matsura Ho-in. Old Ho-in would soon come
rollicking and swaggering home with his boatloads of bravos
from their fantastic exploit of which all had now heard. Him
they knew well enough already; for a fire-eater is the worst of
neighbours to men whose main endeavour is for peace and
plenty.

The padre argued that things were not so bad as they seemed
to the alarmists. The hundred and one petty infringements
of their trading charters which had been winked at for years
would be winked at still—or corrections and adjustments
could gradually be made. The countless junks owned by individuals in excess of the numbers specified by charter could be
transferred from Portuguese and Spaniards to good friends
inland and along the coast. Properties ashore could be simi-
larly disposed of. Gunpowder could be burnt or sunk in the
sea; ordnances and firearms could be buried. Supervision, he
pointed out, need not be particularly feared now. Their
friends of the pre-battle days would be their friends still; they
had all come in, by the mercy and the justice of God, on the
right side.

Arguing these points with arguments that brought some
comfort and assurance to his questioners he knew in his heart
that he was only bilking them, dealing with side issues while
the main problem remained unfaced. He became sore with the
burden upon him, and the burden upon him was, in a word,
Adams. For a score of harsh and hazardous years the padre
had laboured in the Faith. An incursion of protestants into

the field of his labours would be a happening unfitted by the word of even direst tragedy. It was something that simply must not be. The casting up of the Englishman and the Dutchmen was one of those inscrutable mysteries of God whereby He tries the fortitude and tests the skill of His labourers.

A gesture from God Himself could have cleared up the situation immediately. Nothing could have been simpler than the crucifixion of the whole rabble. But God had made no such gesture; He seemed unlikely enough to make it now, after pulling them through to survival against all the odds imaginable—and lodging the Pilot in the shelter of swords like Magome Sageyu's. . . . The ways of God were inscrutable; but the fact of Adams was clear. It was Adams, and Adams alone, who had baulked the simple crucifixion plan. How he had done it the padre had no idea. But that he had done it was as certain in the padre's mind as the knowledge that it had again been Adams who had resisted the kidnapping of the four.

Chafing under this burden of the Pilot, and seeking a relief from it, he was able to thank God that the junks of the natives never left sight of the land. The only vessels that did so were Spanish and Portuguese; so that no word could get back from Adams to the world he had left, to bring others after him. The thought made the padre suddenly happy.

As Ieyasu saw in the Needle-watcher a possible key to the mystery of ships and the sea, so the padre saw in him a key to the mystery of Ieyasu, for he knew of no man who had approached so near to the Shogun as the dumb pilot seemed to have done already. Friendship with Adams would be a service to the merchants and to the padre's country; and through friendship only could he now hope to bring the Pilot's soul to God.

Thus it was that some way of winning him to friendship became the preoccupation of this Portuguese Father.

A Spaniard, too, who had never seen him, was seized with a concern for Adams. He, however, was not a priest but a layman, thinking not in terms of souls, of Catholics and heretics, but of nutmegs from the Philippines and silk from

China, of ambergris and tortoise-shell. All the nutmegs in
the Philippines passed, sooner or later, through his hands;
which was well enough. But the Portuguese cargoes from the
Moluccas prevented his making what he pleased of the market
in Japan. It was the same with silk; his five ships could buy
as they pleased in Cochin China—but Portuguese could do
the same. His flotilla could have cut out and scuttled every
Chinese junk that ventured Eastward, but with Portuguese
on a very lively watch there was many a junk that got safely
through to Nagasaki, adding its cargo to the glut of the Portuguese freights, since neither Spaniard nor Portuguese dared
any enterprise while the other was prowling nearer than the
horizon to carry a tale to Ieyasu whose ideas concerning piracy
and murder were well known. They had come to working
arrangements, the Portuguese and Spanish merchants of
Nagasaki, for there seemed to be no other way. It was when
he saw in a flash that there was another way that the Spaniard
smiled and rubbed his hands together and opened a bottle of
wine with one who was said to be his son, bred in the Philippines and lodged for a dozen years in Nagasaki.

The other way was this English pilot, Adams.

The two of them were amazed that no one else had tumbled
upon anything so obvious. The youth was as fluent in
Japanese as he was in Spanish and Portuguese talk, in Dutch,
Malay and Philippino idioms. His thoughts were as various as
the names by which he was called and the company in which
he moved; but his father called him Concepcion.

They chuckled, as they drank their wine, at the way the old
padre had done for himself and all Portuguese with regard to
him who was now in such good standing with the victorious
Shogun. Already they could count on the anti-Portuguese
prejudice of Adams. Anti-Portuguese was pro-Spaniard. As
colonials they gave little enough consideration to an English
seaman's native hatred of Spaniards; and Concepcion had seldom failed to win the casual liking of men as well as
women.

He had the Philippino breadth of body, its nimble grace with
the swagger of a monied Spaniard. He drank and loved with
natural gusto. His extravagance among friends would have

struck his father in a different light if it had not gone down in his books as an investment in goodwill.

It was a matter for Concepcion, then, to get to Yedo somehow, and with his purse and his bonhomie to show the Englishman that it was he, Concepcion the Spaniard, who was a right good fellow.

CHAPTER XXIV

THE scheming of old Magome Sageyu was on a far simpler and homelier scale. All that he wanted was money—more money than he could get from the fees of a fencing-master. He had it in him to enjoy so many things: a good seat at wrestling matches and the new, livelier sort of theatrical shows. He enjoyed kite-flying and matching the strength and the sharpness of his thread and the skill of his wrist and thumb against those of another cavalero; but only the best of kites and the costliest of threads from his next-door neighbour were good enough for Magome, and he liked to be able to weigh out his lost stake with a gesture of easy and honourable magnificence.

He liked singing girls.

He liked to officiate with tea.

He liked *saké* and he enjoyed the new luxury for the man of distinction which the Spaniards had brought him—tobacco. The smoker needed not only the dark leaf cut to the fineness of spun silk. The pipe for smoking it, to be the pipe of a cavalero, must have a stem that was a legend of history or ribaldry recorded by the hand of a sculptor. Though the pouch was a matter which his daughters could manage with their skill in embroidery, the toggle for holding it to the girdle should be a gem and a masterpiece of minute artistry—the last of the only three jewels with which the Samurai might adorn himself. The other two—the hand-guard of his sword and the stud in its hilt—Magome had had from the day of his father's death, as fine as any in Japan. But a worthy toggle for his tobacco pouch he coveted greatly.

He had always rested in the opinion of retired soldiers that all a man need do in order to become rich is to become, vaguely, a business man; to buy things and sell them. But to one like him the ignoble device of trade was not merely denied, it was unthinkable. Adams had shown him, by the easy way in which he had stumped the self-assured Mitsu and then gone off to return with a skirt-load of tael, that for him, Adams, there was nothing ignoble or unthinkable about making money; for to the simple mind of Magome with his sketchy reading of the document the affair had been nothing but a simple chaffering.

He thought, thereafter, of Adams engaged in vague and general enterprise of buying and selling, backed by the capital they had wrapped up in the sash and hidden away in the heirloom chest. He speculated in his mind about the cargo stowed between the dank timbers of the *Liefde*, feeling that if the Needle-watcher could sell her ordnance so glibly he could sell also her cargo, whatever it might be. He wondered, in the meantime, if there was no work at all that his guest could do— work of some dignity, more fitting for a guest in his house than the mean tavern-sweeping and burden-lifting reported to be so lustily indulged in by some of his shipmates; but work, nevertheless, that commanded its price. . . . Something, for example, that he could teach; for tutoring of any kind carried its distinction as well as its price. But these thoughts, the old man realised, were flung far into the future; for as yet the Pilot could do little more with the language than stumble along in it to demand little odd requirements.

For the present Magome's occupation was not unlike waiting for a child to grow up. The task of the elder was to watch, to guide, to correct—and withal to love. And the last came easily enough to the old man, for Adams had always pleased him. He felt he could get through his guest's adolescence on the presents which he would from time to time accept from one who had a charmingly open hand; for even to the two girls—with a certain amount of embarrassment and in the presence of Magome—he had given two folds of silk.

So Magome, seeing his object clearly enough in the future, for the present could afford to wait.

CHAPTER XXV

WAITING, however, was a matter of less complacency for Bikuni. Her object, unlike her father's, was not always capable of clear and simple definition. At times it was clearer and simpler than his—when all she craved, as an alternative to death, was that the Pilot should cease in his stumbling among needless words and speak with the grace and the might of a strange white body embracing hers, absorbing it till it was nothing but an ecstasy that quivered like a star. At other times her desire was vaguer, for all the terrific force of it, than the desires of all those others whose thought was centred upon the Pilot. It was not for his limbs with the golden dust of hair upon them; it was not for a caress from the lips which smiled in a face that was toughly smooth now that a barber regularly shaved it. Nor was her desire then that he should speak. It was not indeed—when she came to think of it with the sudden stab somewhere within her that would have been pain if it had not been a brightness like the twinkling of a star—it was not from him that she desired anything at all; it was from herself. He need neither even speak nor smile, nor frown upon her. He need not embrace her, holding her body close to the warmth and fiery glow of his own, nor need he put her thoughtfully, but tenderly, from him. He could do all of these things or none of them. The second desire of Bikuni was for nought from within the Pilot, but concerned only Bikuni herself.

What it was that she should do to slake this great thirst, Bikuni knew not. She knew only that she was doing it already and that she would continue doing it for as long as she should live.

When she could do it no longer she would, quite exactly, die.

CHAPTER XXVI

EVEN the captain, placid enough towards all the hazards and chances of his destiny, and the surgeon who entertained himself by making some classification of the little sores that were to be seen upon the shaven pates of children—even these two cronies added their mild desire to the forces that centred and interplayed about the Pilot.

"Four days," the captain once remarked, "it is four days since we have seen Mr. Adams. With young Santvoort taken up with what he calls his marriage, we must not let Mr. Adams go."

The surgeon agreed. "A good man, that Mr. Adams of ours."

"We've got to keep him out of hitching up with these Japonians," said the captain.

"He would seem to understand something of them," the surgeon observed.

"Aye, and of the crew," said the captain. "We need him to hold the crew together. There's not a man he cannot find, if need be. And they pay heed to him, even better than Santvoort."

"Santvoort's fist is readier than his sense," said the surgeon, "and now that there's no occasion for him to use it——"

The captain interrupted. "The Pilot, too, can use a fist on occasion."

"Aye, but always with some sense behind it. Santvoort throws his as a man may toss a stone at anything at all or at nothing." Then he digressed from Adams as he digressed from everything that was not a classification in writing. "He is well occupied in that billet of his. A fine enough girl, his— wife." He was amused afresh every time he thought of Santvoort's marriage. "Captain, we'll have to be thinking of putting up the banns ourselves. There's no need for starvation in a bakery."

The captain was not attracted by the joke at the moment.

"As long as Mr. Adams—but I don't like his rig-out. It's full Japonian from head to heel now. Shaving clean, too."

"Oh, he's got the company's business at heart," the surgeon reassured him. "You'll find him about the quay-side any day looking at the ship."

"The *Liefde?*" asked the captain doubtfully, and shrugged his shoulders. "It's among the natives, as often as not, that you'll see him. At those building slips of theirs; conferring, it would seem, with the shipwrights and carpenters, for he can speak with them with suitable pleasantries. And now that he is shaving to add to his Japonian rig we must look to it. If we lose Mr. Adams we are done, Verhagen; we're stuck here for ever. Even if we could get ourselves afloat he is the only one who could navigate us, even as far as the Indies."

Thus they brooded upon the question of holding Adams. They decided that before they could hold him they ought first to draw him—a thing, the captain suggested, that they had never made any particular point of doing before.

Verhagen, the surgeon, saw things clearer than the captain, and spoke of things of whose very existence the captain was generally unaware. He was no ordinary chirurgeon, this Verhagen, in the generally accepted sense of the term—the somewhat menial type of individual with a gift for bloodletting and leeching. He had been a law-student, with an appetite for the politics of his time—which consisted, for the greater part, of theology. Neither law nor theology, however, provided any ready wages for a young man of his station, and so he, too, had grown to middle age as a soldier. Soldiers, even when sitting in a garrison of the Netherlands, and engaged in no daily, weekly or monthly skirmish, had a way of subsiding with a leg, an arm or a head suddenly broken, with a Spaniard's dagger or an English seaman's knife stuck between the ribs.

Verhagen set bones, washed and cobbled up wounds and dished out physic and purges till he was one of the three appointed surgeons of the Texel Company's Indish venture.

It was he who suggested, while the captain merely grumbled, that they had, perhaps, neglected the Englishman. He and the captain had given each other company; while Adams —now that Santvoort was gone to his new wench—had been driven to this loitering and cooling his feet among Japonians. He was a man of some decency in breeding, too, the surgeon observed—not just a loafing seaman. They must treat him as such, drawing him into their company and the community of their friendship.

They must make him come to dinner.

Then, as they decided upon this immediate move, they found they were already stuck. For it was only Adams himself who could arrange for them any dinner that should be at all out of the ordinary. He, with his loafing and loitering with an old soldier, with kite-makers and carpenters and shipwrights and fishermen, had picked up pleasantries and words enough to say something intelligible to their host.

The surgeon took his cloak and his cane and walked off to find him.

CHAPTER XXVII

THUS, with Magome fidgeting at the time that was being wasted in the Needle-watcher's loitering among workmen; with Ieyasu thinking that it was himself the Englishman would serve; with the padre scheming for a permit to enter Yedo to bind the Englishman in friendship; with the debonair Concepcion already on the road to Yedo, cocksure of the irresistibility of his gay person and his fat purse, with the captain congratulating himself on the fixture of a weekly entertainment of Adams to dinner and the surgeon thinking out little pieces of tact for supporting what he took to be the Pilot's very proper pride; with Bikuni studying his every movement till he went out, and listening to every footfall till he returned—to smile upon her and Magdalena, to hand then some trifling gift, perhaps, or to retire into a silent gazing upon his distant thoughts; with all these forces centred upon him in the wide diversity of their directions, the force that drew him daily and held him till it was time for a meal was the twang of saws, the swish of planes and paring knives, and the clatter of mallets in the yard of a carpenter at the waterside.

Santvoort waited each morning, at ease upon the verandah of the kite-maker's house, to hail Adams as he passed on his saunter to the yard; sometimes he sauntered along with him. A positive happiness had come over the Dutchman; his old pleasure in baiting Adams had turned to a secret of amusement at his fussy seriousness over discoveries so trivial that no one but the Englishman, with his fantastic busy-ness, could have made them. Santvoort gave no consideration to the fact that Adams had been apprenticed to Mr. Nicholas Diggins, the shipwright of Limehouse. After ten years of seafaring the Dutchman was apt to consider two questions only concerning a ship—how much he had to crouch his body walking between decks, and where he could sling the hammock that gave him room to stretch out his legs.

When Adams told him that there was not a shipbuilder in

the whole harbour who knew the first letter of the alphabet of shipbuilding, the Dutchman only smiled.

Carpenters—yes, said Adams. The finest carpenters and joiners he had ever seen. Also the finest timber—some of it like iron; some like steel; some as light as cork and some heavy as lead; some so full of its own natural resin that it held the sharpest chisel fast and clogged the gentlest plane. Yet, with the finest timber in the world, the world's finest craftsmanship was abused in producing nothing handier than great coffins. . . .

"Even if they had a proper rudder, Melchior," he said, "craft of that build would never answer it." There was a note of some feeling that was very near to personal grievance when he said this. They were silent for a while.

"Like a duck, Melchior," he went on, gloomily. "They're more like a duck than anything else, with their broad bellies and great steering paddles, one on each side astern, flapping the water like a duck's feet."

"Well," said Melchior, "ducks have done very well without rudders. Why should you want to put a rudder on a duck?"

"I don't," said Adams. "What I do want is to show them that a ship need not be like a duck at all."

"And when you have shown them, Will?" asked Santvoort, "what then?"

Adams shrugged his shoulders. This was a question that he himself had asked, to find no answer.

"Never mind what then," he said, and Santvoort knew that the tendency was towards huffiness. "The devil of it is to get them to *see*. Those round-bottomed, broad-bellied things are in their blood. I'm scooping out a bit of a model in the yard down there—two foot long she'll be. We'll try rigging her with a lug-sail on the mizzen, square at the main and fore. She'll be narrower than the *Liefde*—you Dutchmen always did run to too much beam . . ."

The tendency towards huffiness had gone, and Santvoort felt easy again in following his normal way of banter. "And your sails, Will?" he asked. "Will you make them of wood, like our good hosts?"

"Wood!" said Adams. "I'll make them of silk, be God, if there's nothing else with which to show them that wood was never meant for sail-making—of kerchiefs and shirts and sashes. Your woman can give a hand with sewing the stuff together—and the girls in my house."

"By your courtesy, Will—and by the law of the land—my *wife*," Santvoort grinned at him, bowing. "Vrow Santvoort-San. And a mighty fine opinion she has of you, my lad. Even your two—nieces—think no better of you than she does, Mineheer An-jin."

The Dutchman's joke of nieces pleased Adams. The relationship to those two girls required some description very like the one he had discovered in foolery.

Nieces. . . . Adams knew how merrily they would fall to work with him, squatting one on either side, their deft little hands eagerly fluttering, their chatter like a brook as they cobbled together whatever stuff he should find for the sails of his model.

"They are grand girls, Melchior," he said, and his pride was avuncular.

"Nieces, I said. Not grand-nieces. But I'll come and see your ship, and give a hand."

"That you will not," said Adams, but he was in good humour. "You can see her, Melchior, but you'll keep your great hands off yet awhile—till the hull is done. Maybe you can help me with the sail plan. Sail-handling is one of the things you do seem to grasp. God knows how you'll do it when the sails are only two foot long, and the tackle pack-threads of silk."

"Well enough," said Santvoort. "Is not my wife herself only four foot long—and mostly silk? Aye, nought but China silk is good enough for her now."

They excited no curiosity as they walked abroad now, the Pilot and the Dutchman. The smiles they encountered, and the nodding of heads, were not of comment but of acquaintanceship; and their aimless talk together was the easiest they had ever had, for Santvoort was now at liberty to think of absolutely nothing, and Adams to think of the lines of his model, of the placing of the foremast, and of his steering gear.

"Melchior," he said, "a ship came up the Thames one day that I was coming down with a wheel on the after-deck for steering, instead of a whip-staff. I believe I can see how the tackle must have been run for bringing the tiller over; hard over the wheel's spindle to a block on each side straight below, and then around blocks to the port and starboard of it, and then back to the tiller's end."

"I daresay," said Santvoort, "but what of it? It would still want a man there. Whether he stands at a wheel, or at a staff, makes little enough odds."

"Little enough odds?" exclaimed Adams. "Why, man! The pilot aboard that ship just stood and turned that wheel over—I tell you he could have done it sitting like a milkmaid on a stool—instead of tearing his guts out at a whip-staff."

"I don't see it," said the Dutchman. "If a tiller could be handled with a wheel and a milking-stool, why aren't ships manned by milkmaids?"

They walked on and arrived at the house of the old carpenter, and went round to the back of it. Only an old man was there, seated under the eaves. His deafness kept him undisturbed till Adams exclaimed, "Melchior, he's *got* it!"

At that he looked up startled, and smilingly held up his work towards Adams.

"Why did you let him have it, then?" asked Santvoort.

"It's the idea he's got, at last," said Adams. "I thought he never would. But he's got it, perfectly." He took the thing from the old carpenter and ran his eye along its sides and then, caressingly, his fingers.

It was a copy of his own rough carving of a ship's hull. The original lay on the ground some yards from the old man; it was still a baulk of dark, tough wood—hewn and carved and split by a man with loose, approximate thoughts in his head, little skill in his hands and tools that were unfamiliar. Old Kuru's interpretation of it was in a chosen piece of white willow; and it was the work of a sculptor.

From the crude bulges and clumsy dents and hollows on the teak baulk lying beside him, from screwing up his old eyes upon the *Liefde's* slowly rotting hulk—with the vision that was still bright behind the eyes' dimness he saw suddenly what lines and what proportions Adams had been trying to record.

In miniature poor An-jin with his great, hairy, square-thumbed paws had been trying to hack it out of teak—the wood which only a master-craftsman could hope to cajole into any sort of obedience to a tool. And so the old man who could still carve a tableau out of a cherry-stone or fit together the timbers of a Daimio's house, took out his little well-seasoned and knotless piece of willow and showed Adams in half a morning exactly what it was that the Pilot, for ten days, had been trying to do.

It was not because it was Adams and the Dutchman that loiterers from the waterside began to form a group within sight and earshot of them. It was simply because an interesting situation between neighbours seemed to be developing.

A workman or two came round the house from the building-slip in front to ask old Kuru some question—while identifying what thing it was that the Pilot held in his hands and thrust towards the Dutchman and became generally excited over.

Old Kuru saw the slyness of them gaping at his work; the gleaming thing was now obviously the hull of a stranger's ship. He sent them about their business, scowled at the idlers looking at them and snatched the thing from Adams. He strutted into the house with it, Adams and the Dutchman after him, away from the prying eyes outside.

In the mind of Kuru, also, the thought was suddenly born that the Pilot was something to be somehow secured and secreted and appropriated to his own use.

Men of Kuru's age had travelled no further than the waterside of Yedo for many years, and the waterside of Yedo was no great place for things that were new. Words came to it in the mouths of fishermen and soldiers and merchants; but the strange things of which they told remained outside the land-locked harbour. The words had been of strange ships that could sail across the wind, could carry the load of a junk and yet outsail it, but Kuru had never seen any such wonder; and what he had not seen he did not believe.

When he saw the *Liefde* rolling into harbour, captive to a score of tow-ropes, if it proved anything at all, it proved that any craft but a junk or a skiff was a futility.

It was only when his hands held in them the things he had carved from the thoughts in the Pilot's mind, when his eye—

the sculptor's eye—took in its lines, smoothly, because they were lines of harmony and grace and balance—it was only then that he believed in the possibility of any ship that was not a broad-bellied soma. Thus it was that he angrily dismissed those others who were prying at the thing that had revealed to him this secret, and with it the greater secret—that the Pilot was a store of possible treasure.

CHAPTER XXVIII

KURU was a man of business; he was, moreover, a man with little time to lose if he hoped to reap as well as sow; for he knew that he was not good for many more winters.

The next day Adams found, instead of the casually cheery greeting in the yard and the master's gesture towards tools and wood, ceremonious gestures into the room at the back of the house. In the room he found a tray of cakes and sweetmeats and drink. The carving of the hull was there, with chosen and polished tools; and Kuru himself took the hull and a tool and sought—in the manner not of a master but of an apprentice—instructions. Adams talked and gave indications with the palms of his hands and his great flat thumbs; and the old man delicately carved.

He had other work, too, however, for every yard in the harbour was busy. Word had come, after the victory of Sekigahara, that many more vessels would be licensed with the Shogun's seal for trade. Three months or four still remained of the monsoon to carry them south, and every vessel with an owner who could make a present that might secure for him the charter and the seal, was trimming and fitting for sea.

He left Adams, with assurance and apologies, to go among his workmen at the slips. At the door a slyness came into his hospitable affability; and his going out was immediately marked by the coming in of a girl.

She slid the door to behind her and secured it and made obeisance to the Pilot as the scum of the earth might make obeisance to an emperor. Adams smiled and grunted and went on chipping timid little pieces from the carving where the master-strokes of Kuru would have taken shavings a foot long.

The formality of her made the girl less human to his eye, more astonishing than were even Bikuni and Magdalena. They, now, were beginning to be faintly comprehensible, for he had seen Bikuni with her teeth unblackened. But this girl was more than incomprehensible; she was incredible.

138

Her throat was burdened to the point of snapping by the brittle architecture of her hair. The movements of her painted lips and hands were no suggestions of a caress, but sheer marvels that called only for a stare—the articulations of a marvellous puppet. Her sudden outburst of singing was hideous. Adams had heard singing enough of the same sort before, coming from houses when he had walked abroad with Santvoort. But he had never been shut up in a room with it; and it was more than he could comfortably stomach. It was not that any musical sense in him was hurt by the nasal squealing of the girl; it was that he felt a fool and would feel a bigger fool if anyone were to come and discover him there. He thanked the fantastic singer and congratulated her. He patted her shoulder; and a momentary thrill held his fingers to the gay silk of the kimono; for under the silk was the roundness of firm human flesh. Then the lips, with their grotesque gilding, smiled—and the humanity of the little creature was again denied. He patted the shoulder once more, took up the carving and the chisel, thrust back the door and went into the sunshine of the verandah.

It was seated on the steps of the verandah that his host Magome found him.

He was not carving, nor was he thinking; for it was only a vague wild hovering of his mind that centred about the flesh of his hand that had rested on a shoulder which would have been the limb of a girl if her smile had not been the grimace of a fantastic effigy squealing somewhere up in her nose with a sound most embarrassing. In the same hand, too, was an unrest for the chisel it could not wield deftly enough to lay bare the lines that were still concealed within the wood of the unfinished carving.

"Ho, then, An-jin," Magome hailed him cheerily.

He answered him and asked, "Dinner?"

"Yes. And late, too," said the old man. "And a good dinner. Come." His eye wandered from the Pilot to the open door of the room behind him, and in the doorway stood the girl. For an instant he frowned—but for an instant only, since it was not his habit to frown for long upon a singing-girl. He walked, most portly, to the end of the verandah and called her and spoke with her softly. All that Adams could gather of their conversation was their peculiar smiles—one idiotically reflecting the other; one with grotesquely painted teeth between lips of gold, the other villainously toothless; one painted with the brilliance of lacquered wood, the other like ancient parchment; but both alike in a peculiar, un-human quality of ceremonial.

The old scamp had his say and appeared to think well of it. The strain of ceremonial gave way to the normal geniality of his smile as he turned to Adams again. Then, when he saw the carving and the chisel, the eyebrow and the cleft lowered, and this time the frown remained. He had suddenly forgotten that there were such things in the world as singing-girls, and had become busy with a problem.

Whose was it? he asked, for Adams could understand well enough now. What was it—and why should he be making such a thing and for whom? Adams explained what he could, and the question became again and now quite specifically, who was the owner?

He; said Adams. Undeniably he himself—An-jin.

The brow and the scar lifted at last. "Very well," said Sageyu, "Very well."

He picked up the carving and thrust it into his breast. "Very well."

Adams did not oppose him; for he was not sure that Kuru could be trusted to cut much further alone.

He walked along beside Magome, who carried against his bosom the first trophy of the only war which he was not yet too old to wage.

In addition to his trophy, he had three distinct grounds for chuckling: Kuru's loss of the good fee he had weighed out to the Kabu-master, his utter failure to please Adams with his generosity, and the Pilot's amazing denial of the simplest and most self-evident of all human laws.

He tried to persuade him, after they had dined, to continue his carving there, in the house of a soldier rather than among the inconsiderable people of the waterside. But Adams made it clear that the work was not his own work, but Kuru's. He himself was unable to do it.

Magome required a few moments for the readjustment of his mind after this information. The disgusting suspicion arose that the fool might have bought it—but on this point Adams soon reassured him. It was his because the thought was his; he had shown Kuru how to make it.

The old man was delighted to the extent of walking with Adams back to the waterside. The carving he had wrapped in a napkin and he handed it to the first loiterer they met outside the house, so that they might walk uncumbered, gentlemen taking the crisp air of a winter's afternoon.

CHAPTER XXIX

AFFAIRS began to press a little on Magome so that he was obliged to slacken his vigilance upon the doings of his guest.

The victorious end of the war brought an immediate movement and busy-ness to Yedo. Soldiers began to arrive and camp-followers to return. Fresh hostages came to the city, till the inns could scarcely hold the sons of Daimio from the south and west with their retinues, and the fathers and families of sons who had remained at their provinces. While the inn-keepers were busy in their attendance upon these, the carpenters were busy upon houses for them, so that Kuru, too, was drawn from his preoccupation with his boat-building slip and with Adams.

Magome himself probably could not have said with any exactness what it was that made a busy man of him. Yet it was the case that when Yedo was empty he was a man of leisure; when it was full he was a man with cares. The commission he held from Ieyasu made of him a man with no particular duty to perform, and yet a man who was always on that duty. He was a secret-service man; and wherever he went he was a policeman. It flitted into his mind, too, that with so many sword-carrying strangers coming daily and nightly to the city he might find that the families of his old friends and unfortunate victims were not such slow bellies as the last twenty years had led him to assume. He walked, therefore, warily, and he walked much. Enemies of Ieyasu were still abroad. There was talk at inns; and there were men in the city whom a retainer had carefully to watch. And for all this there was no reward but the soldier's ration and the soldier's ease of mind in the knowledge of faith kept and duty done.

Reward, materially, came only from the increasing number of fencing pupils. Every afternoon for two hours or three, in the little arena in the yard marked out with poles and screened by hanging mats, the old man worked and sweated as hard as any ancient coolie. The reward was not much greater than a coolie's; but it was enough for a bottle of *saké* for him and Adams to drink with their evening meal.

After the meal—since he was a little out of condition from months of comparative inactivity—there was little for it but sleep.

His muscles soon picked up, however, and then one afternoon a small thing happened which kept his hand light with the *saké* except when he was pouring it for Adams, and his eyes and ears alert.

A strange youth had come that day with three or four others whom Magome knew well enough, and was duly introduced to the master. He came, he said, from far away; from one of the few loyal families in the South of the island of Kiushiu—a family as true as that of Matsura Ho-in of Hirado himself. He answered all questions and even volunteered information so that Magome took him into the arena as freely as he had taken a hundred or a thousand strange youths before.

They chatted as the boy put on the padded jacket and gloves and helmet; and the master tried the mettle of him. He was puzzled a little by the thought that it was not quite in the manner of Kiushiu that he moved his feet in the sand— dragging them so as never for a moment to lose their firm grip upon the ground. Magome pressed him and there was a sound like the drumming of a tattoo from the foils as the youth deftly parried thrust after thrust made by the old man at his throat. At last, cornered and hardly driven to the risk of a last possible chance, he loosed his grip on the hilt of his foil and deftly caught it again hard against the guard to shorten his weapon and so to give a leverage of the long hilt against his forearm. The elbow at the same instant arched high into the air; the blade curved away, downwards and then, in a flash, up towards the short ribs of Magome.

The foil stopped in a clatter against the foil of the master; and they fenced on.

Magome had got the kind of information that other men sometimes get from excited carelessness in speech—an idiom, perhaps; a lengthened or broadened vowel, a trilled or a lisped "r."

It was not from the South of Kiushiu that this young man came.

It was from the Western part of Izumo—whence Sageyu himself had come—bringing with him that trick of the suddenly shifted grip, the sweep of the blade and the quick uppercut to where only the gristle of short ribs protects the vitals of an adversary.

And so he merely feigned with his cup of *saké* that night, while Adams drank lustily.

He admired the Pilot's adroitness in the matter of speech, and he learned much of his doings in the yard of Kuru the shipwright, carpenter and sculptor. Adams showed him a ribald anecdote that Kuru had recorded for him on a peach-stone. Together they chuckled over its excellence and Adams, full of the warmth of *saké* and good-fellowship, pressed it upon the old man as a gift. He accepted it, deeply touched by the other's open-handedness.

Lacquered, it would make a rare toggle for a tobacco pouch.

He produced a pouch now—a makeshift thing as yet, of which a sock formed the basis. So mean a receptacle was it for the finest weed that came by way of the Spaniards in the Philippines that he carried it deeply hidden in his sash. From his room he produced a pipe—also too mean a thing to see the light of day on the person of one so worthy as Magome Sageyu of grace of craftsmanship in any furniture he might handle.

He filled it for his guest, and Adams drank in the peculiar smoke. His head swam and spun; his cheeks paled and reddened; his eyes, that had twinkled already with the light of the good hot *saké*, became round and fixed like the eyes of a suddenly awakened owl. The old man gave him more *saké*, taking the pipe and filling it for himself. Adams, his throat parched and his head still dizzy from the tobacco, drank again and yet again of the *saké*. From Japanese he drifted to Portuguese and Dutch.

It was in English, however, that he told how the model was now done; that it was fully rigged, and balanced to a nicety with a keel of soft iron that they had nailed to her; that he and Santvoort had taken her out in a little skiff that very day and sailed her in the harbour. The sails were not yet right—too

much on the fore as yet, but Santvoort's wife was taking a reef
in it for them—if she was indeed a wife—but what did it matter
to a man like Melchior? Magome must understand him; he had
not a word or a thought against young Melchior Santvoort.
There was not a finer seaman to be found in any ship afloat.
All he meant was that Melchior ashore was a wag. Wife or no
wife—to Melchior it was all one. And, he questioned,—why
not?

For answer the old man smiled and filled his cup again; and
Adams soon yielded to the gentle pointless arguments and the
guiding pressure on his arm, so that he lurched down to sleep
on the mat in Magome's room at the back of the house instead
of in his own.

The old man's sense of hospitality and his regard for the high
offices of friendship were in no way strained by this simple
shift.

After the afternoon's fencing he had brought his pupils to
the bath and then, genially, to the house. Telling them,
trivially and casually, in which room it was that he himself
slept, he noticed that the strange youth had glanced in the
room's direction.

"And a cold enough room it is, too," Magome added. "Cold
enough for the hardness of any soldier. So suddenly did winter
come down that the fastening of the outer door, which has
been missing all the summer and autumn, is missing still. The
door is seldom even closed let alone fastened!" He shrugged his
shoulders. What had a simple old soldier to guard with barred
and fastened doors? His only fortune was his swords; and they
were also the only company for an old widower in his bed. Cold
company, but true. . . .

The youths laughed at the master's joke, paid him his
miserable fee and went off. The strange one noted the door
that was seldom even shut and never fastened. . . .

Magome listened for the mumbling and the discomfort of his
guest to turn from stertorous sighs to the bump of limbs
relaxed upon the sleeping mat.

He told the girls that the pilot was ill at ease and comfortably drunk; and he had given him, for this reason, the greater
comfort of his own chamber and mat and coverlet. They too,

therefore, might go to bed now, since he had no further need of them.

When they had gone, and the house was dark, he stole from the open door of Adams's room to the door at the end of the house—which was not only closed but securely barred. Stealthily he unbarred it and stealthily assured himself that the gentlest push from outside would open it. Through the flimsiness of the other door no more than two yards away came the comfortable sounds of a man sleeping satisfactorily under a burden of drink.

With his left hand he fondled in his sash the jolly gift of the open-handed fellow, the new toggle for a tobacco-pouch; and in all friendship and hospitality he smiled.

He knew, as a fact, that the Pilot was safe enough. So good a swordsman as the stranger of the afternoon would be fully as skilled in all matters of etiquette. Before he struck any blow of vengeance he would rouse his victim and upbraid him in the full and proper manner, so that Adams's heavy and dead drunkenness would have been ample protection for him, without the drawn sword of old Magome's in the darkness of the hall-way.

Magome mused in the darkness upon the luck of soldiers. A soldier's skill, of course, was a different story. From the vengeance of the honourable youth it was not luck but skill that must ultimately save him—as it had saved him before. It was not against the menace of the young man's blade that the old man had put his guest to drunken sleep upon his own mat. He could have cut down the youth at any time and in any place without a shade or a shadow of difficulty. In the narrow hall-way of his house the youth with two or three others like him in support would have presented no great problem to Magome Sageyu; but the successful exercise of skill in the defence of his own old parchment of a skin would have brought him nowhere. The law would have turned his blade upon his own middle, or it would have set him forth again upon the Ronin's road of exile. It was here that the luck of a soldier came in, the brightest jewel in the crown of a soldier's skill.

In defence of himself, the Ronin, he could kill no man. In defence of his guest—the guest, moreover, of the mighty

Shogun—he could kill a dozen, and his reward would be honour and merit.

He wondered a little why the young man should have taken, in a fencing lesson, that infinitesimal risk of discovery; but he saw that the motive was reasonable as well as honourable. With his bamboo foil he had thought to examine and test the skill of the master; with his eye he had satisfied himself beyond the questioning of a soldier's conscience that the old man with the cloven brow was indeed his true enemy.

The door quietly opened and in the slab of moonlight there stood the avenger of a grandfather or an honoured great-uncle. His bare sword was in his hand. A loin-cloth was all that clad him; his torso gleamed naked, a thread of silver outlining it against the blackness of the door like frost on the trunk of a forest sapling. It was well: for it was so, naked, that a thief or assassin would have come.

He left the door open, moved over the mat of steel-cold light and quietly opened the door upon Adams. He spoke; and waited for an answer. But the answer he got did not reach the completion of a single thought in his brain; for old Magome was a kind enough man at heart; one who rewarded piety and honour with the mercy of despatch.

Adams woke up to a dazzle of pain in his shoulder, to curses and a groan from his throat and the warmth of blood slowly trickling down his chest and back; but even before he woke old Magome had laid down again the dead youth's sword with which he himself had cut through the coverlet and half the deltoid muscle of Adams's left arm.

Then he bellowed through the house: "Quick, you girls! Scream at the door! Light lanterns! Rouse neighbours. I have killed a man who would have killed our Needle-watcher—*has* killed him for aught I know; for I see blood."

It was only Magdalena's voice that split the stillness of the night with cries from the front path of "Wake! Wake! Wake!"

Bikuni's was strangled in her throat. Her limbs were stricken so that she could only totter like an aged woman along the passage-way to the door where her father stood, black against the light from the dim lantern in the room, while the aged scullion woman of the household sprinted with a lantern and a bronze tray after Magdalena. She banged upon the tray with her gnarled fist and added the screams of a demon to Magdalena's cries.

"Father . . ." came at last from the taut lips of Bikuni. "Honourable father——"

"Out girl!" the old man snorted. "Out, I say. Go scream with the others. This is no place for women. Go, call men."

Adams spoke: "What in hell's name . . ."

Bikuni went then, like a flash. Her hands had the steadiness of steel as she kindled the lantern in her sleeping-room. Her naked feet were wings as she sped with the lantern over the frozen ground, past Magdalena and the old woman, raising above their screams her calls for the Hollander.

They came with staves and cudgels—the kite-maker and others of his household and Santvoort at the head of them with a torch and a garden mattock.

"He is alive!" Bikuni said, and said again. "He is not dead, Hollander. He spoke to me."

"Not dead," was all that Santvoort got of it as they hurried to the house.

"Put out that torch," Magome shouted from the doorway. He knew what a torch could do in the hands of a rabble such as there soon would be about the house. "There is a light in the room already. The Hollander and his host, and two others only may come. As soon as a soldier comes bid him enter also; for this is a matter for the notary. Others go round to the back of the house." For he was not yet sure that the young man had come alone.

He explained with dignity as they went to the room how good luck and a colic had taken him to the latrine whence he could see a sinister shape creeping in through the open door; how again it was the good fortune of soldiers, coupled with the nimbleness of his wrist, that had intervened at the very moment that the assassin's blade descended on the sleeping Pilot. Again, he said, it was only luck that had left a light burning in the room for him to see these things, for the Pilot himself had been helpless as a babe from over-much wine.

Who the rascal may have been would never, unfortunately,

be known. For the cleaving of his skull had obliterated his identity.

Samurai arrived with other neighbours before many minutes had passed, minutes occupied in taking Adams back to his own room after he had stared upon the strange things about him.

Santvoort took from Bikuni a bowl of water and a length of linen and bound up Adams's shoulder and told him that he had been as near to a dead man as he was ever likely to be.

One of the soldiers took charge of affairs at the house. Mats were laid over the corpse.

Magome took another soldier with him, and his torch-bearers, to make his deposition of the matter at the Secretariat of the Shogun and to ascertain whether Eta—the outcast and pariah scavengers of the city—might at once be summoned to rid a soldier's house of the encumbrance of a felon's carcase.

CHAPTER XXX

THE mind of Adams was clear again as he sat on his mat, looking at Santvoort and Bikuni. *Saké* had an advantage of the heavier liquors of Europe; a few hours of sleep and an inch-deep sabre-cut were sufficient to clear its fumes away and leave the eye alert and steady.

Santvoort, too, was thoughtful. "Will," he said at last, "if it is a Cavalero who now lies without a face in the other room, you may depend upon it that it was jealousy at the bottom of it."

"Jealousy?" asked Adams.

The Dutchman glanced at Bikuni. "She'd pass as a pretty one among these heathen. And if you take a man's girl—and if he's a Cavalero——" he shrugged his shoulders. "They are mighty free hitters, these Cavaleros with their bellyful of swords."

"But I have not taken his girl."

Adams, too, looked at Bikuni.

Sitting on her heels now before him she had none of that quality of grotesque brittleness. Her hair was not a massive sculpture of ebony. The glaze and polish of it were tumbled into hiding under tresses that were ungreased, for the kerchief that held it while she slept had been lost in her scramble for a light. Her kimono was flung about her and held together only by her two hands, so that instead of carven folds its shape was the lissom shape within it.

It was a tousled child that he saw looking with darkly wistful eyes at the blood-sodden rag that bound his shoulder.

"No," said Santvoort, "but they have a shorter way than asking a man and taking his word in answer to such a question. In other matters, too, Will, their way is a short one. He judged you, maybe, as though you were a Japonian. The old man's favour for you may have been enough to rile him if he was in love with the girl."

Adams grunted. "It's my belief," he said, "that the padre is behind it."

"So he is, b' God," said Santvoort, and Bikuni was startled by his exclamation. "The padre," he explained to her, pointing to the bandage and indicating with a gesture over his pate the corpse in the other room; "Bodsu Portingal, Nagasaki. . . . The man ought never to have left the ship, Will, except feet first with a round shot for company—after he had brought the beef and the wine that day." Then he became slow and puzzled. "It's not just or proper that it should be unholy to kill a priest if the priest may play these tricks. Is it unholy, Will?"

"How the devil should I know?" said Adams. "Unholy or no, if it is his trick, as I believe it to be, I'll risk the unholiness one day. It's self-defence."

"An-jin," Bikuni said softly and came to his side. The wound was slowly bleeding and she moved to tighten the bandage.

"Let Melchior do it, lass," Adams said, holding her hands away with his sound one. "His paws are already bloody." His word for Santvoort's hands came easily while he held in his great fist the tiny hands of Bikuni.

She took his meaning as Santvoort stretched out his blood-stained fingers and set to work upon the bandage.

Bikuni smiled, and over Santvoort's stooping back she showed the Needle-watcher that her palms, too, were darkly stained. Smiling still, she closed her eyes upon the friendly stare of Adams. The hands stole into the folds of her kimono. Slightly bowing her head in token of submission, she pressed the palms upon the ache for him in her heart, and upon her small breasts.

"God Almighty!" said Adams, startled by this first impact upon him of the desire she had kindled with the caress of his blood upon her hands.

And Santvoort, busy at the bandage, said, "Sorry, Will. It's a lusty blow, however. We must not let it get to bind you."

"Bind me?" said Adams.

To the flat, amiable face of Melchior, to a shoulder that dully ached about a hotly-smarting gash, he came back suddenly from a blur that had become all his consciousness—a blur that was the mystery of hidden breasts and the shadowiness of eyes that were veiled from him by drooping lids, of tawny limbs that were no more now the articulated members of a puppet, but the warm limbs of a girl, nimble and strangely fragrant.

"Aye," said Santvoort. "It could stiffen and get to holding you. Tight and hard as hell. If Verhaegen isn't here in five minutes to tie it properly, or stitch it, I'll fetch the old lout myself."

"Damn Verhaegen and his stitches!" said Adams. "The thing is nothing, Melchior. It wants no stitches and damme, I'll have no stitches—to-night. Go now, lad—and let me sleep. Bring Verhaegen in the morning. Not to-night."

Melchior, because he was simple of mind, or because he was not, ambled at once to the door. "Sleep then," he said. "But keep the same side uppermost in case of more visitors. No need to have holes made in both arms. Good night then, Will."

"Good night, Melchior."

They heard the fumbling of his feet with his clogs at the outer door, and Adams motioned Bikuni to slide the door. He sat forward and held out his hand. "Come," he said gently.

She came.

On the mat she knelt beside him, but a yard away. She would have spoken, but no words would come. Instead of them, there came only a tumult in her throat, and for a moment she pressed upon it the blood of the Needle-watcher that had dried on her palms. The sound that did at last come to him from her was the sound of stifled weeping. Her back bowed lower till her face was hidden by her tumbled hair. Her shoulders tautened and rippled within the film of silk that was over them, and words as yet made only a great sob.

"Bikuni," said Adams, the blur gone from him now, and in its place a compassion that was a great smile. "Bikuni—here, lassie, look, Bikuni . . ." he stretched out his hand and laid it upon her head and patted it and stroked it. "Bikuni."

The shaking of her became a little stilled.

Her sighs became words at last. "An-jin," she said, "Honourable An-jin." Then, "You are beautiful. Perfect. Lovely." They were words he knew; for he often used them—of the marvellous stitches with which she put together the pieces of his tunic; of her blue and golden sash when it was tied to make those carved fantasies of decoration upon a puppet.

"Little Bikuni!" he said and shuffled on his haunches towards her. Under her fallen hair he moved his hand till its palm lay across the tremor of her shoulders, his forearm against the tears that were warm upon her cheek. He would have drawn her to him and kissed the lips that had once smiled, over grotesquely black little teeth, in the face of a doll; but the contortion of shifting from his haunches and his outstretched legs was too cumbersome an affair—with one hand occupied upon the shoulders of Bikuni and the other held up in the sling Santvoort had made for him.

Instead, he caressed the nimble flesh of her and said, "You, Bikuni, are the lovely one. Lovely . . ." Even the grease that made of her hair a polished block when it was built upon her head, was now an endearment of the little creature as it touched, cool, upon his wrist and forearm.

Again, and suddenly, she collapsed under the burden of her tears and away from the caress of his hand.

"Bikuni," said he. "What is it?"

"*He*," she said. Slowly, and bowing low away from him, "He, whose sword even to-night so honourably saved for me the life of the honourable Needle-watcher."

"He?" said Adams. "The old man? Magome?"

"Yes," she said, and it was awe now that calmed her. "Magome Sageyu. My father."

"Well?" said Adams.

"I must obey my father," she said softly. "Or die."

"Die?" said Adams to her, and in his own tongue he said, "——die your grandmother——" His chuckle gave her his meaning; but she no more yielded the nimbleness of her shoulders and the warmth of her tears to his hand. She rose from the mat and went to the door, leaving him.

"Magdalena will come," she said.

The Pilot's answering thought, which he spoke aloud since his speech kept it as secret as the thought itself was, "To hell with Magdalena."

Magdalena soon came, however—neat and dressed and coiffed with the care and elegance and finish of noon or evening. She sat and prattled; and then, when Adams found that he was thirsty she brought him a cup of *saké*. When he found that he was sleepy she left him to sleep—guarded by the Samurai neighbours whom Magome had left outside in ceremonious charge of the Pilot and the corpse.

CHAPTER XXXI

FEVER came upon Adams for the day or two during which Magome was full of high consequence and busy-ness over the formalities of evidence and depositions.

The Pilot himself was duly questioned by an official and his words set down by a scribe: he had gone to sleep, drunk and sound; he had awoken wounded and sober. A dead man was heaped up beside him and beside the dead man a sword. Over the two of them had stood his host.

Giving his evidence, he saw the scene quite clearly, just as Magome had carefully and vividly described it to him. The corpse, being unidentifiable, had been removed and disposed of by Eta scavengers. Magome's two spoiled mats were replaced at the public cost.

Adams in his fever was restless and disturbed. It was neither the wound nor the fever that disturbed him so much as the vanishing away utterly of the girl Bikuni into the mummy-thing that again moved about with Magdalena (or without her)—all stiff folds and choppy movements, with hair a shining slab that could weigh half a quarter of a hundredweight.

"Bikuni," he said to the mincing effigy when it came in alone with some food and broth for him; "Come near again." He spoke softly and stretched out his hand to her—slowly, as he would have stretched it out to some young, strange creature offered him from a bumboat in a port of Barbary or Peru.

She stopped.

"Bikuni—honourable and little one."

He smiled, speaking not to the shell of paint and grease and folds, to the doll's mask and grotesque teeth of ebony, but to her who had wept and sighed, to the quivering flesh of shoulders, to tremulous breasts whereon had been pressed the dust of his blood.

"Bikuni—for the love of God."

She set his tray beside him and stood away. "No, An-jin," she said. "No."

To her the love of God meant nought. Her own love, however, she did know. She came quickly—craftily too, to the wounded and trussed side of him as he sat erect on the mat. On the back of his head where no razor had touched it but where the hair grew in heavy locks, she laid her hand—as a butterfly would extend and lay its wings, in sunlight. "For me, An-jin——" she whispered over him—"yes. For the trifling Bikuni a thousand thousand times—yes." Then she was gone to the door again. "But no, An-jin. No. My father." And the puppet was gone.

"Blasting," was his morose thought. "Blasting and damnation take your father."

Visitors came to see him.

Old Kuru came, blinking and smiling and humble in so great a house as that of Magome Sageyu the Samurai. He brought his present for the Needle-gazer, wrapped in gossamer paper— another peach-stone slightly more lascivious in its motif than the first one, and finer carving. This one was a box, the two sides of the stone opening apart on the merest speck of a hinge and fastening with a clip pared from a shred of ivory. It was a mean thing, he said; inconsiderable as dirt under a walking man's foot; but it might serve to mark his regard for the Needle-watcher, and for the august house wherein he dwelt. He indicated that the dark brown powder within the casket was an emetic of proved and prodigious potency.

Adams thanked him and asked him to send up the model of the ship.

The Swart came from his commissionairing at the bawdy house; for tidings of a sword-flash travel faster than the flash itself.

The wound upon Mr. Adams's arm was smaller than he had expected; the number of actual victims to the sword of old Magome was vastly exceeded by the estimates that had reached his end of the bazaar. He, too—since he had owed his very life a score of times to his aptitude for adopting strange customs—brought his present. He kept it within his shirt till they were alone and the door slid to—a short dagger with a magnificent blade but rough wooden haft.

"I have another for myself," he said casually, slipping the

gift under the coverlet.

"Do you not know that it is death to be found with a weapon?" Adams asked.

"Aye, Mist' Adams," he said. "I know also that it is often death to be found with no weapon. Keep it, Mineheer Pilot—next your belly, in the sheath which I will bring you to-morrow."

Bikuni came again into the thoughts of Adams as he felt the fine blade and the make-shift handle under his coverlet; for in any scheme for the successful concealment of a weapon one of the foremost considerations for him was Magome. In considering Magome he considered the strange quality the old man had gained from Bikuni's swords. 'My father.' It was Magome, and Magome alone, that brought the new hunger to him and the new, fevered thirst by striking a small lissom girl into a repellent marionette.

"I don't know that I have need of it, Swartie," he said.

"You did not know you had need two nights ago," said the negro.

"Well," said Adams, "it would have been useless. That is just the rub of it. In most cases it would be useless. Death comes—and damme, there you are. Or it does not."

And that, precisely, is the way in which the matter appeared to him. He was neither foolhardy and swash-bucklingly courageous, nor was he over-cautious. It was merely that personal safety seemed to him to be a matter that was of not much concern to the individual. Careful men died and careless survived. A knife—a dozen knives—hidden away on a drunken stomach would have been a futility and an irony. The adequate thing had been the chance of Magome's going off to the latrine, the chance of his having left the lantern alight and the chance of his prowling back in the nick of time. So he had no strong feelings about the Swart's knife one way or the other; and because he had no strong feelings, he thanked the Swart and kept it.

He asked him questions about the crew; for of late, in his occupation with the rigging and sailing of his model, he had seen little of them.

"They go their ways," said the Swart. "They have women of

their own; and their money is gone. I see little of them. It is only the better men of the place that come our way—soldiers and the better men. And wrestlers. You could come, Mist' Adams. You still have money left?"

"Aye," said Adams, "I still have money."

"But you have sufficient women?"

Aboard ship, Adams reflected, a question like that would never have come from the Swart; for a swart would have had no concern in the Pilot's furniture. But shipboard was gone; and the Swart was a gift-bearer.

"Women?" said Adams, and he thought of the singing-girl imported for his entertainment by Kuru. "Women? Swart, I have seen no women—save one or two, perhaps— ragged, lousy strumpets that followed us about at Oita. For the rest they are dolls."

"Ho! Ho! Ho!" laughed the Swart. "You do not know, Mineheer. Never were such women."

"You are a Swart," Adams reminded him.

"But I have been in Rotterdam and Lisbon," said he. "I have been in Plymouth of England and Chatham."

"Chatham!" said Adams. "Have you been in Chatham?"

"Yes," said the Swart. "I was flogged once in Chatham—but never have I known such women as the girls of this place. They sing——"

"Yes, " Adams interrupted him. "I've heard their singing."

"But the singing soon stops, Mineheer."

"And then," asked Adams, "do they become women?"

"Such women——" said the Swart. "And such brawls do the men make for them. But it is a law of my patron's house that soldiers disarm before they enter. They leave their swords with me."

"And so you can afford daggers as presents?"

"They are lusty drinkers," the Swart explained. "You should come one evening; with your host. He is well known and well considered in our part of the town."

And it was at the word of an old rascal with a reputation in brothels that Bikuni drew away from him and said, "No, An-jin—no," and with bated breath—"my father——"!

Verhaegen the Surgeon came, first with Santvoort to look at

the wound and dress it, and then without him.

When his work was done he said, "There is good room for you in our house, Mr. Adams. The Emperor will soon be back now from his wars, they say, and will give you leave to change your lodging."

"I am very well here," said Adams.

"So it would seem!" the other laughed. "By eight or a dozen inches. In the throat—where it was aimed—that gash would have had a different tale to tell. You would not then have been so very well. Living alone with these heathen——"

"But it was one of them that saved me," Adams suggested.

The Surgeon changed his method. He said, "Would there not be some comfort in living among your proper messmates? Comfort as well as safety, Mister. We are the responsible ones of the fleet now, with its business still on our hands. And with the three of us together—well, we could see to it that all three were not drunk at the same time. It would be safer; for one can be drunk only at his peril if he is alone."

Adams saw that the best arguments would be those based on the Surgeon's own grounds. He liked the Surgeon, and as for the Captain, to Adams he was still not only Captain but indeed Admiral-General. Adams was still a seaman, with his reverence for a superior officer.

"As for safety, Mr. Verhaegen," he said; "my host Magome Sageyu is as good a bodyguard as you would find in all the land. One stroke from him cleft a man from his crown to his chin; and in the blade with which he did it there was not so much as a nick."

"For my part," Verhaegen argued on gently, "I would as soon sleep in a powder magazine as the house of a ruffian carrying those skull splitters at his belly."

"But he is our friend," said Adams.

Verhaegen said: "So is the powder in the magazine. But for safety and comfort I'd sooner sleep in a bed."

Magdalena came in, silent and demure with the tray of cakes and sweetmeats arranged for guests. The Surgeon glanced at her and then at Adams, who sat puzzled and a little sullen in his difficulty of opposition to an Admiral-General.

"Adams," he said when she had gone, dropping the sea's

formality of 'Mister' as he drew nearer in friendliness to the Pilot; "a crown or two will buy a girl. The Captain and I—the Swart——"

"I have no mind to buy girls," said Adams, "but these girls are the daughters of a soldier; a Cavalero. They are not to be bought."

"Why should they be?" asked the Surgeon. "There are girls and to spare, without them. Why should any man concern himself with the daughters of a Cavalero?"

Why indeed?

CHAPTER XXXII

THE Cavalero became the greater Cavalero when the news came that the Shogun would soon return, in triumph, to his capital.

Emissaries came before Ieyasu and his army—soldiers of great standing with no exercise but the exercise of their weapons, lesser soldiers with duties of organisation and administration. Hucksters, players and wrestlers came; beggars and priests and host upon host of singing-girls with their attendants and their solemn, lordly herdsmen.

Magome, attending at the palace, was closeted with soldiers and administrators in council; for crowded into the city and all about it was already thrice a city's population.

Nightly there were alarums and excursions and hullabaloo. Swords and dirks slid from their scabbards; lanterns were overturned and torches set, somehow, among the tinder of which brothels and taverns were made.

Nightbirds from the scum and the dregs of the overflowing gutters moved in the din of flames, screaming for the loot and rape and plunder that were their only sustenance.

So by night as well as by day, Magome was abroad. He wore hakama for these sallyings forth—the pantaloons that gathered in the skirts of his kimono and his quilted under-robe, setting his feet freer for their movement in the slush and snow. A glove of soft leather that the girls had made for him with stitchings of silk kept his hand warm for an adequate closing of it upon a hilt, if loiterer or prowler or fugitive should offer within his reach.

It was the houses of the singing-girls, the administrators decided in their councils with the evidence of such as old Magome, whence arose the riots of swords and flame. They drew up a plan, therefore, for setting these houses apart from the others out of the city in the Valley of Delight. Beyond the Valley's boundaries they enacted that not even a soldier might carry a sword or a dirk.

Magome, disarmed, walked beside Adams in high humour on

the evening when he at last felt free to be the guest of his Pilot on the two tael they had taken from the bundle in the strong-box. There was homeliness and a comic nudity about his stomach without its sword-hilts, and he told the Pilot of many jolly things that might brighten the evenings of a prosperous man in that growing city.

They were bound for the new house where the Swart and his patron were established and they soon found it, for most men knew of the Swart. With others they looked through the wooden grille that closed its front.

Upon the silken and painted group that sat within the light of many lanterns there was a carved stillness and austerity that struck a chill into Adams. It was the doll and puppet coldness carried to its logical conclusion of freezing. The puppets were displayed in tableaux; the threads that worked them were dropped or cut or forgotten—till a summons, unheard in the roadway, or an unseen beckoning produced a snap of movement in one of them and she was gone behind the screen.

"Shiratsayu!" old Magome grumbled. "Shiratsayu—White Dew—gone already . . ." and he obviously fidgeted, looking from one to another of the other choice and precious things that might at any moment be snapped away while the Pilot still kept him outside, gaping. But he was the Pilot's guest, and he stood humbly at the grille, awaiting the Pilot's pleasure.

To reach this house they had passed others of the lesser and more vulgar sort where the windows were not groups of still and silent and gorgeous effigies but cages of restless and mis-chievous freaks. For all that, they were more like monkeys than human creatures with their squat stature and their playful gibbering at the bars, they had seemed to be more in accordance with some general law of the fitness of things. Bawdry was, after all, bawdry; and Adams was a little shaken out of con-fidence in his plan by the way Magome moved contemptuously on from robustious and obvious bawds to pause where there was austerity and a devotional quality that could have been found in a Popish church.

Magome clucked and shuffled, and they went in.

They found the Swart in attendance with the Master of the

house. Magome quickly specified his choice; and Adams, superior and magnificent, made it clear that he, for his part, was making no choice. Money had nothing to do with it. That, too, he made quite magnificently clear with the fistful of coins he produced from his girdle. His announcement, however, made none of the dramatic impact he had aimed at; for Magome had bustled over and stood anxiously by Adams, to see that the coins were properly handled and their value accurately applied.

They were summoned with ceremony that again brought to the mind of Adams some vague association with Papish ritual, by a portly chaperone; and before Adams rightly knew where he was, he was following her beside Magome, to an upper room of that magnificent house.

In it were trays for their wine-cups, more ritual between the chaperone and Magome, with Adams being put clumsily through it by the smiling Cavalero—and they honourably seated themselves on their heels.

The girls came in—the second choice of the old connoisseur (since his claim for White Dew had been forestalled) and the Swart's choice for Adams. They played their instruments, and sang.

Magome drank and twinkled and beamed upon them.

Adams drank.

Drink, he knew, could not shake or blur the gesture he was about to make. The music and the singing, the posturing of bodies and the smile of gilded lips that brought little cluckings of delight from the tongue and gums of old Magome struck upon Adams as a cold and bitter taunt. It was none of it for what he yearned; and the warm, muddling glow of *saké* could not touch his yearning. Warmth and muddle in his own heart could not bring life to the stiff and squealing puppets—the life that he had felt so comely at the palm of his hand when it had lain on the bowed little shoulder of Bikuni, at his forearm when it had touched her throat and her tears and her tumbled hair.

A further step was reached in the evening's entertainment; the girls laid aside their instruments and came across the room to them at the trays. It was then that Adams showed Magome the fine and grand stuff of which he was made. He stood up and said to the old man: "Honourably enjoy yourself, Magome my guest. I go below. I drink a little with the Swart; and then I sleep."

To the girl at his tray he gave two benevolent pats on the shoulder and a coin that caused Magome to swallow a sweet-meat without its so much as touching his gums.

"In the morning," Adams said from the door, "when you are ready, tell the servant to call me." And he lumbered off, down the stairs. Magome brooded a moment on the terrible illness that must have been the Pilot's secret; for no mere imbecility could of itself reach so far.

CHAPTER XXXIII

ADAMS found the Swart alone in the ante-room. A party of such obvious wealth and consequence had just arrived that the master himself had gone to over-see the management for its accommodation and refreshing.

Adams said, "Open a bottle, Swart. I'll talk with you awhile. I've left the old man to his frolics."

"And yours, Mister Adams?" asked the Swart.

Adams shrugged his shoulders. As for his plan, that was none of the Swart's affair; and he could not expect a Swart to understand inmost feelings that were no more than a muddle of want and discontent within himself.

"I am very well," said he. "After the bottle you can give me a room to sleep in, till the old man is ready to go home."

"Aye, you can have a lodging room at the back, if this newcomer and his suite have not taken them all," said the Swart. "But if the girl did not please you——"

"Oh, the girl was well enough," said Adams. "But I prefer the wine."

It was all one to the Swart, though for his part he thought well of both. He drank with Adams, easily. For he had forgotten, as he so readily forgot all things that were past and done with, the old status of Pilot-Major and ship's Swart, and took naturally to his own high status of household servant. As such he was a bigger man now than a shop-keeper and as big as an artisan or craftsman.

"Swart," Adams said thoughtfully. "Soon the Emperor will be back, his wars finished. If you had a home would you want to go back to it?"

The Swart was puzzled. Adams explained what was meant by 'home'—a place to live in, where there were friends; a wife and possibly children.

"I have a home then," said the Swart, "and I shall therefore stay in it. It is true that I have all the matters you mention."

The Master returned. The wits and the ears of Adams and

the Swart easily combined to get the meaning of his obvious pleasure. The party he had just accommodated had come not only for accommodation but for his personal assistance. The young gentleman of such obvious wealth was from Nagasaki, and his object in coming to Yedo was to seek out and to pay compliments to the lost Pilot of the Holland ship. Here, honourably drinking his poor wine in his miserable house where even the women who delighted lesser men were beneath his august notice, was the Pilot himself—An-jin Sama.

"Oh," said Adams, "the women are the finest I have seen. But this man? Is he a padre?"

"No," said the host. "A merchant."

"A Portingal?" asked Adams next. The Swart's present to him was in its sheath against his stomach.

"No."

"But a Jesuit?"

"A foreigner of one sort or another," said the other casually. "Spaniard perhaps and Filipino, but dressed as we are and speaking our tongue. He comes honourably, bringing me word from good men in Nagasaki, friends of mine. And good money."

"Is he armed?" asked Adams.

"No," said the other. "How should he be armed? When even your honourable host, the soldier Magome Sageyu, disarms before entering here? I tell you, An-jin, he comes as your friend."

Adams felt the knife-shaft that rested against his skin. He was awake and sober. The chances were good enough.

He followed the Master to the room of Concepcion.

The youth welcomed him with the gesture that Adams now knew to be a ceremony of deference and respect, shaking his own hand and nodding, welcoming An-jin Sama of far-flung fame to the hospitality whose wretchedness was due not to the resources of the house but to his own mean inability—through the haste and dishevelment of travel—to set the best of it before him.

Adams answered that that was all right, and asked him if he could speak Dutch or English instead of Spanish, and if he was a Jesuit.

"Of me also," Concepcion answered in slow Dutch, "the Jesuits are no friends." There was something pleasing about his sly geniality. "The Jesuits," he went on, "are friends only of—the Jesuits. I, in my small way, am the friend of whoever may care to find any small convenience in my friendship." Some subtle thing in his manner indicated a simplicity and a sincerity. He had also one thing already in common with Adams—they were both obviously in fancy dress—foreigners tricked out as Japanese.

"Well," said Adams, "what need can a Philippine merchant have of me—or I of him—I who am no merchant of any sort?"

"All men have need of friends," said the other. Without Concepcion's cheery smile the words would have been the utterance of a pompous old man. "For how, otherwise, can enemies be dealt with?"

"You mean the padre?" said Adams. "The way old Magome Sageyu my host deals with them. By chopping faces in two—brains and all."

"Your understanding of Spanish and even Japanese is better than my speaking of Dutch, Mineheer Pilot," said Concepcion, and they squatted to the trays that were set for them. "I understand you have already taken your entertainment, so we will talk a while. Such service as the soldier's I myself cannot give you. I have no swords. But I know the people and am known to them—all the big ones of Nagasaki and some even here in Yedo. And I know the Portingals. There are certain comforts and conveniences that only knowledge can bring. And we have an abundance of money——"

Adams said, "Have you come all the way from Nagasaki to make me a present of money?"

The other shook his head, but he did not at once answer. He poured some wine from the bottle he had brought with him. "To a Japonian," he said, "I would answer, 'Yes.' Perhaps he would not believe it, but he would accept the answer with the present. You, however, would not believe it; and the puzzle would prevent your accepting the present. Am I not right?"

"That's right," said Adams; and they drank some wine. "That's right. A Papist might have come to convert us to

Popery. But you look more heathen than Papist. So what have you come for? To buy the cargo—if we could sell it?"

"No," said Concepcion, "we have goods already more than we can sell. Your broadcloth is of little value. It is only as an act of charity that we would buy that."

Adams was already accustomed to business methods. He thought now that it was surely to make a bid for the cargo that the young man had come.

"I have a buyer for our broadcloth already," he said, casually. "We only wait for the Emperor's return, to get his permission to sell. The price is a good one."

"Take a deposit then, quickly," said the other. "And have a deed firmed. I will undertake it for you if you like, being accustomed to these matters. We will say, too, if you like, that I am competing with your buyer. It may get his deposit the quicker."

Adams had wasted a lie.

"What *have* you come for?" he said.

The young man became thoughtful again. "It is difficult to say," he admitted. "We are enemies of the same people. They want my business and your life. So it seemed well that we should meet in friendship."

"Do you want me to sail a ship for you then, to save this business of yours, and my life?"

"No," said the other.

"Then what in God's name do you want?" It was perplexity and not impatience that moved him. "As long as I do not sail a ship I am a prisoner. 'Okyaku Sama' these cavaleros call it; but it's 'prisoner' that it means. To-night is the first time I've been as free as this since we landed here, and I know well enough that I could not escape from this house without— perhaps—a chopped skull or a ripped belly."

"Escape?" said the other in some alarm. "Do you want to escape?"

"No," said Adams. "I mean that in escaping I should be doing the only service I can do to any man. I should be sailing a ship."

Concepcion shrugged his shoulders. "In Nagasaki alone there are a score of men who can sail ships, in the Philippines a thousand or more. I myself, for that matter, can sail a ship."

"Oh, you can, can you?" said Adams. This he knew was nonsense. The fellow was either a liar or an idiot. "Do you, too, call these duck-bellied craft that crawl along the coast—ships?"

"They pass for ships," said the other. "And they are sufficient. But no, señor. You can do more than sail ships. You can talk, it seems, to the mighty Ieyasu himself—even before you can speak his language."

Concepcion stopped. It was the first time in his life that he had ever told a man what was really the bare truth of what lurked at the back of his mind; and the phenomenon startled him into staring afresh at the man to whom he had told it. He, with one eyelid a little drooped and teeth parted under his closed lips, was savouring the Spanish wine with movements of his tongue, and judging it against *saké*.

Adams swallowed the wine and said, "What is it you would have me tell the Mighty One of you?"

This time Concepcion could only shrug his shoulders, for there was no formed scheme, even at the back of his mind. In his difficulty he reverted to his method of general palaver. "It is sufficient," he said, "that we should be friends. You, as my friend, could serve me in one way or another, for I have no friend in the General's presence. I, as your friend, could perhaps be of service to you—for you, Señor Pilot, have no friend in all this world."

"Ho!" said Adams, "don't you run away with that idea!" It was great wine the young man had brought. "There's Melchior the Hollander to start with; and if you know a better man than Melchior, I'd like to see him. There's old Magome Sageyu, my host."

"The Hollander is like yourself," said the other. "A foreigner and helpless. Magome Sageyu is an official."

"There's Mitsu," said Adams.

"Mitsu?" said Concepcion. "He of the Bodyguard who was found to speak a little in Spanish and Portuguese and Dutch?—coming from Izu?"

"Maybe," said Adams. "God knows where he comes from; but he is a good friend."

"He is dead," said the other.

"Dead?"

"Dead," said Concepcion. "After the battle some few prisoners whom he was guarding succeeded in making away with themselves, so he cut his belly. The story is well known and much told."

Adams had tilted his wine-cup till the wine from it had spilled to his lap. He slowly put down the cup again. Slowly, he again said, "Dead."

Concepcion watched the movement, listening to the words.

"Truly this man was your friend," he observed.

"This blasted belly-cutting——" Adams exclaimed. "Mitsu to go and perform such a foolery!—If they were prisoners, what did it matter if they made away with themselves?"

"They had been specially saved," Concepcion explained, 'for other purposes."

"The whole damned lot of them——" said Adams morosely, "are mad."

"That is very true," said the other. "They are incomprehensible."

Incomprehensible. . . . Adams took some more wine. There was no need to keep brains even fairly clear when greater sanity made greater nonsense of the incomprehensible. Death from one cause or another had always been a fair and normal risk; but it came to Adams as a sheer revelation as he drank his wine and mused that death was not even a risk. It was something that must, in some way or other, be ignored altogether; and the manner of death was equally negligible.

"I suppose you are sure of this?" he asked. It was the last chance by which the revelation could be denied.

"It is common news," said Concepcion. "If the man had been of greater importance it would have reached you here. We knew of it because he was newly discovered to be a linguist. So you see, Señor, you still have need of a friend."

The fellow was not in the least offensive with this solicitation; he made it so quietly and so good-humouredly. "There are so many things; comforts, entertainment, women——"

"Women!" said Adams. "A man needs no elaborate or particular arrangements in this island to get women. Look at

Santvoort—and the lot of them. They find no dearth of women—wives or wenches."

"But you?" asked Concepcion. "Have you no need of women?"

"They are not women!" he snorted; and then stopped, suddenly, to think. This man said he understood the people. Adams would test him. "My friend the Hollander is said to have married the daughter of his host. Can such a marriage be according to law, and good?"

"Perfectly," said the expert. "All marriages are according to law, and good."

"Then," said Adams, "why should I not marry the daughter of my host?"

At this the expert laughed.

"Why not?" Adams repeated. "Is it because in my own country I am married already?"

For this the expert had more laughter. Then he explained. "Your host, Señor, is a soldier. The daughter of a soldier may marry only a soldier."

"To hell with that!" said Adams. "I have done as much soldiering one way and another as old Magome. I've shot off a musket and let blood and broken a head with the best of them. Is that not soldiering?"

"Your host is a nobleman," said Concepcion. "A caballero."

"I, too, am a cavalero for aught he knows," said Adams.

"He knows that you are not a known caballero," the other explained. "It is enough for them of his kidney—the two-sworded ones. Señor, my first act of friendship is to caution you; say nothing of this love of yours for his daughter to the old man. He would take it greatly amiss."

"Would he indeed!" said Adams. "The lascivious old dog! I know enough to set him holding his tongue. He'd have no face to take objection to me."

"You do not understand," said Concepcion. "A nobly born girl may go only to a nobly born soldier among these people. Even a nobleman of Spain would not be considered suitable."

Adams could have answered this tersely, but politeness kept him quiet.

"But what of the girl herself——" he began instead.

"There is no such thing as the girl herself," the sage young man explained. "A girl—any decent woman—is nought, according to the writing, but three obediences: to her father, her husband, and when her father and her husband are dead, to her son."

Adams had no more to say.

"It is in my mind to have a house in this city," the young man continued; "you could no doubt gain permission to be my guest instead of his. There are comforts and women in this country, Señor, other than those under the roof of an old Samurai."

"Damnation take these Japan women," Adams mumbled.

"But there are others to be had from the Philippines," said the son of the nutmeg king, "Spanish women."

"——Spanish women," said Adams.

Spanish wine and Spanish talk had driven him back to his mother tongue; but even there he found no clear expression for his thoughts. The question was not the very simple one to be answered glibly by the word "woman." It was the vague irksomeness he found in mincing dolls and stiff marionettes who talked in clicks and sang songs like the wailing of the damned. They were concealing something; and a libertine's talk of "Spanish women" was oppressive, not because the talker was a libertine and the women Spanish, but because it was beside the point.

"You will find, Señor," Concepcion said suddenly, "that your broadcloth is utterly worthless. What the rats have not already eaten in the holds of your hulk, they might as well eat. The only market in this country is for the light stuffs—silk and cotton—from India and China."

So the cargo was another thing gone; and the young man had not been taken in by the tradesman's story of a buyer.

Adams saw that only a muddled bleakness remained at the end of nearly three years of survival against probabilities. Bare life had been preserved by a series of unconnected pranks, but all the stuff for the feeding of it was gone. The ship was as good as gone. The broadcloth was worthless; Mitsu had had a peculiar value and he now was dead. Santvoort still held good; but Santvoort—the best of lads as he was—had an inherent dullness and inadequacy about him. There was no glimmer from him as there had been from Mitsu. He thought again of that glimmer. . . .

About Bikuni, too, there had been a sudden glimmer on the night of his wound that had haunted all the nights that followed it. But he now had his doubts of that glimmer—the same kind of doubts that had sometimes arisen in his mind about the value of the broadcloth. The ripple of shoulders under the silk of her kimono, her neck and the quiver of her breasts as she wept within his arm, the glow of her wet eyes and the tremor of lips that were painted then only by her youth—these, too, he was willing to believe, had been only a false calculation on his part. . . . One thing, however, did survive—the only surviving thing outside himself. It was small enough and trivial enough. Three spans of his hand more than covered its length from rudder to bowsprit—the ship he had made and rigged and sailed with Melchior—he and old Kuru. About that one thing, as about the life that was starkly preserved within himself, there was neither doubt nor question.

It was a fact.

CHAPTER XXXIV

It was at the bath that they met Magome in the morning. Lordlings and soldiers, merchants and scribes and the better artisans greeted one another with easy but particular courtesy; for the houses of no night that made all men swordless made them very near to equals.

"Introduce us, Señor," Concepcion said; and the old Samurai, rubbing his paunch with the palms of his hands, was soon exchanging pleasantries of the morning with the nimble young merchant from Nagasaki.

Adams looked on and listened, noting the slickness of the young man's tongue and his glibness with the right phrase to answer phrase, which counted for more in the speaking of that language than the mere uttering of words.

Concepcion placed the wretchedness of his hospitality at the condescending disposal of the renowned warrior as to breakfast.

The inconsiderable and much over-rated soldier was astonished to humility by the unparalleled generosity of so magnificent an invitation. He accepted it.

Adams was glad of this palaver while he dressed himself; for his dagger was among his clothes and had to be negotiated, unseen, within them.

While they ate their rice and tea and pickles and preserves he heard the old cadger accepting open invitations for them both for future evenings. Concepcion issued them so that geniality was tempered with profound respect.

Magome looked upon the Pilot with a new benevolence, thinking with fresh happiness of the lucky day that had brought him, and with him this fresh source of entertainment.

When he had assumed his swords again as they walked home Adams said, "Why did you not tell me Mitsu is dead?"

The old man stopped. His shock came from the sudden realisation that Adams was already independent of him, already grown to the extent of having access of his own to the world about him. On the strength of this thought alone he immediately distrusted the Filipino.

"Why not?" Adams repeated.

Magome's face softened. Correct and splendid phrases would have been wasted on the Pilot.

"He was your friend, An-jin," he said softly. "It was not seemly that I should distress my honourable guest and my own friend."

They had continued to walk on again; but it was Adams who now stopped, for it was he who had been startled. The old soldier, when he spoke without phrases, and softly without a smile, had some quality of the same glimmer that had been in the flesh of Bikuni when it had rippled to the touch of his hand.

"God!" he said. "They're an odd lot . . ." and then, "He too is my friend." He jerked his head in the direction they were leaving.

"The Filipino?"

"Aye. The Spaniard," said Adams.

"Spaniard or Filipino," said Magome, "it makes no matter, so long as he behaves fittingly."

"And spends handsomely." Adams suggested.

"And spends handsomely," Magome agreed simply. "For he is a young man of substance. And it is fitting; for how else can merchants move among men of the better sort?"

"He will build a house for himself to live in here," said Adams. "A very fine house. With women."

"No doubt," said Magome.

"He has asked me," said Adams, "to live with him as his guest. It would be fitting, since I too am no Samurai." This, he thought, would get some kind of answer that would bear thinking about.

The old man said, "But, An-jin, you have already in me a friend—Magome Sageyu, the soldier who has cleft a skull for you from crown to teeth. Already you need no merchant for a friend. And soon, with Magome Sageyu to guide and protect you, you will need none for a host. You yourself will have money—enough for a good house; and women."

The old fellow had missed the point, but his very missing of it was a starting point for some thought. Adams did not answer.

"You would not leave the poor house of this person, An-jin?" Magome asked, and in his wistfulness there was again that quality of glimmer. But there was in it, too, an encouragement to Adams. He ventured further.

"In your honourable house," he said boldly, "there are no women."

The old man said, regretfully: "True." But he was unable to contemplate for many moments together any side of things but the bright one. "True. But outside my house there is a multitude; and the multitude grows daily, as the soldiers return from the South. Already you have money enough, An-jin—if you would spend it. And your friend the Filipino —and mine—has more than enough for all. But"—and he now spoke sadly, wagging his head and lowering the scar over his eye-socket—"you, An-jin, would honourably appear to have a distemper for women."

Adams would have said, if the language of Japan had any contemptuous word for it, "It is for your *bawdry* that I have a distemper." If there was such a word he did not know it, so he said nothing.

Towards the end of their walk he made one more move towards the question.

"If I am a merchant," he said, "and not a soldier, it is fitting that I should live among merchants and not in the house of a great soldier with daughters."

Phrases disposed of this: "So negligible a person as this poor soldier," said Magome, "is honoured by the presence of one so illustrious as the Needle-watcher. His dismal and comfortless house is warmed and brightened by the presence of such a guest." It was approximately the same kind of thing that the old man had said to Concepcion. But he had not invited the Filipino to enter his dismal and comfortless house. Adams noted, therefrom, that he stood better than the Filipino.

The girls treated their father and his guest on their return as though their night out had been a day spent fishing. Their only concern seemed to be that the time had been spent to the satisfaction of the spenders, without unduly tiring them.

Adams had wasted his gesture of chastity, but was not content to let matters rest there.

The old man soon was engaged with a pupil behind the mats of his gymnasium. The girls and the old woman, about their morning's work, were in the other part of the house, and in the yard. Their tasks were light and brief ones—the stacking away of night-shutters, the fetching of water from the well, the moving of charcoal and of kindling wood.

Adams went out to Bikuni in the yard and said, "I was conversing throughout the night with a Filipino merchant."

She said, "It is well." But whether she considered it well or ill her words did not imply. It was preposterous; but it was not to this utterer of phrases that he had anything to say. It was only to the creature that had lived and quivered; and vanished.

"Yes," he said. "It is well. And your father knows. *He* did not spend the night in conversation with a Filipino merchant."

"What would my father have to do with a Filipino merchant?" she asked simply.

Adams mumbled to himself: "Mighty little when there is drinking and whoring afoot."

She was lifting a bundle of faggots from the stack. Adams grabbed it from her and picked up another as well. "I'll take them," he said, but she thrust herself in his way. She implored him to lay down the second one and give back the first to her, twining her fingers into his. He closed his together, holding her and waiting.

"An-jin," she said softly, lowering her eyes to the caress that held her hand. "An-jin—condescend——" or something of the same vague sort.

Suddenly her fingers seemed to shrink, for they slipped easily from between the Pilot's, and he turned to look towards the gymnasium.

Magome had thrust aside a mat and roared one syllable, and was coming towards them. Bikuni stood back from Adams, her hands folded in her sleeves, her head bowed. Magome spoke shortly to her and she went into the house. The old man jerked the bundles from Adams and flung them on the pile.

"Come with me, An-jin," he said, and turned again towards the mats.

Adams, in his mother tongue, said "Go to hell!" and stooped again to the wood-heap. But the old man turned upon him. Instead of anger in his face there was a smile. And he spoke softly. Obviously he was carefully considering what he said. "That is work for women, An-jin; and coolies. I will teach you the craft of a highly-born man. Come." He thrust his little hand out behind him as though to lead a child; and Adams lumbered after him.

The old man drew the mats together behind them and again stripped off his kimono and the garment under it. "I will teach you," he said, "to use a blade. It would be well for you, also, to strip."

Adams was in a fix, with the secret dagger under his clothes. But—sooner or later, he supposed—something would have to be done about that dagger; and sooner was as good as late.

He need not have bothered. Magome Sageyu was capable of miracles. He studied the hairy torso of Adams as he stripped, with his usual wonder and some admiration. He looked at his navel—a neater and more compact affair than the same detail in the average Japanese. Adams left the dagger haft for him to look at. The old man looked at it; for many moments his eye rested on it. And while it did so he performed his miracle. He omitted to see it.

He was doubtful of the Pilot's deltoids—the left one with its newly-healed scar; he was doubtful, too, of the tight heavy casing of his shoulder-blades. They were well enough for a wrestler or a wharf-coolie; but what a swordsman wanted was muscles that were as a light fluid, not great daubs that might have been emptied out of a shovel and allowed to solidify on the joints of his frame.

He handed him a bamboo foil, however, and showed him that it was fashioned, and weighted with lead, to have the form and the balance of a sword. He showed him the first three weapons that a mere shifting of the grip on the hilt could make of it—a short rigid blade for a lunge or a thrust; a lever with a fulcrum in the holder's wrist and the weight of all his body, through his forearm, upon its butt; and the delicate thing to flash through the air and flesh and bone by the grace alone of its curve and balance.

CHAPTER XXXV

NEVER before, in all his experience, had Magome seen a bamboo foil in any hands for the first time. It was only in matters of the art's very highest subtleties that a pupil ever came to him—boys and youths and sometimes a contemporary, whose style—a delight or a horror to the master—were styles already formed. He had to take, in them, the materials and the foundations or the stupid distortions that were already there and to work at this bad habit or that, and so leave the matter. Ahead of him, with such pupils, there were no possibilities. There were fees, perhaps, if the pupil had money enough and the old tutor nursed him properly; but for the artist in him there was nothing.

Adams might have had no particular aptitude beyond his quite general training in the use of tools and implements of one sort or another; but he had the charm for old Magome of having nothing to unlearn. The master gloated in his sheer virginity. Even if he had had the foot of an ox and a hand all thumbs, he had the ox's humble docility and the thumb's firm strength.

He put him through exercises that he had designed in years of reverie—movements that should be the basis of all true swordcraft; but which he had never been able to thrust upon pupils who counted out their candereen per lesson without a coin to waste upon an old man's pedantries—things they ought to have known before they were a dozen years old.

Magome wore no mask, and Adams sensed that same glimmer again as he lunged and stepped and swayed; as he clucked and snorted or clicked approval, and sweated in the frosty pale sunlight. The old man's glimmer made communion out of loneliness.

It reminded him while he, too, glowed in the chill morning that elsewhere there was another also with whom there might be some communion.

"Magome Sama," he said, smiling and panting, "I must go

now. Kuru will soon be home for his rice. His boys are working for us, without him I can do nothing with them."

"It is enough for one day," said Magome, hanging up the foils. "More would make your limbs even stiffer and harder, till we have softened them. . . . But you will not do it by working with Kuru and his boys."

"Oh," said Adams, "it is not my limbs that work with them —but my head. I only show them what to do."

"Is it another toy you are showing them how to make?" The model had disappointed Magome by its valuelessness; for Adams had made it clear in answer to all questions tactfully thrown out that he fantastically intended to turn it to no account, but to keep it for himself.

"No," said Adams, "not altogether a toy. They are making a boat big enough for men to sail in, two mats long."

"Ho!" said Magome in his throat, "let us bathe ourselves, An-jin, and I will come with you to the house of Kuru. I would have slept a little after to-day's rice, but I will first see to this affair."

"There is nothing yet to see," said Adams as they went towards the bath. Magome had attended very carefully to the straightening of the foils on their pegs while Adams picked up his clothes to conceal the dagger.

"There is less that I have not seen already," said Magome.

As they walked down to the waterside after their meal there was more than the usual pomposity in the bearing of him, with his hands rubbing one against the other in his sleeves.

Such a man, it is true, could not unbend himself to the extent of forgetting that his life was all invested in the two magnificent blades at his girdle, and to haggling and chaffering for money with a carpenter and boat-builder.

But he was the host of a guest; and there was nothing more fitting than that a soldier should protect with the keenness of his wits the financial and spiritual interests of the guest entrusted to him. If ultimately the guest, from the kindness of his heart and a proper sense of gratitude, should make a present—or a series of presents—that, too, was fitting.

Kuru the shipwright, harangued in courtly and portly phrases by the Samurai, saw the justice and decency of the proposition. He agreed that the Pilot, for his design and his overseeing of its execution, should receive a royalty of one-fifth of any price or remuneration that Kuru might receive for the job he was now doing, and for any contracts that might succeed it. It was fitting that Magome Sageyu, the man of justice and honour, should be present at all meetings, as referee without prejudice, and at the final striking of any bargains between vendor and purchaser.

If vendor or purchaser (or both) should contemplate some small deed of gift to the referee and arbitrator—that too was well.

Magome drank a cup of *saké* that night to the good health of his pupil—once the Needle-watcher and now architect to a small firm of speculative shipbuilders in the harbour of Yedo.

This contract turned out, in the course of three days, to be a provisional one. When the keel was properly laid and futtocks scarfed together for the vessel's ribs, loungers about Kuru's little slip went away talking, and in their place came one or two serious ones who stayed only a little while and went away in thoughtful silence.

A present of fruit and wine was brought to the house of Magome; a present of fruit to the Pilot. Magome listened solemnly to the bringer of the present. Thereafter he tucked his robes into his hakama and departed again in the slush of a thaw to the house of Kuru.

It was a simple matter to tell him how a rival had outbidden him for the services of the Pilot; and how he, Magome, bound by the honourable duty of a host, must consider above all ties of personal regard for Kuru, the interests of his guest.

The architect's royalty was raised from one-fifth to a fifth and one-half of a fifth—to thirty per cent from twenty.

So Magome and Adams again drank to the good health of the architect—eating also the fruit brought by the rejected employer.

CHAPTER XXXVI

IEYASU the Mighty made no great show of his return from the place of his victory to the place of his government. He came simply as a man who had been away to do a certain work, and had done it. One day it was said that he would now soon be back, and a day or two after that he was already come.

"He *is* dead then, Will," Santvoort said as he walked with Adams past loungers who discussed the news. "He is surely dead enough, or he would have been to see us."

No bleakness had come to the Dutchman till now; for he was never hit, as they used to say on the *Liefde*, till a bone was broken. Adams, since the revelation had come to him that death had become something as far beyond comment as it was beyond calculation, said shortly, "Aye, our Mitsu is dead enough."

"If his Majesty ever claps his eyes on us again," Santvoort went on, "we'll be parleying through Portingal scum again, or Spanish half-breeds."

Adams stopped in his surprise. "God alive, man!" he exclaimed. "Will nothing ever wake you up? Have you not noticed that we can now speak this Japonian tongue as well as Mitsu ever spoke your Dutch, or even Portuguese? And you can speak it better than I."

Melchior smiled. "What you do not realise," he said, "is that my talk to Vrow Melchior van Santvoort is not the same talk that one would address to his Majesty an Emperor. Nor is yours that you speak to the carpenter lads and your host."

"It would do well enough. And he will certainly clap his eyes on us again, for I mean to see him and have this matter of our bondage clear with him."

"Bondage?" said the Dutchman.

"What else is it?" said Adams. "I intend to get our leave."

"To go home?" asked Santvoort.

"Aye, to go home!" and the Dutchman was startled by his sudden vehemence and his astonishing words. Adams went on, and Santvoort referred later to his outburst as a fury. "How much longer do you think I can abide it—you with your wife, and your grinning at your household, and sleeping away most of your time. I've got a wife and children—probably starving —and here I am, cooling my feet with a lot of carpenters or sweating my guts away with an old clown, learning to fight like a farmyard-rooster—with a stick."

"But, Will," said Santvoort, "you like this country, and the people?"

"You fool," said Adams. "I *hate* it."

It was out of him at last. He had snapped out to the amazed Dutchman, to whom he had not spoken of home for half a dozen months, the conclusion of thoughts that had been busying his mind for some weeks. The conclusion was a surprise to himself. But there it was.

Things which Santvoort simply did not consider in any way his concern, Adams either believed or disbelieved. As simply and as firmly as he believed in latitude, he believed in the Protestant's Almighty God.

He believed in sin.

Drunkenness and gluttony and adultery, as occasional indulgences, counted for not very much more than the slightly more casual sin of profanity. Occasional and casual fallings into sin seemed a normal and a vaguely proper sort of risk for a man to take. But the adoption of, for example, adultery as a steady way of life was a different story.

And so, for some time now, he had fought a little shy of Bikuni herself and of the whole question of Bikuni. There were other aspects, too, to the question of Bikuni than the aspect of sin. He could see well enough how Melchior could frolic about in the way he was doing. His girl was a merry enough creature. . . . If he had been Santvoort and Bikuni had been such another girl, he doubted not that he would have done the same as Santvoort—falling into the Dutchman's sin. But it was Bikuni herself that was the other aspect of the question. The glimmer that had come to him from her was no lightly frolicsome enticement. Other enticements had found in him the happy fact that sailors don't care—not even married and Protestant sailors. But the enticement of Bikuni thrust him remotely away from the immediate moment, and it made of him a distant contemplator of he knew not what. The sum of it was an irritating puzzle. Bikuni was only one factor in it with the many others; and now that Ieyasu was back, he found that he was sick of it.

His announcement came from the bottom of his heart, "I hate it."

Santvoort said quietly, "You can take it that your wife and children are not starving, Will. My uncle will have seen to them by now. There is not only your indenture with the Company, but also a special request left by me, and he will abide by them."

"And if he does," said Adams, "all they will have got is a pittance."

"Well," said the other, "and if you go back they will not get even that. We came here to make our fortunes. Our going home in rags would bring fortune to no one; and there are no fortunes to be made at home."

This would have carried more conviction if Santvoort had ever before given evidence of being much concerned with fortunes or futures.

"I will see the Emperor," said Adams.

"Let sleeping dogs lie," said the other.

"That I will not," said Adams. "But it is only for myself that I ask his leave to go. You can stay—and all the others. Maybe I'll come back. I've sailed here once and can do it again. Merchants will not be wanting to send out another ship and cargo."

Santvoort was aware of a basic fact: if Adams went they would all, for some unknown reason, go also; and he hated to be disturbed.

"Well," said he, "you had better let me come to the Presence with you if his Majesty gives us an audience. I may be able to put in a word here and there if ever you should get stuck for them."

"I shall not get stuck," said Adams.

"When?" asked Santvoort thoughtfully.

"As soon as may be."

Santvoort was as jarred by this talk as he had been by anything since they had avoided crucifixion. He went therefore, while Adams was with the boat-builders, to sit in the little garden of Magome, waiting for the old man to dispose of a pupil.

"So," he said, when they were seated by the brazier in the front room, "so your Pilot would leave this honourable roof."

"What?" exclaimed the old man. "For the roof of that Filipino?"

"For his own poor roof," said Santvoort, "his own roof half a world away. I thought he would have told you."

"Are they his own words?" asked Magome.

"His own," said Santvoort. "This morning. When we heard that the Emperor was returned, he said, 'I will see the Emperor and get leave to go home to my wife.'"

Magome seemed to have been struck into a coma. Heavily, and unseeing, he unfastened his embroidered tobacco-pouch that was fastened to his girdle by a peach-stone most enviably carved into an obscene sculpture, and delicately lacquered. He filled his pipe. It was, in the decoration of its stem, an advance on his first pipe. But it was still a simple thing. He smoked out the pinch of tobacco and filled again, and again smoked.

Then he spoke from his coma. "In two years from now—or even less—he would be able to use a sword. In three months from now, they tell me, the little ship would be built—and sold. Already there are three possible buyers. . . . In six months from now he would be able to use our tongue for any speech that is in his mind . . ."

He stopped and then woke suddenly out of his coma. "Hollander!" he said, "he must not go. It is only that Filipino with the boats from Nagasaki that could get him away."

"It is only the Emperor that can stop his going," said the Dutchman.

"Very well, then," said Magome. "I myself will see the Emperor."

It was a tall order; a big resolution for the old man to make— it meant presents in a series of progression that began at the castle's outermost gate and ended at the door of the audience chamber. But somehow he would find them. The shampooer would have to be touched for another loan. . . .

Santvoort said, "Good."

But already a messenger was on his way from the castle to Magome, bidding him attend with the Pilot that same afternoon upon the presence of Ieyasu.

While barbers shaved them after their midday meal and made a fresh and splendid knob of the hair at the top of Magome's head, the girls took out and laid ready for him the jacket with his magnificent crest.

For Adams they produced the coat that was Ieyasu's gift to him.

Magome gave an impression of full-sail as he walked beside him, full of consequence. He explained to all who asked, and to any who did not, that he was taking up his honourable guest the Needle-watcher, to introduce him to the Presence.

At the door of the chamber, however, his sails were furled, and his portliness collapsed. The doorkeeper told him he might rest himself in the pleasant sunshine. It was not he, the illustrious soldier, but his guest the Needle-watcher that the General wished to see.

Because of a faint hope that had gone on persisting in Adams, the first thing he said to Ieyasu was, "So our friend Mitsu is dead?"

He expected a smile of assent so immediate that he scarcely even looked for it. He only asked the question because of that absurd, restless hope. They were alone in the chamber, he and the other whom he always called "the Mighty" or "the Emperor of all Japan"; and instead of any syllable or any faintest gesture of assent there was silence and utter stillness.

Adams noticed, when there was a thudding at his ear-drums, that his breath was held. He had been staring into the face of Ieyasu; but he did not see the beginning, in any feature, of the smile that had come there. He let out the breath he could no longer hold. The smile was not a gesture of assent, but friendliness.

Ieyasu spoke very softly. "No, An-jin. Your friend Mitsu is not dead."

Crazed and fantastic as they were in every detail, there seemed to be no impossibility among those people—nothing that was even improbable; so Adams made no loud exclamation.

He was satisfied to find that that vague, pig-headed hope of his had not been so imbecile a matter after all. And he went on with his breathing.

"Then——" he said, and he looked about him, peering into the corners of the dim room; "where——"

"Ah——" said Ieyasu, "that, Needle-watcher, is a different pair of sandals. It is enough that I have told you, in token, that he is not dead."

"Token?" said Adams. "Token of what?"

"Friendship," said he.

The word jarred with the same ironic quality of a joke that they had found in their learning of "okyaku sama"—their style of "guest."

"Friendship . . ." he repeated slowly and thoughtfully.

"You learn words easily," said Ieyasu. "Yes, friendship. One other knows, besides you and me, that Mitsu is not dead. I know because the plan was mine—a very simple plan for him to do some work for me which he could not have done so easily if he were known to be alive. A mere child's plan. The other one knows because it was necessary; he was an accomplice. You know, because I have told you. It is the handsomest gift a man may give a man, when no gain can come of it, but only loss. A secret."

Adams thanked him.

"Have you understood clearly—all?"

"Not all perhaps." said Adams. "But enough."

"Good," said Ieyasu. "So that in another two moons, or three, you would understand all—every word."

"Another two moons——" and Adams suddenly stopped musing. He had come to say one thing and one thing only; and for that reason he said it. "I would go home, my Lord. In two moons I would be gone from here—I and whoever of the others would go with me."

"An-jin——" said the other; and he clucked and frowned. It was clearly not at Adams, personally, that he was clucking and frowning, but at a perplexity. "An-jin, throughout the length and breadth of this land there are now no prisoners——"

"No," said Adams, "just guests."

Ieyasu frowned on till he saw that this was a joke; then he laughed.

Serious again, he came nearer to Adams and said, "A secret for a secret, my friend. Tell me—you yourself—inmostly—do you desire it—to go?"

And Adams said, quietly and unintelligibly, in his own tongue, "God knows——"

It had seemed clear enough while Santvoort was quibbling with him, and trying to thwart everything he said, talking nonsense. Gillingham in Kent with the fog rolling up from the Medway. . . . It slithered over the mud flats and the grounded barges, and prowled up the street. On the hillside it enveloped the little house and the family in it, that had been—in the teeth of Santvoort's stupid opposition—a call that was flatly undeniable. But it was in the words of Santvoort himself that he now seemed to see the greater truth; they would be well enough in that little house. The Dutchmen in Rotterdam, with Santvoort's genial uncle among them, would see to it. And Mary's relations would see to it. . . .

Ieyasu touched him upon the shoulder; and before he could say again—defiantly and for the simple reason that he had come with the purpose of saying it—whatever it was that he had come to say, Ieyasu said, "It is no matter, An-jin. Whether you desire to go or whether you desire to stay, is no matter; so meditate no more upon it. From to-day there is one prisoner in Japan. I make this law: if he attempts to run away any man may honourably kill him. Any man omitting to kill him will himself be killed. So you have no need of worry. You are free."

Adams considered the revelation which had come to him with the first report of Mitsu's death; death was, in the sum of things, a thing utterly negligible, because it was sheer vagary. The conviction was in no way shaken by the news that Mitsu was not, after all, dead but smiling away somewhere, listening and watching and thinking. And this easy and amiable talk did not shake it—of casual killing, and being killed, as though by the quiet operation of some fantastic machine.

"So . . ." he said, and Ieyasu said, "Even so."

"You treat your friends," Adams observed, "with great and honourable benevolence."

"It is written," said the other, who saw no irony, "that there is but one measure for right and wrong—benevolence of conduct only."

Adams had to grin, to show that his observation had been a joke. "The benevolence of cutting a man's throat for wanting to go home to his wife and children!" he said.

"The benevolence of depriving him of doubt upon a point; and giving him peace," said Ieyasu. "That matter is settled now. If you would live at all, An-jin, you must live here."

And the astonishing part of it all was that this cool threat of execution came from Ieyasu as a princely gift; it had the charm of that benevolence of which he quietly boasted.

A few seconds gave Adams more than enough time to see that there was no way out, under the sun.

The men who wore them pulled out their swords and used them as briefly as they sneezed.

He shrugged his shoulders. Only one question remained, and Ieyasu answered a part of it before it had quite formed itself in the Pilot's mind. "Mitsu," he said, "is dead. You understand that?"

"Yes," said Adams. "I'll tell no one."

"Very well. I require in his place a man who can sometimes interpret to me the sayings of Spaniards and Portuguese when they have cause to speak with me."

"Have they not their own interpreters?" asked Adams. "There's that man Concepcion——"

"Aye," said Ieyasu; and he smiled. "They have their own, as you have cause to know. It is sometimes well that other ears also should listen to them."

"Am I to leave the house of old Magome Sageyu then?" It was not till this moment that the question had acquired any importance.

"No," said Ieyasu. "That is as you wish. He will be told to see to it that you have every comfort, and complete supervision. And I would talk more to you, An-jin, when your speech is readier, of ships and such matters. I will send for you when I have need of an interpreter."

Adams turned to go. At the door he stopped. "Oh—" he said; "the others will ask me. Are they also—guests?"

Ieyasu thought a while and then said: "It is a small matter. But there is no reason why even they should suffer doubt. They might as well be prisoners, too, like their Needle-watcher. Their heads, too, will be cut off if they swim further than a league from our coast. Are they, too, learning to speak our tongue?"

"The Hollander is learning," said Adams. "He has taken a wife, according to your law."

"*My* law?" mumbled the philosopher as Adams left him. "It is the law of the birds and the fishes. . . ."

CHAPTER XXXVII

For the benefit of the sentries Magome was familiar in his greeting of Adams as he joined him in the courtyard. For the benefit of his own soul he was deeply respectful to him who came from the cloistered presence of the Shogun. For the itch that was in his mind he said, "Tell me, An-jin, how the Great One spoke to you. I shall make clear any of his sayings that were hidden from you."

"There was nothing hidden," said Adams. "It was all quite clear."

The old man cleared his throat. He had had difficulties with the Pilot before; and the visit from the Dutchman that morning had confirmed his view that when the Englishman's face became like a slab of wood and his gait became the gait of an ox it was not always due to his misunderstanding of mere words.

"He was—benevolent?" he ventured.

"There is but one measure of right and wrong," Adams answered with fine pomp. "Benevolence of conduct only." The old man's agony of curiosity, his cringing humility were too good a joke to be destroyed by satisfaction. Adams grinned and said, "Aye, Magome. He was most benevolent. He asked me if I was comfortable with my host."

This was something; and Magome seized on it for the moment. "You spoke well of me, An-jin?"

"I told him that there could not be such another host in all the island. Such a good friend to his poor guest; so fine a servant of his Emperor."

"You did well," said Magome. "For there could not be such another guest in all the world. A man so generous. One who speaks out his inmost thoughts and most secret plans. One who so honourably shares with his poor and trivial friend whatever there may be in his purse. *Or* his mind."

"The meagreness of his purse and the emptiness of his unworthy mind——" Adams began; for he was becoming competent at this business of bandying phrases and giving no change; but Magome could not stand it much longer.

"Poor An-jin." He said sadly. "You do not yet know your fate then." He shot a glance at Adams. Getting no answer, he said: "He did not say what is to become of you?"

"On the contrary," said Adams. "He told me very clearly what *is* to become of me."

"What then?" asked Magome.

"In the course of years," said Adams, "I am to become an old man. In the course of more years, I shall become an older one."

Magome might have been a testy old soldier, irritated to the point of exasperation, but he was a host, and he chuckled and bubbled at the brightness of his guest's fine wit. Adams knew that it was only a matter of hours before Magome should have, through official instructions, the information for which he begged. So he said, "He told me more, too, Magome. I am a prisoner. More than ever I am a prisoner. You, or any other cavalero may cut off my head if I so much as move a finger to leave this country of yours."

He realised now, when he had said it, that he was at last a free man. There was no obligation in all the world that claimed him; no burden to weigh upon him; no bond, anywhere, to hold him. The wife and the children and the house in Gillingham—whatever they were, or ever had been, they were cut off from him now as surely and as cleanly as his head would be cut off if he made the least gesture towards them.

Whether the sudden feeling in him was regret or despair or happy exuberance, it was enough to produce a dizziness in him.

Gone also, as a load lifted from his shoulders, was his obligation to the *Liefde* and her rotting cargo. . . .

"Your ship, then," old Magome was saying thoughtfully; "the little ship you are causing Kuru to make—has he forbidden your finishing that, lest you sail away in it?"

"No," said Adams, light still in his head and his heart. "I may go on with that. But we will make a little banquet to-night at my expense, for the Dutchman." Magome could only think the Dutchman a liar; for here was his Pilot making a celebration of fruit and fish and wine in acceptance of his captivity and durance. He could not think that it was the way these crazy people accepted adversity; for it was not thus that Adams had behaved at the news of Mitsu's death.

Obviously the truth was that the Pilot was utterly happy.

Santvoort himself could understand him no better, for Santvoort, in all his life, had never experienced the lifting from his shoulders of a responsibility.

He did not question him for long. Adams's first answer, and his second, and his third were identical. "Here we are, Melchior. And here we stay, lad."

Later, when they were drunk and digesting food peaceably while Magome puffed, over the brazier, at the pipe his guests had declined, he told the Dutchman a secret.

"Melchior," he said, "it is *here*."

Melchior looked round the room. "I see nothing," he said. "Nothing new."

"You great fool!" said Adams. "Fools, all of you never to have thought of it. Chance has brought us to the one place in all the world where it is most likely to be found."

"What is?" Melchior still scrutinised the corners of the room, the ceiling and the screens.

Adams lowered his voice. "Melchior," he said, "the *Passage*, boy. The North-West Passage. It was the beginning of it that the others failed to find. But here we are set down at the very gate of it."

The numbskull took the information as though it had been nothing. "I daresay," he said amiably. "I daresay. For you were right about that old matter of our latitude."

"Latitude indeed!" Adams shouted, so that old Magome blinked towards them through his tobacco-smoke; for he could not yet be quite sure when it was anger and when goodwill that set the hairy ones bellowing at each other.

From indignation Adams swung into delight at the Dutchman's apathy. It was only the *saké's* hazy warmth that had melted the secret of his discovery out of him; and Santvoort's glum smile restored the secret to him, intact and gloriously unshared.

The girls came in, about some business of removing dishes

and attending to the brazier.

"Now," Santvoort yawned, smiling very amiably upon them; "if you were to tell me you found the way to celibacy— but God knows how you've done it—with the odds so big against you, for she is a very handy one."

Adams did not answer. The *saké* was again urging him towards secrets that it was useless trying to expound to the smiling, sleepy Dutchman. For how could young Melchior have understood the peculiar tenderness that yearned to pet and lightly caress the elegance of the creature that was concealed in the trappings of Bikuni? The fellow would only have winked. Even for her shrinking fantastic horror of her father he would have had one of his grins.

"You lecherous fool . . ." Adams mumbled.

"I'd have you know, Will——" For in Santvoort the *saké's* product was dignity. "I'd have you know that I am a soundly married man. It is recorded by the notary. Married as you are, more married than you are. For the man who can nullify your country as this Emperor has done to-day has nullified your wife. I'm a properly married man, and you're a widower."

There was something in it; and it was a sombre loneliness.

The day had been a big one; for you cannot, without giving a man a distinct shock, set him down in a place some ten thousand leagues from home and tell him that his head will be chopped off or his trunk ripped open by a passing acrobat if he tries to move. Setting upon him the shackles of this captivity, you cannot also give him a limitless freedom from the bonds of all life without again shocking him. You cannot burst it in upon him that a peculiar friend who was casually dead is, as a matter of casual fact, not dead at all; and you cannot then—without again shocking and shaking him—suddenly reveal to him that what even Frobisher had failed to find is plainly in front of his own nose. Then fill him with good *saké* and he will clearly see the fatuous pomposity of one man like Magome Sageyu the famous snob, and the impenetrable stupidity of another like Santvoort.

They sank in their wine, those two, as happily and as smoothly as a brace of fishes in water.

Adams meanwhile floated on his, nimbly and somehow aloof

from it, like a gull. Separated from them, he was separated
from all else, alone in the loneliness of the thought that had
come to him of the Passage—the straight waterway lighted
by the midnight sun, that should, at last, link East with
West.

CHAPTER XXXVIII

FROM a simple loafer Adams became, before he knew it, a busy man.

The sentence of Ieyasu upon him was of moment to no one, so far as he could see, beyond Magome, Santvoort, the Captain and the Surgeon, so it was to them only that he spoke of it.

They, accepting it calmly enough, since it seemed so reasonable a continuation of everything, mentioned it to no one at all; and yet, among neighbours where every man was an agent or a principal of secret service, an impression was made as though by public proclamation.

Obscure men (and women equally obscure), with the vaguest of intentions, made ceremonial gifts to the Pilot and the three other hairy ones lodged by the waterside, and even to the crew scattered in the bazaars.

There were fruit and fish and wine in the house of Magome of quality high enough for the cavalero's most elegant of appetites, and of the second quality—in quantity sufficient—for his paying off of many an outstanding and anciently rankling obligation.

The old man fell with a fresh zest into the tuition of the Needle-watcher in the art of allowing the grace and balance of a sword to do their work unhindered by clumsiness from the man wielding it.

Before either of them had stirred from the house in the morning the old man would say, "Come, An-jin; I have leisure. Let us take our exercises." Or he would turn over the little tablets of wood on which his memoranda were made, and say: "I finish to-day a good space before the midday rice. If you could conveniently return from your boat-making, I should be honoured to test my poor skill . . ."

And already there would be Kuru himself waiting below the verandah, or one of the younger men from the yard, with a small timber and a question about the cutting of a mortice or the rabbeting of a plank.

If he lingered with the carpenters after the sun had passed its height Magome would surely appear with his smile, to see whether, by chance, so trivial a thing as an appointment with his inconsiderable self in the fencing arena had honourably slipped the Needle-watcher's memory.

For Magome was given up to this business of making a swordsman in much the same way that Adams was given up to the business of making a miniature ship. What would become of their work when it was done, neither of them knew, nor particularly cared. They knew only that now at last they had the finest of material, and endless time. And so their respective works shaped.

Men began to say of the Pilot that on afternoons when he was summoned to the castle he went freely and without formality into the chamber: that Ieyasu conversed with him, not seated upon his dais, but strolling about the room or leaning over the papers whereon the Pilot drew straight lines and circles and squares; and charts.

In the Shogun, at least, Adams felt that there was one who would listen to his secret of the Passage. He drew seas, and sailed them with his thumb; and Ieyasu digressed from seas to the properties of circles and triangles; so that Adams was discoursing to him of the easier problems of geometry. Simply, the mighty Ieyasu was entertained by the Pilot with his instruments and his drawings and his brass globes, one of which always remained now in the Shogun's chamber.

Adams tried to tell him of John Rut who had sailed from Plymouth seventy-five years before, of his long disappearance into the ice, and of his defeat. He told of the death of Willoughby a quarter of a century later, and of the half-triumph of Richard Chancelor, who returned from Muscovy by way of the White Sea with a letter from the Czar of Russia.

As a twelve-year-old apprentice in the shipyard of Nicholas Diggins, Adams had seen the heavy smoke-rings and heard the bangs from the *Michael* and the *Gabriel* when Frobisher shot off his ordnance in salute of her Majesty as he sailed with his fleet of fifty tons for Cathay.

A piece of black stone, a sick Eskimo and the naming of Frobisher Bay were all that immediately came out of it; and the undiscovered thing remained "the onlye thinge of the world that was left yet undone, whereby a notable mind might be made famous and fortunate . . ."

Of these three, and of the failures that followed them, the essence was the same. All had succeeded in finding the way into the wilderness of the Polar Sea where even the compass-needle followed no law. It was only the exit from that sea that had baffled the fumbling of their frail prows. What Adams had to tell Ieyasu was that here, by sailing first Northwards and then to the West, they would be upon the doing of that one "onlye thinge of the world that was left yet undone . . ."

The mighty Ieyasu, however, was a contemplator of truths and of the essence of men. His interest was but slight in the accident of whether they did or did not come upon a doorway that was hidden somewhere in a wall of tumbling ice. It was more to him, for the moment, that the interior angles of a triangle appeared to be equal to two right angles. This truth seemed to be one of several possessed by the Pilot that had not come his way before; and so, for the moment, it was of geometry that Adams had to be content to discourse to him.

Concepcion the Filipino began at last to wonder whether the time was not ripe for him to be getting some return—or at any rate some promise of return—for his expenditures. His father had written, too, asking for a report. He said that the Portuguese padre was on the point of setting out for Yedo.

One of the young man's difficulties was that Adams himself had benefited little from the generosities. This had not reduced his expenditure, for old Magome made up for the Pilot's deficiencies as a guest.

Concepcion had not yet made up his mind whether the Englishman was an invalid, a monk, or an idiot. His next banquet was planned, therefore, with some desperation, to put him to the test.

It proved that he was neither invalid, monk nor idiot, but as good a man as the rest of them.

Concepcion himself had a pleasanter evening of it and Magome was delighted; for in some mysterious way he con-nected the Pilot's progress in tavern-deportment with his pro-gress in swordsmanship. It signified, too, that the Pilot was settling down to the broader verities and becoming generally tractable.

The meeting together in the morning for their early rice found them all in appropriate good humour.

An idea had recently come to Adams: this young Filipino had intelligence, and money, and he had ships. Neither the Muscovy Company nor the Cathay Company of London had had more than these for Willoughby's lieutenant and for Frobisher. It behoved him, therefore, to be gracious and genial to the young man who was himself so genial.

The talk turned easily from phrases to a discussion of Concepcion's immediate plans. He explained that he had waited till now, shaking down in that passable place of entertainment, considering sites for the great house he proposed to build. He was attracted by Yedo itself, for Yedo seemed to have an immense future as a growing city. In that future lay a demand (amounting to a dire necessity among men of such breeding) for the elegances in which he and his father traded to make their poor living. By the present Charter they—Spaniards—could sell their wares only in Nagasaki. The extension of this charter—or, better still, the granting of special trade licences to a select few traders—would bring a direct supply into Yedo itself—Yedo the new city of gentlemen and fine soldiers for whom only the best was good enough. For these same gentlemen and soldiers of quality it ought also to be made a reasonably cheap city by the elimination of countless rogues of middlemen.

Middlemen, he explained, meant not only an inflation of price, but a lowering of the quality of the goods. Wines—good Spanish wines—were tampered with; spices and ambergris were adulterated; silks and cloths were stretched by means of wedges slowly driven between the two boards on which they were rolled when damp. A local warehouse of the importer himself—or his son—would be an immediate remedy and a safeguard. Did not the Needle-watcher think so?

The Needle-watcher slaked his throat with fragrant tea, and did think so.

It was only, then, the formality of the licence that stood in Concepcion's way. A word, he supposed, would be enough to obtain the gracious consideration of the Shogun—provided the word were graciously spoken by the right person. Such a warehouse, he pointed out quite incidentally, could possibly be of some insignificant service to any man who himself had some otherwise unsaleable wares to sell—the old cargo, for instance, of a derelict ship. Did not the Pilot, perhaps, agree?

He did.

Concepcion turned from him to the old, thoughtful Samurai at his side; for Concepcion seldom made mistakes of diplomacy.

Since they were all honourably agreed, Concepcion went on, as to the principle, all that was required was the condescension of one so illustrious as Magome Sageyu to place the negligible tradesman in a position whence he could dispense gratitude on a proper scale. It was no close secret, he said, how Magome's lightest word carried a load of weight with Ieyasu; it was a fact known to the meanest coolie in the remotest bazaar.

Magome sucked his tea with a rattle and crackle of decorum, pondering the young man's lies and the admirable cunning of him.

He was, he said, nothing. Only an old soldier. Those words of his to which their host had graciously alluded—the words by which the mighty Ieyasu was pleased to set so much store— were only words concerning their craft spoken by a soldier to his general. With the elegant performance of trade he had no concern, and of it he had no knowledge. His brain, presuming to occupy itself with such a subject, would be no greater than the brain of a louse. Any words that he might speak about it would be as the braying of an ass.

Would he not speak, then, to his Lord? asked Concepcion. He was ready to turn, as soon as the proper moment should have come, to Adams.

The proper time did not come; for Magome staggered him by saying, magnificently, "Assuredly I will speak."

He drank tea once more, and continued: "Of my countless opportunities for conversation with his Excellence I shall seize the next one and adjust the matter to your satisfaction. Let us go now, An-jin; for this very day is a lucky one for doing this small thing for our friend."

CHAPTER XXXIX

"How can you so easily get an audience with the Emperor?" Adams asked when he and Magome had left their host.

"That," said Magome, "was but a manner of speaking, to the young man. It is you that will see him and not I concerning a matter of trade. We must talk a little of this plan."

"But young Concepcion seems to have made his plan already."

"It is not a good plan," said Magome. "It is not, in fine, the plan to be adopted. There is no need in this city, An-jin, for hucksters from Spain and the Philippines with their loud talk and swaggering manners; for this is a city of soldiers—the work of soldiers and the comfort and entertainment of soldiers. What the young man said, however, is true: there are too many hands as yet between the unloading of wines and stuffs and spices in Nagasaki and their delivery to us here."

"Yes," said Adams. "That is why he needs to come here himself."

"What that young man needs, my An-jin," old Magome said, "is what that young man is going to have: an agent in this city. An honourable man, with some knowledge of Spanish wine, and a little of the Spanish tongue. It is this agent that shall have the Shogun's licence to trade in Filipino goods, despatched to him from Nagasaki. That such a man should know but little, as yet, of the ways of the people of Yedo is no matter. Whatever little knowledge is lodged in the head of his poor host is at his disposal; for a host is no host unless he have for his guest the solicitude of a father."

"You old dog!" said Adams; and his laugh conveyed some of his meaning.

"But it is well," Magome said; "even for the young man it is well. To get his licence and to establish himself in the esteem of this place would cost him too heavily in presents. By my plan he will have but two presents to make. The presents will be so much the better for it; and so will he. One present only,

I should say—for a soldier has no concern with trade."

Again Adams said, "You old dog." But again he laughed, and he added intelligibly and thoughtfully, "But he will not agree to such a plan. He won't sell to us."

"*Sell* to you?" said Magome. "*Sell* to you? There is no talk of your spending money, An-jin. The goods shall be his till you have sold them—and the risk also; for he is a tradesman. And if he will not thus send goods here, there are many others of his kidney that will. It is only poor, addled and worthless wits such as mine that could not have thought of this thing before."

"There's little enough amiss with your wits, my friend," said Adams; and the old man smiled. He said, "A host shall be worthy of his guest."

Later, when they had walked a mile in silence, he said: "An-jin, a thought has at last deigned to enter this dullard's mind. That young man ought to have a licence to visit this city at his will. He would thus have need of a small boat to bring him swiftly and honourably from Nagasaki. The niggards of this place, so the ancient Kuru tells me, are unwilling to pay even a bauble's price for your masterly work."

"Who told Kuru he could sell it?" said Adams.

"He asked me," said Magome, "to use what little influence I may chance to have with the Pilot. He desires an association between him and your honourable self. It seemed fitting to me, on my guest's behalf, that thirty hundredths of the price should be paid over to you for any goods sold that are made under your direction. Scribes have, in fact, prepared a deed for your firming—if it should seem fitting to you."

"Aye," said Adams; "it's fitting enough—and I shall not forget a share for the negotiator of the business."

"I am no negotiator of businesses," Magome said with great dignity. "Nor have I shares or interest in them. If I protect my guest's interests it is as I would protect his life—as a soldier and host."

"You're not going to sell that cockle-shell as a seaworthy craft, Magome," Adams said firmly. "She's a toy, man."

"*Sell* it as a toy, then, An-jin," he answered.

"To run that coast from Nagasaki in some of the gales I've

seen here? Man, it isn't three spindling toy masts that you want on a craft that size." He thought for some minutes and then suddenly said, "It's one short one, a little forward."

"Give her one, then," said Magome agreeably. "One short one, a little forward."

"Be God! I believe she'd do!" He stopped again, and then went on in the language he knew, "—for'ard, with a lug-sail. She'll look like hell, surely enough, with those toy decks fore and aft; but with a Dutchman's lee-boards, and in any sea but one of these hell-brewed furies of yours, she'd do." He stopped and turned to Magome again. "Aye, Magome, I believe she'd do."

"Good," said the old man. "It is clear, then, you must obtain licence for the young man to visit Yedo by sea. You must see his Excellency without delay. He will give you sanction to trade in Filipino goods."

Adams grunted. "It's a fine thing!" he said suddenly. "It'll look well, won't it! A man asks me to obtain the Emperor's permission for him to trade here, and I get the permission for myself."

"It was me he asked," Magome corrected him unctuously, "not you. And it is I who shall have achieved this thing for him. An-jin, it is fitting that the next meeting should be between the young man and me alone. I can tell him then of the delicacy of your feelings in the matter."

Adams became very emphatic now, tending to become wooden-faced and ox-footed. "That young man is not to be thwarted," he said. "I require a service of him far greater than the selling of wine and nutmegs and a few fardels of cotton and silk."

"A service? What service, An-jin, that your host cannot render?"

"Never mind," said Adams; and then, more gently: "You would not understand, Magome. And I shall not be requiring it yet awhile. Not—not for years perhaps. But—I must do the handsome thing by him."

"Yes, indeed," said Magome, "most handsome. By my plan you would be doing the handsome thing by him—not once, since one short deed of however great kindness is soon forgotten—but for many years. Thus only is gratitude made and friendship cemented—by not one brief service, but many."

Adams saw the force of it.

CHAPTER XL

CONCEPCION protested at first that the arrangement was inadequate, and of no great advantage to him; that if the most he could do in Yedo was to appoint agents it would be sounder for him to appoint not one but a dozen.

That, Magome pointed out to him, was not the Shogun's concession. The concession was for one only, and that one already specified to be the Pilot and no other.

The cavalero unbent to the tradesman. He told him secrets of the court: it was not, most regrettably, for the sake of him, Concepcion, that Ieyasu had been persuaded at all. Concepcion and his fellow Spaniards Ieyasu considered to be well enough entertained already with the freedom of Nagasaki. Their prosperity was a byword throughout the world. It was only for the Pilot's sake that he had allowed this thing; and if Concepcion were to consider the appointment of any man but the Pilot, the concession—Magome was regrettably sure—would be immediately withdrawn from him. Ieyasu, as all the world knew, thought well of the Pilot—so well, indeed, that he insisted on his being made, without delay, the prosperous agent in Yedo of some well-named Nagasaki merchant. Magome here mentioned a Spaniard and a couple of Portuguese. He shrugged his shoulders; they were good enough men and had recommended themselves to the court at one time or another with services and gifts. However, his own negligible influence with his Lord added to the illustrious reputation of Concepcion the Filipino for fairness—and generosity—had made of him, happily, the successful candidate.

The young man, in his heart, had one sound consolation: his father could have done no better with so hard a nut to crack as Magome Sageyu.

Magome next made a highly confidential suggestion. Kuru the carpenter had built a small boat in a peculiar style, and it was the stubborn wish of the Pilot to buy this work from Kuru and offer it as a present to Ieyasu. Adams had the money laid by in Magome's charge—a trifling eighty ducats—but the expenditure of it would be sheer waste, when it could form a handy little item in the capital required for a new business. The Pilot stood well enough with the Shogun already. He himself stood well enough; particularly since the happy chance which had placed under his blade the skull of a rascal who would have killed the Pilot. Otherwise, of course, it was he who would have bought the boat from Kuru and offered it to his Lord. Ieyasu would think well of any man who made him such a gift; and since neither he nor the Pilot was in need of ingratiation he offered the chance to Concepcion.

He could almost guarantee that Kuru would sell for eighty ducats.

His father, Concepcion now knew, not only would have done no better, he would have made a mess of it; for there was in his father some peculiar blood and some spleen that made it hard for him to knuckle under to little, old swashbucklers and sharpers.

He said, "Excellency, an agent with advice and forethought such as yours at his disposal would be a prize worth any merchant's winning. This Pilot and I are truly fortunate. You must permit me a great pleasure. I have noticed how, out of kind consideration for the feelings of those lesser folk with whom you are obliged to mix, you smoke a lesser man's tobacco-pipe. I have with me one carved by the Hunchback of Kioto, bought against just such a happy chance as this. If you would deign to accept it, you could smoke it in private or among your few peers when none by comparison would be made to feel small."

He went to the wall-cupboard, and unrolled the paper of a parcel.

Magome's eye started. The work of his head was, for the time being, done; his heart became full of kindness and love for this open-handed youth.

"Sir," he said, and the old deft fingers caressed the coils of the dragon that were his new pipe-stem; "even princes will be small now, when Magome Sageyu drinks tobacco . . ." The pipe, wrapped again in its paper, snuggled into his girdle where his sword also would go when he redeemed it at the frontier of the Valley.

"As to the boat," he said; "you need not lose it by making a gift of it to the General. The matter can be arranged so that the use of it is always yours. The question of its licence will thus, of itself, be solved; and it will be a worthy vehicle to carry you hither. And your agent, the Needle-watcher, shall have a house and establishment that shall be worthy of the guest who visits it from Nagasaki."

"Have you the documents with you?" asked Concepcion. "For I will set my hand to them; taking with me the Shogun's licence. Your forethought has obtained for me, no doubt, the further concession of freedom to come and go as I please?"

"All has been obtained," said Magome. "We wait, as you might say, for the drying of the scribes' ink. Three days— perhaps four—maybe a week—and all will be ready. Even the boat itself should be nearly done."

He hurried home, and from home to the house of Kuru, to find Adams; for now that he had dealt with Concepcion satisfactorily there was no reason why they should delay further in approaching Ieyasu. To have said or done anything before could have been mere waste; for a demon of hard foolishness might have entered into the young man so that he rejected the plan. And then, the gaining of the favour from the Great One would have been the heavy reproach of fruit picked when there is no basket for the carrying of it away.

He primed Adams as they walked up to seek the Presence.

"Tell him, An-jin," he said, "that you would bring the comforts and elegances of the islands and of Nagasaki into this city without bringing also the earth's scum who deal in them."

"Aye," said Adams, "I'll tell him."

"Tell him that the friendship of this young man and of his house will serve his interests well in Nagasaki, where the other hairy ones have not always fostered loyalty to himself."

"I'll tell him," Adams grunted.

"Tell him also," the old man continued, watching his pupil for any expression that might disturb the thoughtfulness that had once more turned the face to wood. "Tell him also that with this person to counsel you, and supervise your doings, there need be small fear of any mishap."

"I'll tell him," said Adams. "Have no fear."

He was soon given leave to enter. Magome stated that he would be at hand if his help were needed, and sniffed the cold air for any fume that would lead him to a brazier where he might smoke his pipe in the presence of soldiers.

Adams stated his request briefly—that he might do a small trade in the city, in such articles as a young Spanish-Filipino might send him from Nagasaki. Concepcion's name and the name of his father appeared to be known already to Ieyasu. The subject of the Pilot's talk and of his own questions seemed to be as remote as usual from the Shogun's mind, while the focus of his interest was peculiarly upon the Pilot.

"So the Needle-watcher would get money!" he said with a smile.

"Yes, Excellency," said Adams. "A lot of money. I have need of money." His face was still the wooden-face of thoughtfulness that had blocked Magome on the way up.

"Then you have found uses for money in this city?"

"There are uses for money everywhere," Adams replied; "——if you have enough of it. With money I should want no help from others in finding the road by the North. I could do without Spaniards who hold all other roads already. It would be *my* road, when I had found it . . ."

"Yours, An-jin?" Ieyasu again smiled.

"Mine," he answered. Then he, too, smiled. "And yours," he said, "for the permission to find it would be graciously given by yourself."

"Yes," said Ieyasu, "if I gave the permission, the road would most certainly be mine."

"You will surely give it," said Adams. "When I have bought a ship from the Spaniards or Portingals or trimmed and fitted what is left of the old *Liefde*; when I have victualled her and manned her, you will not withhold your sanction, Excellency. Finding my road, I shall return; and with me I will bring goods to trade whereof you and your country have need. And I shall bring my countrymen."

"But why buy new ships or trim old ones?" Ieyasu asked. "Have you not caused a new one to be built?"

"A ship!" Adams exclaimed. "No, it is not a ship that I am building, but a toy; to pass time in which I had nought else to do. But now, if I may trade and make money I am done with toy-making."

"Yes, you may trade, An-jin," Ieyasu said. "Make little ships, or big money—or any other toys that please you. The old man your host shall see the Secretary for the necessary documents."

"Thank you, Excellency," said Adams.

"It is nothing," said the other. And it was obvious that he thought it nothing. "Some day you shall give up toy-making for a space, and make real ships for me."

Adams laughed. "I am no ship-maker. Sailing a ship is not making it. Yourself, Excellency, the best swordsman in Japan, you are no swordsmith."

"You are no tradesman, An-jin," said the other; "yet you are about to trade."

"Ah," said Adams, "that is different."

"We shall see," said the other. He said next that his rude manners and dull speech had bored his guest sufficiently for one day.

Adams withdrew and Magome tapped out his pipe and sheathed it; for a busy afternoon lay before him.

CHAPTER XLI

He soon made it clear to Adams that the point had been arrived at when a start should be made in the judicious investment of some capital. The official documents required to legalise and regularise the business were virtually Letters of Patent. There was first the Shogun's licence to Concepcion to consign goods from Nagasaki to Yedo. There was the specification of a junk to be licensed with the Shogun's red-seal—the ensign of a protected merchantman—which might carry the goods by sea; and an inventory of the personnel of a train that might transport them overland. These documents—and the old man smiled amiably—were the affair of Concepcion; so that the Pilot need not consider the cost of them. His affairs were only the licence to himself to store, handle and sell the goods from Nagasaki; the indenture between him and Concepcion defining and limiting his responsibility as the Filipino's agent; and lastly, a trifling lease between himself, Magome Sageyu, of the one part and his guest, An-jin Sama, of the other part: for it was obvious that the Pilot should rent a substantial, fire-proof godown for the safe warehousing of his stock; and there was no godown handier than the one at the end of Magome's garden; and there was none sounder in all Yedo than his should be when a day or two's wages had been paid to a workman for making good the holes and cracks in its thick clay walls. Adams was made to see how necessary was the small formality of this document: no soldier, and thus no property of a soldier, could be involved in the honourable vulgarity of trade. By the terms of the lease the godown and warehouse would cease, for the time being, from being the soldier's property and would become the property of the Pilot.

Adams handed over the sum from the roll in his host's strong-box. Five tael, the old man estimated, would handsomely cover the gifts that would pass in exchange for the documents. They made a memorandum on the receipt Magome had given him.

Adams went to find Santvoort on the way to Kuru's, while Magome bustled off again towards the castle braziers where the palms of waiting hands were warmed—the palms of scribes and lesser secretaries.

The Dutchman had been playing for a day or two with the carved model, re-rigging her for Adams with the single mast set forward instead of its original main and fore with the small lateen sail on the mizzen. Adams knew he could trust him at such a job; for the lazy eye of Melchior had a sudden and bright gleam in it when it rested on a sail. He did not have to measure canvas that was bent to a yard, or to make a pedant's calculations. When the spread of it was right, or the fall of it unhandy, he simply knew.

The model rode among jags of broken ice on the little pond at the back of the kite-maker's house. Melchior and the kite-maker chafed their hands together in their sleeves as they stood and watched her. Adams stood behind them, also watching, as the sail bellied and her bows dipped and rose and dipped again in the glint of bergs and floes, gathering herself together, then plunging away from Santvoort's feet to the North.

That plunge, her handsome righting of herself into the smooth, clean rhythm of steady headway caused Santvoort to clap his hand upon the shoulder of his father-in-law; and the two turned, smiling, to see the smile of Adams.

"She'll do, Will," said the Dutchman. "The old man wouldn't have it. He tried to show me with a kite—forgetting that the pull of a string at a kite's middle is not the hold of a hull at a mast's bottom. But there you are!" The craft had made through the broken ice and was aground now on the pond's northern shore. "She'll do."

"We'll take her out in Kuru's boat," said Adams. "And give her a fair run in the harbour."

"More ballast is all she wants," Santvoort suggested. "A pound or two amidships and astern to steady her nose a bit."

"Aye," said Adams, "Kuru will have a handful of great nails for us or some old tools. Come on."

They took the toy from the water.

"I'll want a jerkin, out in a boat," said the Dutchman, blowing on his fingertips. Adams had his seaman's cloak; and on his half-shaved head was the cobbed-up piece of old woollen stocking that he always wore among the lads at Kuru's.

Santvoort went into the house and came out with his kimono bulging with his old moleskin jacket under it. "Some day, perhaps, we'll have grown Japonian hides," he remarked. "It wouldn't surprise me to find that they've fur on the inside, the way they'll turn off a nor'-easter, and grin at the fun of it."

When they were near the waterside Adams said, "You untie the boat while I go to the yard for that handful of ballast. We'll have to hurry; the light won't last above another hour."

In the yard Adams found the two youths peculiarly hushed in their work. They nodded to him, and frowned and grimaced towards some mystery on the other side of the cradle.

Adams went round it, carrying the model, watched by the boys with great awe.

Seated on a stool which they had brought for him was an old man. Even without the awe and the grimaces of the carpenters Adams would have known him at a glance to be a cavalero of consequence.

Old Magome Sageyu, with his threadbare efforts to maintain it, had taught his guest how to sense nobility; so that Adams would have recognised this old man, even in a bath tub, as a nobleman. The queue of his hair would have been enough, his smile and the inclination of his head. Now the magnificence of his sash told him; as did his sword-hilts and his crested short jacket.

"An-jin Sama," he said, "you do honour with your presence to the unknown Shongo."

Adams was equal to it. He said, "To a man so ignorant and insignificant as this one it is regrettably true that even the illustrious name of Shongo is unknown."

The smile of the other was now a specific one. He was pleased and relieved by the Pilot's fluency. "No matter," he said. "I am not unknown to your host Magome Sageyu. I carried him in a boat with other soldiers many years ago to the Korean wars. I, too, An-jin, was once a sailor—in days when there was need of sailors and my limbs were lusty as yours are. But now——" he stooped to pick up a crutch that lay on the ground beside him.

He laid the crutch on his knees and Adams stood looking at him. A sailor; this was something new. Adams had not seen any sailor in this country before with the swords of a nobleman, features as nobly carved as the gold studs on his sword-hilts, a man to set the couple of cheery carpenters whispering and hushed in their work.

"It is a fine afternoon," the old man went on. "The warmth of the sun and the thawing of the ice tempted me out upon my crutch to the impertinence of prying into this work of yours whose fame is exceeded only by its grace and elegance."

He was looking at the nondescript little craft in the cradle.

"She looked neater with the three little masts," said Adams, "than she will with one—like this." He threw aside his cloak to expose the model.

"Ah!" said the old man and he held out his hands. "Ah. . . . It was the mast that I came to see; and the sail, and your manner of raising it. Men have told me of it—lies; how it may swing this way and that, taking the wind first upon one face of it and then the other, turning the boat about to sail into the wind's very teeth."

"Not *all* lies, Shongo Sama," Adams said with some pride. "She'll sail—she'll sail——" and he stuck for the words to tell him that within six points of it was the nearest she would sail to the wind. "Not into the wind's teeth," he went on, and his smile exposed his own teeth which he tapped with his thumb-nail. "But—— " and he moved his hand so that his thumb swerved aside from his teeth and grazed his ear.

"As near as that?" exclaimed the visitor.

"Aye," said Adams, "as near as that. But, sir, you must excuse me. My friend a Hollander has a boat ready. We go out into the harbour, to try this sail—it is new."

He would have hurried off, but the old man rose to his feet and tucked the crutch under his arm. His breeding should have provided him with a glib phrase and an appropriate gesture for every crisis in his life, great or small; but he stood before Adams now, overcome with mere shyness. It must, Adams thought, be due to his lameness and he himself hesitated in a search for the proper way of offering to carry the little fellow to a palanquin that was surely waiting somewhere. The difficulty was to do it without casting any aspersion on his honourable poor physique.

The old man suddenly looked up like a small boy not sure of anything where an adult is concerned; "An-jin Sama," he said, "would you consider permitting a guest to attend you in trying this new sail? My crutch will carry me with my painless leg to the boat-side. It is only then that I may require some assistance. You and your friend——"

Adams interrupted him, for he had the kind of phrase for such a situation as this. "This person," he said, "and any friend of his would be honoured to carry such as you upon their shoulders from here to Miaco."

Santvoort was sitting in the boat, blowing on his fingers and slapping his hands on his shoulders. He, too, immediately recognised an august presence. "You can go no further than this, Will," he said. "You have brought the Pope himself this time."

"Give a hand with him," said Adams. "Whoever he is, he's coming with us. I couldn't leave him behind, for all he's as lame as a cripple. I believe he'd have cried, Melchior."

"Ripped you up, more likely!" was Santvoort's comment as they lifted him into the stern and offered him the courtesy of the steering paddle. "I've seen him," Santvoort went on; "months ago he came buying kites, and father-in-law nearly bowed himself underground at his greatness—as a kite-flyer at any rate."

"He's a sailor," said Adams.

"Likely enough," said Santvoort. "They mix the two games freely. Their sailing is no more than the flying of a kite with a junk made fast to the bottom of it."

Their guest looked benignly upon them as they talked.

They shipped their paddles and Adams invited his attention while he made his adjustments of the model's sail and rudder so as to put her hard on the wind. The guest watched as only a sailor could.

They had a kite-flyer's spool in the boat with a silk line whose end they made fast to a little ring at the model's taffrail. Adams trimmed her ballast while Santvoort made a suggestion or two, and the old man himself approved. Then Adams

shoved her off with the bamboo wand to which one of Kuru's
boys had lapped a minute boat-hook.

The old man chuckled and clapped his hands together as she
settled down to her course. He reminded Adams of the gesture
he had made with his teeth and his ear and showed his delight
that the promise had been made good.

"We'll have her in again, Melchior," Adams said, for it was
the Dutchman who was paying out the line from the spool.
"Handsomely, son; we don't want to spoil the trick for the old
man by capsizing her. We can haul that sail a little closer yet.
That will show him."

He lifted her from the water and turned, smiling, to their
guest. He tapped his teeth again—the teeth of the wind; and
he indicated not his ear this time but his cheekbone, to show
that she would sail still closer.

"Never!" said their guest incredulously. "Never!"

"We shall see," said Adams. As he put her over the side
Santvoort slipped another lump of iron into her stern. "That'll
steady her, Will. We mustn't disappoint his holiness even if
we've got to burst her hold with cargo."

It was successful enough to satisfy Adams. It delighted the
old man so that he insisted on taking the spool from Santvoort
and himself hauling her in. The spindle of the reel fell between
the finger and deft thumb of a great kite-flyer, and his eye-lids
wrinkled over knowing, dim lenses that peered at the movements of the sail as he drew it nearer.

Adams helped him from the boat while Santvoort held her
steady to Kuru's landing-steps.

The carpenter-boys had not wasted a minute of the last
thirty or forty. A crowd of loungers waited on them as they
turned from the quay into the roadway, like the crowd that had
waited on the old hairy ones when they first staggered ashore
from the *Liefde*. They made obeisance to him who lurched
on his magnificent crutch between the Pilot with his threadbare cloak and stockinged head and the Dutchman with his
moleskin jerkin bulging his kimono.

The old, little cripple was the great Admiral who had carried
the soldiers of all Japan to Korea when Adams was a baby in
Gillingham and the Dutchman was as yet unborn.

The crowd fell away from the waiting palanquin, but stood watching as the old man stopped and spoke.

"It is a great game of play that you and your friend have given me to-day, An-jin Sama."

He slowly unfastened his embroidered tobacco-pouch from its toggle. "Permit me to make a small gift."

Adams handsomely declined it; saying that what he had done was nothing, and that all the pleasure of the afternoon had been his and Santvoort's.

The Admiral pressed the fine tobacco-pouch upon him. "It is only a nothing that I beg you to take."

"But there is nought," said Adams, "that I can give you in return."

The old man's eye was on the model. "That little toy," he said. "Some day, perhaps, you will have no further use for that toy. On such a day it would make a gift most princely to an old sailor."

"Take it now," said Adams. "Its use is already fulfilled."

They exchanged their gifts.

The Admiral groped next in his palanquin and drew out a small cushion; for the crowd was looking at Santvoort who stood by, smiling. To him the cushion was handed as magnificently as the pouch had passed to Adams.

"My trifling gift, sir," said the Dutchman, taking it, "must be the mast and the sail of the boat. . . . I've nought on me but my shirt and my jerkin, to exchange . . ."

"Let there be no thought of exchange," said the Admiral kindly. "For that is the way of trade, not friendship."

His bearers carried him away and Santvoort remarked, "They'd give you their shirt, these cavaleros. There goes his holiness without a cushion to his hunkers, rather than leave me out in the cold after giving you his tobacco-bag. . . . What'll you keep in it, Will?"

Adams answered, "Tobacco."

"And *smoke* it?" asked Santvoort.

"Surely," said Adams. "It's not so bad when you've weathered yourself to it. It's strange that we never tried it before, for there were many that smoked it ashore in England."

CHAPTER XLII

MAGOME had already heard the news when he set out for home in the evening: Shongo Sama, the old Admiral of the fleet in the Korean War (and father of the young Admiral of a non-existent fleet), had gone forth with his crutch, notwithstanding his lameness from rheumatism, to pay a visit to the Needle-watcher. He and the Hollander had entertained him by carrying him to the harbour in the leaky old boat of Kuru the carpenter and playing with a toy ship. The Admiral himself had flown it like a kite on a thread. They had landed him, the Pilot lifting him in his arms like a child; the Admiral had given to the Pilot, with an embrace of friendship, his jewelled tobacco-pouch and to the Dutchman a gold-embroidered cushion: they, for their part, had given the Admiral the toy.

Magome's mind was therefore busy.

The Pilot had shown some aptitude towards a liking for tobacco-smoke. He had exercised it, so far, upon that old pipe of Magome's which had been superseded by Concepcion's gift.

Magome's gift-making for the documents had worked out well under the estimate of five tael; and Magome with loose money surviving in his girdle was as generous a man as any in the land. He left the straight road that led to his house and went to the house of a wood-carver where he bought for Adams a worthy pipe. From the wood-carver's he went to the herbalist's a little regretfully, since the time was so short now before the finest of tobacco should be stored in his own godown. He went, nevertheless; and the tobacco he bought for his guest was from the same jar that supplied Shongo the Admiral himself—it was not from crumbs in the Admiral's pouch that Magome wanted his guest to learn what tobacco could be.

The Pilot was with the girls and the old woman when he arrived with his parcel and went to the kitchen-end of the house to look for him. He saw at once that it must have been in his shabby, shapeless old cloak—no credit to the house of any man—that the Pilot had entertained the Admiral. He accepted the fact, however; for there was something to be said on both sides of this—as there was on the probability that the Pilot had worn, on his head, the piece of stocking.

They went at once to the living-room, for Adams was anxious to know more clearly about his visitor than the girls had been able to tell him.

Magome quickly presented his gift and hurried Adams in his unwrapping of the paper.

"Magnificent!" said he. "Magnificent! How did you know of this other thing, to match your present so well?" He handed him the pouch.

It was, Magome saw, in no way jewelled, but just plain soft leather from China with a few beads and a silk tassel.

"Know?" the old man said; "I knew nothing. But what need had I to know of other presents? Was it not sufficient that I should know my guest's honourable wants? In due course I would have begged him to accept a pouch also. But since some unknown other has already given it, following my own poor offerings—it is well. But tell me, An-jin, who is the giver?"

"I don't exactly know," said Adams. "An old man, lame. He said you would know him, Shongo Sama."

"Shongo——" the old man repeated thoughtfully. "Shongo —ah, yes. I remember a Shongo. We were comrades in the Korean War. He sailed a boat."

"Bikuni tells me that he commanded all the ships."

Magome shrugged his shoulders. "It is a manner of speaking," he said. "We say of him, Shongo, that he sailed a boat as they say of this person, Magome Sageyu, that he plied a sword."

"He is in truth a great sailor then?" asked Adams.

"The Korean War, An-jin," said Magome, "was many years ago. He also, at that time, was not inconsiderable; so it is natural that he should speak of me with some brightness in his memory. We will go one day to call upon the old man and take him a suitable present."

"I gave him that little boat we made," said Adams; "he seemed to want it."

"Oh, you did?" said Magome. "That was suitable, An-jin. There is no further obligation in regard to his pouch then. Let us fill it worthily with the leaf I have brought you, and when the girls have fed us we will savour it. Let us bathe now, for it is cold."

They bathed and dined and smoked; but Adams persisted in bothering his host by not accepting his easy dismissal of the Admiral.

"But you have no need to concern yourself so," the old man said at last, almost peevishly. "In a very short time now you yourself will be a big one in the city, with all its trade from the Philippines and China in your hands."

"I'd like to go and see him, all the same," said Adams. "If it would not be an unseemly impertinence."

"It would be most fitting," said Magome; "if I were to conduct you."

"Conduct me, then. You need not stay if you do not esteem him highly."

"How should I not esteem him highly?" asked Magome. "He who is so estimable, so worthy of the friendship of the General."

"So he, too, is a friend of the mighty Ieyasu?" said Adams. "I thought as much . . ."

"Friend enough." Magome had had enough of the topic for the time being. "But you yourself bid fair to being as great a friend as any man."

"All the more reason, then," said Adams, "for me to have some talk with one who knows these seas; for he has sailed, you say, Northwards."

"Aye. And returning he brought back nothing but a wild prisoner or two—women as hairy as foxes. There are men, however, in the city, whom your black man at the tavern could bring to your notice, well versed in the city's trade."

"For them, too, there is time," said Adams. "I do not suggest spending the rest of my life in talk with Shongo Sama."

A remark like this always reminded Magome of the possibility of the wooden face on the Pilot.

"Tell me, An-jin," he said (for he had succeeded in getting the tobacco he had brought into the pouch before they had tried any of the Admiral's that had remained in it), "is it good tobacco that I ventured to offer you?"

"Good indeed," said Adams. "It is on such as this that Melchior should weather himself."

That Dutchman was another interest of the Pilot's which demanded thought from Magome, and produced an irritation; but the Dutchman was less formidable than Shongo; for he was, in a manner of speaking, nothing while Shongo was most illustrious.

It is better, however, to have a hold upon the stirrup-strap of him who is mounted on a good horse than to offend rider or horse and receive a hind-hoof in the belly and be left with hunkers grounded in the mud. . . .

"When we call upon Shongo Sama, An-jin," he said, "—and we will do so very soon—our gift to him shall be some of this same tobacco. He is a big smoke-drinker."

Adams went with him, two or three days later, to the herbalist and paid for the handsome parcel of it on their way to the Admiral's house (for the herbalist was no mean retailer of imported goods—spices and herbs, nutmegs and ambergris).

There was no ragged old sea-cloak and stockinged pate about Adams now. Magome had seen to it that the coat he wore was the one given to him by Ieyasu, and Magome's barber had done his best towards a top-knot with the Pilot's hair; so that the Pilot was thankful when they had made the herbalist's without encountering Santvoort and his possible comments.

Magome took charge of all ceremonies as they entered the noble house.

He took charge, also, of the parcel of tobacco.

The Admiral did not himself come to them in the front room. His message was a regret for his boorishness in not doing so and the hope that guests so famously generous of heart would overlook it and follow the servant to his hovel of a private chamber.

He sat on cushions, his sound leg tucked under him and the rheumatic one stuck out. There was a vase of blossoms on a lacquered stand beside him, and on another stand the boat-model. Cushions were brought in for his guests, and a brazier apiece.

Magome, holding forward the gift of tobacco, apologised for

his presence, saying that only the expressed orders of their Lord, enjoining him to attend the Pilot in all his goings abroad, could have suggested that he should obtrude anything so trivial upon the attention of the illustrious Shongo.

The Admiral said it was yet another instance of their Lord's beneficence that any orders of his should have produced such pleasure for Shongo the inconsiderable, as a visit from the illustrious Magome Sageyu.

Magome, with the tail of his eye, watched this speech sinking into his Pilot.

The Pilot, said Magome, he believed was already known to their host.

"We are old friends, the Pilot and I."

Already Magome and distended phrases were done with—except the few that disposed of the gift of tobacco.

They squatted to their braziers, and trays were brought in with cakes and wine cups. Shongo called for a jar to take the tobacco from the parcel and invited his guests to fill their pouches from it.

"The Pilot is a tobacco-drinker?" he asked.

"By the happiest of chances," said Magome while Adams nodded, "I had presumed to make him an unworthy present of a pipe at the same moment that yourself were conferring upon him the inimitable pouch. Yes, he is a fine smoker."

"Let us first drink *saké* then, and thereafter smoke," said the Admiral, and they sucked hospitably and appreciatively at their *saké* cups.

"That sail," Adams observed, looking at the model, "is set wrong. The rudder is dead against it." He got up and swung the yard over, indicating with one hand the thrust of the wind and with the other the thrust of the rudder. "That's better," he said, and returned to his cushion.

"You must take me out in the real boat, An-jin, when it is finished," said the Admiral.

"That too, sir, is only a toy," said Adams; "but taking you would be a pleasure, for I would talk with you."

"Let us talk now," said the old man. He glanced at Magome, and there was a gesture of his features as secret as a wink towards Adams as he said, "Magome Sageyu the warrior will forgive two ruffians who have already sailed a ship together if they divert their lumbering wits from matters of graceful interest to matters of a boring sort."

Magome tossed out a gust of smoke, and said, "It is an honour for him to be present at a communing between such masters of a noble craft." The answer was a fair safeguard against dismissal, and Magome hugged his brazier and re-filled his pipe.

Adams started immediately at the beginning of his story of the North West Passage, and of the magnificent attempts that had been made, from the wrong end, to find it. Having already gone through it for Ieyasu (while Ieyasu thought of geometry), he dealt with his theme more fluently now. And the Admiral listened.

The point he was most anxious to make was the one that seemed to elude the old man, or not to impress him with the same stupendous impact with which it had impressed Adams.

He asked for paper and a brush and ink. The Admiral clapped his hands and called for them, and Adams left his brazier and shoved his cushion to the Admiral's side. Quickly he slashed the broken coasts of the Arctic seas upon the paper. They were unanswerable challenges, a muddle of insoluble riddles as he scrawled them down. His brush moved, and hesitated, and moved again; and stopped, as doomed ships had moved with doomed men, among a score of possibilities whereof there was only one that was not frustration.

He abandoned, with a flourish of his brush that had in it some drama, his prodding and plodding in the muddle he had made of the Arctic Sea's wilderness.

Remote from it, where the paper was clean and clear, he flung upon it a simple line that was the coast of China; and hard by it the island of Japan.

His point was made.

There, obviously enough, was no confusion of alternative failures. The entry was one only, with no dead ends and false starts.

The old man smiled, and took the brush from Adams. From its point there slowly sprawled another island to the North of the Japan that Adams had made; and to the North of this more islands still.

China began to bulge and spread and break—till Adams took back the brush from him, and thought—and then slowly laid the brush down.

It was words he wanted now.

The old man laid his hand on the Pilot's shoulder.

"What I have set there, my son," he said, "I have myself seen."

"You've sailed there?" exclaimed Adams.

"Until men's fingers parted from their hands, cleaving to the black ice that they fended from the boat-side. Your host, Magome Sageyu, could show you three or four pairs of such hands in the bazaars now. Beggars' hands. I myself have a leg that is a dead crutch when it is not a living pain. We found no open road, An-jin."

"Did you look for it?" asked Adams.

"We looked for whatever we should find," said the Admiral.

"Yes—In a *junk!*"

Adams thought he had hit it now. "——a pot-bellied thing that can go only like a barrow where the wind pushes."

"A good stout thing," said the Admiral with a smile, "that even millstones of ice could not grind between them."

"Had you needle-watchers with you?" Adams challenged next. "Men who could read the stars and guide you?"

"There were no stars to read. Only a cold sun by day, and by night a colder light where the sun had set."

Adams was looking at the chart they had made between them. It was small wonder, he thought, that the junk had got nowhere in particular, with the old Admiral's sense of scale and latitude to guide it. North of the Pilot's Japan he had drawn an island whose extremity went degrees further than a latitude of ninety.

"Shongo Sama," he said; "with a good ship and victuals and charts and instruments——" while he spoke he moved his finger about on the paper, surmising that fifty degrees was as far North as the old man could ever have got—and he had glibly drawn an island that would have curled right over the world's very crown and spread down to the shores of Frisland!

"Instruments——" he said again vaguely; and the Admiral came very leisurely into the pause.

"It is fitting, An-jin," he said, "that you should converse with my son. He has some instruments, got from Portuguese and Spaniard sailors. To me, an old man, they are nought; but he sees something of the use of them. He also has a son of some intelligence and spirit, a pupil of our Magome Sageyu the swordsman. It was he who told me of Magome's execution of that—enemy of yours."

Magome did not turn a hair.

"Your son is a sailor?" asked Adams.

"He would be a sailor, if any war demanded it. At the moment he is on a journey. But when he returns you must talk with him of your hidden roads, and your instruments. I will send word to you, if you will come."

"Perhaps," Magome suggested, "he would accept the hospitality of our—of my—poor house."

"His instruments are here," said Shongo; "and here the sailors' talk would not disturb the business or the leisure of a soldier."

CHAPTER XLIII

Magome cursed himself and he cursed the devilry of language.

It was language that had delivered the Pilot to him in such docility; and it was language that threatened to rob him now of his prize.

If he, Magome, had learned the language of the Pilot instead of encouraging the Pilot to learn the language of the land, he would have had him still, his unassailable property. There was no justice in his cursing of himself, for the men who had mastered even a smattering of the alien thoughts and alien tongues that came to them in ships were geniuses who could be counted on the fingers (without the thumbs) of one hand.

But he was an old man, and when a fact went against him it became a fault. Nought but sheer indolence had prevented an intelligence so nimble as his own from becoming an exponent of the Dutch and English languages; so he cursed his indolence.

It was too late now. The damage was done. He himself was dispensed with, left smoking and idling in guardrooms while the Pilot conversed in the most private chamber with Ieyasu. It was only by dint of cajolery and the assistance of a fluke that he had got the final negotiations with Concepcion into his own hands; but now he was dispensed with again. Shongo the Admiral, a visit to whose house was itself a matter to be talked about among cavaleros, had said plainly enough that Magome need take no part in the next one. If he went on the pretext of attending bodily on his charge the Pilot, he knew that it would end in his smoking by himself or with other hangers-on in the room hospitably set aside for such in the great house, furnished with small braziers, with cakes and *saké* and tobacco of the second sort.

The Pilot would be in the room of intimate honour with Shongo the younger whose lustre in Yedo was as the lustre of his father. They would talk of this nonsense of a road for ships through the ice of the North, a road that could lead the Pilot only away from the easy money which he, Magome, had caused to tumble into his very lap. For he knew that wooden face of the Pilot as he trudged home beside him in the melting snow. The one person in the world on whom every word was wasted—whether the word were of cajolery, raillery, lofty courtesy or sheer, stark wisdom—was the Pilot when he wore the wooden face.

Adams mumbled a word or two and went into Santvoort's house, while Magome went sullenly home.

The brazier in his room was as cold as a dead lizard and he roared the fact out to the girls. Bikuni came, and knelt with the blow-pipe to rekindle it.

"And the Pilot's," he snorted. "That, too, neglected, I suppose. . . . It is small wonder that the man would be gone from a house where the women, left to themselves for an hour, cannot keep a brazier alight."

"Gone, Father?——" Bikuni looked up from her blowing. "Gone—where to?"

"Where to—who cares where to?" He rubbed his chilled feet with his chilled hands. "And the bath where a man should be able to warm himself—is that, too, cold? No?—Good. Who cares where to? Who *knows* where to? Even he can only write marks upon a paper and say 'Here,' and 'here,' with Shongo also writing marks—like a pair of boys playing at some game."

"But, Father," said Bikuni, her blowing done, "why should the Pilot go—anywhere?"

"Why?" winced the old man. "Is not that what I myself keep asking—'why?'—when in a year he could be a man of consequence and wealth. 'Why' indeed! You had better ask him 'Why'."

"Very well, Father," said she.

"Very well!" He was snorting again. "Is it for nothing that you have been taught—or has no one ever taught you?—that a woman shall not concern herself in the affairs of men? 'Very well, Father,' indeed! You will do no such thing."

"Very well, Father. Would you deign to eat a cake and drink a little wine?"

"No," he said, and opened and closed his hands over the brazier. "I have eaten cakes and drunk wine till my stomach is solid—listening to their talk. And it is for the return of the

younger Shongo that we wait now. One word from him to the
General, and the Pilot would become *their* guest instead of
mine. I—mark you—who have made a son of the man. I have
taught him to use a sword so that he could already give some
account of himself to two or three men out of every ten. I have
given him a tobacco pipe that is no shame in any company. I
have guarded him in transactions with Kuru the carpenter. I
have placed a tree of money above his lap, so that all he needs
do is sit here and wait till it ripens and falls from the
branches."

"And he is not content," said Bikuni.

"Girl," said her father, "it is I who am telling you that he is
not content."

Bikuni trembled on the verge of the possibility to which the
old man's fuming had brought them. She knew his tempers;
sometimes it was possible to say nothing at all to him while he
wriggled his hands open and shut over the brazier; sometimes
things could be said then that would have been likely to cause
an apoplexy in a quiet moment—things like asking him for
money.

She stooped again, blowing the fire. Then, peering into the
shimmer above the charcoal, she said: "Perhaps, Father, since
his contentment is so much to you—perhaps I, Bikuni, could
give him some content."

It was said now; and her trembling was stilled. Even the
shimmer in the charcoal fumes seemed to stop as she waited for
his answer. His fingers ceased their clutching for the meagre
warmth that rose from the brazier and wheezed, acrid, out of
the room through a score of chinks and crevices.

The answer came, the thought of a surprised man dealing
thoughtfully with his surprise.

"You, Bikuni? How?"

"I have read writings, Father," she said, looking at him;
"how that even—sometimes—a woman——"

Magome leaned back, away from the brazier, and his bellow
was laughter. "Writings!" he roared. "Writings! Men are not
writings, Bikuni San. I have watched that Pilot when women
have tried to bring him some content. One whom old Kuru
hired for him—a most pleasing girl; another whom that black

man had concealed for him so that no other visitor might see her beforehand. It may be true that once—the last time——"

He stopped and there was more laughter. There was in it this time a little tenderness for the pathetic idiocy of his daughter. "But there have been other times, many. With my own eyes I have seen."

"I, too, Father," she said softly. "With my own eyes——"

He sat forward, compelling her to look at him; and as she looked she shrank in awe and sudden terror of the greatness that was his alone, for he was her nearest ancestor.

"Girl," he said, "what are you telling me? Is this man a beautiful actor that you should say such things? Are you not the daughter of a soldier——?"

"A soldier most illustrious, my Father," said she.

"And you speak thus of garbage washed up by the sea. You speak of love for such a man!"

"Yes, Father. It is of love I speak. He is your own honoured friend. Your lord the General also loves him, and the great Shongo regards him well."

"He is a hairy survivor from the ocean's scum."

His hands dropped to rest on his sword and dirk; and Bikuni saw again the heap that had lain beside the tousled Pilot—torso and doubled-up legs, skull cleft in two like a broken dish.

"He is your friend, Father, and guest," said she.

"And is there love between this parentless fellow from anywhere and you, the soldier's child?" He rubbed his palms on the hilts, for they were still cold.

"No," said she; for she interpreted the question as strictly technical.

Her father scowled at her. "What is it, then, that you say you have seen?"

"His discontent," said she. "In the books of my reading there was another such—a prince and nobleman. There was no rest for him, or any comfort in all the world, save in the love of a certain lady——"

Magome was trying to keep an open mind; and it seemed to him a probability worth any wager that the prince of whom she told was not of the sort that would have spent the night drinking with a black door-keeper and gossiping with a Filipino, if the choicest creature of the second-best brothel in Yedo had come to him with a song and a wine-cup. . . .

"And who," he asked, "was the girl?"

"A princess," said she, "the daughter of a great and noble house that was become poor."

"She was beautiful, I suppose?" He was studying his daughter with very close attention that led him away into a weary, dejected reverie.

He woke from it with a sudden start at the sound of sandals on the path.

"No word of this disgraceful thing!" he rapped out to the girl, "——this thing that would ruin the name of Magome Sageyu. Friend or no friend, he is a product of no parents and you are the daughter of a soldier. Let him go to the sea he came from, and let it swallow him rather than that he should perish at a soldier's wrath. Let him go, I say—or his blood will be spent in this very house; and I shall be set upon the road again. D'you hear, girl?"

"Yes, Father," said she; and Adams came in.

CHAPTER XLIV

NOUGHT but big drinking could promise any solace to the old man in his perplexity that night. And the prospect of drink with his guest was itself another perplexity; for there were thoughts in his mind and words held in behind his tongue which drink might loosen. Within him, too, were anger and indignation and fear which a sober man could choke down so that his hands remained folded and still upon his girdle, whereas drink might give to them a yearning and an itch for the grip of a weapon, and to his eyes a blazing and a blinding vision of the greatness of the family of Magome Sageyu. . . . And there was that other thing in him also, the peculiar softness that caused the tough old swashbuckler to smile openly in answer when the Pilot smiled, to smile within the bars of his fencing-mask when the fellow parried deftly or lunged true; to see a beauty in the great white barrel of his chest and ribs; to call him, sometimes, 'son'——

He was glum at their bathing. He ate morosely and drank sparingly at their meal.

After the meal he excused himself as being ill at ease and went off to his room, where Bikuni had placed for him a cup and a bottle (for there were, nowadays, always bottles in hand).

It was a disappointment to Adams; for he had, now that he came to think of it, looked forward to company and talk this evening. He had wanted to hear more of the Admiral, and of his son. He had wanted to talk of the consignment of goods that would some day come from Nagasaki, and of the herbalist who would buy from them. He would have talked of trying the boat and of some possible ways of getting it to Concepcion at Nagasaki.

He wanted, in short, to mix, and there he was—left squatting alone in the room while the old man shuffled off to bed, sulking; and Bikuni flashed silently from one trivial deed of house-keeping to another, heedful that the walls of that house were of

paper, that the only impenetrable mask to a man's soul in that
country was the shape of his conduct.

There he was. . . .

There, by the rules, he was to remain in that lantern of wood
scantlings and paper; for without the attendance of a soldier he
might not stir abroad now that it was dark. The sheer nonsense
of that, however, was rather more than he intended to bear
with, since the house of Santvoort was scarcely more than a
stone's-throw away; and Magome in half an hour would have
changed places with the bottle that held a quart of *saké*.

He waited the half-hour and decided not, after all, to go back
to Santvoort and the kite-maker; for he had drifted into
thoughts that kept him squatting peaceably on the mat.

He filled his pipe and smoked it; filled and smoked; filled and
smoked the dozen whiffs at a time that exhausted each load of
tobacco in the little copper bowl. The tappings out of the ashes
and the endless refillings were in accord with the restlessness of
his peace.

He was waiting.

It was only in the yard of Kuru that he himself did things.
For the rest he was waiting: for the goods from Nagasaki; for
the return of the Admiral's son; waiting for Magome to be
amiable and sober; waiting, as he tapped out and refilled his
pipe, vaguely for Bikuni to come in.

In due course she came, the handmaid to see whether the
wants of a lord were fulfilled. She glanced at the brazier and
the tray and at the easeful disposition of Adams upon his mat.
She would have gone again, but he smiled and beckoned to
her.

"Come, be seated, Bikuni San," he said; "give An-jin your
pleasant company."

It was precisely that that he would have said if Magome had
been there; for he had learned to say it of old, when she and
Magdalena had come in on the old wineless evenings to sit with
the men, and work.

She hesitated. "Talk," she said quietly, "might disturb my
honourable father."

"Your honourable father," said Adams, "is as drunk as an
owl by now, and I doubt the crack of doom would disturb him.

Would that I were too." The last was a mumble of sheer peevishness.

"There is a bottle, An-jin," she said. "Would you that I bring it for you, and a cup? Or set it in your room?"

Thoughtfully he said, "No, Bikuni." Drink, he saw wearily, would not meet his case. . . . Begod he had a mind to rouse the old rascal in the other room, to shake him by the shoulders and bid him listen and talk to him—of the goods coming from Nagasaki; of the deeds of old soldiers if he preferred—in battle or in bawdy-houses; of the things Ieyasu had done; of kite-flyings and of wrestling-matches—of anything that made the talk of cronies. . . . Alternatively, having shaken the old man, he could tell him to go to hell with his pomposity and hollow swagger; for he, Will Adams, was as good a man as he or any other and he wanted his daughter and there was no reason on God's earth why he should not marry her, for he was, in point of fact, on God's earth no longer, but cut off from it utterly by the smiling word of one man and the blades of a thousand others. The short-cut back to it was at his hand; but it was closed—with the ice of black-frozen seas and the ice of imbeciles' apathy. And thus he was made a single man again, one who could virtuously marry.

So he would have talked quietly and reasonably to the reasonable old man of his want of Bikuni. He could have explained how the mighty Ieyasu, annulling his country had annulled his earlier marriage also; a man with only one want that was not a matter of waiting for the action of others—and that want the wistful little creature who so meekly and so cheerfully had offered to fill him with drink if drink had been his desire, and who had gone back, meek and dignified, to the kitchen when he had grunted that his desire was other. . . .

He could have made it clear to the old man that his intentions towards Bikuni were, in the phrase, honourable. His caresses would be the caresses of gentleness and protection, not the romping of a sea-dog. Arguing quietly he could have got him to see that Bikuni would be as well with him as with any fantastic cavalero of Japan; as well if not, indeed, better—for permanence, in the Anglo-Saxon or generally European sense, was a quality in situations for which Adams himself no longer looked. Richer and poorer, better and worse, sickness and health—these a man could still specify as fair and assessable chances. Only periods of years or months or even days were altogether outside his speculation. Death could come on a man at any time and in any manner; from the sword of a cavalero, a word from the Emperor; from earthquake or fire, from the cudgel of a footpad—or the equivalent of death could come, so far as one life or another was concerned, through the contrariness of wind and the pressure of sea.

These were things he could have argued out with old Magome; but Magome was drunk as an owl, grunting and puffing and snoring away with his anxieties muddled and stunned to a turbulent peace; and Adams went to bed.

With the routine of a man winding up his watch or placing a pair of boots outside his door, he took the Swart's dagger from his waist and placed it under his head-cushion.

An hour later his hand closed suddenly upon its haft.

His door was opening.

Inch by inch a slit of darkness widened less dark than his room, as a hand, skilled and stealthy, worked the frame back upon its slides.

Noiselessly, holding the dagger to him, he rolled over in his coverlet, away from his sleeping-mat; and waited.

All he could see was a blur of the hand moving from the top to the bottom of the door-frame; then a whisper said, "An-jin, it is Bikuni."

He rolled back to the sleeping-mat and replaced the dagger under the pillow. "Good," he said.

From the doorway a perfume came to him and in a moment the perfume was in his arms, with Bikuni whispering, "An-jin most honourable—An-jin—it is not unmaidenliness that has brought me to you thus, but fear."

Adams felt the throat of her in his hand as she said it; and when he cupped his hand it took her chin and jaw, and he felt that they were trembling.

"The fear is for you, my Lord, " she said. "For myself there is none. I am ready, if you think it well, to die; since living I must only love you."

"Love away!" said he, and drew her to him and closed his

eyes to be more at one with the fragrance and the nearness that
enveloped them. "Love away, my little one. A moth . . . a
moth, moving so softly in the night . . ." And thus was the
peace for the unrest that moved behind the unrest of waiting—
for the goods to come from Nagasaki, for a ship to come from
anywhere with victuals and water and men who would sail with
him to find the Passage.

The slight and lissom all of her was a caress, and the gentleness of him was the fear of one who would hesitate to crush a
flower.

"If he should kill you——" she began, but he stopped her
with, "Kill me—indeed . . ." Then a thought came to him; a
solid, sober and feasible idea.

"There'll be no killing, girl." His fingers moved lightly on
her brow and cheeks; they touched her lips, and from her throat
they drew once more some little quieting of his unrest.

"But how, my most loved great one?" said she. "How?—
how?——"

The necessity for not chuckling aloud was a hardship, but he
bore it.

"*How*, poor baby thing?" said he, and now his fingers patted
the shoulder of a ridiculously frightened child. "Have you
forgotten that my very good friend is the mighty Ieyasu
himself?"

"But what can even Ieyasu do to my father?"

"He can set the old rascal slinking belly-to-earth like a
beaten pup by the very presence of him a mile off. He can
make even your honourable father see reason, if any man can."

"But even his Excellency cannot bid a nobleman let his
daughter go to a—a—to you, honourable An-jin."

"Can't he?" said Adams. "We'll see."

He would say no more, for he was superstitious. He had
never yet counted chickens before they were hatched. And he
was satisfied, to date, with the results of his policy.

She, dreamily now—almost sleepily—as she nestled closer to
him, said, "An-jin, beloved one, I could bear you a son perhaps."

"Perhaps you could, my beauty," he answered. "Perhaps
you could. And perhaps you will. But we'll leave that yet
awhile, till we have settled with the old man. But that is no

reason why you should not come to me again as you have come to-night. Even sober the honourable one is a good, honourable sleeper; and I have money enough for *saké* to fill him any honourable night that we care to pour it into him. Bikuni San, it is very sweet to hold you so."

"And so to lie, An-jin," said she, "is all sweetness."

"You'll come again, then?"

She knew that she could, alternatively, die—and at any moment.

So she said, softly, "Yes. Again."

And the Pilot again said, "Good."

CHAPTER XLV

THERE was a keen and placid sense of enjoyment in Adams the next morning. He had, in his sleeve, a magnificent joke.

The old man, still huffy in his perplexity—still, as Adams put it to himself, with pepper in his nose—was a comical mockery of his own pompous dignity.

He was a breathless enough wreck from his solitary debauch, but he went to the bath with the swagger of a wrestler at the top of his form. Obviously he hated the world and every prank in it that was man, woman, food or drink; and he remarked, unctuously, that the morning was fine and the day of good omen. He trusted that his guest had spent a satisfactory night in the hospitality of his wretched hovel.

"Aye," said Adams, thanking him, and adding a warmth of geniality to the phrase, "never a better. Never a better, honourable host; for it is the hospitality within a room that brings the brazier's warmth; not the gilding of the tiles upon the roof's ridges. Is that well said, Magome?"

"Aye," said he—morosely, for phrases had gone as far as his choler could follow them; "it is well said." For, he was thinking, what was he to do? It was a race now between the goods from Nagasaki and the Admiral's son from heaven knew where: he was denying and dismissing the nonsense that Bikuni had spoken. The goods from Nagasaki would hold the Pilot.

Adams let him rest, with his spleen and his sore head, till they were squatted to their trays.

Then said he, "I have a matter of importance to discuss privately with his Excellency. Your distemper of last night is most regrettable, for you are still, no doubt, too ill at ease to accompany me to the castle."

"On the contrary," said Magome. "I myself have some business with the General. It was my intention to go up this morning. But since your matter is urgent—too urgent, it seems, for discussion first of all with myself—I will allow you to occupy the Presence."

236

"You could wait, as usual, among your friends outside," Adams suggested playfully. "I could ask him to permit you to enter to him when I have done."

"A soldier may obtain that permission at any time by petition," said Magome. "And one with my standing need only signify his wish—through the usual official channels."

"Yes," said Adams, "and the usual gifts."

Magome sucked in a dish of tea and said nothing for a time. Then, "To a man in my position, An-jin, the making of gifts is a privilege."

"And to a man in *my* position," Adams said very amiably, "the privilege is to save his honourable host from such unnecessary expenditure."

The old man saw now the full slyness in the Pilot's manner. He was behaving in the way that he himself so often behaved, grinning complacently within his mask, playing upon the other's clumsy blade, trouncing his ribs, prodding his padded breast, whacking his helmet, working him into a sweat of exasperation just because he had a trick to show him that he had not shown him before.

This new annoyance, the slyness of his guest, was as irritating as the fellow's occasional face of wood. There were certain attitudes in a man which, when they were applied to certain large and grave matters, could be met only with very drastic means. Wooden-faced obstinacy was one. Slyness was another.

When verbal statements on any subject whatever were made to Magome by any person they fell on a completely open mind. Magome neither believed them nor disbelieved. He treated them as one item only of evidence. So, Bikuni's having told him that there had been no love between herself and the Pilot meant neither that there was not nor yet that there was. It meant only that there might be, and that, if he wanted to know the accurate truth, he must find it out for himself by means of other evidence. And a sly man was as hard to squeeze for evidence as a man wooden-faced with obstinacy. However, if the Pilot was absorbed at the moment in his secret purpose with the General, the moment might be a good one for surprising him in another direction.

He had found him once absorbed in some drawings upon a paper with a writing-brush, and had asked him for the honourable loan of a mace or two. The Pilot had grunted amiably and gone on with his drawing. Magome had asked again, for the matter was a pressing one; and at that the Pilot had frowned, quickly jotted down some calculation to do with his absorption, dug in his sash and handed over a whole tael. He might well do the same sort of thing again now while he went on secretly smiling and thinking of the other matter.

"An-jin," he said with sudden vitality, "your friend the Hollander finds much comfort and pleasure in the woman he has taken to wife."

"Aye," said Adams; "for even you have said she is a comely one."

"You alone seem to have found none to satisfy you," the old man said next.

Adams wondered for an instant if the old rascal had not, perhaps, been as satisfactorily drunk in the night as he had seemed to be. But the slackness of the pouches at the old jowls reassured him.

"Has our last evening as the guests of Concepcion already faded from your memory?" he asked.

"I was not referring to the passing entertainment of singing girls and wine-cup fillers. I was thinking rather of the permanence and the greater convenience of a woman of your own."

"A wife?" said Adams.

"Yes," said the old man. "A wife. You should have no difficulty in finding a suitable wife. As a man of means you will have some standing." That ought to have tripped the fellow up into an admission of the outrageous and perplexing kind that the old man dreaded his making.

But Adams, still with that smile of inscrutable slyness, said: "Ah—it is the finding of her that is the difficulty. That is why I go to his Excellency. He must find my wife for me."

Magome jumped on his broad haunches so that his back was suddenly straight. "What?" he exclaimed. "The Shogun find a wife for you? Why should he be the one to do such a thing?"

For months now Magome had been thanking his luck every

day that Ieyasu commanded nothing and did nothing to move the Pilot from under the thumb of his present host. . . . He had a quick, wild thought of a deed of formal adoption that could make of the Pilot a son; but he could not cope with it with all the food inside him resisting digestion and the Pilot grinning in his face with his secret joke.

"Who else?" asked Adams innocently. "Who else can give me a wife that would please me?"

CHAPTER XLVI

THE men about the castle were accustomed to the Pilot's visits by now—with old Magome or without him. He went unchallenged till the last stage of the approach to the Presence, when he stopped to smoke a bowl or two of tobacco at the guardsmen's brazier, while one went to see if he might enter.

The only words he wasted on preamble were phrases of formal courtesy. Then he said, "My Lord, I have come to-day to ask you for a gift of swords."

"Swords, An-jin?" asked his friend. "Why? Whom would you kill that Magome cannot kill for you?"

"I would kill no men," said Adams. "I would beget them."

"The swords with which men are begotten, An-jin——" but the mighty Ieyasu saw that his joke was good enough to be left unfinished.

When they had done with this ribaldry Adams said, "You are mistaken there, Excellency. These cavaleros set great store by the furnishings in a man's girdle outside his shirt. With swords I may take a woman suitably. Without them I am dirt."

"You ask me to make a soldier of you, my friend?" Ieyasu said it slowly and very thoughtfully.

"Aye," said Adams. "A cavalero."

Ieyasu said, "Do you know how much you are asking?"

Adams said, "I know how much I am willing to give." He explained this quietly. "It is all yours in any case, as you well know. My life is yours so long as I am here; and I could not get away if I would. I am your prisoner and your servant. As a small man I can do but small work for you. As a big one I could give you the service of any of these gentlemen—better service than some and as good as most."

Ieyasu fell into very serious thought and then said suddenly, "Who has sent you to ask this thing? Who is it with a daughter requiring a husband such as you?"

"No one has sent me," said Adams. "No one knows the

errand on which I have come. But the daughter requiring me
as a husband is the daughter of Magome Sageyu."

"Ho!" said Ieyasu. "So it is Magome Sageyu who sends
you!"

"That it is not," said Adams. "It is I who come secretly,
and of my own will. His is the nose that I would pull with
your gift of swords before the old ruffian should know that a
swordless one is seeking his daughter. I know him too well,
Excellency. He would not sit down to think on the matter till
he had first cut the impudent one in two in his love for his own
great name; and ripped up his own fat belly in his regard for
you."

"So you know your host?" Ieyasu smiled.

"Aye," said Adams. "A handy one with those fine blades of
his."

"And you want his daughter to wife?"

Adams said, "Why not? It is no wrong; for I am as good as
dead; and the other side of the grave there is no giving in
marriage." This point was now quite clear to himself, and his
God-fearing conscience was at ease. It was not the same point,
however, which was bothering Ieyasu.

"One sword, Anjin," he said after some thought, "I could
allow you easily."

"I know," said Adams. "But one sword would be nothing
for Magome Sageyu. No lesser man than a Samurai could
approach his daughter and keep a whole skin."

"Why not take some woman where there would be less
difficulty?" asked Ieyasu.

"Why not give me the swords?" asked Adams, "and so
remove the difficulty—as your Excellency removes all difficulties?"

Ieyasu, where Adams would have paced the floor in similar
thought, sank his chin a little and sat quite still. Suddenly,
where Adams would have stopped in his pacing, Ieyasu jerked
his head and said, "Indeed, why not?" and again, "Why not?"

"The swords themselves, you understand," Adams said, "I
would of course buy."

"That you would not," said the other; "for the blades and
scabbards, the hilts and their furniture would be the least part

of this gift. I have swords, and to spare."

"Do you doubt my loyalty, then?"

"No," said Ieyasu thoughtfully. "I do not doubt your loyalty. For it is rarely that a man knows beyond all doubt that the man upon whom he is looking is altogether his friend. Looking upon you, An-jin, I have always known that one thing."

"Very well, then," said Adams. "The giving of swords to such a man can make little difference to you. To me it would make a great deal."

"The only difference of which you have told me is that it would give you one woman rather than another." Ieyasu was not chaffering now in the manner of a bargain-driver. He seemed to be assessing the matter for his own satisfaction.

"Is that of no account?" asked Adams.

"A great deal, no doubt—to the woman," was the answer. "But to you—the receiver—the gift would be less than its value to the giver. Swords are a large matter."

"It would make a bigger man of me," said Adams.

Ieyasu said, "Ah!" and thought further. "As a bigger man what is it that you would do?"

At this Adams burst out, "Do?—I would do whatever you would let me do. I would sail a ship with your old, good friend Shongo the Admiral. I'd find that passage to the North West and open a trade on a sea that has no pestilence of Spaniards and Portingal robbers, with my own country. I would bring men to this country who should be friends to you as I am, and goods that your country lacks. I'd bring you ships and stout seamen."

"Seamen I have already," said Ieyasu. "Ships you can build for me here."

"That I cannot," said Adams. "I can sail ships, but I cannot build them. I am no shipwright."

"What of the vessel you are now completing?"

"That!" said Adams. "It lacks a thousand things that must be in the architecture of any proper ship. Only an architect can make them, and I am no architect, but a sailor. I have never even tried to make them."

"Try then," said Ieyasu quietly; "now."

"It would be a waste," said Adams solidly. "A waste of time and of timber."

"Waste them, An-jin," said Ieyasu. "It is no matter." He smiled; "The time I have already given you, and I can give you the timber and the workmen."

"And what about my swords?" The question startled Adams himself back from a muddled and prodigious contemplation of the interweaving of great timbers and of little ones into the structure that sun and water could not warp nor the stress of wind distort. . . . There was still the old *Liefde's* hulk; it could, perhaps, be copied in all its details by old Kuru and those lads of his. . . . But there were no proper nails for them, and their dowels would not serve; their joinery——but he came quickly back. "What about my swords?"

"What about my ships?" Ieyasu countered, and they were silent.

Each of them was beholding a suggestion quite fantastic.

"For you, An-jin, to try building a ship," Ieyasu went on, "is a no greater matter than my trying to build a Samurai. The material we both have is good. It is only that we have never tried."

Adams looked up from his problem of building a proper ship.

"Let us try, then, Excellency," he said.

Ieyasu smiled at the hardihood that was demanded of himself, rather than at the Pilot's enterprise. For, as he had said, if the Pilot's effort were to waste a parcel of timber and the time and wages of a score of workmen it was no great matter. Whereas if he, the judge and assessor and lover of men were to misplace one faith and so break another that bound him to a host of noble vassals, it was a matter great indeed.

"So you would be a bigger man, my friend?" he asked. "And you would have the first woman you have properly seen in this country?"

"Aye," said Adams. "Who would not? I would find that road of which I have spoken. Men less instructed than I have adventured it. And as to the woman—is it not nature?"

"Are they not both nature?" was the answer. "For the thirst of man craves both wine and water, and is utterly quenched by neither. But swords, An-jin——" he paused in a suddenly divergent thought. "Swords. . . . You must know that even I would be justly laughed at for giving a sword to one who cannot make a pretence of wielding it."

"I do not ask you to give it to such a man," said Adams; he was a little testy at the suggestion that he could have been such a fool as to have suggested it. "Twice——" he went on; "twice—I won't say that his wrist was not shaky and his old eye fogged by nights of big drinking—but twice I have touched the throat and once the lower ribs of old Magome Sageyu with the foil. And that, Excellency, is not nothing."

"So you have fenced with Magome Sageyu and you say that he knows nothing of this request of yours?"

"Nothing, my Lord," said Adams, and he suddenly chuckled. "I would give much for you to see his face when I first hail him with sword-hilts at my belly. He will burst an honourable blood-vessel and throw an honourable fit—and there will only be Santvoort to see it, the Dutchman who sees nothing. . . . Yes, for many months I have used the long foil with Magome, and learnt to draw the dirk and thrust and cut with it."

"We shall see," said Ieyasu, and he suddenly warmed to the smile which was his for things near-by. "We shall see. For there is a man here—a man young as yourself—indeed younger —who can put you to a test."

He struck his gong and ordered the one who attended to bring foils and the other furniture of fencing, and to summon the honourable one who was but lately arrived from Suruga.

*　　　*　　　*　　　*　　　*

Adams had time to fidget now, waiting for his adversary. He flexed his toes stealthily in his socks and privately thanked God that he never (for some reason so vague that only pure luck could account for it) carried the Swart's dagger when visiting The Mighty One.

He saw that Ieyasu was watching those movements of his feet, for he said, "At any rate, An-jin, you are aware that nimbleness and sureness of foot are as great a matter as wrist and eye in the handling of a blade."

"Aye," said Adams, "I am aware of that. Old Magome says

that no man should draw a sword till he can spin himself about
on the ball of one foot with his eyes shut."

"And have you attained to such grace?" asked Ieyasu.

"No," said Adams. "Nor never shall. If you expect me to
win any bout with a man who is not also a novice——"

"This young man is no novice," Ieyasu smiled; "nor do I
expect you to win."

"Well," said Adams, "that is fair." He wished the young
man would come, so that he might openly stand upon his toes
and stretch his calves and his thighs and straighten the tendency to twitch out of his fingers and biceps and forearms, as
every swordsman did on taking up a foil without exciting
comment, since every muscle in his body must be nimble and
alert.

The adversary came in, bare-shanked, jacketed, gloved and
already masked. Behind him was the bearer of foils, and the
gloves and jacket and mask for Adams.

The Pilot untied his sash and slipped his body from his robe
and under-robe. He stood naked before the two clothed ones,
the ruler of all the land in his gold and blue and silver, the
other one an unknown engine of force and lithe skill already
taut and girt for the exercising of them.

The attendant laced the jacket upon the Pilot's nakedness.
The face in the mask smiled at the length of Pilot for which
there was no protection in the jacket's shortness.

"Spare his behind," said Ieyasu amiably, and the voice from
the helmet amiably assented.

Adams's helmet was secured to the tabs on the jacket's
breast and back and shoulders. The gauntlets were laced to
the jacket-sleeves. Ieyasu had taken the foils from the
attendant and was squinting along their lengths, playing with
their hilts, balancing them, tapping their blades one against
the other.

"It is well," he said to the attendant, and the man withdrew.

"You shall have the choice, An-jin," he said, and turned to
the other—"with your permission."

"Most certainly," said the mask; and it was obvious that for
one such as he there was little to be gained or lost by a hair's
breadth of perfection or imperfection of a weapon in the hand

of such as Adams. . . .

"Most certainly."

For all his eagerness to be started, Adams gave the punctilio for the choosing of his foil that he had seen exercised by swaggering young men in the arena of Magome. It was, he knew, part of the game—and it was the one part which he could play as well as any man. So he squinted down the curved lengths of the weapons, first one and then, thoughtfully, the other. He tried the balance and the swing of them, holding them first at the hilts' end and then close against its guard. He swung them and flicked them—and the others watched him; the eyes behind the bars of the mask and the eyes smiling in the wrinkled face of Ieyasu.

"It is well, my Lord," he said when his choice was made.

The adversary took the second foil from the Mighty One, and a single shifting of his hand upon its hilt gave him the balance of it, and his grip.

"Fall to, then," Ieyasu shrugged his shoulders benignly upon them and hugged his hands together in his sleeves for the enjoyment of a joke.

In the salute, also, Adams felt that he was as good a man as any of these cavaleros.

The blades clicked together; Ieyasu's joke was started.

The other one, thought Adams as he shuffled flat-footed about the centre of a circle whose wide circumference was the twinkling steps of the adversary—the other one, thought he, could do all the shooting-off of fireworks. For himself he would do well enough in doing nothing but answer as best he might with steady parrying.

The other dealt fairly enough with him at first, demanding only the simplest of moves for the stopping of his blade. Ieyasu, the joke enjoyer, smiled as he saw the possibility of a future deftness in the present clumsy twitch of the Pilot's wrist at every parry to save the razor-edge of a blade, by presenting its soft back to the impact of the attacking one. He smiled also at the slithering of the great feet upon the mat, seeing that it was not ineptitude but stratagem that kept them fastened upon the ground in the firm hold that was necessary to carry the bulk of the Pilot—the trick of men schooled to fighting on sand.

Foil snarled against foil a dozen times as Adams was in the nick of time to save his throat, his crown, his ribs and his shoulder from the waspish blade flashing about him.

"Well done, An-jin!" said Ieyasu. "Well done . . . late. Every time the fraction of an instant late, but—well done!"

He smiled again, for Adams in grunting his reply slacked nothing of his attention to the matter in hand. . . . For had not Magome told him that cities may collapse in earthquake or go up in flames or vanish into the sea till such time as the good swordsman has earned leisure for such matters by cutting his man to the spine? Had not the old fox coughed sharply in the shuffling silence of a bout, or suddenly roared the explosion of a sneeze to startle Adams? Did he not sidle against the mats enclosing his arena and suddenly rattle the whole contraption with a kick?—and reward the straying of the Pilot's attention with a trouncing of his ribs, a whack upon his helmet and a lunge against the padding of his jacket that would have spitted a bullock and did, in effect, plant the Pilot's bottom in the sand? Did he not thereafter dance about the disarmed and breathless one in a bellow of laughter and a whistling of the blade that would have minced him to nothing? . . . So Adams answered his Lord with a grunt in his throat only, but with eyes unwinking and a mind taut upon every flicker of the other's blade.

His adversary went from fairness to generosity. He offered chances to Adams—an open side, his breast, his throat. But Adams took no chances. He stuck his feet faster still to the mat and drew in his blade to command it better in its work of guarding him. Again Ieyasu smiled.

"Have at him, An-jin," he suggested. "Fights are not won by the simple act of not losing them."

"Maybe not," said Adams, wary as ever. "Maybe not . . ." A click of blade meeting blade showed that his wrist was still alert at the hilt while his tongue was answering in talk. "Maybe not, my Lord. . . . Nor did suicide win fights. If I can guard——" but the adversary began to press him now. The tapping and clicking of the foils ran together into a clucking rattle. The attacker circled about Adams; and Adams could feel the warmth of friction through the soles of his feet. He would have liked, he reflected, to see old Magome matched against this cold fury in the jacket and mask. . . . He knew that it was a matter of time only. Sooner or later—but it came sooner. The blade flashed to his side with a clean swing that would have glanced, as Magome had so often explained to him, between his ribs, to slice his heaving heart in two. The next instant it was upon his helmet's top in a descent that would have cleft a skull to the chin. In the next the foil's point was at his breast—but this time he was ready. A sudden nimbleness came to the great feet whose only work till now had been the work of an anchor's flukes. They flashed to the same life that was in his wrist, to bring his own weapon clicking upon the weapon of his adversary.

The point grazed his jacket. An arm shot by him, a neck was outstretched within the helmet that was now at the level of the Pilot's thighs—and the Pilot's blade spun through the air to come to rest upon it.

"Good, An-jin!" said Ieyasu. "Good. Good. Good." His laughter then became as the bellow of Magome himself. "But——" and again he laughed. "But—the pity is that you were twice dead in the time you required for the doing of it. . . . It is enough, however." With laughter still in his voice he turned to the adversary and said, "You I thank most honourably."

He would not have spoken thus to an ordinary soldier, and Adams was proud in the observation.

Ieyasu himself untied the thongs that held the helmet to the other's jacket; and the face that Adams saw withdrawn from the mask was a face more obviously noble than the face of even a palace soldier. The youth laid down his gauntlets and foil and himself untied the Pilot's helmet while Ieyasu took his foil and played with it again.

Adams, wiping the sweat from his eyelids and his brow, said in his best manner: "Sir, you have done great honour to this person. In his most humble opinion you are a finer swordsman than Magome Sageyu, the noble Ronin of Izumo."

The other uttered a politeness.

"He is, in fact, a better swordsman than all others in the

land," said Ieyasu. "Except—and then only possibly—his father."

"His father?" asked Adams, for he had heard the names of most of Japan's famous swordsmen.

Ieyasu smiled. He said quietly: "Exaggerated tales of my skill with a blade may have reached you in idle gossip; for it is with my son that you have measured foils."

"God's life!" mumbled Adams; for many were the tales he had heard of this young man's swordsmanship.

Then he made proper obeisance to Hidetada, the mighty son of the mighty Ieyasu.

And Hidetada was smiling at him; not with the smile of his father, who had a great love of things and a patience that was already a legend. The smile of Ieyasu was a communication; the smile of Hidetada his son said no more than the bars of bamboo in his fencing mask. It conveyed not hostility, since it conveyed nothing.

"As to your own skill, An-jin Sama," he said, "the reports of it that are abroad in no way exceed it. You have learned well. Its excellence is that haste does not seduce you from the method. Its fault is that you are slow. Keep the method; and when you have speed——"

"Speed——" Adams interrupted him with thoughtful humility. Sweat trickled under his jacket and down his thighs. He pulled off the gauntlets and cooled his hands by closing his fingers and slowly opening them. "—I cannot look for speed such as yours. We are junks, we Englishmen and Hollanders. We have the better ships, but your men are to us as our frigates are to your junks. You could have finished me, I daresay, in a minute . . ." He shrugged his shoulders. To Ieyasu he said, "But I can do *something* with a sword, my Lord."

"Indeed!" It was Hidetada who spoke instead of Ieyasu; and he spoke handsomely. "Indeed, An-jin, of the half thousand men about this palace you could stand up to a good hundred. Twenty or thirty of them you could cut—keeping your head and your feet as you kept them now."

"Perhaps he would not find the stake so high in another encounter," Ieyasu said slyly, for he was back at his joke. "He has heated himself in this bout, for a woman. See how he still sweats and heaves!"

"A woman?" asked Hidetada.

"Aye," said Ieyasu. "No less. And no more. He would take the daughter of our old Magome Sageyu. He knows his Magome Sageyu, however. For him to take her as a merchant or a craftsman would fill the old man's nose with pepper and his fists with swords . . . So to give him his woman we must give him swordship to-day and make of him a Samurai."

A sudden indrawn breath of astonishment was heard to whistle, till the young man checked it, through the teeth of Hidetada. "The Pilot a Samurai?" he asked. And still he smiled.

"Why not?" said Ieyasu. "He has served me well, in friend-ship. As a Samurai he says that he can serve me better."

Hidetada shrugged his shoulders, and the very shrug was the gesture of profound obeisance of a child to a father, of a vassal to a lord.

"Is it not well?" asked Ieyasu. What he meant most clearly was, "Is not the joke a good one?"

"It is well," said Hidetada. "Let us bathe, An-jin."

Stripped of his jacket as they stepped into the bath there was a greater friendliness about him than there had been in the chamber. Adams noted with some satisfaction that the smooth torso, the colour of dark honey, shone with sweat even as his own. The round had not been mere child's play for him.

He would have given much, snob that he was becoming, for Magome to have seen him seated in the bath-tub with Ieyasu's son. . . .

"You smile at some lucky thought," said Hidetada. "A thought of the girl perhaps, that my honourable father gives you?"

"A thought rather," said Adams, "of the old man. It would be some small recompense to my Lord for the generosity of his friendship to this person if he could see the old man's face when he hears of the honour that is to come upon me."

"Yes," said Hidetada, "my father enjoys a joke."

"But the swords," said Adams, "do you think he will allow me to obtain them without undue delay?" He laughed.

"Magome could assist me in the buying of them."

"My father," said Hidetada, "is not slow in action when once his action is determined. I have little doubt that he will have given you swords, and good ones, before you are dismissed his presence to-day."

"God!" exclaimed Adams; and before he knew what he was at he had committed the hideous discourtesy of leaping from the bath to the ground before his host.

"My Lord," he said sheepishly, "you startled me." He glanced in the direction of the corridor leading to the chamber. "Perhaps it were better for me to hasten the boredom of this rude company from you."

Hidetada stepped leisurely from the steaming water.

"I come too," he said. "I would see the swords." If curiosity could have been friendliness his words would have been friendly. He clapped his palms together and two attendants came out of the corridor with napkins and their robes.

II

SAMURAI

II

SAMURAI

CHAPTER I

It was as Hidetada had said it would be.

Upon the low writing-desk before Ieyasu in the chamber lay a long-sword and a dirk. The hilts were simple enough weapon-handles, and of no great consequence as gauds. Instead of the dandy's favoured sharkskin rubbed down and dressed to the semblance of mottled and polished ebony, they were lapped with cord of black silk, shiny and a little worn. The guards were bronze, lightly engraved in the form of lotus petals. Only the studs in the hilts' centres were gold; but they, too, were simple in design—tortoises not much larger than the Pilot's thumbnail, minute heads and feet just protruding from the shells, emblems of longevity and good luck. The silk of the scabbards was faded and, here and there, torn so that the shell of old wood showed through.

The eye of Adams ran over these details while his mind, peculiarly, hesitated at them, so that he stood quite still. He had heard talk of swords from Magome and his cronies and his pupils. He had heard it from old Kuru the boatbuilder and from Santvoort's kite-making father-in-law. He had heard it from loafers at the water-side, and before any of its words had been comprehended to him he had heard it in the rabble about the execution field at Oita. Even till yesterday, when only a few words in any talk of swords had been meaningless to him, the trend of all of it had not been so much nonsense.

Yet now—looking down upon these clean curves that were death and immunity from death, that were love of a most peculiar sort or hate and unflinching enmity—words stirred within him for utterance; yet, uttered, they too would have been nonsense.

"They are shabby things, An-jin," Ieyasu said, smiling at the way his joke was going.

The speech of Adams in reply was no more than a sound in his throat.

Hidetada, also looking upon the swords, knew that they had

once been the girdle-weapons of Ieyasu himself, and before
Ieyasu of an old man who had died in the service of Ieyasu.
He knew that for many years they had lain in a chest for the
reason that no man had occurred to his father as worthy of so
handsome a gift. So from him, too, there came no full-fledged
word.

"Something has made you dumb, An-jin," Ieyasu said.

"My Lord," was all Adams could say—"something has."

"It is a suitable quality in a soldier," said Ieyasu. "There
is but one undertaking required of a soldier by his Lord; he
gives his word to keep it, even as he draws his sword but to
use it. You understand?"

"Aye," said Adams. "I understand."

He signified more than any speech of his had signified
before; and already he knew it.

Other words he had once said with great solemnity and a
similar sensation of prickling about his neck and below his
ears. He had said them to the parson in the church above the
wharves of Gillingham, as he fumbled a gold ring upon the
finger of Mary. But those words, he had suspected even as
he mumbled them, exceeded the possibility of accurate
achievement by human man.

It was as a formality and, in a sense, as an exaggeration that
he had conceded them to the parson. They had not been part
and parcel of life itself. . . . Of a parson's life perhaps, or of
a woman's, but not—when it came to the detail of living things
through to their logical conclusions—of a normal sea-going
pilot's. Thus, in making his undertaking to the parson at
Gillingham, he had meant one thing while the parson had
meant another. But in making his undertaking to the Lord
Ieyasu the parties of both parts meant, exactly and accurately,
the same thing. It was no fantastic evasion or hyperbole.
Ieyasu was himself no fantastic matter like a woman or a
parson. He was, put in the simplest terms, a friend; an oldish
man with a smile and an understanding and—it appeared now
—a generosity that was staggering.

"Aye," said Adams, "I understand. I give my word, to
keep it."

"It is well." was the short reply of Ieyasu.

Then, moving the two weapons so as to lift them together and hand them to him, he said: "Take them. No ——" He replaced the dirk on the desk and held up only the sword. "First regard the blade." He slowly withdrew it from the scabbard, and Adams at last moved forward.

"Is it good?" Ieyasu asked, as Adams took the hilt and gripped it and ran his eye along the blade with the edge that was sheer length without breadth that human eye could see—steel that twinkled like a jewel or like a rift in grey clouds against the dull soft metal of the blade's body. It was the first real sword his hand had ever held; and the feel of it made the remembered feel of a bamboo fencing-stick the memory of a dead thing.

"My Lord," said he, and his eye followed the coils of the graven dragon that swayed along the blade's curve, "how should I know?—except that it is you who give it to me."

"We tell you then," said Ieyasu with the boastfulness of a boy, and he smiled to include his son in the telling—"it is a good blade. As also is its fellow here." He tapped the dirk, and returned to the sword in the Pilot's hand. "Regard this." Close to the hilt, where the blade was thickest, he indicated a stain—a faint, dull smokiness in the metal. "By this mark you may always know these blades as yours. It goes through the metal from one side to the other. In the dirk it is the same. No man can remove it except the master who put it there. Both blades were forged in the house of Yoshimitsu."

To this Adams could say nought but "God!"

It was only nonsense that he had heard talked concerning swords by old men and youths and artisans and loafers; but even nonsense itself was no great wonder when he held in his very hand the wonder of such a blade—he a craftsman with a craftsman's recognition of perfection in a tool. Among the nonsense was the tale of luck carried by every Yoshimitsu blade in the girdle, or in the hand, of any friend of Ieyasu; for it was with a dirk of Toshiro Yoshimitsu's forging that Ieyasu had sought to cut his belly after his defeat at the river Tenrin. The young General struck, but the metal turned from his skin as though the blade had been not the finest metal in Japan, but dough. . . .

A sudden thought drew Adams suddenly back from Ieyasu and he said: "These blades—a soldier——" He could put the startling question only in its simplest form. "Do soldiers—sword-wearers—do they never trade?"

"Trade?" asked Ieyasu. "Why should soldiers trade?"

Adams suddenly gazed very far away, in thought. He closed his hands upon the hilt and lowered them slowly to the full length of his arms.

"To-morrow!" he said, "or the next day—or the next—I am—I was—about to begin trading. The goods will arrive from the Filipino. But if a sword-wearer may not trade . . ."

"An-jin!" exclaimed Ieyasu in great laughter that fitted the climax of his joke; "would you forgo your trade with the Filipino, to have the swords and the woman and the laugh on Magome Sageyu?"

It was not with laughter that Adams answered laughter. To himself he said "God knows!" and then to Ieyasu, "I had not considered it." He considered it now, and slowly said, "I think so. . . ."

"But may a soldier trade then?" Hidetada spoke at last, directly to his father. "Has such a matter ever been known before?"

"In one of us," said Ieyasu quietly, "it would not be seemly or permissible—but neither would the haunches of a stallion nor the chest of a fox. . . . Yes, this soldier may trade. So go, An-jin, honourably. Do not at first show the blades to your Magome Sageyu; keep that till the jest has somewhat ripened."

Adams smiled. It would be a jest indeed, this one with Magome Sageyu; but his smile at the moment was for the thought of one other who should see him swaggering home with the hilts sticking out at his middle . . .

Other thoughts, too, came to him as the scabbards passed within his girdle and his friend Ieyasu showed him the turn of the knots that should hold them firm. They were of the big men of his profession, Raleigh and Drake and Frobisher, of the rewards that had come to them also, of nobility bestowed by their sovereign; of the things these men had done and of the Passage Northward and Westward—the one thing only that still remained in all the world for a sailor's doing.

III

1613 AND AFTER

CHAPTER I

AFTER a dozen years of wearing those swords in his girdle—in their scabbards peaceably, since they were the work of Toshiro Yoshimitsu and not of Muramasa with the ill-repute of all blades from that forge for knowing no rest till there was marrow upon them—after a dozen years he was able to say, "If it be that there cometh a ship let them enquire for me. I am called in the Japan tongue An-jin Sama. By that name I am knowen all the coast along."

There was no exaggeration in the claim; for it was to An-jin Sama in his lordship of Hemi-Mura near Yedo that a despatch was delivered which set him at once upon the journey to the most Westerly point of Japan. At the end of the journey he sat in the shade of some timber at the waterside of Hirado, looking across the water at the ship *Clove* of London. He had seen no English ship for fifteen years, and never before had he seen such a flag as was flown at the *Clove's* peak.

The *Clove* struck him as a stout and handy vessel. She was not unlike the ship he had himself built for Ieyasu eight years ago—the ship which never went adventuring North because she went South instead on an urgent political mission, sailed by the Spaniard who lost her. But the *Clove* was a better ship than that first attempt of his at shipbuilding; drawing rather more, she would be steadier in heavy seas, solider among ice-floes.

More nearly to the little *Clove's* pattern had been the second ship he built, two years after the first one. In this one he had sailed North—as far North as the fiftieth degree with old Shongo the Admiral, there to watch his reading of the cross-staff and astrolabe. Together they had compassed the wild island of Yezo and sailed South again in the Sea of Japan. The Admiral saw again the coastline of Korea; and Adams accurately carded the islands of Lintschoten.

Then they turned North-east again for Yedo. . . . But thereafter the ship was sold by Ieyasu as a point in policy, to the Governor of the Philippines.

Reports came, in time, in the mouths of Spaniards and Portuguese, of Chinamen and Japanese and nondescript Swarts that there were English merchants as near at hand as Java. Instead of building more ships to be lost by fools or sold by Emperors, Adams gave his attention to the writing of letters and to the finding of men in the crews ashore at Nagasaki who might be induced to carry them.

The first of them he had written eight years ago, the second but six months. To one or other of them he saw in the *Clove* his answer.

And he was tired.

He had come by land—on foot to rest his buttocks and his thighs, on horseback to rest his feet—and he had averaged, for seventeen days, a rough fifty English miles a day. His age was close on fifty. The country's food and the life were beginning to get the better of him. He had an occasional fever and he made his water, at times, with difficulty. So he sat quietly looking out at the *Clove*, thinking of very little beyond the probability that his cook and his scribe, whom he had dropped with the jaded ponies of their last stage at an outlying tavern, were beyond any use for the next twenty-four hours.

From where he sat he could see the same strange flag that was flown by the *Clove* over a house, so he had no need to ask any man the way.

He stretched himself and hitched the girdle to his scabbards and his waist, and made for the flag.

On the verandah of the house were John Saris, Captain-General of the *Clove* adventure, and Richard Cocks, who was to remain in Japan as Cape Merchant—the East India Company's resident Managing Director in Japan. With them, for it was near dinner-time, were their chiefs-of-staff—Eaton, sober for the time of day and quiet in a new resolution; the magnificently named Tempest Peacock chatting to his friend Cawarden; young Edward Sayers, who was there because of family influence on the Company's Board, and tough Nealson, who was there because he had been, at one time or another, in most places to which men were carried by ships.

They saw what they called a "Natural" cavalero walking up

the road to them; and when a coolie stood aside to let him pass they saw that he was, indeed, a cavalero but not a "Natural"; for although he walked with the waddle of unshod, precariously clogged feet he was a head and more taller than the coolie. Under the great straw hat, as he raised his face to look up at the strange flag, was a beard as full as Richard Cocks's own.

He saw the group on the verandah and stopped for an instant as though tripped up by something in the road; and then he hurried forward, prodding at the ground with his staff.

The group already knew something of the significance of a brace of sword-hilts; of coolies' amiability, too, when it became suddenly an obeisance. The coolie, incidentally, had stopped and turned fifty paces after passing Adams and had become a dozen or a score of men—other coolies, peddlers and general loafers—all quietly staring at the house. Instinctively the Englishmen drew into a knot about Saris by the room-door. The twinkling eye of Cocks saw whatever there was of drama in the situation. If he had followed the impulse of one of his greatest passions he would have set the gunner to loosing off a piece of ordnance. Instead, he said, "So . . . He has come."

"Aye," said Saris. "It is he. And by the look of his robe and his pantaloons he's run and slid and rolled here." For Adams was shabby and dirty. It was twenty-four hours since his clothes had been washed, and the roads were ankle-deep dust.

He strode to the verandah step and dropped his staff and the canopy of rice-thatch that was his hat. It disclosed a crown that was stubble where it had been shaved, crested by a tightly bound top-knot. On the steps he shed his clogs.

"Captain Adams," said Saris, genially. Stepping forward, he held out his hand. Cocks was only a shade behind him, his hand also held out.

Adams stopped as though again tripped by something. His stare was wide and a little unfocused—for the light in the verandah was subdued after the glare of the road. Moreover, that at which he stared was a crowd of Englishmen, and no such phenomenon had struck his eye for fifteen years.

He looked at the two hands held out to him—but the hand he grasped, from fantastic habit, was his own.

His salutation of his countrymen was a wringing of his own hand and the words he gibbered to them were the bare-toothed clicks and hisses of Japans.

But he saw what a fool he was making of himself, and shrugged himself out of the ceremonious side-ways shuffle of Japonian greeting.

"God's love!" he said. "Look at me!" He took the hand of Saris and shook it, although he would not be presentable to any man but a coolie till he had bathed. "So . . . They have come."

"My own words!" said Cocks the dramatist. "My own very words!" His hand, after the hand of Saris, was warm and spacious, and it pumped the hand of Adams up and down and then directed it to the hands of the four others.

They drifted into the room; Saris took the head of the table and Adams, still consciously unwashed but embarrassed beyond the ability of asking for water, sat on his right, with Cocks opposite to him.

"We did not look to see you, Captain, for at least another fortnight," said he. "Perhaps you were already on the way and met the King's courier?"

"No," said Adams. "My journey took seventeen days. Nigh on three hundred leagues. I came with—pleasurable—haste." His hesitation over the phrase drew their attention to its peculiarity. Glances were exchanged at the lower end of the table. Cocks repeated "pleasurable—haste. Ha!" and Saris attended to his carving of the leg of pork.

It was only in Nagasaki taverns that Adams had spoken to Englishmen in fourteen years, and then only four times—thrice to discover that his listener was drunk beyond any understanding, and once to find a reasonable chance attached to drawing the stoutly packed and sealed letters from his own girdle and thrusting them into the shirt of the other.

He heard for himself that the phrase was somehow foreign. "Aye," he said to correct it, "I hurried."

But even his "hurried" did not strike quite truly on the ears of the listeners. His teeth and his lower lip had done something to the "h" of it, even as Japanese lips and teeth did to all aspirates, so that Saris and Cocks both recorded "King" Ho-in in the journals as "Fo-in," and Hirado as "Firândo."

Saris wanted no clownings over that meal; so it was his own steward who attended them. He poured the General's wine, stared at the chief guest as though wondering how it should be administered to such an one—sitting with the great spars of sword-hilts that fouled the table's edge, with the beard of a normal human being and a head that was half hedge-hog, half Japonian twist and top-knot.

"Wake up, man!" said Saris, and the man filled Adams's beaker.

Saris stood up when all were filled and ceremoniously proposed the King: "James. The Sixth of Scotland and First of England."

They drank the toast and sat again, and Adams suddenly said: "Ah! The flag. It is St. Andrew's cross with the George!"

Saris did not at once see what he was talking about; but Richard Cocks did, for he saw also the drama of it and it warmed him.

"You have much to hear from us, Captain," he said; and before Adams could answer—if, indeed, he had any answer—Saris said, "And much time to hear it in, now that he has come. But we, meanwhile, have much to hear from Mr. Adams."

Adams saw how one man called him Captain while the other now called him Mister.

"Aye," he said, "there will be plenty of time."

"Nevertheless," said Saris, and he spoke amiably again, "we are somewhat impatient to hear you. We have waited several weeks for your coming."

"For my part," said Adams—amiably enough, if not quite as amiably as the young man at the head of the table—"I have waited twice as many years for yours."

He drank his wine while the others laughed with the ease that came to them all from his retort's easy humour; and he pushed aside the trencher from which he had taken but three mouthfuls of pork.

Saris glanced down at the gesture, but Adams immediately disarmed him. He smiled and said: "Pardon my rudeness, Captain. When we were first made prisoners in this country such meat was eaten only in Nagasaki, generally in secret, among the Portingals and Spaniards, and we were elsewhere. My Hollander friend prayed that our guts would shrink since there was not food enough in half-a-dozen meals to fill them. His prayer was answered; for a trencher like yours would now burst either him or me with the colic."

"So there is another of you?" asked Saris.

"Of me?" said Adams. He did not know that his letters home had got no further than the privy councils of the Company.

"You came not alone to this country, breaking adrift from a galley or carrack?" Cocks asked.

Adams drank more wine; and while they ate their pork he told his story.

"Santvoort is left," he concluded; "he is now a junk-master in Nagasaki. He had leave to go home, but went only to Bantam. The Captain went eight years ago; but it is said they gave him a fleet at Bantam for the Moluccas where he died in a fight with Portingals. The Surgeon is still in Yedo, compounding salves from herbs and spices for the scab upon the heads of children. There are others, too; a Swart with a great tavern in the bawdy quarters of the city, and there is one Yoosens—a vile, dirty fellow. These remain."

"And you among them?" It was Cocks who put the question; and he put it thus in innocence and good faith. All he had meant to signify beyond his insatiable curiosity for detail was pride in the survival of Adams. But Adams took it otherwise. Already he knew that if any good was to come of an association between himself and Master Saris there would have to be a declaration of a certain sort. There could be no underestimates of weight or prestige on such a ship as he had visualised. So to the innocent and wide-eyed Cocks he said: "Think you, Sir, that I am a waterside-prowler or a bazaar-dweller?" Whatever more he might have said or done remained unsaid and undone in the languor and comfort that any man found who looked at the geniality and hurtlessness of the adventurous master-grocer from Northampton, Richard Cocks.

"Nay," Adams finished softly. "It is not among such that I have stayed."

"Indeed no, Captain," bubbled Cocks. "We are not so blind, Sir—nor indeed deaf neither—my question was only—well, Sir, why did you stay? Dutch ships have been here two years and more—*three* years—and they would have given you room. They think mightily well of you, the Hollanders."

"And well might they," said Adams proudly. "It was I who got leave for Santvoort and the Captain, and the boat for them from the Lord Ho-in here to go to Bantam and bring their ships. It was I who got for them their Charter from the Emperor, and the friendship of all the land. But I—myself, I had to stay."

"Why?" asked Cocks; for most of the soul of Cocks was "why?"

"Because," said Adams, "because—myself I had not leave to go. To the Emperor I had given a word—I also—I waited for your coming . . ." He broke suddenly away from the preoccupation of thoughts that seemed to have been holding him a little aloof and hesitant. He exclaimed, "And now, Sirs, you have come! And brought the ship."

"Rather let us say," Saris put in very calmly, "the ship has brought us; with our cargo."

Again Adams gave them reason to stare at him. He said, "—— a cargo? . . ."

Whether the man had tramped his wits away on his journey, or whether they had shrunken to the boasted nothingness of his guts, Saris felt that it was time something was done to rouse him.

"We have most assuredly brought a cargo!" he said. Adams noted the pomposity of him. "The Worshipful Company did not fit out the adventure to give us the only pleasure of seeing your country."

If there was a jibe in Saris's "your," Adams accepted it. With Cocks he would quite willingly have shared a country; but he was satisfied to stand apart from Saris.

"Nevertheless," he said, "that pleasure will also be yours. Before undertaking business such as ours it will be necessary for you to pay a visit upon the Emperor at Yedo. You stated in your despatch to me that you have letters and gifts from our King." He had nearly said "your" King from the same vague antagonism that had caused the other to say "your country." He added, "And your Company."

Saris was the business-man waiting for the suitable moment in the processes of nourishment and digestion. He recognised it now, and laid his knife aside and wiped the fingers of his left hand on the cloth. "There will be no difficulty in the way of the business then?" he suggested. "These Hollanders here, and the Spaniards and Portingals in the other city—Nagasaki——"

"Hollanders?" said Adams. "Spaniards? Portingals? What are they in this country but tradesmen and hucksters! Many years ago—as soon as I had word that ships and men of England were as nigh as Java—I saw then that these others might have the paltry trade that the country has to offer, leaving the other matter for us."

"Other matter?" asked Saris. "What other matter is there here than trade?"

Adams stared at him and he stared at Adams; for one was as incomprehensible as the other. One was a guy of a man—fair of complexion but peculiarly sallow as though his very hide were going native; decently bearded and yet heathenly shaved, speaking familiar words with a curious clumsiness, to all appearances famished and yet with no stomach for good victuals; the other was a coxcomb of a lad stuffed with pork . . .

They continued staring.

"For tradesmen, the Captain means," suggested Cocks. "Seeing that it is as tradesmen that we have come——"

"Oh!" Adams shifted his eyes from the meaningless eyes of Saris. "So you are tradesmen?"

"Are we not the East India Company?" said Saris.

Adams rose from the stool that was comfortless to buttocks grown accustomed to the support of heels. Then he sat down again. "Be so good," he said to Saris, "as to give me the letter from your Honourable Company."

"The letter to the Emperor of Japan?" asked Saris.

"No," said Adams. "The letter to me."

At last, thought Saris, they would be able to proceed with the business in hand.

"There is no letter to you," he said. "Whatever the Company may have to say to you, Sir, will be said by me—me, the Captain-General, and Mr. Cocks our Cape Merchant. For our guidance we have the instructions and the remembrance of the Council."

"Very well," said Adams, and he moved straight to the main point. "Who, then, is to command the ship?"

"Command the ship?" Saris could add nothing to the force and the breadth of his staring. "As the ship came commanded by me, with her master; so she will return."

"So—return?" Adams shifted his eyes again from Saris to Cocks in search of some spark of intelligence in an English face.

"But there *is* a word of you also, Captain Adams——" Cocks said hastily; and he turned to Saris whose proper place it was, so long as he was present, to speak the words of their employers.

"Yes," said Saris, "for you there is a cabin and every courtesy of entertainment and comfort. The Company has heard well of you. And for your return with us to your country——"

"Return . . ." mumbled Adams; and his stare now saw nothing of the other pairs of eyes boring into him. "——Return. . . . God's love!—Return . . ."

Cocks spoke softly, and awkwardly: "No doubt you have come to find great comfort among these Japonians."

Adams came back. "Aye," he said slowly. To Saris he said: "The matter of which I wrote to the Company was a finding of the Passage to the North-West. It is from here that it is to be found. What word is there of *that* in your Remembrance and your Instructions?"

Very simply Saris said: "None."

Adams rose. His legs were cramped from sitting upon the stool. One leg tingled and prickled; the foot at its end was numb and useless. He stretched the toes and tapped the sole upon the floor, steadying himself with knuckles rested upon the table. He found, in his mind, some idioms and translated them: "Your hospitality is great to this mean person. His rude presence should now be taken . . ." His foot was sound again. He pressed his hands together against his thigh in salutation and moved towards the door.

"But——" Cocks began as they rose from their stools; and Saris said, "We have made lodging for you here. A bed—are you not tired?"

"Aye," said Adams. "And I have a bed. . . . Thank you."

He took up his hat and his staff from where no flunky had had the grace to remove them.

He went down the steps and away from them, his gorge rising and his stomach heaving against men who stuffed themselves full of pork; whose bodies were verminous and foul, stifled to the point of stinking in clout upon clout of unwashed wool and linen and broadcloth; men who carried the dirt and the dung of roads and gutters into their house and trod them into the furniture of their mats with their great sea-boots and clod-hopping shoon. . . .

Saris noted the group of outsiders hanging about the verandah—gift-bringers of the more decent sort; among them a servant from the Dutch house. At the roadside there was another group—loafers and coolies and wastrels who made way for Adams, and made obeisance to him. His journal says: "Divers weare inquisatyve, I know not for what cause, whether Ange would lodge in our howse. . . . Manye proferring after he came downe to go along in companye with him in love; but he intreated the contrarye, as some weare not well pleased, thinking that he thought them not good enoffe to walke with him."

Those of the rejected escort who had nothing of greater urgency to do, followed him at a comfortable distance and saw him do no strange thing. For years now the Pilot had had a regular lodging at the end of his many journeyings to Hirado; and to this he now repaired. It was the house of one Zanzeburro.

He passed into it, under—according to Saris—his 'cullors, which he had put out at an ould wyndo, being a St. George made of coarse cloath.'

The house, however, had its amenities. Adams accepted

from Zanzeburro an emetic. After the emetic he bathed. After the bath he ate with Zanzeburro and drank warm *saké*; and when anger was dispersed and comfort had come to him again; when he saw that there was still hope—that all he, for his part, had still to do was wait—he drank one more cup of *saké* and retired to his mat and slept upon it for twenty hours.

CHAPTER II

In those twenty hours matters settled themselves in his mind. The first point was the clearest and the hardest: Saris must, somehow, be stomached. More, for he was going back to England; he must be won over and convinced.

That which had appeared to a man trying to digest pork and heavy Spanish wine as a cause for disgust and anger slowly began to have in it some reason.

For eight years now Adams had waited for an answer to his letter putting before the East India Company his secret of the ease with which the Passage could be found. He had demanded a ship, and a ship's full equipment of material and victuals and men. The ship had come—with neither material nor victuals nor men for the expedition; but only the cargo for a paltry trade.

Much, therefore, depended upon his handling of Saris. If the Company had not had his letter and his map it was through Saris that they must get their information. If the Company had had the letter it was equally on the shoulders of Saris to take them a good report—of the project and of Adams himself. So he was sorry already that he had taken the man and his doings and sayings in dudgeon. . . .

And Saris, too, was regretting the way in which that "short dynnor" of his journal had gone, with Adams stumping away before the prying loafers to his mean lodging with the tattered old St. George's cross. Even if the man was, as had been so obvious to those in the English house, a naturalised Japanner, he was the fulcrum of all their future movement.

Says Saris himself: 'I conferred with the Merchants concerning some fitt present to be given Mr. Adams, wheare by he might have some feeling of his brothers. For that no peny, no paternoster in this age. It was resolued on these parsells viz:—4 yeardes black culler No. 169. 4 yeardes Stamet culler No. 206. 3 fine Chauters' (this was his own corruption of the Hindustani 'chaddar,' for shawl). '5 blew Birammes. 10 white

Baftas. 5 Alleiayes. 10 Redd Sellas.' (The choice suggests a closer consideration of the gift's value as travellers' samples from the cargo than of their acceptability to one who could cover fifty-odd miles a day on his bare feet and his bottom.) It cost the Company a debit of forty-seven crowns. Saris's own personal gift he entered as a debit against himself, four times the value of the debit against the Company. Some of the items he bought from the cargo—the 'fine sashes. 4 bookes fine Callico. 1 Symmian Chautter . . .' But for the rest he sacked his own wardrobe. There was '1 white hat and band. 1 very faire Bande and Cuffs. 1 shirt of fine Holland. 1 paire of worsted Stockins. 1 pare silke Garters. 1 pare Spanish leder Slippers. 1 Handkercher of fine Holland. 1 Turkey Carpett.'

The tenancy of Adams in the house of Zanzeburro extended to a godown. In it he kept some stock of the goods consigned to him by Concepcion the Filipino-Spaniard; and to this were now added such junk as the white hat and band, the band and cuffs, the silk garters, the unwearable, toeless worsted stockings and leather slippers.

His own gift was ready and it went back to Saris forthwith, 'a Salvitarye and plaster box for a Chirurgion of Meacko ware, which I kindly accepted (worth heare 6s.).'

Poor Saris! It was at great cost that he must learn how it required no more than six shillings in gift from a Cavalero to balance a hundred and eighteen crowns expended by himself.

But the gestures of good-feeling had their immediate result. Adams dined that night at the House, and thereafter slept there. Saris would have done the normally handsome thing in hospitality and sent for the "dancing-bears" as the English House called them ('for all men of any Ranke have their drink filled to them by Women') but it seemed, at the time, a superfluity. Instead of singing-girls he mustered the *Clove's* orchestra, as he had mustered it for King Ho-in—the viol, the tabor, and the pipe which he had bought on Middleton's flagship in the Persian Gulf. Eaton behaved well in his pots, and all were merry enough to sing. From singing they drifted to talk of business. Adams explained that prospects were satisfactory enough for tradesmen, though not wildly hopeful. The country was a poor one and its wants modest. It was more by buying there than by selling that visitors could hope for big returns on money. Saris, doubtful of the value of any information that would have discouraged him, was delighted to find that when the hard facts of business were being discussed Adams could talk with the best of them. He knew the facts and he had the figures. He knew how the market in calico and broadcloth had declined, mace by mace, over a period of a dozen years. He told them how the prices of small ordnance, of fowling-pieces and murthering-pieces, of powder and shot was steadily rising. Saris was happily amazed by the balanced soundness of him—for Saris did not yet know that for a dozen years he, Adams, had been the central exchange for the bulk of foreign commerce in Japan. Adams did not tell him; nor did he tell him that at the end of those dozen years of commerce he was not a rich man. He only made it clear that these adventurers must not expect too much.

"What of cloves?" Saris asked. "What of nutmegs and other spices?"

Again the picture was neutral-tinted as Adams painted it. The market was good enough, but it was held by the Spaniards and Portuguese; and now also by the Hollanders in the Moluccas. Saris laughed and said that the *Clove* also was in the market with cloves and nutmegs and spices. He walked about the room as Adams squatted at ease on his heels; and he came and stood above him and slapped him on the shoulder. "I've cloves, man—by the bushel! bags of them smuggled aboard under the very noses of the Dutchmen. And if Mr. Cocks and I could do that with one ship—and she not half the size of the smallest Dutchman—if we could do that—say I——" he again laughed and rubbed his hands together and flung into his chair. Then he became calm and serious, and calmly showed how that the bee in his bonnet was a trade not in cloths and stuffs from the Indies and in trumpery from England, but in spices from the Moluccas. He visualised an alliance ahead of the Englishmen at Bantam with the Hollanders at Patani. He saw them, together, thrusting the Portuguese from their precarious hold on the Moluccas, the source of the wealth of cloves and nutmegs. . . . And Adams let him talk.

Spaniards came to the house in the course of the evening,

seamen from Nagasaki who had learned from Zanzeburro that the Pilot had moved his lodging. They importuned him for an audience, and at length he gave them a short one in the corner of the verandah. He apologised to his hosts on his return to the room, saying that the men had waited long for his coming South and had come a long journey to see him. They were good seamen, he added, if the master of the *Clove* should be in need of hands to make good the casualties of the voyage out; they were fugitives from the mutinied crew of a Spanish vessel that had been about to set Northward in discovery of the Passage.

They had killed the Captain and burnt the ship.

Saris said that the *Clove's* surviving crew was ample.

Other visitors came after them—Portuguese with obvious seamen among them and others who were as obviously half-Japanised tradesmen from Nagasaki; and a young Hollander from the Dutch House. This last one said that there was a matter of the most pressing urgency upon which his Captain Brower desired to see Captain Adams. His innuendo made it clear that Adams knew well enough what the matter was, and how pressing; but Adams said handsomely that he would see him in the morning as he could not now leave his friends. Then, said the young man, would not his friends go over with him to the Dutch House? They would all be welcome to a round of wine and entertainment by singing-girls. Saris saw that the young dog had been sent over with a broad hint for an invitation to get Brower across the road, so that he might see for himself how things were going between the newcomers and the one who had preferred the mean house of Zanzeburro to the Mess of his long-lost countrymen.

To this young man Saris made it clear that they were all on the point of retiring, as Captain Adams was still doubtless weary from the prodigious journey he had made to join his countrymen. (In his journal it was with immense satisfaction that he noted how Adams did not leave the house for any summons, but remained their uninterrupted guest throughout the evening. It did not strike him that for thirteen years the life of Adams had been such—the peace, if peace it ever was, at the centre of forces of contentions big or little. It was

Cocks who at some time noted: 'frenship there is in diuers quarters for Mr. Addames, even padrés, their style for pristes and fryres heare, seeking him in affaires, whome notwithstanding had served him so ill in other times as I have heard per his own accompt and of others likewaies'.)

CHAPTER III

It was no easy matter to maintain a prolonged harmony with Saris. Adams tried to explain to him that the one obvious place in all Japan for the English settlement was in the East of it, in the Bay of Yedo—close to his own small Estate and close to the Court of their friend the Shogun. Saris only looked at the map, to see again that Hirado was the natural base for operations in the Moluccas which were to him the source of all wealth in those seas. The map told him also that at Yedo they would be remote from the enemies in Nagasaki—the Portuguese and Spaniards—and too remote from the peculiar friends in the Dutch house ruled by the smooth-tongued Brower. As for friendship, what greater friendship could they find anywhere in the land than the friendship of rollicking old Ho-in?

Cocks, too, was enthusiastic for Hirado as his headquarters, and dead against any movement towards the remote East; for already there was a dream in the mind of Cocks, of the thing he should achieve for the Worshipful Company when once Saris had departed with the *Clove*, and his own actions should be free to follow the sweep of his imagination. The dream of Cocks, like the Moluccan dream of Saris, was vitalised by the merest glance at the map which Adams had spread on the table before them. Andace the Chinaman had been at Cocks, for Andace spoke some Dutch; and so the dream of Cocks was represented by the three words that are the leitmotif of ambition that runs through the two volumes of his Diary— *'Trade into China.'*

Neither Saris nor Cocks, however, argued their points with Adams. Saris merely told him that the matter was already settled: the house had been firmly leased from Andace "the Captain Chinesa"; that private and personal arrangements (amounting to contracts which neither he nor they could now deny) had been made between the English and Ho-in, and that these were an alliance against the two enemies at Nagasaki and the neighbour in the Dutch house across the road. For old King Cole, Ho-in, had told them how Spaniards and Portingals and Hollanders were one in deranging his stomach, while the yearning of his whole life, ever since the Pilot had told him it should one day be his, had been for the friendship of Englishmen.

Adams also did not argue. He could afford to be silent, and in his beard to smile. He had means in his sleeve for settling such a detail as this one: Ieyasu would decide whether it was at Hirado or at Yedo that the English factory should be planted, since Ieyasu could say, in a single word, that it must be Yedo or nowhere.

Andace the Chinaman went on with his talk to Cocks. He told of the brothers he had in China, in addition to the prosperous merchant, Whow, in Nagasaki. They all stood well among the merchants of Tonkin, and well at Court. Carefully selected presents delivered to the Nagasaki brother would find their way to those that mattered at Court; and so China, forbidden to merchants of Japan and all other countries of the world, would be opened to Cocks and a selected few Englishmen.

The presents that should in due course come to himself (on their way to the Emperor of China) were only a secondary consideration in the thoughtful mind of Andace. He and his partner, or brother, Whow at Nagasaki were, in fact, the chief shippers for the trade in silk and carved ivory from China to Japan. The laws of both countries were a muddle of restrictions and prohibitions which only philosophers could understand, and with which only the more adventurous among financiers and seamen could cope. Whatever the philosophers might have made of the tangle, the financiers and sailors achieved the fact that cargoes left China in certain junks and arrived at Hirado and Nagasaki in the junks, generally, of Andace and Whow. But there were exceptions to the general rule—and it was the exceptions that provided the food for Andace's thought. Junks and their crews were often lost at sea, and it was on Dutch vessels that their cargoes came to Japan. It was as a neighbour to the Dutchmen that Andace wanted vigilant Englishmen to ply freely in the proper monsoons between Hirado and Bantam.

"King" Ho-in likewise was shocked at the idea of the new men's sailing away to Yedo, taking with them the new ship whose cargo proper was still unexplored, and whatever ships might follow her. The Dutch, so far as the old Daimio was concerned, were explored and exhausted; Ho-in, moreover, liked for their own intrinsic value men who moved about the world carrying with them good mastiffs and falcons and fowling-pieces; men who would set a crew to helping with the netting-in of the waterway so as to enjoy with him a day's fishing with his renowned and beloved cormorants. . . . He saw with Andace how good it was to defeat the Yedo scheme of Adams, for Adams himself had been a fine friend to them in Yedo while he had been unbothered there by the nearness of fellow-countrymen.

Afternoons were spent by Adams in the house of the Chinaman over rolled documents and flat documents and documents bound into books. The Scribe managed the books and writing-brush and ink-block. Adams held the ivory stick to push the coloured beads of the calculating abacus—for the marvel of this device had never ceased to please him since old Kuru the boat-builder had shown him how the shifting of half-a-dozen beads would work out a sum whose answer was the quantity of timber required for a job, and the shifting of another two would tell its cost. . . .

After these sessions Andace would refresh him with *saké* or tea and tobacco, and he would talk—disinterestedly and quietly and as a detached philosopher—of the Yedo scheme. The chief point he made was that Adams himself—far-sighted, law-abiding, honourable and completely admirable man that he was—had lived for more than a dozen years in great harmony and peace and content with his illustrious and charming household at Hemimura, so near to the Shogun's court and among the noblest of the land. But they knew what sailors were. . . . Was it wise or proper that Adams should saddle himself with the responsibility of neighbours and countrymen who might, from ignorance and sheer lightness of heart, bring grievous trouble where even the smallest trouble was conspicuous by its contrast to the general decorum? Were it not better for these others to remain the guests of good friend

Ho-in, who interpreted laws with unique liberality and assessed men by their motives rather than by the accident of their deeds? . . .

Adams argued not a single word, but went quietly about his affairs. The only men who waited upon him without records of merchandise and money, who conferred without his scribe or his abacus, were the Spaniards from the burnt ship whereon the Captain had died. Conferences with them were brief; for as yet he could tell them nothing. His days were filled by Andace, by Brower, by Portuguese and by the now somewhat portly Concepcion, who had suddenly arrived from Nagasaki.

On his second morning at the English House, Adams had told Saris that he would go, forthwith, to look into the matter of the rascals Evens and Muffet at Nagasaki. That same day Concepcion had arrived from there with business that could be done at Hirado (with a saving of two days of travelling); and Adams at once said that the matter of Evens and Muffet, who had mutinied and deserted to Nagasaki, could wait. Saris was of opinion (and made no long passage of saying so) that the matter could not wait. Adams retorted that it was, as a fact, waiting already; for he had sent word to Nagasaki that the men must be kept there. Word?—exclaimed Saris—had not word been sent before, again and again?—by him, the Captain-General of the English, and by Ho-in the King?

Adams smiled. The matter was in hand; it could wait; he had other matters to deal with besides the catching of runaways, after a journey of three hundred leagues.

He walked off with Concepcion to the house of Andace, and from the house of Andace to the Dutch house. And the Englishmen wondered if the Japan heart of him had turned Hollander or Chinese, Filipino, Portingal or Spaniard?—or was, indeed, a bastard hybrid, begotten out of Japan by the lot of them. They could make nothing of it; as they could make but little of the food he most genially pressed upon them, prepared by his own cook working beside the Norfolk youth in the kitchen who had at last found how to spread charcoal satisfactorily beneath a gridiron and gobbets of beef.

He served them well, however, in the matter of Wickham;

for neither Saris nor Cocks had been able to get anything out of this Wickham but oaths and rancour against, Damian, the Spaniard, as he sulked and skulked aboard the *Clove* in his "natural proud humour." He stuck to his contention that no man had a right to forbid him the use of his sword; but only, with a better one, to dispute it. His parole was all they wanted from him; but all they could get was his undertaking to run the Spaniard through so soon as he could get him near enough.

Adams went aboard for an hour, and when he returned to the house Wickham was with him, his empty hand instead of his weapon addressed to the Spaniard.

They asked him what Adams had done to him, and young Edmund Sayers kept tormenting him with the question till it suddenly looked as though the cure had been achieved only specifically as to the use of steel, but that his fist was still diseased with the old "proud humour."

Young Sayers moved from the side of Wickham to the side of Adams; but Adams did nothing to satisfy the boy's curiosity. "You will see it, lad, for yourself," he said, smiling. "Aye—it will come to you without any telling, if you stay long in this country; for you have come young enough."

"What is it that I shall see?" He was eager and earnest; as curious about this mystery of pacification as he had been about the price of women.

"All of it," said Adams, and made a sweep with his arm; "and it is more than the way of the law here, which is swift and straight enough in the matter of blood-letting and brawling. It is more than the law that you will see."

"And you, Sir," Sayers smiled; "you who carry *two* swords can upbraid the villainy of blood-letting to men who carry but one, or none at all!"

"This," said Adams, and he tapped the hilt of his long-sword, "is for the killing of an enemy. This"—and he tapped his dirk, "is for the killing of myself. For no man may profit himself by the killing of another. That is the law."

"And is that all I have to learn in this country?" the young man asked.

"Not all," said Adams, "you will learn more. You will learn that death is no great odds; whether the death be yours or your enemy's—or your neighbour's grandmother's brother's, whom you have never seen—it is no great business. You will learn that; and you will not wish greatly to fight with men; and danger will not heat you greatly or chill you overmuch. You will become neither hero nor coward, but——" he would have left the thought there with a shrug and gone to bed—to the real bed that he now occupied, with a pallet of straw. But Sayers pressed him. "What can a man be," said he, "who is neither hero nor coward?"

"A Samurai." said Adams.

Only young Sayers heard him, or saw the stolid swagger with which Adams spoke. And thereafter, even during the period of exasperation when others were disputing the Pilot's title, to young Sayers Adams was "Captain."

CHAPTER IV

SARIS patiently kept his journal and impatiently waited for the return of the courier whom Ho-in had sent to Yedo. It was possible that he might bring back the Shogun's licence to unlade the cargo.

Adams meanwhile was busy from morning till night.

The courier returned. The despatches from the Shogun were to the same effect: he welcomed the Englishmen and their General to his poor country and thanked them for their courtesy. He awaited their personal visit in the company of their esteemed countryman, the Pilot.

Ho-in announced forthwith, with a gift of fish and wine, that galleys were ready manned; palankeen-bearers, horses and a bodyguard were standing-to for the immediate start of Saris. Cocks bustled about Adams, and Saris fell upon him with the demand that they start on the morrow.

"To-morrow," said Adams, "I go to Nagasaki."

"Hell's eternity!" said the General. "Your friends can hold them there for us—or let them go. What are two rascals that they should keep us now?"

"Rascals?" asked Adams.

"Aye, rascals." Saris always came a little near to shouting now if Adams appeared to require explanation of anything. "Evens the gunner, and Muffet his mate. The runaways from the crew. But they can wait."

"They need not," said Adams. "To-morrow I shall find them, or the next day—for I have other business that takes me to Nagasaki."

"God's life, man!" protested Saris. "Is yours the only business in Japan?"

Adams said quietly: "It is the only business I have had since coming here. Mine and the business of his Majesty."

"For the business of his Majesty of England, then, you see no urgency?" It was a grand sneer; but the result of it was a shrug of Adams's shoulders.

283

"Where," he asked lazily, "was the urgency in your taking eight years to get here?" This distortion of fact had fixed itself inflexibly in his mind. It was eight years since he had thrust a letter into the shirt of a sailor. Saris was the paltry answer to it, and he had taken eight years in coming. . . . "When men are moved by urgency, Sir, they travel fast and straight." There was a comfort in bragging to Saris. "I myself moved some twenty leagues a day for seventeen days because of—urgency."

"I would have a straight answer from you, Mr. Adams," was the challenge of Saris to this. "On what day do I leave for the Court?"

"You, Sir," said Adams, "leave for the Court on whatever day you please. King Ho-in has already given you skiffs and bearers and horses and pikemen to run before you on the road. You have your presents for his Majesty and you have your linguist. For my part I have small need of these, and I shall start my journey light as I came, my dunnage in a wallet, my cook and my scribe for company—when my business is done. To-morrow I go to Nagasaki."

"Your business!" snorted Saris. "May I take it that your business will leave you leisure enough for the business of your countrymen in Nagasaki? Will you bring back the rascals Evens and Muffet?"

"If they have not been justly cut or crucified," said Adams, "I shall bring them."

The three days of waiting were difficult and irritating ones for Saris. When the skiff of Adams was sighted in the harbour by some loafers and reported to the house, he called to Cocks and they walked together to the jetty. They heard the chanting of the oarsmen and saw the flutter of the Pilot's rag of a St. George's cross. Adams himself had the steering-oar at the stern. On the thwart in front of him were two huddled figures, bearded and unkempt, but robed in mean kimonos. The sight of them with Adams lording it at the tiller was enough to bring a mumble of oaths to the throat of Saris.

"He has a weight, you see, General," said Cocks with his amiable tactlessness. "Neither your demand nor the letter of

the old King here could get the King of Langasaque to surrender the rascals."

"If he will lend me his skiff," said Saris, "I will take them
aboard to the master. A whipping for them now is the best
service we can do you, if we are to leave them with you and
start our journey in the morning."

"Will he start, think you?" asked Cocks.

"God knows," said Saris. "It depends only on his humour
now, since all here say that their business with him is done."
He looked to his pistols as the boat approached. "If those
villains are armed——"

"Armed, Sir?" said Cocks; "under those robes they are
stripped to the hams. The doxies of Langasaque, as ordinary,
have seen to the fleecing of them. Cold backs for a flogging,
General."

"Perhaps our Captain Adams will have worked his magic on
them," sneered Saris; "as he did on Wickham. The Master's
magic may help his spell."

The skiff was alongside and Adams stepped ashore. Evens
and Muffet stood up and treated their General to a ragged
salute.

"By your leave, Mr. Adams," said Saris, moving towards the
boat, "I will take those men aboard into custody."

"You need not put them in custody," said Adams. "They
cannot by any means go back to Nagasaki."

"Oh?" said Saris, and he looked at Cocks; "more magic?"

"Not magic," said Adams. "An order of the King that no
man or woman may harbour them; and I have told them what
would happen to any breaker of that law."

"Nevertheless," said Saris, "I will put them aboard." He
stepped into the boat.

Adams spoke to an oarsman, and the man took the flag from
the little staff in the bows and handed it to his master. Adams
folded it up and stuck it in his girdle. He spoke again and they
shoved off from the jetty and rowed Saris with his deserters to
the *Clove*.

Cocks in his red-heeled, buckled shoes, his cloak and his
plumed hat—stumpy and ready to be breathless after the first
dozen paces—made no attempt to keep step with Adams as

they walked back from the jetty to the house; for Adams in his sandals appeared to slide through the dust as though propelled by no stepping of his feet but by the action of the staff he carried. Loungers and loafers in their roadside knots saluted him, and he turned suddenly to Cocks and said: "What is amiss?"

"Amiss?" said Cocks. "Nothing is amiss, Sir. There has been much to-do with the King over this journey, and the General has been much put about. But there is nought amiss. If a man took note of every crowd that gathers in this country he would think—but pardon me, Sir, for speaking so to you who are, if I may so put it, a master of this country and its ways. Briefly, Sir, nothing is amiss that I know of."

"Nevertheless," said Adams, "all is not well. I can see much in the faces of loiterers—which you, too, will soon be able to see . . ."

They entered the house. The sandals detached themselves from Adams's feet and remained on the verandah while Cocks stumped in in his shoes. Adams went through the living-room and corridor to the yard, to find that there was no fire in the cylinder of the great bath-tub. The water was cold.

He scowled and clapped his hands and called to his cook.

There was no answer.

He went to the kitchen and said to the Norfolk man who was filleting and cutting up a fish, "Where is my boy?"

"Gone, Sir," said the man. "Gone like a streak of lightning when the General cuffed his ears yesterday; and not a sign of him since."

"How came the General to cuff his ears?" asked Adams, and it would have taken sharper wits than those of a cook from Norfolk to sense anything but normal—if not, indeed, idle—curiosity in the words of Adams.

"Two bottles of wine were gone," said the man. "The boy and I knew where they had been put, with three others. I never took them. So the General cuffed him."

Adams went back to the living-room and stood silent for a few minutes. Cocks had discarded his cloak and was standing against the door-post, looking thoughtfully into the road.

"Mr. Cocks," said Adams, "how came it that it was the General who banged my cook, and not you whose business it is to manage these matters in the house?"

Without turning, Cocks said, "The General has busied himself with many matters that are not his affair in these last days of waiting." Then he moved to look at Adams, and smiled. "But he banged him soundly enough; you could not yourself have done it better—for he was in a great fume. Will you start your journey to-morrow?"

Cocks was disturbed by the manner of the answer. It was not the word itself that disturbed him, for "Maybe" was all that Adams said. It was the vastness of some burden that weighed upon him so that his shoulders were bowed in his Japonian robe, his brow twisted into a frown and his eyes scowling into the twilight beyond Cocks—where a group loitered in the roadway, looking first at the house and then towards the jetty and then again at the house, and chatting.

"Maybe."

"You have found something amiss, then?" asked Cocks.

"Aye," said Adams. "But you can do us a service in the righting of it. The General will soon be back. The others are all out; I beg you to keep them from the house; and to go yourself also, taking even your cook while I talk to the General. What I have to say to him may muddle him with anger if others also hear it."

"Great God!" Cocks exclaimed, "you would quarrel with him now!" He danced up to Adams, amazed and indignant and incredulous.

Adams quietly said: "No. There will be no quarrel. We do not quarrel here, such as I." Some invisible movement of him made it clear to Cocks that "such as I" meant a Cavalero with swords at his belly; and Cocks, for all his bewilderment and the bother that tormented him at the way things were going between the interesting Adams and the nagging Saris, felt that some sort of a joke could be found in that pompous claim coming from a girdle of weapons more sinister and villainous and lovely than he had ever before seen. He did not make the joke, for none but a buffoon could have gone on smiling while Adams stood there, looking sightlessly before him, travel-stained and shaggy, morose with a thought that bowed his shoulders.

Cocks tried to unbend him. He said:

"Would you not wash and refresh yourself while the General comes?"

"Thank you," said Adams, but he stayed still; "no. I can neither wash nor refresh myself till the business with your General is done."

"But—dinner," said Cocks; "if I take the cook away——"

"There will be no dinner either," said Adams, "—till it is done. Go if you would eat, you and the others, to the Hollanders. Victuals are never wanting there. And go soon, I beg you; the General is coming." He had read this fact from some ripple of movement in the loiterers outside.

The uneasiness of Cocks was mollified by the knowledge that any quarrel with Saris was made less bitter when the quarreler was the only witness of the General's demeanour. He took his cloak: "If any of the others should come in," he said, "beg him to join me at the Dutch house." He hurried to the kitchen and Adams heard him going, with the cook, into the yard, as Saris came up the steps.

CHAPTER V

HE came in and flung his cloak and hat to the bench. "No table!" he snorted, for the table was bare of all the furniture of dinner. "And no light! . . ."

"There is no need of light," Adams said out of the gloom. "If you will sit down, Sir—or stand if you prefer it—there is much I have to say to you. To explain——"

Saris liked the tone of that. He sat down. "To explain?—will you not sit?"

"No," said Adams.

Of that Saris did not like the sound. "It will soon be time for dinner," he said.

"Maybe," said Adams. He moved a step nearer to Saris and said: "Listen. And have no anger. Anger can bring nought but ruin to us both. Have a care; and be quiet. Outside, yonder, there is a group of idlers with ears acock for the sound of blood from a severed throat like the bursting of wine from a barrel with the plug torn out. I myself have seen and heard the like. Behind the group is a whole country that can see nothing but your death at my hands for what you have done."

Such words as these could produce but one result in a man of Saris's time and temper. His hand jumped from his belt to his rapier; but in Adams the result produced by this movement was a sneering chuckle that became the sounds, "Fool—keep still."

He himself did not move, and Saris shifted his hand back to rest on the thumb stuck into his belt.

"And, pray," he said, "what is it that I have done?"

"As I thought," said Adams; "you do not even know. . . . Yesterday, in a fume of anger, you struck me in the face—me, who am a nobleman of Japan."

"God's body and blood!" said Saris, "the man is mad! Or are you drunk? . . ." He would have got up and shouted for a light and for dinner and told Adams to go to the devil, or sleep himself sane or sober—the fool who talked of having been struck in the face when he had but returned from Nagasaki within the hour. But Adams said: "Listen; I said, no anger—for I myself have none. In striking a man of mine you struck exactly me—a nobleman."

An oath was all that Saris had for dealing with such nonsense.

"You must learn that," said Adams with the utmost patience. "The country's peace is built upon it, and its builder is a finer man than you have ever seen. We start to-morrow on our way to see him, if you live. No—do not toy again with that yard of metal at your belt." He slowly drew out a paper napkin from his girdle and crumpled it lightly in his hand. "Your blade," he said, "would scarcely sever this if it were placed on a butcher's-block for you to cut at." He sauntered away to the far corner of the room where there was no chance of being observed from outside. Saris saw him toss the light ball of paper into the air. He heard a cleaving of the air, sharper and briefer than the whine of a musket-ball, fainter than the snapping of a lute-string. He saw a flash of steel.

Adams, his sword once more in its scabbard, was slowly shifting the paper across the floor towards him with his unshod foot. Instead of one twist of paper there were three smaller ones.

"It was but a poor performance," he said. "I missed the third cut. My son of twelve can do as well with his grandfather's blade, and you will see better tricks than that from a dozen good-for-nothing, idle swashbucklers at any country fair. It was not to flaunt my own mean skill that I performed the trick, but to show you that my talk is not of fighting; but of execution."

Saris said calmly: "You do not frighten me." And it was the truth. Men did not attain maturity and remain in professions like his if they were frightened by, approximately, anything. "The rascal you left in the kitchen filched some wine; and I cuffed his ears. If you require me to fight—very well, I fight. But you would have cuffed him yourself."

"But man! Can you not see the difference?" Adams exclaimed. "He is mine. I may cuff him. I may kill him—and a hundred others like him—greater or lesser—and their families too."

It was fantastic. Saris was sure that some single word, some one particular turn of thought was all that was necessary to set it all straight—if he could but find it. It was like trying to discover the trick that would pacify a child—a child that had to be pacified to make life possible for adults. "Is it not possible," he suggested, "that such a Lord as yourself should have given sanction to me to cuff your servant?"

"No," said Adams. "It is not. A Lord's duty to his underlings is as binding as his duty to his Lord."

"Well," said Saris, and it was sheer diplomacy that prompted him, "if I must die I must die." Out of the bewilderment when he looked at Adams, dim in the twilight, still and morose and weary, any anger that threatened to rise subsided again when he looked away from Adams at the absurdity of the business. It was impossible as yet to take it seriously.

They were silent, since there was nothing more to say; Saris staring through the dusk at Adams and Adams staring at nothing; till Adams himself in his weird turn-out of beard and top-knot, his robe and sash and sword-hilts and his passionless silence began to bring some impulse of pity to the heart of Saris.

"Come, Mr. Adams," he said, and he remembered suddenly the miracle of the suddenly peaceful Wickham, "I am ignorant of this country's laws. What can I do, other than die, to satisfy them?"

"The only other thing you could do," said Adams, "I fear you cannot do, because of your stiff neck. It is to seek out the boy and make amends to him, and obtain his forgiveness."

"His forgiveness indeed!" Saris was on his feet now. "Have I no honour, that I should go creeping for the forgiveness of a thieving scullion—forgiveness for catching the rascal at his thieving? Damnation take him—and you, with your sword-tricks! I'll fight, man—here and now, or where and when you will."

"That you will not," said Adams quietly. "I am making no fight of it. When I kill you, if kill you I must, I shall do it in the same way whether you have drawn that thing and pointed its bungling end at me, or whether you have not. It is no odds. But you should consider. . . . You have done a wrong——"

"I have done *no* wrong."

"If you have done no wrong, the righting of it will also be nothing."

"Nothing!" snorted Saris. "Nothing it may be, but my gorge will not take it. I will fight."

"Not fight," said Adams. "You will die."

Suddenly laughter came from Saris. "Did I say I know *nothing* of these laws? I do know that you can kill neither me nor anyone without straightway cutting out your own guts if you are a Cavalero, or dropping your head in the Justice's bucket if you are not."

"I did not say otherwise," said Adams. "If it were otherwise I could have killed you without talk, and so put an end upon the matter. But no . . ." Fantastically it was with himself only that the fellow was arguing in the darkness, while the chatter of the loiterers outside came stealthily nearer, so that whispering voices were mingled with the taut flapping of the house's paper sides. "No," said Adams. "It would serve nothing. Your Company's venture would be lost utterly. My friend the Mighty One would have nothing of men whose countryman and commander had caused the death of me, his friend. If the others got away with their lives and the ship it would be by luck alone. And as for me—I——" he hesitated in his words because of the weight of sadness that was upon him. "No other man—no Englishman—would find the Passage. . . . No!" Of a sudden he spoke loudly and sharply. "Saris—*General* Saris—or John Saris, or Jack Saris—whichever you will—man, you must make amends to that boy. You *must*, I say. It is the only way. You must. You shall . . ."

His wits, perhaps, were leaving him. But Saris stood firm.

"That," said he, "I will not." The movement of his hand to a grip upon his rapier was unseen, for the room was now dark. "I will fight."

"Fight. . . . Fight. . . . Fight," grumbled Adams. "You and your Master Wickham. Fight . . . ruin . . . destroy— everything. God damn you . . ." He said it slowly and gloomily, his last words before action.

Saris was no fool; nor was he sluggard in the drawing of a rapier for whatever any rapier might be worth against a katana, which was not one weapon but a dozen in the hand of any man who knew it. He was aware that he had one chance, and one only against a hundred, as his grip tightened and his feet moved stealthily to a position whence he could readily lunge. But he neither drew nor lunged, but sat back aghast at the next movement of Adams.

For Adams tossed back his head which was dark against the pale wall of the room, flinging his beard up from his chest, and roared with sudden laughter. "God save us!" he said at last, when Saris was sure beyond doubt that his wits had utterly gone. "God save us!"

The strained tensity had gone from him and he ambled loosely about the room, chuckling. "Saris," he said; "Captain or General, John—or Jack—whichever suits your fancy. . . . This country's very blood has entered my veins as it runs in the veins of my son, that I should talk so glib of death, and stare it in the face when there is no need of it. Here, man!—steady, I am not drawing my weapons; I am handing them to you. Look! I surrender."

Saris watched dimly, as he laid upon the table before him the sword and dirk that had seemed to be a growth upon his person.

The voice of Adams was gentle as he spoke. "You need make no amends to me, the nobleman whom you struck in the face yesterday. I am no longer nobleman or soldier. I have given you my swords. I go now, to my lodging in the house of Zanzeburro, where I fly my flag. It is not with you that I go to the Court of the Emperor. I go alone, having forfeited all that he gave me. Among the words I speak to him there will be no word at all of you and your ship and your Honourable Company; for my speech with him must be all concerning myself, and the giving up of my swords. Your honour has chosen."

He was at the door, pausing with his hands resting in his sleeves upon his swordless girdle.

It required less than a minute for Saris to see exactly where they now stood. He could at least have drawn his rapier and made some gesture with it against the imbecile's katana; but against the lumpishness of a rock he could do nothing.

He said: "What are these amends that I must make to that

rascal cook-boy? Take your swords. Go tell him what you will; and then come back. Dinner will be ready."

"Nay," said Adams. "I am no messenger. Amends are only made by the party making them. If you would make them—to give me back my honour and my swords, and your hospitality and your company to-morrow as we journey to the Emperor—to have my introduction and my support for the trading of your company, 'tis you alone who must make them."

"What in God's name is there that I can say?"

"What you would say to any man you have wronged," said Adams. "But before that, there is a formality of the country by which you must say first that I, the principal, have forgiven you already and that I, with you, seek the forgiveness of the boy."

"Oh, so you speak with me?" Saris was a little relieved. "Will you send for the boy that we may get it done?"

"No," said Adams. "That cannot be. You must seek him out. You will find him at my lodging where he will have gone to bide my coming, and my commands. Go and speak as I have told you, crave him to return with you—walking beside you and not behind you—in token that he has forgiven both you and me. Your excuse—of all excuses the most valid in this country—is that you were in liquor."

"I am to say all that—since you will not come with me—to my linguist, the Malay?"

"No," said Adams. "More suitable than the Malay is the boatman you have had working about here, whom your men call John Japan. I will tell those outside to call him—and I'll lay he is within earshot."

It was as Adams said. Within a minute John Japan was in the room. He hustled out again, at the command of Adams, to the kitchen. Saris could already accept the fact that a man who had appeared to work only outside the house and in the godown could find and light a lantern in the kitchen without any difficulty.

"Here, man——" he said uneasily, "your swords, before the light comes. We do not want this foolery——" he looked uneasily out of the door.

"Ah, but we do," said Adams. "They must have it, in the

light, for all to see. You will hand me my swords, and I will
hand you your hat and set your cloak upon you. We will then
shake hands and I will command John Japan to go with you
and translate your words faithfully, for the calling of interpreter is an honourable one in this country. He will understand
anything but English, for he has sailed on Dutchmen, Spaniards
and Portingals."

In the light from the lantern they gave their shadow-show
on the wall to those who had so patiently waited. In the
doorway they shook hands.

"You have done well, Saris," Adams said, bringing a vitality
to the puppets who had made the shadows.

Saris grunted. "You make a joke of all life in this country,"
he said.

"A joke?" said Adams, and he leaned against the door-post,
his beard and his chin sunk into his fist. "A joke?—Maybe.
. . . But I am not the maker of it."

CHAPTER VI

It was not Adams who caused the two days' delay in the party's start for the Court, for he was now free of all old obligations, to devote himself completely to the newest one.

Proud Wickham and young Edmund Sayers were his own nominees among the ten Englishmen besides Saris who were to form the party. As a salesman of twelve years' standing he knew the value of samples, so it was he who also chose the weapons that the ten should carry—good pistols and the best of the flint-lock 'murthering-pieces' that the *Clove's* cargo would yield. It was he also who chose and valued and listed the gifts that were to fill two great chests.

It was Ho-in who made the delay, for it was he who provided the skiffs and pinnaces to carry them as far as Osaka, and to Ho-in—when the objective was not an immediate battle or a fishing-party with cormorants—postponement was the breath of life. He inspected boats and men and told his guests that never before had he seen such a sorry lot of either. Such fussiness, had it been not royal, would have been beyond the stomach of Saris; for Ho-in took the whole of the second day to choose the one officer and the three men of his Samurai who should be second to none of the hundreds or thousands they might encounter on the eight-score leagues of Royal Road they were to travel. From a host of candidates he chose the pikeman to walk before the litter or the horse of Saris. Himself he chose the dozen women who were to go on the skiffs and pinnaces, the section of the journey devoid of taverns. Himself he tasted the wine.

The pinnace with Saris and Adams aboard flew the St. George and St. Andrew, with the faded work of Bikuni's needle that Adams carried in his girdle or hoisted above his settled presence anywhere.

Brower ordered a salute from the Hollanders' jetty as the oars of the flotilla dipped. It was taken up by the three

Dutch ships; and Cocks, aboard the *Clove*, 'shot affe peece for peece with them,' giving a salvo of his own in final 'complemento.'

It was perhaps the greatest of all days for Cocks in all his eleven years in Japan—friendship everywhere, hopes undimmed, and the ship under him bouncing to the roar of complimentary ordnance.

Saris, too, was in great humour. Adams had agreed to the inclusion of cloves and nutmegs and pepper in the gift-chests, and this showed either that Adams agreed that good would surely come of it, or else that he was subjecting his own opinion to the opinion of Saris.

The cook-boy, in the large manner of his forgiveness, had made of the idiotic and grotesque farce an affair of royal magnificence. His speech in the house of Zanzeburro, translated by John Japan into Malay-Portuguese-Spanish, had made Saris feel, as Adams himself had just failed to make him feel, that they had verged on mysteries as vast and deep and inscrutable as life itself. . . . And then he had sprung suddenly to smiling nimble life again, and to agile and attentive service, making of service a beneficence and a delight.

Adams smiled and chatted as he squatted on his heels and smoked his tobacco on the pinnace's afterdeck beside Saris; and the heart of Saris was softened by some pathos he saw in him: the best of showmen—if he could be steered clear of the humours that were apt to come upon him—for the strange country they were about to enter. A sound business-man. A good seaman. A good swordsman, it seemed, with that fantastic blade and his trick of slicing crumpled napkins as they fell through a yard of space—sound and good all round, in a sense—yet. . . . Peculiar. That was it; peculiar. The shaved head and prehensile great toes were housings of a thinking-apparatus that was quaint, and of an apparatus for thrusting foot-gear along paths that were tortuous and unbeaten. The easy way he sank his haunches to his heels and rose up again like a spring uncoiled were the movements of a mastiff. . . . As a show-piece, a tamed lion, Saris had never seen the like of him. He could imagine the wonder of Sir John Smyth and the Directors of the Worshipful Company when Adams, at the request of Saris, did his trick with the sabre and the ball of paper. He could see himself conducting the lost Pilot to the court of King James himself—even as the lost Pilot, on his haunches, conducted him now to the court of the heathen Ieyasu. Adams in England, Saris could visualise perfectly and very happily. Adams left in Japan as the representative and champion of sane Englishmen he could not visualise at all. The man was more than peculiar, sucking his lungs full of smoke from a tobacco that would have strangled a Swart; he was impossible. Saris would most verily have believed—if the thing had not just been incredible—that he would have sliced his throat or the throat of any man for punching the head of a cook-boy, if he had not been diverted from it by an inspiration of fantastic blackmail.

Business, Saris very well knew, was done best by business men; and not by freaks.

"Adams," he said, for they were on terms now of easy informality. "It will be a great day for you when you set your face for home again."

"Aye," said Adams; for it was by way of the North and West that he proposed to set it.

"It is now more than thirteen years that you have been among these people," Saris went on pleasantly. "Fifteen since you left home."

"Aye," said Adams. "Fifteen years, and a half—nearly."

"By middle-November," Saris went on, "our mission should be done, and we returned to the *Clove*."

"Aye," said Adams. "Easily. There should be no delays."

"The monsoon will be blowing for us by then."

"Aye," said Adams, "it will."

His talk upon other matters had run easily enough; and Saris wondered what had so suddenly come to him, letting only sparse words out as though through a sieve.

"When you have settled our countrymen here in friendship with the Emperor, your work will be done." With these words there was a gesture from Saris, as though rousing Adams to behold some fine thing that was set before him. "It is with a light heart that you will become the *Clove's* guest and passenger."

"That," said Adams, "I will not."

"You will not?" exclaimed Saris.

"Rather," said Adams slowly, "I cannot. I have not leave to go. I am held here. By the Emperor Ieyasu."

"But you have said yourself that Ieyasu is no longer Emperor," Saris retorted.

Adams looked up at him, and for a few moments stared at him and then said, "It were better for you not to meddle in such matters, Saris." He repented, perhaps, of the shortness of his words; for he went on, "It takes more years than you have been here weeks to understand how Ieyasu may be only Regent, and yet Emperor at the same time."

There he went again, thought Saris—more Japonian in his thought than English. The opportunity was a good one for getting to the root of this matter. "If leave *were* to be given you," he said, "would you not go?"

"Leave," said Adams, "will not be given."

"But," said Saris, "if it *is* given?"

"If the Emperor Hidetada should give leave," said Adams, "and if his father Ieyasu should deny it, it is Ieyasu that I must obey, for it is he who is my Lord. But enough of this, Saris. Yonder in the Straits you will presently see a great dockyard I caused to be made for the Emperor; and a junk of eight-hundred tons burthen, sheathed in iron, for the carrying of soldiers. There are women divers hard by it, who dive for fish and catch many that are missed by line and net——" but Saris had no ears for showman's patter now. He had suspected before that it was not only the command of Emperors that held this man to his beloved island of Japan.

He tried him again on another day when the hills of Shikoku were sinking into the sea again, astern of the flotilla. "This estate of yours, Adams," he said, "and your possessions here— they would fetch a good sum if you were to go home?"

"There is but little money to be had," said Adams, "for estates and possessions in this country." Then he made a slip. "And it is not for estates and possessions that I would stay here awhile."

Saris was now satisfied; and so he pursued the matter no further. The lying of Adams would soon be at an end when he himself, through his own interpreter, should have obtained permission for the Pilot to go home. Adams also was willing to let it rest, since a word was all that Ieyasu need give to relieve him of all further responsibility and argument—as a word would suffice to bring the Englishmen from Hirado to Yedo.

CHAPTER VII

IEYASU was now seventy.

Mitsu, his secret mission achieved, had emerged long since from the character he had publicly played of the dead and buried soldier. He waited now upon the presence of Ieyasu in his retirement at Suruga. Together they greeted Adams when he paid his visit in advance of the formal presentation of Saris and the ten Englishmen.

"He has come, no doubt," Ieyasu said thoughtfully to Mitsu, "to ask me again—after an interval of eight years—if he may return home. Is it not so, An-jin? Have not your country-men seduced you with their talk?"

Adams said, evasively, "My Lord, only a fool persists in seeking that which he knows he may not have."

"And only another fool," said Ieyasu, "thinks that because the cuckoo sings not to-day it will be dumb to-morrow, and again to-morrow."

"You would let me go then?" Adams recoiled as though his friend had struck him.

"Let us be seated, An-jin," said Ieyasu. "It is long since we have drunk tea together, and smoked tobacco. For the affair-less man is seldom in the road to meet with men of business."

Adams peaceably sat, smiling at the way Ieyasu had startled him.

"Aye," he said, "they make a load of business, these visitors. Spaniards, Portuguese, Hollanders, the Chinamen—and now my friends and countrymen. There is one among them, my Lord, whom you shall some day see and assess highly. He is to stay here as Cape Merchant. I will bring him to wait upon you when this other has returned home."

"Oh," said Ieyasu. "So the other returns?"

"Aye," said Adams, "when the monsoon is good he takes the ship and goes again."

"Oh," said Ieyasu; and he and Mitsu regarded each other and from each other they looked at the Pilot.

Tea was placed before them by unregarded girls who silently withdrew.

"Oh . . ." And then he said, "An-jin, has there been no word from these countrymen of yours of taking you also—home—on this ship?"

Adams first exclaimed: "God Almighty!" and then said: "Speech with my countrymen has brought our oaths back to me, my Lord. . . . Aye. There has been word. This man Saris has had scarce any other word for me these last days. He is instructed by his Lord of the Company—a great cavalero in my country—to make a great and honoured guest of me aboard the *Clove*. Aye, they would have me go."

Ieyasu said thoughtfully: "You could go; and return."

"Return?" said Adams, "after four years—or three—or five—return?" The thought was a new one to him, a possibility never before considered. He considered it now, only to let it go. For even three years were a long time, and a great hazard—with himself away in England, and the gate of the Passage left unguarded. Like a fool—and who is not sometimes a fool among pot-companions in a tavern?—like a fool he had talked again and again in the past dozen years. Spaniards, Portingals and Hollanders all knew what he had jealously guarded as a secret when wine was not in him. Hollanders and Portingals both talked now of an adventure Northward. A Spanish ship had come, victualled and manned; and it had actually sailed to the point of Shinzani on the fortieth parallel, before word had come to him; then certain of the crew had fired it and coasted down in a stolen skiff and hidden themselves in bawdy-houses, to await the coming of Adams to Hirado. . . . Thus the new possibility of going home was no possibility at all; for he could not be spared for a single month from Japan. In a month could come some ship other than an English ship and sail with men other than his own shipmates to the discovery of his secret road.

"And what have you said to him, An-jin?" asked Ieyasu, recalling him from his thoughts.

"I have told him," said Adams, "that even if I would, I could not; for you will not give me leave."

"And it is that that you would have me say?" asked

the thoughtful old man.

"Aye, my Lord," said Adams. "I would."

The look which Adams saw on the face of his Lord was one which neither he nor Mitsu had seen before. It was a look of fear; the fear of the weak for the strong.

"It is a small thing, my Lord," said Adams quietly, to soften some hardness of which he himself knew nothing. "A small thing. When I have asked before for great ones you have given them; and smiled—as you gave me my swords and my wife and my Lordship. Or you have refused them; and smiled—as you refused me leave to depart Southward and West eight years ago on the Macao ship with Lopez the Spaniard, or Northward and West on the ship I myself had built, with Shongo Sama the Admiral. Always you have smiled. But now——"

"Now," said Ieyasu, "the matter is a different one. At other times I was a man, and you a child. You had neither thoughts nor speech. Now you are the man and I the child, for you have speech enough for all our thoughts; and I am old. It is true that I also have speech and thought; but I have nought else."

"You have need of nought else," said Adams. "It is only a speech that I ask of you."

"You ask that my word should substitute your conduct," said the philosopher; and the Pilot could only shrug his shoulders.

As soon as the corollary of Ieyasu's proposition had become clear to him, he stated it: "If you command me to go, will not your word become my action?"

"I would command no such thing," said Ieyasu. "Staying or going would be of your own choice; the shift of a grown man with regard to his destiny."

"And your advice?"

Ieyasu said, "Ah. . . . Advice . . ." He drank more tea. "An-jin, we are very free of advice, some of us old ones, for we can see facts and probabilities without the desire that makes illusions of the facts, and certainties or impossibilities of the probabilities. But we would be better employed with writing in our books; for it is only when set down on paper that facts can live without desire. We waste our time in talking to the young."

"Young?" said Adams. "I am fifty."

"Fifty, or five times fifty, you are young: You would still achieve a thing—move a thing from one place to another, look upon this thing rather than that one. You are not yet concerned with yourself being of such a constitution rather than another; you are not yet concerned with contemplation rather than thought and action."

The speaker was indeed, thought Adams, becoming an old man.

"Yes," he admitted, "I would still achieve. I would still move a thing from one place to another. I would move a ship from here to England, and I would move it by way of North and West. You could help me. And will not."

"An-jin," said Ieyasu, and once again he smiled. "When I could have helped you, I did not. Now I cannot. Twice I thwarted you—when you built those two good ships for me, thinking that it was for your adventure that you were building them, with the wild old Shongo at your elbow. I thwarted you from friendship; and in the manner of a soldier you submitted. You acquired merit thereby; and I acquired use. What was it to me that you and Shongo and a hnndred others should go and freeze your guts in the black waters of the solid Northern Seas? There were strangers in my country, lying and posturing and cajoling and corrupting; and you, An-jin Sama, the Needle-watcher, were the only stranger whose heart was visible to my eyes, and to whose eyes the other hearts were visible with all their lies and posturing and cajolery and corruption. You were eyes to me; ears; a tongue and a heart that understood contortions of thought and desire that were beyond my own heart. You and Mitsu have served me well. . . . But one Lord's man is not another Lord's man; and I am your Lord for but a little while longer—and then only in the most trivial matters——"

"Great God!" said Adams; "you are still the Mighty One. The honourable son, Hidetada—he might be——"

The smile of Ieyasu became laughter now. "Behold, how you yourself have said it, An-jin! One man, one Lord, is the law of fealty. Yourself you cannot stomach the thought of another, even though he be my son. How then can my son take a man as fully as I myself took him, for the only reason that I am my son's father? . . ."

"Oh!" said Adams; "so your honourable son is not well-disposed to me? . . ."

"He is amply well-disposed to you," said Ieyasu. "He is your friend as you well know; but he is, as you yourself said, Hidetada while I was Ieyasu. In keeping you of old I kept you for a purpose that was clear to me. You were a tool, a weapon for which I had specific use. It were unseemly for me to keep you now that I have not the strength to wield a weapon or direct a tool. For I am old, and the weapon has, as it were, acquired a life of its own. I have told you all, An-jin; so that now when I speak to my old weapon, the weapon can answer me with its own strength and the ring of its true metal."

Adams stood up, silent.

"Will you not speak, An-jin?" said the old man. "Will you not tell me what is in your mind? To-morrow and again we will be busy, with other men about us—young men with affairs on hand—your countrymen and mine. In leaving this land now, which has given you for a dozen years the produce of its earth and of one of its honourable women, do you leave with the satisfaction of service well and truly done, and of friendship well served?"

"Leaving the land!" he exclaimed. "Do you think I'd leave it now? My countrymen have come; they will presently send a ship. . . ."

"Oh—a ship! a ship! a ship!" the old man was a little peevish. "Do you still talk of that ship—you, a grey-beard—as you did when you could say so little more than 'ship,' and 'Northward' and 'West'? Be at peace, man. Hidetada will no doubt give you any ship you may build, even as I took your ships away. You shall have your ships and your frozen bowels and an old soldier of Japan frozen beside you. Is it well? But chatter no more 'ship, ship, ship.'"

Mitsu laughed.

Adams said, "It is well, my Lord—I cease to chatter; for the ship shall be an English one. The mighty Ieyasu's ship—yes, with his ship I would have adventured it. . . . But as you yourself said—one man, one Lord. Now I wait a little longer for a ship from England. In the friendship of yourself and the hospitality of this country, I wait."

"Well said, An-jin," said Mitsu, chuckling.

Ieyasu very thoughtfully said, "—or go, An-jin, peaceably —home."

"Go?" Adams snorted now. "Go?—with young Jack Saris, who thinks that the secret of this country is cloves and nutmegs and pepper! Go?—with nothing done in all these years, and when now it can be done?—I'd cut my belly first."

He made obeisance to his Lord and went back to the lodging where Saris awaited him.

"Will he see us to-morrow?" asked Saris.

"Aye," said Adams. "He'll see us."

CHAPTER VIII

IEYASU sat still and thought. At length he said to Mitsu: "I will thwart him in that other matter also. I will allow his countrymen to stay in Hirado; and they surely will stay there. We know how they have disagreed with him from their first meeting, when he left their house, unbathed, and repaired to his own lodging. They will continue to disagree with him, and will stay in Hirado if we permit it. We will permit it; and then perhaps—in dudgeon—he will return home."

"My Lord," said Mitsu, "you could command him to go."

Ieyasu shook his head. "I verily believe he would cut himself; for he has a proud spirit; and he is mad. 'Ship, ship, ship!' And 'North, North, North.' It is that pride of spirit that I would save for him, by persuading him to go now, while we are still here—you and I—to see his honourable going. But if he will not, he will not. . . . And perhaps his destiny will direct that the weapons will again be foils of bamboo when Hidetada fences with him. He has served us well, Mitsu."

And Mitsu said, "Yes, he has served us well. It were better for him to go now."

CHAPTER IX

It was with a light heart and brightly open eye that Saris went about the pompous business of the next weeks. The countryside was kindled with the tints of early autumn. He saw the Daibutsu Buddha, "made of Copper, being hollow within, but of very substantiall thicknesse. It was in height, as wee ghessed, about one and twentie or two and twentie foot, in the likenesse of a man kneeling upon the ground, with his buttockes resting on his heeles, his armes of wonderful largenesse, and the whole body proportionable. . . . Some of our people went into the bodie of it, and hoope and hallowed, which made an exceeding great noyse."

His short audience with Ieyasu had gone splendidly. His gifts had been graciously accepted, the letter from King James read, and graciously answered. His requests had been denied in only two particulars: permission was withheld for the bringing of Chinese prizes into Japanese harbours; English law-breakers ashore were to be tried and punished by the English Cape Merchant and not by the local Justice. Neither of these points particularly bothered Saris. The demand for freedom to bring in the prizes had been made only half-heartedly, and only at the suggestion of Andace; and the future discipline of the "House" was Cocks's affair. For the rest, Ieyasu had indicated no obstacle in the way of his settling his factory wherever he pleased, and of trading freely anywhere in Japan. Nor—and it was Adams himself who had slowly translated the words—nor was there any reason why the Pilot should not now go home.

Mitsu had listened while he spoke, and John Japan . . .

Confirmation on all points, said Ieyasu, would be given at the court of his son Hidetada in Yedo.

So it was with a light heart that Saris admired the Daibutsu and estimated its height and "hooped and hallowed" to hear the reverberations in the cavernous interior of it.

Yedo he found a "very glorious appearance unto us; the

ridge-tiles and corner-tiles richly gilded the posts of their doores gilded and varnished." It was not thus that Adams had found the city as he shambled up with Santvoort and Mitsu from the *Liefde* to knock at the door of shabby-genteel Magome's bungalow. It was not thus that he saw it now—gilded tiles and door-posts, varnish and lacquer and bunting. He looked, instead, to Uraga—the little bay outside the bay of Yedo—where he already had a small warehouse of his own beside a jetty to which a small, unrigged hull was moored. For it was beside this same warehouse and this same jetty that he desired the English House to be built. It was on those sands that he had found a basin where hulls could be built in a dry cradle and launched by digging a waterway to them from the sea. . . .

And Saris said to him, kindly—for those gilded tiles and garish door-posts, the glowing maples and azaleas, the cool of the shadowed harbour glimpsed beyond the city, the warmth of the rabble in the streets below them—these touched a chord in the heart of Saris that was not deaf to the sweetness of lute-strings. "So this has been your home."

Adams said, "Aye—this. More or less."

Adams, as Saris knew well enough, from their evenings in the Mess, was no musician. It was reasonable to assume, therefore, that the impact upon him of miraculously coloured leaves and flowers was a dull one. He watched him with some interest as he said lightly, "There would seem to be people enough in the city below to buy your goods and your property, and set you free of them."

Adams turned not a hair. "Among my goods," he said, "there are some that you yourself might buy for the Company; good Meaco ware—candlesticks, screens, writing chests and such. I have a hull, too. I've set no masts or rigging till I should know the style of seamen manning her. I will show you all to-morrow, while you wait for audience with the young Emperor."

"Would you yourself ask him," said Saris, "or shall I—for your leave to go home?"

"There is no need for any to ask him," said Adams. "It has been granted by his father, whose affair it was."

Saris was content to let the matter rest thus. There was a soft, dull Adams and a hard bright one—a quiet man and a man in humours; so he smiled in friendly fashion and left well enough alone.

Adams took him to Uraga next day and showed him his jetty and his warehouse and his hull. He sold him screens and candlesticks and fine writing-boxes. Over the hull they came to a discussion, and Adams went warily, since now he had only his own persuasiveness to help him.

"I built her, as you see," he said, "with a great belly of a hold to carry cargoes, coasting; and for Cochin-China and Siam. With your factory here you would need some such craft to collect merchandise of the Spaniards and Portingals and Dutch at Nagasaki and Hirado. No other ships but ours would be permitted to enter this whole harbour."

Saris answered, "At Hirado we should not need any such craft?"

"No," said Adams. "But you would pay portage for every ounce of goods sent up; and you would have no stock here. . . . Saris, this is the place for trade. Many years of peace have altered its character so that it is no longer a barrack for soldiers only. At Hirado and Nagasaki all wants have long been supplied—and there are already three peoples supplying whatever wants are left. Here the wants are new and there is only myself with that small godown supplying them. Think on it, man."

Conscientiously, Saris did think on it.

In the journal he noted: "A very good harbour for shipping, where ships may ride as safely as in the River of Thames before London, and the passage thereto by sea very safe and good. . ." He had an open mind for the moment as to whether Adams could, or could not, be forced to return on the *Clove;* but whether Adams went or stayed, Uraga struck him as a little too near to the Court and the Officials of Yedo. The winking eye of old Ho-in at Hirado, the smile of Andace and the proximity of the Dutch house counted for more than a safe riding for ships at anchor.

"It is well enough, Adams," he said. "We will consider the ship when our charter is clearly given."

It was the turn of Adams now to let a matter rest, despite its pressure on him; for he placed Saris, roughly, in the mule class of men—a good mule he might be; but, nevertheless, a mule.

In three days the charter was granted, a confirmation of the terms Ieyasu had laid down. The important item was, of course, that a free choice was left to the settlers in the place of their settlement. Adams englished the document; the last clause of all ran, "Item, we will that if in discouerye of anye other places of Trade or retorne of their shippes, they shall have neede of men or victualls, that yee our subjects furnish them for their monye as there neede shall require. And that without our further passe They shall set out and Goe in discouerye for Yeadzo, or anye other part in, or aboute, our Empire."

The work of Saris was now almost done. The rest was for Cocks to do in the course of years; and in this Cape Merchant Saris had every confidence, for Cocks was most magnificently normal. Even Saris, who expected bluff and valour as normal from his fellows and subordinates, had been impressed by the poise of the stout little man when he had mustered the half-dozen shabby musketeers from the *Clove* and paraded himself with a fine umbrella before the Dutch Company of swashbucklers in the Moluccas. The only menace for the Company, as against the hard head of Cocks, was the fantastic heart of Adams. Murder *could* have come out of that punching of the cook's head. . . . And how could Cocks or any Englishman be expected to make profit in a country to which the door was held and blocked by such a freak as Adams? The remaining duties of Saris became the single duty of taking Adams home with him; and now was the obvious time for tackling it while Adams was near enough to his home to go to it and set any matters in order that might need his personal attention, and say whatever had to be said to the woman there.

Adams meanwhile continued, with persistent tact, to champion the little harbour of Uraga and the possibilities of business in Yedo. Saris began to see some sense in it; but he saw, as more important, the great store set upon it by Adams—a store great enough to form the basis of a bargain. It would be worth the Honourable Company's while to settle by Yedo instead of Hirado (for a time, at any rate) if that should be the price of the Pilot's going home.

"Adams," he said, "are you permitting me to visit your Lordship and your estate, and to deliver our presents to Mistress Adams?"

Adams said, "The hospitality of my poor place is at your disposal. But we have business to do here. You have not yet seen all my goods. There are more that the Company may care to buy."

Thus an opening was presented sooner than Saris had hoped for. "I thought," he said, "that in your estate also, and in your house, there may be articles which you would care to sell—or take home now that you may go."

From the steady look that Adams gave him Saris was quite unable to guess what kind of thing it was that Adams was about to say. He spoke very quietly: "Saris, why did you yourself not turn about at Bantam, and sail for home again?"

Saris was puzzled. "Why sail home from Bantam?" he asked. "It was for Japan that we were making."

"Aye," said Adams; "and if any man had urged you to go home before you had made it, you would have thought him a fool. As I think you."

Saris shrugged his shoulders. Temper was the one thing to be avoided with this Adams. "You have nought to fear in going home. With our factory here at Uraga the affairs of your estate and your family could be watched by Cocks and the others."

"And I?" asked Adams.

"In the service of the Company you could return here. The Company would give you what you desire."

"Would you go back to your country empty?" But Adams himself answered the question. "You would not, Saris. You would do first what required doing. You would not go with nothing done—as indeed you did not go fron Bantam, because you were set for Japan."

"Nothing done!" exclaimed Saris. "Man, you have become a Lord in the place. You have been the friend of a great Emperor and of many people. You have explored a land and set it down truly on a chart. You have made some fortune and begotten a family—and you speak of nothing done!"

Adams responded to the geniality, and the policy behind the Captain's words. "Aye, it is well enough," he said. "But there is more still to do."

"What more?" He was still genial.

So Adams said, "Find the Passage to the North-West."

"God's life!" said Saris, able to bear no longer with a man who talked of passages to the North-West when it was Southward and Eastward in seas already charted that the world's great problem lay; for it was there that Dutchmen, unchallenged, were able to filch the world's cloves and nutmegs and pepper, and grow fat upon their filching. "God's life! *That* keeps you!"

"Aye," said Adams; and his eyes narrowed upon the fool who could see only his contemptuous *"that"* in the dream that had obsessed the Pilot's mind through the years wherein some other parts of that same mind had chaffered with tradesmen and ambassadors in four tongues, with princes, carpenters and coolies; while he himself had loved a woman and begotten a son and a daughter in his fief at Hemimura, and a daughter in the house of Zanzeburro at Hirado . . . "Aye," he said. "That does keep me." It was as clear to one of them now as it was to the other that further palaver was impossible.

"Go you with your ship," said Adams, "—to England or to the devil. I stay here."

"The factory then stays where I have placed it," Saris retorted. "At Hirado."

"Go, then, to it," said Adams. "Our business here is done."

"And do you not return with me?"

"No," said Adams. "I go home. I shall overtake you on the way, travelling light."

So, Saris realised, he was not to visit and assess the Lordship after all.

"And the Company's present to your—wife?" he asked.

"That," said Adams, "is wages for my journeying with you. I myself will take it."

Saris wrote in his journal: "It was thought fitting, and was bestowed upon Mistris Addams for a present in regard to hir husband's kindnes, these parcells, viz.

"One silver and Gilt Cup, poiz 6 oz., at 7s. per oz.

"1 peece of bafta of 10 rials per corge.

"1 peece of Byrames at 15 rials per Corge."

Twelve rials-of-eight covered the value of the present—about fifty shillings.

CHAPTER X

Bikuni San washed and wiped the miniature ritual-furnishings with which she had observed the absence of the Pilot. They were a small tray and tiny cups, bowls and dishes for the service, by candle-light, of meals to the homing spirit of the absent one.

Magome Sageyu clucked sardonically when his eye gave him the dim image of the Pilot walking up the path, his ears the blur of the Pilot's voice in the garden calling to his son Joseph.

It was Magome's other son-in-law, the one-sworded, bright merchant from Nagasaki, who had started the tale of the Pilot's probable returning to this place no more. For the Pilot, so far as this man whom Adams called Andreas could see, was all that stood between himself and the full management of a good business in Yedo. Concepcion the Filipino had sent this man North in the first instance; and Magome, whose thoughts were turning at that peaceful time from fencing to indirect finance, had felt that a single sword was, after all, something, when the Pilot was daily giving less time to business and more to affairs that were the affairs of other men and productive of great enough honour to all, but little profit to himself. Let him, with his two swords—thought the old soldier—see to the honourable standing of the household, while Andreas, one-sworded, looked to its finances.

There was little love lost between the Pilot and this husband of Magdalena. Andreas usually regulated his visits to Hemimura so that they corresponded with Adams's absences therefrom—for, after six years of brotherhood-in-law, Andreas still could not believe that the old watchman who guarded Adams's warehouse at Uraga was as stupid as he made himself out to be, or that old Magome's awe of the books and tablets which he kept in his chest for the Pilot was not a superstition that would one day pass. . . . But for six years these things had persisted against the wheedling of Andreas; the watchman was still as deaf as a post, his face as impassive as a carving at the end of it. Magome kept guard over the Pilot's books as though he were a heart carrying a dark, but faintly amusing secret; and he answered with nothing but a peculiar grin the most innocent of questions that Andreas put to him concerning those books.

Even when this one-sworded son-in-law arrived hot from Nagasaki with the news of how the Pilot had tumbled into the arms of his countrymen and was seeking leave of the General to depart with them and abandon his local interests, the old watchman remained deaf and carven, Magome sat unmoving on the chest of ledgers; and Bikuni continued in silence to tend the small feast set out for the Pilot's spirit.

And so at length Magome clucked sardonically when he heard the voice of the Pilot calling to his son in the garden; and he cursed the dimness of his eyes, that they could not give him a sight of the discomfiture on the face of Andreas, the one-sworded.

"So An-jin," he said, "your business is done and you have returned?"

Adams was patient with this formula that had been the old man's welcome at his home-comings for a dozen years.

"Aye, father," he said. "And all are well?"

"Your son you have seen," said Magome. "Your wife is well to welcome you. Her sister is better than when you left. The husband——"

"I met the husband," said Adams, "on his way to answer the sudden call that he received from Nagasaki. I hope that nought is amiss."

"All is well," said Magome. "My own digestion functions with smoothness. When you have bathed, the women shall bring us drink. And food."

"I will see the women," said Adams. "For Bikuni I have a gift from my country—the first English drinking-cup that has ever entered here."

Bikuni followed the course of ordinary decorum in not obtruding her presence upon the Pilot till it was required of her.

He found her squatted before her toy dishes and the shrine's small candles, weeping.

"These are not tears," she said, as she rose and smiled at

him; "they are my heart's secret laughter at the return of my lord."

Adams lifted the mother of his son in his arms and held her to his breast, and kissed her.

"So master Saris was not the only one," he said, setting her down again, "who expected me to pack up and sail home with him!"

She knew that when he mumbled thus to himself in his own tongue he was either pleased or puzzled or angry; and now that he was neither angry nor puzzled, she smiled.

"Have you journeyed well?" she asked.

For answer he said, "Regard me, little one. I do not return to that first country of mine. I tell this to you that you may know it, whatever others may say."

Her heart was warmed by her love of him and by a duty well and truly done; for a secret word had come to her from the mighty Ieyasu himself when she was great with the Pilot's first child that she should add whatever she might to give him content among them so that the country of his birth, and its women, should disturb him not with any lure of things that are far away.

"You are pleased to stay, then?" she asked.

"Aye," he said. "I must stay. They have not done what I asked of them. There is much for me to do here. I must bathe and eat and rest. I must see the Admiral—for he, too, waited upon their coming and upon another matter of a Spanish ship that has been burned. I must prepare a large writing also for the Lord's merchants of my country; and I must return with it to Hirado. I had thought to bring my countrymen nigh here, and settle them at Uraga. But they will not come."

"Is that well," she asked, "or ill?" For herself it was well enough; she feared the nearness of men for whom she had watched his yearning. Word of an Englishman in a galley's crew ashore at Nagasaki had always been enough to set him upon a journey.

"God knows!" said he; and she knew that those words had the same meaning as the shrug of his great shoulders. "They are fools," he explained. "They will need tending . . ."

It was thus that he had found the Spaniards and Portuguese

at Nagasaki for the past ten years, and Dutchmen at Hirado for the past three—fools that needed tending. So that the old haunches of Magome had grown flattened in those ten years to the lid of the chest that held the Pilot's ledgers; for the foolishness of other men had left the Pilot little time for business that was his own, and only intervals of time at home.

"Perhaps it is well," he said thoughtfully. "But there is one among them whom I would have you see some day. He is not as the one whom I would not bring here—the one who struck the boy, so that I would have killed him if I had not thought of another way of adjusting the matter."

He went to the bath. Bikuni meanwhile saw to his change of tunic and robe and pantaloons and socks, and despatched a messenger for the barber.

CHAPTER XI

BEFORE settling down to the evening's drinking with Magome he despatched his present to Shongo the Admiral, and a message that a visit to him would be his first pleasure as soon as he had rested and attended to one or two pressing duties at home.

These pressing duties became, by next morning, one duty only—the writing of his last "large" letter to Sir Thomas Smyth of the East India Company. He was sure now that the other letters had never reached him; so the first part of this "large" writing came easily enough to the paper. He said little in it that he was not able to take from the copies he had of the last ones. He remarked, incidentally, that the *Clove* herself would do for the adventure if no other ship could at once be found, and he went on to specify her necessary equipment. Men came first in the list; he demanded eighty to a hundred of the better sort. Poledavy was next in importance, enough for two spare suits of sail; with all cordage of good hemp. He asked for a surgeon and for the latest charts of all the world, with anything new that had come out in the shape of instruments. As to the victualling, all he required was good store of English biscuit. It seemed little enough to be asking for, in the light of the glib and easy arguments that followed in support of the request; and it was only when he had finished setting them down at large and came to the rest of the letter that he found himself stuck. It would not have been easy— even if his language had not grown rusty in a dozen odd years of disuse—to admit that he must stay sitting in Japan so that any ship setting out upon the passage, that was not an English ship, might be scuttled or burned. And he had to refuse the Company's magnificent invitation for his return home, and the refusal of any invitation had acquired for him, after his thirteen years in Japan, the significance and weight of ceremony. . . .

The *Clove* from Limehouse, and the men in her with their

English talk, had brought a suddenly pressing life again to the family in Gillingham. The problem, then, was not only to refuse the Company's invitation but also to set about, with the same reed whittled to a fresh writing-edge, and beseech the Company's charity for his English wife and daughters.

Phrases came not easily. He paced the house and the garden in search of them, and walked the acres of his lordship among azaleas and niggard plots of rice and millet. With a nod he took in the salutes of men, the obeisance of women and the hail of children.

He went to see Shongo. He was toothless now, but still able to go abroad in fine weather, to walk a gang-plank and stand firm upon a deck with his crutch under his arm. To Shongo he said briefly, "It has not come. My letter did not reach them. I am writing another, which they will get, and within three years—or, at the widest reckoning, four—the ship will be here."

Three years, or four, were nought to Shongo now. He nodded and said that it was well; and Adams returned to his letter. Over the conclusion of it that had so bothered him he now found it possible to hurry. As to the Company's fine invitation, he said that "terms" had arisen between himself and John Saris that made it impossible for him to return on board the *Clove*. It was more fitting, he wrote, for others to explain what those terms were than for him, who was personally unknown to the Honourable Company, to be setting down a specific complaint against its chosen "Captain-Generall" . . . It was a neat way out, and he smiled at the thought of Saris explaining away the inexplicable. . . . And he added that he was still a poor and an unsuccessful man; not one who could return to his country with the dignity of any achievement behind him. That which he had striven to find in Japan was not yet his; so he must wait their Lordships' pleasure for other ships, and a ship that should bring him their answer.

For the girls and wife in Gillingham he asked, in the end, no charity. Instead, he unhorsed old Magome from the strong-box and took from it certain documents. Magome clucked and smiled at the Pilot rummaging in the safe, for he had never known him go far wrong in any transaction with those papers. But the documents which Adams then sought and found were bills which were due, and nearly due, in Nagasaki and at the Dutch house in Hirado. Whatever kind of poltroon Saris might be, Adams knew that he could trust him in the matter of money. He would deliver the cash to his wife and daughters. With his "large" letter now certain of delivery he was assured of a ship and canvas and tackle and men; so he had a light heart in tapping the investments he had made towards the possible necessity of equipping a ship of his own.

The boy Joseph could now stand up to his father and his grandfather with a *saké*-cup as promisingly as he could with a bamboo foil. Bikuni and Magdalena waited upon their drinking which was in the nature of a rite, since Adams was again ready for a journey.

They drank and talked easily and pleasantly together—the old man, the Englishman who was neither old nor young and the boy with the nimbleness of wit and limb that were from Japan, with the skull and thigh-bones over-long, the brown eyes and out-thrust chin that were from England.

After their drinking they slept; and in the morning, with his cook and his scribe, Adams took the road for Hirado again.

CHAPTER XII

In the two years following that day, the taverns on the great road to Yedo began to look for their most frequent news to the meagre retinue of the Pilot. When the road was empty of travellers by reason of snow and flood, the tavern-keepers might still expect its emptiness to yield to them a brief gossip with the weather-beaten An-jin, with his cook and his foot-sore scribe. When the road was a living tide that rolled from Yedo Southward to the very sea, they might still expect him—his long shanks or his pressed pony wading to outstrip the tide's ambling pace, towing behind him the cook and the writer.

* * * * * *

For two years the Road was his home more constantly than any other place; for Saris, before sailing away with the letter in the *Clove*, had cajoled and chaffered him into the firming of a contract with the Company. By its terms he was entertained into the Company's service at a salary of a hundred pounds a year. The nature of his service was not specified; and the extent of it seemed, at first sight, negligible. Even at Yedo no particular duty was imposed upon him; for proud Wickham was set up in the capital officially to represent the English House of Hirado.

The idea of Saris was sound enough. In appointing Adams he blocked him from open service to the Dutch or Portuguese or Spanish, and by giving him Wickham as his local protégé at Yedo he was giving him, thought Saris, enough to keep him busy.

One further provision he made for the superfluous and eccentric energies of the pilot. Cocks had pestered him in his last busy days to sanction a small adventure towards China. Saris agreed at last, and set down in the "remembrance" which he left with Cocks that a small expedition might be sent, as soon as all other matters were found to be running smoothly, commanded by Adams.

Cocks, when the junk had been bought and furnished and laded with a cargo suitable for the fulfilment of his dream, saw suddenly that there were better men than Adams available for the job. He defied the remembrance of Saris and sent Tempest Peacock, because he, too, was a dreamer, capable of glimpsing his own bright vision of El Dorado. With him went Carwarden—because he was no dreamer, but a hard man pickled in brine. Adams he kept at hand—at Hirado, at Nagasaki, at the end of the nine-hundred-mile road where he could keep a weather-eye on Wickham, or else moving upon that road from the bothers that were Wickham at one end to the worries that were Cocks at the other.

There was other work also for the Pilot in those journeyings, besides the adjustment of prices for Cocks and of quarrels for Wickham. The country was ripe again for war. It was fifteen years since Ieyasu had slain the hundred thousand who had sought allegiance to the infant Hideyori and rallied to the standard of Ishida Mitsunari. Hideyori himself was now a man. For the hundred thousand slain at Sekigahara in allegiance to Hideyori and the legend of his mother, there were now a hundred and fifty thousand sons grown to manhood with that weight of blood upon their shoulders. Their home and their councils were in the South, neighbouring upon the Road and the sea-shore which Adams travelled, watchful and thoughtful. Curiously, in all those journeyings, no man as yet had killed him.

Winds, from snarling in the teeth of the Pilot and his men as they travelled South and West, shifted to smite at their backs. The sting in them was the parched dust of summer, the tang of frost, lashes of sleet or the cold caress of snow. From North-East the winds fell to calm or swung full East on their way to mobilising Southward with the changing of the seasons.

It was only Adams and his retinue that moved upon an invariable and inflexible line.

CHAPTER XIII

At the end of those two years it was known that Peacock and Cawarden had been swallowed in the mystery Westwards.

When Cocks admitted this, he admitted a crisis. Business had been going ill enough; for Brower the Dutchman had spoiled the local market in every item of merchandise that the *Clove* had brought. Broadcloth was worthless; the price of lead was down, very nearly, to cost. Yet Cocks had to sell to turn his money over. A junkload of the cursed stuff was sunk a cable's length from the jetty, in transit from the store. The thirty Samurai divers who failed to recover it cut their bellies upon the order of "King" Ho-in; and Cocks, dazed by the loss and aghast at the romance of the slaughter, wrote off some five hundred crowns in his ledger. But as easily as he was depressed by one accident, he was cheered by another. Adams arrived from Yedo with a commission to buy whatever he could for the army of Ieyasu. By a stroke of luck unparalleled in the history of the English House the *Hozeander* arrived from Bantam and was able to land "4 chistes guns, also two fardels steel containing 166 gads." Even better business than this was done, not out of the hold of the *Hozeander*, but by stripping her of ordnance and emptying her of powder and shot. She had nothing else from home, Cocks thanked God, to clutter up his godowns. What she had brought from Bantam was sold at once, and for cash: ivory, ambergris, coral, silk and some gems.

It was clear from this to the man who was so readily allured, that whither Peacock and Carwarden had gone to failure others must go to success. He had the ready money now to furnish another venture, and he put the matter to Adams. Adams, however, could not stay to discuss it with him then. He had to convoy his purchases by sea, in his own junk, to Yedo. Cocks offered him all he could to get out of him some days of talk—seamen from the *Hozeander* to man the junk, the first mate to command and sail her so that Adams might stay a while and talk. But Adams shook his head and left him doubting him and cursing him for one who loved all men in the world better than his countrymen and brothers.

Adams, his guns and munitions landed at Yedo, had to hurry forthwith to Suruga where Ieyasu waited for him with some pressing matter.

Ieyasu said to him, "An-jin, your indenture with this Company of tradesmen has been expired for some months now. I myself have work for you to perform."

"I am very ready to perform it," said Adams.

"It is in Yedo," said Ieyasu. "And it would leave no room for any masters other than myself only—and my son."

"I am bound, my Lord," said Adams, "bound and beholden to serve my countrymen."

"But is not the indenture expired?" asked Ieyasu.

"It is true," said Adams. "In a sense—yes; the indenture is expired, but there is still a bond . . ."

"They have been here long enough now to fend for themselves in their chaffering and bickering," said Ieyasu impatiently. "The work I would have you do is better work than the running of errands—and the pay is better than a messenger's."

"What," Adams asked simply, "is it that you want me to do?"

"That ancient and everlasting question, An-jin!" said Ieyasu; and he smiled as a father remembering some infant trick of a son. "It is the one question of yours that I have never been able to answer truly. I told you once what was in my mind—that your work should be the building of many ships for me, and the development of some power at sea. But matters turned out otherwise; I had no need of ships and your work became the reading of men's hearts and the interpretation to me of their crooked words. You found friends in your old enemies the Portuguese—for me and for yourself also; and you found enemies in new friends. Those men who came to measure our coasts and sound our harbours, saying they came in friendship—you did well there, An-jin, in discovering their aim and causing me to send them back to Spain. But I could not have told you beforehand that that was to be your work. Likewise I cannot tell you now. A man cannot say before an encounter, 'I will parry first, and then cut or thrust or lunge, or step this way or that.' So I can only say that I have work. Will you do it?"

An exact answer to a vague question would always have gone against something in Adams. For decent vagueness's sake he said, "Whatever I have been able to do for you, I have always done gladly and faithfully."

"That I very well know," said Ieyasu. "Listen. Your countrymen paid you for two years less than it has cost you to conduct their business. With me it shall be otherwise. My work will cost you nought but vigilance and thought; and for pay the paltry gift I made to you of an estate shall be trebled. Forthwith you shall be among my Eighty Thousand—and my son's Eighty Thousand after me. Indeed, An-jin, you shall rank among the first half of that number."

"But, my Lord," said Adams, "what need is there for entering afresh into the service of him whom I already serve?" It was Cocks that was holding him back—Cocks fretting and fuming for his return, and hopelessly blundering among any rascal junk-owners who had old hulks for sale.

"The need is that these others should no longer have you at their beck and call," said Ieyasu. "It is for that only that I would increase your Estate to place you in the first half of our Eighty Thousand."

He was asking the one thing that Adams could not give him—the last of his freedom. Shrewdly he said, "What would he say of it?—your honourable son?"

Ieyasu laughed, and Mitsu chuckled. "It was he himself," said Ieyasu, "who suggested it."

Adams saw again the bars of a fencing-helmet. He saw behind them the glint of eyes, and he saw a nimbleness which caused flashes of movement that were beyond his understanding and beyond his own poor skill. . . . "The nature of the service," Ieyasu continued gently, "so far as we can say, is only that you stay in Yedo, or wherever we may send you; that you cease running about the country and disappearing on errands that are not ours."

Adams walked about the room, mumbling and frowning till he was stopped by laughter from Ieyasu.

"Man," he said, so that even the single word sounded like a part of his joke, "this is no walking matter. It is but a small thing either way. You need not accept."

"Thank God," said Adams in his beard, "for that." To Ieyasu he said, "You leave me free then—to serve these others, if need be?"

"Certainly," said Ieyasu, and the shrug of his shoulders made a very easy matter of it all. "You have said that you will return to your country on the next ship that comes from it. No doubt they will reward you there for these services you do them—as they do not reward you here."

"Possibly," said Adams. "But I must return to Hirado now, for there is an urgent matter in our Cape Merchant's mind of sending a junk to trade in Siam and Cochin-China. But after sending it I shall return, for there are matters in Yedo also, from the cargo of our ship from Bantam. I could then——"

"Perhaps you need not return," Ieyasu said thoughtfully. "We would have used you in Yedo to dispose these guns and munitions that you have brought, and to instruct more men in the use of them. But perhaps it would be as well for Ho-in's men to have the handling of these weapons. I will confer with my son."

Adams grunted. "So I'll be taking all that tackle back again?" He expected no answer from Ieyasu, and got none; for the question was of the trivial sort whose answer comes not from individuals but from destiny. He accepted it. "I will go to my home while you confer with your son," he said, "so that my return may not be delayed unduly."

He had made a decision in those minutes that altered the shape of his life; and he passed out of the chamber and went to his lodging conscious only of having managed to arrange immediate details in such a way that Cocks need not be left fretting and blundering, Ieyasu's little task need not be neglected, nor affairs at his home unattended. He had declined the specific service of the Lord of Japan and assumed the unspecified service of their Lordships of the East India Company.

CHAPTER XIV

Ho-in found the men for Ieyasu—pike-men and archers of the less efficient sort—one hundred in number—to be taught the craft of artillerymen. A cove eight miles south of the town of Hirado gave them the nook they required for their practice. The pieces were mounted on the beach where balls could be buried harmlessly in the cliffs' sand, or flung out to sea at rafts and targets of timber.

Cocks himself was able to subscribe towards the work. He notes it thus: "The Scottsman which came out of the Spanish ship is called Henry Shankes and is a guner per his profession." The runaway, naturally enough "out of money and aparell," took kindly to the idea of an immediate job. With him went the gunner and his mate from the *Hozeander*, the powder-men and Adams; and behind them the hundred whom Ho-in could spare from the ranks of his archers and pikemen.

Carpenters and coolie-masters were in conference with Adams while Henry Shanks and the *Hozeander's* gunners instructed teams in the laying, the loading and the touching-off of pieces. There were fishermen also in these councils, with masters and coxswains of junks and skiffs. They, too, centred their various ingenuities upon pieces—sakers, culverins and demi-culverins. They had to make slings and handspikes, and to drill squads for shipping the dismounted guns and landing them again. They made cradles and hammocks to carry them, on the shoulders of coolie-teams at the travelling-pace of archers and swordsmen. They made also boxes and crates for the powder-barrels and balls.

Thus were the batteries made and equipped that bombarded, in due course, the great free-stone walls of Osaka.

There was a road from the beach which held the training-grounds and the experimental workshops. It twisted for eight miles over the hills, among maples whose flame was consuming the last twilight glow of chrysanthemums. For weeks there had been but little traffic and no song and laughter upon it, for the last mushrooms had been gathered from the woods, so that when Adams hurried along it, he was alone. Hirado was at the other end of the road, and at Hirado was the old junk for which Cocks had paid two thousand tael—and another two thousand had already been spent towards refitting her.

There, also, was Cocks himself fretting him at every possible meeting to leave the gunnery and undertake the adventure for the Honourable Company instead of Wickham who had been summoned from Yedo and was hanging about waiting for the trimming of the junk, sulking and sneering at the fantastic name which Cocks had given her—*The Sea Adventure*. Adams said "No," and stuck to it, explaining it with the single word "Emperor." Yet he knew, even better than Cocks, that Wickham was likely to bungle this adventure as Peacock and Cawarden had bungled the last one. He knew—and this too, better than Cocks knew it—that he himself could have made a success of it; and a success that could be measured in silk, in ivory and in gold would cheer those hucksters towards that other voyage in his mind whose success should be immeasurable.

Brooding thus as he walked his road one evening, he fell in with a fisherman of Oita.

Adams asked him what news there was, and the man said, "The news is for you alone, An-jin. He Himself is in the South, within a dozen miles of Sakai, with Mitsu and half a score of others. No man but you must know."

"And how come you to know it?"

The man smiled. "Many years ago I did Mitsu a service, at the time that you and the other hairy ones lay on your ruined ship. It is he that sends me to you with the word."

"It is well," said Adams. "Are you lodged, and have you bathed and eaten and rested? For there is hospitality with my men for any close-tongued server of Mitsu and his Lord."

The fisherman said, "The gentleness of the Pilot's hand upon his friends is as famed as the weight of it upon his enemies. This person thanks you. All is well with him; he has done good business, by the way."

"How long have you been on the road?" asked Adams.

"We had the wind," said the fisherman, "and sailed—my

son and I. Three days from Oita. From Sakai to Oita I was seven."

Adams calculated. He knew, within a league, every distance in that country which he had so laboriously carded. He saw four hundred miles of road before him; for not a boat could sail Eastward or Northward during that monsoon. That meant nine days going—or ten; and five days returning, or six—in a boat with fair wind. Fifteen or sixteen days of monsoon would be lost to the *Sea Adventure*, but a master might be gained for her who should be competent to get the best out of her— and the best also out of the timber- and ivory-merchants of Siam and Cochin-China; one who might be able, moreover, to get to the bottom of the Peacock and Carwarden business with the tales that shrouded it, of piracy and murder.

"What man of Sakai," he asked the fisherman of Oita, "could provide a boat and men for the return of a servant of his Excellency?"

The fisherman gave him a name.

Cocks reaped the fruit of his "kinde wordes" and his turbulent patience when Adams said that night, "I will sail in the *Adventure*, Captain—if I may."

"If you *may*?" exclaimed Cocks. "Man, have I not entreated you to take her?"

"I mean if the Emperor has no need of me," Adams explained. "If I sail, we sail in a fortnight. I can get word in that time—but no one must know. I go to-morrow. And if I am to sail I will bring back my royal permit for the voyage."

The Adams now speaking was the one of whom Cocks wrote, "Trulye I could live seven yeares with this man without falling into termes with him."

CHAPTER XV

ADAMS took papers with him into the presence of Ieyasu in the tavern at Sakai. They were lists of guns and munitions, and nominal rolls of the men he had chosen as fit to command the detachments of gunners. Among them also was the original invoice of the material he had taken with him to Yedo and carried back again to Hirado.

Ieyasu took these things from him and tossed them to Mitsu and smiled, and said, "So, my friend . . . was it to present a tradesman's bills to me, who am a busy man in hiding, that you have travelled so far and so fast? Was it to give me these names of men who are competent to set off fireworks? Or was it not rather to take leave of your old friend?"

"I came to see," said Adams, "whether my Lord has further need of me; for these countrymen of mine press me with their blundering."

"An-jin," said Ieyasu, "you are now your own man. For many years I have kept you by me, thinking 'some day there will be a purpose for this man.' But the purpose has never come—beyond the small doings of every day. For me the season of purposes is now spent. There is but one matter still left before me."

"Will it soon be accomplished then, so that I may be free?" Adams asked.

"You are free already," said the other. "You have already done towards it all the service you may, in mustering and instructing and naming for me these fireworkers. Henceforth, An-jin, you are free. I am your master no longer."

"I am dismissed," Adams exclaimed, before the thought had settled into a solid contemplation of a solid fact. And it was not that he was hurt by the quiet statement from Ieyasu. It was merely as though he had made an idle gesture towards his girdle and found it to contain no sword. In a tone of slight bewilderment, as a man might wonder where those swords had got to, he repeated the words, "I am dismissed."

"Rather," said Ieyasu, "it is I who am dismissed; for it is I, not you, about whose head there is no longer the buzzing of possibility of purposes. For is it not with a purpose in your mind that you have come to me?" Suddenly he ceased to be the thoughtful old man and became a lively good fellow of robustious laughter. "Ho, my friend!" he laughed; "we know our An-jin after these dozen years of him! When he comes to us with a face so long that the fox's brush at his chin conceals his belly—when his face is heavy with anxiety for what *we* would next do, it is because his heart is kindled with some thought which he himself would follow."

Adams smiled. (It was as though the swords had been there in his girdle all the time.) "Purpose!" he said. "Aye, they consider it purpose enough to be venturing a junk and a cargo to Siam; and they will lose it as surely as they lost the other, unless I can take them. As for my own purpose, that must wait—till the winds are from the South. The same winds that bring us back from Siam will bring also a ship from England with the answer to my letter. I can wait as well on board their Siam junk as cooling my feet ashore."

"And your place?" Ieyasu asked.

"Magome Sageyu most competently manages my place," said Adams.

"Some men," Ieyasu observed, "would consider the management of an estate a greater matter than the navigation of a junk belonging to neighbours."

"There is more than the sailing of the junk," Adams admitted. "There are other countrymen of mine as near as Bantam. It would be as well, perhaps, for me to see them."

"Will they give you a ship," asked Ieyasu, "if those in England do not?"

"But how should they not?" Adams demanded. "They will have had my letter."

"An-jin," Ieyasu said, "make your own ship and go from here with my old Shongo. Do not wait for these others."

"The waiting is nearly done now," Adams said. "This monsoon will soon pass for one who has a boat's crew to command, and matters to deal with. It is well that I should give my mind to commanding seamen for a while, after these years of idleness."

"But you commanded that ship of ours, and seamen, to Macao six years ago," said Ieyasu, "and you found it no great matter."

"No," said Adams. "That crew was a crew of your vassals. But this lot that I shall take on the *Sea Adventure* know no master but the master of their ship—if he can command them. They are Englishmen, with some Spanish renegades among them; Swarts and a few Japans of my own choosing."

"So your eye brightens," said Ieyasu. "Even as the eye of a fish returning to its water, after lying and leaping upon land."

But Adams denied this. It was not in any sense as a prank that he saw this *Sea Adventure* business. He saw it mainly as the necessity he had pointed out to Ieyasu for some man of ordinary sense and soundness to step in among a lot of fools. It had occurred to him, on one of his walks from the gunners to the shipwrights, that Santvoort could have been induced to undertake it; but he lacked confidence in even Santvoort now. He loved him still as Melchior the Hollander; but, from irresponsibility the mind of the widower junk-owner had become nothing but a solicitude for the daughter who was the goddaughter of Adams himself, and the invariable shipmate of her father. Women, Adams had reflected to put an end upon that thought of asking Santvoort to go—women of one size or another had always set young Melchior a-stagger in any latitude . . .

Mitsu came out of his reverie to say, thoughtfully, "An-jin, you are a fool."

The observation was of the kind that calls for no immediate comment. Mitsu elucidated it in due course. "If it is a ship you want to go Northward, make the one which his Lordship has now said you may make. Take the men who are, you say, the better men, and go. It would be an honourable end."

"It is not an honourable end that I am seeking," said Adams. "You and your honourable ends! It is enough for you to stick your dirk in the left side of your belly and draw it out at the right and then shove it, if you can, in your throat, grinning at your friends the while till you topple over! But I have other work to do."

"You become a coolie," Mitsu suggested.

"It is his affair," said Ieyasu.

But the exact situation of Adams was that he had no affair at all. He could not rest sufficiently, at that moment, even to ask Ieyasu the full significance of his saying that he was the Pilot's Lord no longer. He could not see that Mitsu had diagnosed him truly as a coolie; for all he could do was feel the weight of a burden on his shoulders—a burden that was not his own—and know that he must trot on to the burden's destination.

CHAPTER XVI

THE burden was the *Sea Adventure* and upon him it was tied by the official licence for the voyage which was issued to him in his name of An-jin.

They were "stowte seamen," according to Adams, the men of Japan. But of such he had no more than twenty in a personnel of a hundred and thirty aboard the junk. For the rest there were half a score of English roughs whom the *Hozeander* had collected as the spare men from the factories of Bantam and Ayuthia. The junk and the voyage made good sanctuary for the Spaniards who had killed their Captain and fired their ship, so they, too, were on the pay-roll; ship-mates to them were certain swarts who had swum ashore from galleys in the Philippines and stowed away in junks to Nagasaki and begged their way to Hirado.

There were passengers also—for the mind of Cocks was not the only one that was fired by a thought, or word, of China. As the rumours of this thought and word of China, of silk and ivory and tea had mustered a crew of fifty, it filled also a passenger-list of eighty souls.

Chief among them was one Shobei of Nagasaki. To Cocks, while Adams was away seeking Ieyasu, this respectable junk-owner and merchant with credentials in perfect order meant a good lump-sum in plate bars of silver as his fare, with a properly executed contract assigning fair royalties to Cocks's Honourable Co. on any business that the good merchant might do. To Adams, on his return, the rascal's name on the list meant an immediate fix; for his fame at Yedo was greatly enhanced by the fact that there was nothing, legally, against him in any official record. Adams knew, therefore, that it was impossible to nullify the contract which Cocks had signed. He knew also that among the eighty small hucksters and women who filled the rest of the great list there must be a score of Shobei's own especial thugs. For years Adams at Yedo, in the handling of sailing-silences, had observed the series of peculiar misadventures that had dogged the career of this same Shobei. His own junk, at critical moments, was found to be laid up in dock for some vital repair, so that he was forced to sail on his business as the passenger of Spaniards or Portuguese or of some neighbour. The boat that had carried him on these cruises had generally returned, during ten years, as a derelict towed in by fishermen. Typhoon had battered it or pirates sacked it. Its cargo had gone, looted or jettisoned; the crew was no more—the seas or the pirates had destroyed it to a man. Shobei, however, and a few nondescript passengers survived. Though a ruined man he was ever thankful to whatever powers had so beneficently saved his poor life—and the lives of a score or so of inconsiderable passengers—hucksters and women. Curiously, as time went on, Shobei was seen to be not a ruined man but a plodder who rebuilt his shaken fortune. The silk and ivory and coral and ambergris on which he did it came from God only knew where —but, nevertheless, it came. Only on the last of Shobei's lucky escapes from the perils of the sea had it occurred to guardians of the harbour not only to search and seal the battered wreck, but to arrest and search one of the rescuing skiffs also. In it were bales and jars and crates, silk and ambergris and pottery; but Shobei and the other survivors were found blameless: men so battered and foredone could not be held responsible for the guarding of bilge-sodden holds.

Adams could only curse at the name of Shobei on the list and at sight of the man himself, smiling and affable, thankful to the lucky day that had brought him aboard a vessel which no less a person than the illustrious Pilot of Yedo himself was to command. Adams could do nothing. He had to accept the man against whom nothing had been proved. So he looked to the fowling-pieces set handy in the rack of his deck-house; and he mounted a small saker on the afterdeck, its muzzle laid on the orlop-hatch. In lieu of balls he lashed beside it a barrel of small grape.

It was too late now to repair the oversight of Cocks, and to search the dunnage or the merchandise brought aboard by the eighty passengers. He could count absolutely on but twenty men—his "stowte seamen" of Japan in the crew. The rabble

of whites and swarts were only a possibility. Instead of raising
any hullabaloo he included, in the furnishings of the deck
house, a chest of thirty short swords whose fashion had been
brought to English ships by encounters with the Portuguese.

Skiffs towed the *Sea Adventure* from the Harbour, with
Cocks loosing off seven pieces from the *Hozeander* "in farewell
and complemento," and Adams brooding in the satisfaction
that disaster might be averted since he, who had the measure
of Shobei and knew the treachery of those seas, was in command instead of sulky Wickham or the boy Sayers.

These two, with the Spaniard Damian Marin (now on easy
enough terms with Wickham), occupied the deck-house with
him and stood, approximately, in the position of officers.
There were personages among the hundred and twenty odd
whose status was a mystery to the other three; one who was,
Adams told them, the Japan Captain; a purser; a master of
the carpenters: a portly, unsmiling individual who was the
spokesman of the merchant-passengers so that even Shobei
communicated only through him with Adams.

In addition to the adornment of swords in his girdle Adams
now wore at his breast the sailing-permit with the Shogun's
great red seal.

After a very few days at sea it was reported that passengers
were tampering with the cargo, and half a dozen hucksters
were brought before him by his watchmen. It was Shobei who
defended these simple fellows, through their officially appointed
spokesman. It was water, he said, that had set the poor
wretches anxious for their shabby and worthless goods. The
vessel was said to be a-leak.

Adams took young Sayers with him, for Sayers at the
moment was wearing his sword and pistols. They called for a
lantern and the sounding-stick and went below. Crawling and
scrambling among the bales and chests in the hold, they roused
hidden sleepers and sent them, blinking, into the twilight
above. Men and boys and women were dug out and sent up,
Adams smiting any bottom that presented itself handy to his
sounding-stick.

Young Sayers sweated coldly in his palms and gulped the
retching in his throat; but the stomach of Adams was hardened

to any stench that the hold of a junk might offer.

He sounded the bilge and they went up again.

"In two hours," he said to the passengers' spokesman who stood with Shobei and others at his elbow, "I will measure the water again. All men's goods are safe—raised well above the water on the ballast of stones, and upon faggots. In the meantime no man is to go down."

While he still stood there the foreman carpenter battened the hatches and the watchmen squatted upon them. He added to their number two Englishmen and two Spaniards.

When they were in the deck-house again, with Wickham and Damian the Spaniard still somewhere on deck, Edmund Sayers drank some wine and said, "Is there trouble, Captain?"

"Lad," said Adams, "have you ever known a ship that was not trouble? Englishmen, Dutchmen, Spaniards, Portingals and Japans—I've sailed them all, and they are all the same. They are all trouble."

He, too, drank some wine and sat down.

"But is she a-leak?" asked Sayers.

"Aye," said Adams, and peculiarly he smiled. "Aye—and I am obliged to Master Shobei for the thought. She is a-leak." His smile tended towards a grin.

"I did not think you took a fair sounding," Sayers observed.

"And I," said Adams, "did not think you had a thought down there beyond vomiting." There was obviously more in this boy than met the eye. "But say nothing of it, lad. I'll tell you more when we're ashore."

"Ashore?"

"Ashore," said Adams. "But again say nothing. We'll make the Great Lu-Chu forty leagues to South. It's good anchorage and I have some friendship with the king."

"But if there is no leak——" Sayers began.

"If there's no leak," Adams interrupted him, "there shall be a leak. And the pump shall be lost in the night—or ruined. You yourself shall see to that. And we shall have to anchor, and land the cargo, to trim. And in re-lading the cargo we will examine our passengers' goods, for arms."

Sayers was merely puzzled.

Adams said quietly, "There are some pirates aboard us. If

we leave them their arms, there could well be mutiny and murder."

"Then why all this business of a leak?" asked Sayers. "If you know of murderers aboard——"

"Because," said Adams, "Japan is a country well governed by laws. It is only according to the law that any man may rule another. And understand this, lad: a shipmaster is somewhat of a servant to his passengers." He smiled now. "It is Shobei, the chief of the passengers, who has given us this leak, and so in landing we shall be lawfully following his wish. I will see to it now that their spokesman and my scribe record that Shobei and certain others first reported a leak to us. My soundings will confirm it."

Before he went out Sayers said, "Shobei is the rascal, then?"

"Aye," said Adams.

"If I should find him ashore," Sayers suggested, "—or aboard when all others are ashore—shall I kill him?"

"You might," said Adams, "but you are scarcely knowing enough yet—in the law and other matters. Only luck could put him readily in your way—but there is no harm in your looking for it. I, too, shall be ready for such luck, if it should come my way. But remember that the law is stronger here than men—decent men no less than rogues." More thoughtfully he added, "Cut him rather than stab him, if it should so happen. For stabbing in this country is the obvious work of a foreigner."

CHAPTER XVII

AFTER going again into the hold with his lantern and his sounding-stick he assembled the passengers on deck and addressed them. First he thanked their astute and worthy Shobei, whose sagacity had discovered what his own poor intelligence had been too dull to find: to wit, the leak in his ship. His indebtedness to master Shobei was unbounded, and no pains would be spared to set the matter in order. Regardless, for the moment, of his own inconsiderable objects in this voyage he had already followed the wish implied by the report of his passengers, and altered the vessel's course. He was making for a harbour, they would be gladdened to hear, where the damage would be repaired. Thus, said he—and he smiled benignly upon his passengers—any damage that might already have been caused could be at once recorded, and claims fairly entered.

He wished, as he spoke, that young Sayers could have followed, to learn something of the manner in which any man of sense comported himself. . . . He concluded: No man need have anxiety meanwhile for the safety of his goods. They were under battened and sealed hatches, and there they would remain till the time of landing.

The spokesman murmured a suggestion from Shobei that it were better for men to have access to their property, lest the water rise to destroy it. Adams smiled and said, No, the water would not rise sufficiently. Of that he gave them his word, and his word was known from Yedo to the end of Satsuma, to be as good as his bond. Any damage to their goods from water should be upon himself. Against any other risk also he was prepared to guard them. The watchmen would be doubled in number and would be armed, the foreigners with pistols and the natives with swords. Anyone attempting an entry to the hold would be shot at sight, or cut in pieces.

Shobei himself led a sudden applause at the end of the

speech, and even Adams could not see that any in the rabble below them, rather than any others, hesitated or hung particularly on his words or movements, to mark them out as the thug's adherents.

He said later to the spokesman that it would not be fitting for him to accept the offer of Shobei and certain other volunteers to relieve the sailors at guard over the hatches; for passengers were honoured guests and should honourably sleep while wage-slaves properly laboured.

This settled Shobei; but Adams was cheated, by the flat inscrutability of the faces, of any discovery of accomplices.

They were more cunning than even Adams had expected of them, and more closely knit together in their scheme: the arms which he had found in the hold incriminated no one man. They were swords and dirks of adequate forging and workmanship, but of no distinction to identify any of them as the property of a particular man. They were stowed together in a single hamper instead of distributed and concealed in the property of individuals. With them were half-a-dozen short bows and bundles of arrows, and pikeheads that could be fitted to the staves carried by most of the travellers aboard.

They made land; and as soon as they were fast to the small jetty Wickham and Damian the Spaniard went ashore with Adams's scribe and a seaman carrying an umbrella, a mirror and a set of glass bottles they had brought from the *Hozeander* for just such a contingency as this. With the presents despatched to the King of the Great Lu Chu, work was immediately begun.

Ashore, so ran the law of Japan, every man's property was his own affair. So Adams stood at the hatch, attended by young Sayers and the passengers' spokesman. They held the list and checked the tallies as each man claimed his chest or bale and bundles. The women these men had brought with them were already busy ashore with their braziers and cooking-pots. The baggage passed smoothly enough from the hold to deck and from the deck, along the gang-plank, to the shore. The Japan Captain was below to supervise the labour of his men. It was he who had seen to the loading of the cargo, and Adams knew him of old for a good hard sailor, a man to be trusted with cargoes, with a sword and with the tiller, as with secrets.

When he reported that all the tallied goods were up Adams called a halt. "We will search now," he said, "for the leak.' He turned to dismiss Shobei and the spokesman whose goods had gone ashore on the shoulders of flunkies. "When we have found the damage and repaired it," he said, "I will ask you to condescend to see that it is good." For this was the formality; the passengers were entitled to see that the vessel carrying them was seaworthy.

Shobei was bland but hesitant, glancing quickly down the hatchway so that an inspiration came to Adams that it would be well for Shobei to be kept out of touch with the seamen.

Shobei wore at his girdle the single sword to which his standing entitled him; the hilt and scabbard indicated a serviceable blade. The spokesman also stood well enough in affairs for the same distinction of a single weapon; but his potbelly and splayed feet placed him in a class where there was no swordsmanship, and the thing at his girdle was an obvious dummy, carved and decorated and useless trumpery.

Adams got them ashore, thanking them for the great courtesy that prompted Shobei to linger in his anxiety to be of possible service.

Some of the white crew were already ashore, concocting the gallegalle of lime and oil for caulking; for Adams meant to dramatise this business of the leak. There was enough water in the bilge, as there always was in the bilge of any sea-going junk, to justify a systematic trimming. While the sailors and carpenters and smiths caulked and trimmed, the passengers would be ashore cooking and drinking, talking and quarrelling. Adams's cook would be among them—listening and watching. There also would be the scribe and with them the few others, seamen or passengers, whom the cook and scribe had chosen. . . .

"Your men," he called down to the Japan Captain, "may go now and eat and rest themselves." They came up, sweating, and gladly went ashore.

"And you?" Adams asked the Captain.

"It is well with me, An-jin Sama," he answered. "By your

leave I stay here awhile."

Adams casually drew the gang-plank aboard.

"Deign to come below," the Captain said, when Adams was again at the hatch. "There is somewhat here for you to see. Let no others observe us." Adams told young Sayers to sit by the hatch, allowing no one to enter, and went down to the taipan standing with his lantern, thoughtful and lonely in the loneliness of command.

"By luck," he said, "I alone saw it and allowed none of the others to see."

He beckoned Adams to crawl abaft with him to the store of weapons.

"I, too, have seen it," said Adams. "You have done well."

"Aye," said the other, "well enough. For if any of the crew had seen, there would have been commotion and possibly an immediate killing of some passengers; for my men are lusty fellows, with small patience for assassin tradesmen. And regard this." He tapped the boards above his head. "Here is a concealed hatch. Your small gun on the poop is laid upon the forward one. This one is indeed under the very brow of the poop-deck; from it a very good sally could be made."

"Who, taipan," asked Adams, "would be the men to make such a rush?"

"Ah," said the little Captain, "if I knew that—or if you knew it—I could have handed these things to my men and so made a short work."

"It is not yet, however, that they would strike," said Adams. "Yet why should they have stored their arms thus ready?"

"Who is to know the way of tradesmen?" asked the sailor. "But the loot, as you say, would be richer when we are returning."

"Anyhow," said Adams, "we have disarmed them now. If we can learn, while they are ashore, who are the parties with an interest in this hamper, it will be easy to watch them when we have got to sea again."

"Unarmed," said the Captain meditatively, "my men could doubtless throw them from the deck."

"But are they unarmed?" asked Adams. "Will they come

aboard again unarmed—*all* of them?" For it was not seemly to name any man under suspicion.

The Captain recognised this. "For any among them," he said, "who is entitled to wear a sword, I also am entitled to wear one." He tapped its sweat-polished wooden hilt with his thumbnail, and smiled.

Adams had made many such friends as this new one; so he passed on from the achievement, saying, "It would be better, perhaps, to leave these, undiscovered, till we have sailed again. If we were to throw them overboard now, quietly, word of it might get to them ashore. A fight in the camp would not be so smooth a matter, for they could arm for it from the bazaar. We will trim and put to sea again peaceably. Whoever inspects our work of caulking down here will see, if he looks for it, that this armoury is still intact. When we are out to sea it can smoothly be tossed out."

CHAPTER XVIII

MATTERS were not, however, as easy as this. The king, Sho Nei, was hostile and disgruntled. The monsoon was already well advanced. Sho Nei was aware how much easier it was to land a rabble of seamen and passenger-hucksters and disperse it in his bazaars than to assemble it again on board and put it out to sea. It was not that he had any kind of objection to seamen or men of business turned loose in his bazaars. He himself was, in fact, one of the very shrewdest; and so it was only the time of year that bothered him. With the very first of the West and the South-West winds each spring there came to his island a great junk from China. Sho Nei had no particular love for Chinamen; but he did most particularly want to keep the exclusive handling of that junk's cargo. Purses so long as that in the custody of Adams on the *Sea Adventure*, and in the chest of Shobei from Nagasaki, were direct rivals too potent for entertainment by him who flourished as a middleman. Adams found, instead of the genial host he had always found before, a testy and outraged monarch. For his breach of the formalities in having landed men before actually getting the royal permit, Adams found himself weighing out plate bars as a further present to his Majesty; and he hugged the reflection that if he had waited for the permit he would never have got it.

Shobei the thug, meanwhile, was making his own friends in his own way. He bought from the king's godowns whatever rubbish still cluttered them from the Chinese cargo of the year before.

The king was able to explain, even to Adams himself, why he was so anxious for him to be gone: if they waited for the China junk the austere pride of China would be injured beyond the possibility of repair. Never again would a rich cargo come to him from the mystery of that dark land if any from it should find him entertaining a cavalero, together with merchants and a shipload of merchandise, from Japan. Adams willingly undertook to go as soon as his leaks were caulked; and it was then that the trouble began with the crew.

At first it was nothing more than Adams could easily accept as the normal villainy of seamen ashore. The Englishmen started it with a demand for money on account of pay. Adams refused it, pointing out that the indenture stipulated for a first payment in Siam. The indenture, retorted the men, specified Siam as their first anchorage. Since, for reasons of his own, he had violated the indenture by bringing them into this God-forsaken backwater, he must meet them with the compensation of some cash—following out the indenture by paying at the first port of call. Adams saw that there was reason enough in this to make a case, so he paid them. One of the men, mumbling at the coins in his fist, said they knew well enough what the leak was worth; and Adams saw that Shobei had been at them.

Their immediate vanishing into the bazaar had its bright side, for the Japan Captain employed a dozen native artisans and apprentices for the work of caulking, who neither would nor could assess the leaks they were mending. But the business of trimming turned out to be not all pantomime for the benefit of Master Shobei. Neither Adams nor the Japan Captain was of the sort that could prowl for long about a ship laid-to without finding work that called for real doing. The mast-case was shabby; worms had been at the housing; the fit of it had been made good with the sheer dodgery of wedges; and they both knew what winds could be between the Lu-Chu and Siam. They would have had the mast out and overboard to give room for a new one if the king had been in a different temper—if, perhaps, Adams had been the one to buy up his remnants of stock instead of Shobei. As it was, the king would sell them no tree; and in the end it was only Shobei who could get for them, out of the bazaar, timber enough for a new case and for partners to reinforce the housing of the old one.

The men began to come back from the bazaar in groups of a sullen half-dozen at a time. The first lot skulked about ashore among the passengers' women and the cooking-pots; and Adams was content to let them skulk, for they were of no immediate use to him—sore-headed Englishmen and a

Spaniard, the type he had not handled for fifteen years, and
not a craftsman among them.

When two of his carpenters came back the Japan Captain
lost no time in hurrying them aboard to work upon the timber.
But after a night ashore among their messmates and the
bivouacked passengers they came aboard in the morning, not
to work but to demand pay for the paltry hours they had put
in the day before. The Captain was puzzled. He turned to
Adams, and from Adams back to the sullen men. "Pay?" he
asked. "Hours? Are you no longer seamen but bazaar-
artisans that you should chaffer for wages by the hour, instead
of by the voyage, or by the sea?"

Neither of the men was anxious to answer the jibe, for both
were well known to Adams; but they were being watched from
the shore by the others who had primed them and shoved them
forward. One of them mumbled and cleared his throat and
began afresh to rehearse what he had thought would remain
quite clear in his mind: "There are no seamen at all here. This
is no voyage. As the casual workmen on shore that we are,
we require full payment before we render further service. Not
only we, sir, but the others also—to a man. The hairy ones
and all." He had spoken his piece and was obviously relieved.
Adams smiled at him and then thought it worth risking the
insult—provided that he laughed not too loudly—of allowing
the smile of friendship to become the laughter of scorn. "Ho!"
he said, chuckling to the Captain and ignoring the men, "the
palaver of coolies is a funny matter when it comes from the
throat of a deep-sea-man!"

The Captain turned to them. "Since when," he asked
gravely, "have my men made of me a coolie-master?"

The answer came from the one who had not yet spoken; and
it came with a cool insolence bred of the taunt from Adams.
"Since you elected to sail with us as a coolie-master instead of
as the commander of deep-sea-men. Such a commander should
have a proper boatswain to carry his bidding to his men."

"So——" said the Captain, and the question was put quite
inoffensively as merely seeking information, "you would
become boatswain?"

"That I would not," said the man. "I am a carpenter, and

what I would now do is draw a carpenter's pay."

Adams turned to the Captain. "Is it true that they have no boatswain? I did not know of it."

"No!" the carpenter answered very smartly. "You, An-jin Sama, who commanded the whole affair, did not even know of it. You brought us to sea without the means that are the right of every sailor for obtaining whatever is his due."

"And of what dues have you been cheated?" Adams demanded.

"We have been cheated of a boatswain," was the answer. The rascals ashore could not have chosen a better spokesman than this one; for when an idea had once been forced into his head it stuck there. "We have no boatswain," he repeated stolidly.

"Very well," said Adams. "You have reason in your talk." He had lived but a very short time among those "stowte seamen" before learning what Santvoort had never learnt— that a heavy fist and loud oaths among them did not make the discipline of a ship. The deep-sea-man of Japan was a man apart from others. Obedience in him was not a blind habit of his spirit as it was in the spirit of a landsman to his feudal Lord; it was an intelligent gesture, a matter of confidence and consent. The thing of which this carpenter had now got hold was a fact for proper consideration. In the general busy-ness of the bungled start from Hirado a formality had obviously been omitted. No boatswain had been appointed; and without a boatswain the men had no way that was honourable and strictly proper of communicating with their Captain; for the status of boatswain was something unique. The properly appointed boatswain could address the Captain as a man addresses man, while to him any mariner in the crew could speak any word that was in his mind without slight or embarrassment to either party.

"How comes it, Captain," Adams asked, "that they have no boatswain?"

"As it comes, An-jin," the Captain said sadly, "that the ship itself has an unsound mast. There has not been weather enough to show us the oversight in the ship. And there was not weather enough—till now—to show us the oversight in the crew."

"Well said," Adams grunted. To the men he said, "You have heard him. As we are repairing the one, so we will repair the other. You shall have your boatswain before you come aboard again."

But the matter was not thus dismissed. The man who had seen and taken the insult in the Pilot's laugh said, "That is as it may be, a matter for the others to decide. But we two have the other matter for settlement. We have come for our pay."

From the tail of his eyes Adams watched the lounging, muttering lot on shore; and he did not like it. He drew the purse from his girdle and from the purse some coins. "No," said the man sullenly. "Pay. Not charity from a Lord."

Never, in fifteen years, had a man thus spoken to him, unchidden by himself or unthrashed by a flunkey. "It is pay I give you," he said quietly; for he could not replace coins and purse at the fellow's rebuke with the sulky crew and half a hundred passengers watching him. "It is no Lord's charity. For indeed I myself am but a seaman here like your Captain and yourselves, and no Lord at all. And as to charity—I feel but little when the friendship of old shipmates is lost by the talk of peddlers and the hospitality of brothels." The men still hesitated at the money. "Take it," said Adams. "It is big pay, I grant you—the pay of perhaps six men instead of two. But the work you did yesterday was good—the work of six."

Adams knew well enough that tact such as this—(old Cocks would have called it "complemento")—would have brought back cheeriness to the two sulky men in any ordinary circumstances. But the circumstances were not ordinary, with the crew and passengers mixed into a hang-dog rabble ashore.

He allowed the carpenters to go, and himself stood with the Japan Captain. Both knew that they must not, in policy, leave sight of the crowd as though to go into furtive consultation; for thus are enmities declared. They exchanged words quietly, Adams saying, "I'll speak to them now," and the Captain, "I, too, An-jin. I am at fault for not giving them a boatswain. I will repair it. They are a good crew."

Adams went to the side and beckoned the crowd nearer. They came—his Englishmen and swarts and polyglot Portuguese and Spaniards thrust forward by the others. He started with a bluff, so that he might get from them their grievance before admitting that they had one. "The leaks are mended," he said with unconcern. "They were slight enough, and they are now caulked. Yesterday we began work upon the mast. To-day we will have the sails ashore for mending. There is some little discontent in the Japan crew, because they have no boatswain—or some such matter beyond my understanding, which their Captain will adjust. But our time is getting short. We must work while the weather is good." He realised now the want of officers; for there had been no organisation at all—just a rabble of seamen flung together with himself to command them and young Sayers to give casual, unspecified help. Sayers himself was missing at the moment, ashore somewhere with Wickham and the Spaniard Damian. One man, however, an Englishman named Hargreaves, had stood out from among the others since their sailing as a natural Number One. Adams called to him. "Hargreaves, bring the sailmakers aboard. Not the Japans—only the two English and the Spaniard."

Hargreaves muttered, "Can't be done, Captain." He turned his broad back upon the *Sea Adventure* and moved away among the seamen towards the passengers. Then he turned again, shoved and prompted, and said, "We want to talk to you of our indenture."

"Come then and talk," said Adams.

Hargreaves came forward, pressed and followed by the others.

"What is your talk?" asked Adams.

"We want our pay," said Hargreaves. "Without our pay we will do no work."

"Man!" said Adams, "you've had pay. Your indenture of service was to go for Siam. You have come now less than one fifth of the way and you talk of pay. Though you are entitled to nothing, you have had some pay already. You have drunk it and whored it—and now you ask for more. It is mutiny."

"Mutiny it may be," said Hargreaves. "But it is sense.

It is not the indenture that brought us here, but your own service to the Japan Emperor—to spy out this island for him. It is you that brought us here, contrary to agreement. Pay us, and we will go on."

"You will work for your pay before you get it, or you have declared a mutiny." Even in the mind of Adams this word and the thought still stood for a dire thing among men who followed the sea. He shouted it—"Mutiny"—as the greatest threat he could hurl at rascals.

It shook them. For Hargreaves said, "Not *us*, Captain. It is the Japans. They have declared it. And if they will not work, we cannot. Give us our pay and get the Japans to work. Then we will work also."

Adams said, "You are at sea. I am your Captain. Any man disobeying me is a mutineer. When I give you work to do, you must do it. What the Japans do is no affair of yours."

"It is very much our affair," said another man in the crowd, "if half the crew will do nothing, putting all the work on us."

"All the work!" sneered Adams. "There has not been a hand's-turn of work for a man of you since we weighed our anchor. Our sail was set and a good wind brought us here— passengers and all—with only me and Mr. Sayers on deck, and the Japan Captain, and a Japan boy at the helm. Work indeed! Had it not been for that paltry leak——"

"Aye—we know that leak," sneered the man. "The junk was making no more than a pint of water in a day."

Adams spoke more quietly to them, motioning them nearer to the boatside. "Neither is the size of the leak your affair. There are things in this country of which you know nothing, and of which I may not yet tell you. I have them in hand, however; and when we have made our voyage and returned home—to Japan—I will perhaps tell you of them. In the meantime we will straighten out the crew. I will make mates from among you, according to the service you can show, and according to your wishes. I am in good standing with these Japans; you need not fear that they will not get their fair share of the work. As soon as they are come aboard——"

"Aye!" laughed the man. "Get them aboard first! Or get

any of us—without our pay—if you can."

Adams remembered, in the rage that was rising in him, the effect upon those scoundrels of the word "mutiny."

"I have talked enough," he said, "with a rabble of long-shore foot-pads. If mutiny you must, let the manner of it at least be in the manner of seamen. Send three men of you aboard to parley with me. If you have anything to say that is fair, I will hear it. If it is nought but villainy——" but no; the time for that had not yet come. "Send them aboard!" he shouted. "I am waiting for them—your chosen three."

He went aft to the deckhouse, to await the answer to his challenge, and his mood was not so much the mood of a man whose solitary wits are matched against a mob or against destiny, as of one who is baffled by the refusal of a simple machine to do its work. . . . It must work; on that he was determined, for the machine was of the same material and the same type as the one that was to do his later work, Northward. There was, too, a more immediate object before him in the handling of the *Sea Adventure*. In the making of Siam he could also make the English factory at Bantam and the acquaintance of the Cape Merchant there, Spalding. This man, he suspected, was more open-minded than John Saris of the *Clove*, and in better standing with the Company. For Spalding had written him a letter three years before in very friendly sort, encouraging him to await the arrival of an English ship. At Bantam also—at the disposal of this open-minded and friendly Spalding—were ships and victuals and seamen.

His swords were of more use to him than pistols; so he sat down upon the lid of the chest that held the firearms. He was alone on the ship, for the Japan Captain had gone ashore to hunt up his men and to get them, if he could, out of the hairy rabble of Englishmen. Presently the *Sea Adventure* rocked to the weight upon the gangplank as three men came aboard.

Adams called them into the deckhouse and they stood, with their caps in their hands, at the doorway. To his pleasure and relief Hargreaves was one of them, and both the others were English. He said at once, "This discontent among you—did it start among the Japans or the others, Spaniards and Portingals and Swarts?"

They were not to be caught. All were thirsty with parching and terrible thirsts. All were penniless where a bazaar offered no hospitality except for cash, for it was a bazaar accustomed to every kind of sailor. All had dealt with officers, in tight situations, before.

"The discontent, Captain," said Hargreaves cannily, "came to all alike from unfair treatment. We come to a voyage's end, and get no pay."

Adams saw clearly enough that there was no guile in them. All they wanted was to get into the bazaar. But he saw also that there must be a limit to the humouring of them, as there would never be, so long as they lived, a limit to the thirsts that drove them.

He smiled. "How much money is it," he said, "that you want? If I give you the chest we carry, there would still be the cargo left."

But the officer who could wheedle those men where he could not command them had yet to be found.

Hargreaves answered solemnly. "We want our fair wages and no more. We sailed for Siam. It was not our doing that we came here, but yours. Our wages should stand, according to the indenture of our service."

"We have come now one-fifth of the way to Siam. You have had one-fifth of the money due to you in Siam—more or less. If it is less, I will make it up."

"It is not for a fistful of shells one way or the other that we are asking, Captain," said Hargreaves. "It is for the full wage. We sailed to draw it so soon as we should come ashore. We have come ashore."

"In Siam will you not again want money?" asked Adams.

Hargreaves shrugged his shoulders. The shrug meant—and reasonably enough—that there was much between the great Lu-Chu and Siam; and that for seamen sailing a junk towards the turning of the monsoon the morrow could well take care of itself.

Adams drew his tobacco-pipe from its case and then put it back again; for the cook was ashore and there was no brazier from which he could light it. "And if I will not pay it?" he asked.

"Then we will not sail."

"And if I consent to pay you half?"

The men hesitated. Hargreaves had his eye fixed on Adams, seeking an answering glance so that he could convey some meaning by his stare. Adams felt the stare and the reason for it; and so he looked everywhere but at Hargreaves. One of the other men said, "It is not for us to make a bargain. There is firm agreement among all ashore that our pay shall be the full wage to Siam." There was no understanding between this man and Adams of the sort that was ready to exist, at any moment, between Adams and Hargreaves.

"And if I do not pay it?" asked Adams. "Is there firm agreement ashore as to what you will do in that case?"

The man mumbled, "We will not come aboard to sail your ship."

"Very well," said Adams. "You have been appointed by your fellows to do their bidding, and you have consulted them. I also must consult, and receive bidding; for I also am a servant like yourselves—except that I have not yet mutinied against my masters. They will soon return from taking the air ashore; and I will lose no time in telling you their bidding." This was neat; and Adams saw the neatness of it as two pairs of feet shifted upon the floor, and the jaws in two faces dropped. Hargreaves moved neither his feet nor his jaw. Only his eye shifted to a fresh glint in another search for the eye of Adams. But it found nothing: Adams knew the dog must have his drink and his women—or promise of them—before he could become an officer.

"They will come back drunk as the Lord Mayor," grumbled one of the men.

"We will do them the courtesy then of waiting till they are sober." Adams smiled amiably as he added, "They have already done as much for you."

They took it as coming somewhat from the strange Japan heart that was in him when he said, "I thank you for your waiting upon me." He was thinking of his machine. These three—or at any rate two of them—would presently be his officers. When they had shuffled out to the deck he called after hem, "Have the kindness when you are ashore to send word to my cook to bring my dinner aboard."

"Aye, sir," said one of the men, his habit of obedience over-coming, for the moment, his habit of mutiny.

The Japan Captain was aboard before the cook, and Adams got little enough cheer from him. "How much of it is the work of certain passengers, and how much of your hairy ones, I cannot yet say. But the trouble is great, An-jin. I had all but gained the forgiveness of my men for the discourtesy in the matter of the boatswain when they began a loud talk of pay. Of that I could not speak with them, for I myself am, like them, a wage-earner. But they say they will not come aboard till the hairy ones also come, to do their share of the work."

"They are in mighty close league," said Adams. "They have talked well together—with no linguist."

"Or the same vile tongue outside them has talked to both," the Captain suggested. "But it is always the same with a mixed crew, An-jin. Either there is quarrelling among them and daily bloodshed, or there is a close league of villainy. As to pay, the money you gave them two days ago was ample for any man of sense; but those men of yours swaggered to the taverns and flung their money out, paying thrice the value of every bottle and every woman they took, setting the price—for all others—of one night's entertainment at the price of three. It is small wonder that they want more money!"

"If it is only money," Adams said, "the dogs can have it. And when they have drunk it, we will go. But there is the matter of the passengers. We must search them as they come aboard; for they may have armed afresh, not knowing whether we have found their store below."

"They know that it is where they left it," said the Captain. "While I was ashore and you were in the house with your three I saw a man swim from a fishing-boat and crawl aboard to spy. No doubt there have been a dozen others. It is better so."

They stood on deck where all could see them. Ashore there was great bustling about braziers and cooking pots in the lee of chests and bales and bundles, under awnings rigged to poles and walking-staves. The farther fringe of passengers and crew mingled with hangers-on from the bazaar along the road which twisted inland from the beach, and was lost to the *Sea Adven-*

ture's view behind a low bluff.

Adams liked a problem stated in its exact terms. It made calculation possible instead of speculation. Six days at least, or eight, would be necessary for the spending by the crew of the pay they demanded, for he feared trouble in the bazaar if he allowed all to go and drink together. The king was in no amiable mood and Shobei was on the prowl. . . . Relays, therefore, it would have to be; and the men would have to settle the order of them for themselves. With Hargreaves slaked and tamed he would have ample time at sea to make a crew that was a real crew before trouble came from Shobei; and the Japan Captain's trouble, he knew, was only family trouble—for he and his men would be united and loyal again as soon as the petulant ones had been humoured and the slighted ones had been restored to dignity by the appointment of their boatswain. . . .

As he began to wonder whether the men had sent his message to the cook he saw an agitation stirring through the gabblers on the road, and presently the cook came, running. He thrust by any who would have stopped him, and came aboard.

"They return," he said, "carrying a body on a litter—Master Sayers with them."

"Whose is the body?" asked Adams.

"Not *his*," said the boy. "For he walks with them, lustily as ever."

"Shobei?" Adams suggested.

The boy nodded. "Yes, Shobei walks beside the litter, assisting the one who is not dead. For he has a considerable wound."

They were presently aboard, pressed as far as the gangway by those ashore whose cooking was not at a moment of crisis. Young Sayers came first; by the happiest of flukes, or because drink made his movements a little ostentatious, the salute he gave Adams was a most elaborate one. "They have had their fight out, Captain," he said quietly, as one who seldom criticised the working of natural laws.

"And is the Spaniard dead?" asked Adams.

"Not he," said Sayers cheerfully. "He still bleeds, however —blood or *saké*. Wickham got him in the chest just as he got

Wickham in the thigh, and I ran out with Shobei to part them."

"Shobei was not injured in the pell-mell, then," Adams observed.

"It was little enough pell-mell, Captain," the youth explained. "They went out of the room where there was drinking and singing, all friendly; and in a minute there was their swords knocking together and Wickham swearing, and the other bawling back at him; and I ran out to knock their blades away, and Shobei came after. And besides, Captain——" he had dropped his voice, and was speaking very solemnly; "—this Shobei——"

"I know—a very fine fellow," said Adams. "The best of friends, and a good host no doubt. But you attend to those wounds, lad, if you are sober enough, while I eat my dinner on deck. The Japan Captain will bring water and rags to the deckhouse to help you if he has fed; for he understands such matters. Then sleep; I will deal with Master Wickham later."

"Deal with him?" asked Sayers.

"Aye," said Adams. "Deal with him. It is not enough to get a man's own consent in this country to let his blood."

The litter-bearers had passed them, going to the deckhouse, followed by Wickham on the arm of Shobei. A bloody napkin showed through the gape of his breeches where Sayers or Shobei or some bawd had slit their leg to stanch the wound. Adams looked at the napkin and at the pale, drawn face of Wickham (for the fellow had bled considerably). But he had no answer for Wickham's attempted smile—a grin of pain and sheepish, stupid pride.

In the log he wrote, "Mr. Wikham & damian did fight to gather . . . I muse solitari and walk melancholie on the shoare."

CHAPTER XIX

THIS record of himself was no attempt at dramatisation. It represented one fact as accurately as the closing entry for the day stated another: "It rayned the wynd at no no Eest Clloudi and foull wether."

In the melancholy of those hours of pacing the beach in the foul drizzle he found a peculiar oppressiveness. It came from the mystery by which alone so accurate an understanding had been arrived at between the two crews. There was professedly not a man in either of them—Japan or Ingari—who had any word in the tongue of the other, unless it was a word that stood for some hard thing of their common craft or a normal requirement at a tavern. Of any elaborate thought of past or future none but his scribe or himself could carry a meaning from one group to the other. And yet they had come to a detailed agreement.

Adams sent for Hargreaves when he had talked again to the Captain, and Hargreaves slouched up to him on the bluff of the hill. Adams tried to make an officer and a colleague of him at once, by saying: "The men ask too much, Hargreaves. Half the Siam wages would be a possible payment. Unreasonable enough, but possible. That much I could put before the Company."

"The 'Company'?" said Hargreaves; and Adams knew that if he looked frankly at the man's grin he would be admitting the farce that brought it there.

"You must tell the mutineers the half wage is the most they can hope for."

"The full wage," said Hargreaves quietly, "is the least we will accept. The Japans also."

Hargreaves went back and Shobei came to him as he walked and continued musing. He brought some raisins and a sweet cake. "An-jin Sama," he said, "seeing the wretchedness of the sky and the air, I ventured to think that the rude company of this person might not be so complete an unattractiveness as otherwise."

358

Adams accepted the raisins and the cake with proper thanks and said, "The same considerateness which sent you out to me prompted you, no doubt, to leave your spokesman comfortable, and in some shelter." They drew about them their cloaks of greased paper.

Shobei said, "I came purely for the insolent indulgence of my desire for the Pilot's company; and not for the transaction of any business."

"The gratified desire," said Adams, "and the pleasure are the Pilot's."

"If any small assistance could be given to one so powerful as the Pilot by one so insignificant as the prattler, the chance would be a happy one."

Adams chewed raisins and said, "I know well that in the event of any trouble I should find immediate help from my passengers. But at the present moment, for myself, all is singularly well. What trouble there is, is not mine but the crew's; and neither you nor I can cure it, but only the tavern-keepers and singing-girls. If it is to get to sea again that you are anxious, your anxiety will soon be ended. As soon as the men are paid, and spent and sober again, we will be trimmed, and away."

Shobei smiled and said, "It is indeed well. All men of any sense have known from the first that the justice and fairness of heart that have made the name of An-jin Sama a legend in our land would clearly show his colleagues the propriety of the men's demand. In myself there was never the briefest instant's doubt. So sure was I in my heart, that as soon as I saw the first signs of this black turbulence among the men— seeing also that our Pilot and Commander was one so greatly put about by other pressing affairs—I myself presumed to quiet the rascals. Their temper was ugly enough, but I knew— knowing so well the fairness of An-jin Sama—that I ran no material risk in undertaking to them, as I did unhesitatingly undertake, that the money would be paid to them. By myself if by no other."

"In your haste to render me this service," said Adams drily, "you overlooked the law which forbids a passenger to meddle in matters concerning a ship-master and his crew."

Shobei took this blandly. "With men gone lawless," he said, "it is expedient to apply new laws."

"Aye," said Adams, hoping to get something out of the retort, "it is." But there was small comfort to be found in the triviality of a cryptic retort; for Shobei had scored already. All that the rascal had to do now was swagger back to the camp, saying not another word to the men. It was Adams's own action that would do the damage. In paying the men he would be making good the promise of Shobei to them, and establishing the villain as their champion. He cursed himself for his shilly-shallying. As soon as the men had beaten him he ought to have admitted it. Now the defeat would look as though it had come from Shobei.

Shobei had more to say. "There is another matter concerning which I had done better, perhaps, to have approached you formally through our spokesman. It is a graver matter than the handing of a few tael to lecherous and thirsty seamen; for it concerns the security and the peace of all. It is not for myself that I speak—for I myself carry a sword lawfully and am competent to draw it. It is therefore only on behalf of the others—the unarmed crew as well as passengers—that I open my mouth to speak."

He paused, looking portentously and very solemnly at the ground. Adams smiled, because he was not going to be rushed into saying things this time. It was a pleasure, too, to watch Shobei digging the sand with his toe, stuck for words. He said, "Speak, then; for as yet you have said nothing. The opening of your mouth has been concerned with the great courtesy for which you are so justly famous; but of your own distress it has told me nothing."

It may have been that he saw the insult of the Pilot's amusement at his discomfiture; for it was a little testily that he answered, "The distress is not mine. Some of your Ingari carry swords openly suspended to them. To-day has shown us how glibly they will draw and use them. It is known that every seaman of the hairy ones carries somewhere about him a knife or a dirk or a dagger. Cheek by jowl with these armed ones on a small ship where the shortening of tempers is a daily matter, you have some five score helpless men, unarmed as babes."

Adams saw the possibility of a joke, and made the best of it. "So," he said, "you would have me arm my whole crew—native as well as hairy?"

Shobei made it clear that this was no fooling matter. He said, "Nothing but the prodigious stupidity of this blunt merchant could have obscured his meaning from a mind so famously alert as the Pilot's. What I meant, simply, is that all must be disarmed before we sail." He had stopped scratching about in the sand now and took a square, solid stance.

"Oh!" said Adams; "must they indeed!"

Slowly, and frowningly stubborn, Shobei said, "Yes. My meaning is now clear."

"Perfectly clear. And I thank you." Adams smiled. "But to such poor wits as mine it comes very strangely that advice to sail a ship with an unarmed company should come from such as you. It is well known that Shobei Dono has never hazarded these seas without encountering pirates and robbers and murderers. A dozen times or more nought but the luck of Shobei has saved him from the fate of his fellows, to send him home a ruined and a broken man with nought but his life in his hand and his shirt upon his back. But this Shobei is truly dauntless! He suggests that hazards which are survived barely, or not at all, by crews fully armed, should now be faced by men naked of all weapons."

Shobei was equal to this. He shrugged his shoulders. "The suggestion is not mine." He said: "I merely repeat what is said among the others. They will not come aboard again to sail among ruffians who are armed. The worst of them are the very ones that share your place and guard the chests of swords and murdering-pieces enough to slaughter the whole company in a dozen minutes. These reckless men must be stripped of their weapons; the magazine and armoury must be given into the custody of the passengers."

The cool impudence of him was beyond any of the words in the various languages that were commonly at the disposal of Adams. All he could do for some moments was whistle. It did not amount to anything of a tune; and if Shobei had not heard, in tales that were told of the Pilot, that a snatch of whistling sometimes played a part in his conversation, the sound would have puzzled him. Then Adams said, "So. I must do that, must I?"

"Yes," said Shobei, still standing square. "You must."

"And if I do not?" Adams suggested.

"In that case," said Shobei, "they will all refuse to sail. Certainly all the passengers, and probably most of the crew."

"And in that case," said Adams, "much as I should miss your amusing company for the rest of the voyage, I shall leave the lot of you behind."

Shobei said, "Again most luckily an honour has lighted upon me. I who am worthy of neither part nor share in the Pilot's plans or counsels, am happily the one to bring him the first word of important matters. Certain trifling affairs of trade have brought me in touch with certain of this place, merchants and officials. Over the tea and the tobacco-pipe or the wine-cup at a bargaining, remarks are passed and words are allowed to fall. A two-sworded one would not know the way of it; but so it is. And thus, in the plying of my mean affairs I gathered words that might be of service to the two-sworded one. The king has taken this tarrying of yours on the island as pepper in his nose. You must therefore go, An-jin Sama; and right quickly. The edict, even now on its regrettable way to you, lays down not only that you must go, but that you may leave not a thing on these shores—neither man nor girl of passengers or crew; nor indeed a stick or packet of merchandise." He became more deeply thoughtful. "It were a pity," he said, and looked over the camp and at the *Sea Adventure*, "to forfeit so good a ship and so rich a cargo in confiscation, for the dis-obedience of a law."

"The king has been a friend to me," said Adams. "I will see him concerning this fool's order of which you speak."

"He is in the castle," said Shobei.

It was but four miles to the fortress. "What of it?" said Adams. "Can I not see him in the castle? The door is open to me in the castle of the mighty Ieyasu himself." Something about Shobei was beginning to produce the peculiar annoyance in him that led to bragging of this sort.

Shobei very solemnly shook his head. "An-jin Sama," he said, "if the honour of offering advice may be added to the honour of carrying information, this person would humbly suggest that you do no such thing."

"And why not?" demanded Adams.

Shobei hesitated. "At the expressed wish of the Pilot I repeat again what is said. The Pilot's skill in measuring a place with his bare eye, and in charting his measurement that other men may be guided thereby, is famous. A suspicion has entered the mind of his Majesty of the Great Lu-Chu that it was not for the purpose of repairing a leak that you put in here at all. It has even been said by certain in the taverns— 'if leak indeed there was' . . ."

"It is recorded," Adams snapped, "that the leak was reported by you and no other. It is recorded also that it was in obedience to your complaint, and for no other reason, that we put in here."

"His Majesty would perhaps wonder," Shobei suggested, "that the nervous fussing of a trivial landsman-huckster should so easily have ruled the judgment of an illustrious seaman."

There was an unpleasant sensation of warmth and tingling about the back of Adams's neck. "Is the law of *my* making," he snorted, "that a sailor at sea may be put about by any gang of landsmen who have paid for their passage? It is the law of your country, and you know it. And so does the King of Lu-Chu. If he does not, I can very soon tell him of it; and show him the record of your complaint."

"My complaint—yes," said Shobei. "An open investigation of my complaint would have fulfilled the law amply. I did not demand a landing. That also is recorded."

"So you have made a spy of me before the King!" The warmth was spreading on Adams's neck; the tingling was now in the palms of his hands. But if he slapped the little monkey's face, the trouble could be endless.

"I?" said Shobei innocently, and greatly shocked. "Who am I to talk with kings upon such matters? If my ears have been placed where they have heard words that may be of service to the Pilot, only the happiest of chances has placed them there. When they talk here of the war that is waging between our Lord Ieyasu and the Prince Hideyori there is nought that I can say. If it is said that the Pilot is over-zealous in the service of his Lord Ieyasu——"

The insolence of this was treason. With it said before witnesses of the right sort Adams could have cut the scoundrel down and had done with him for good and all. But the rabble that would come scampering up from the beach was too speculative an asset in such a venture. . . . Adams did not consider the matter very fully or very far. He saw on the face of it that, whichever way it ended, such a course would mean a thundering lot of trouble by the way—the passengers tinctured with cut-throats of Shobei's own careful choosing, and both crews in such a temper that any fresh happening would not be overlooked as a possible item for blackmail. . . . Ieyasu had told him once that when a sword has been drawn and used, except in general battle, it can be of no further service to its wearer in regard to that particular enemy. He had remembered this at odd crises in the past fifteen years, to be struck by the good sense of it; and what he most particularly wanted at the moment was not hullabaloo and pother, but some straight way of getting that rascal crew on board again, sober and alert for master Shobei's pranks. So in his own mother tongue he bade him go to everlasting damnation and to hell; and in the tongue of his listener he bade him good-night.

For his own part he continued to walk a while, solitary.

In the deck-house, when he had written up the log and found his bunk, he listened to the robust snoring of young Sayers sleeping off what liquor had not been dispersed by the brawl, to the mumbling of Wickham who probably had some fever in his wound from the rag that had been clapped upon it, and to the gurgle and wheeze of blood in the lung of the Spaniard Damian. He listened also to the whispering of the cook-boy and the scribe on deck, the *Sea Adventure's* sentries while he himself should honourably sleep.

The only companionship for him in his solitude and his "melancholie" was the wind in the junk's standing tackle: it was holding—as he had noted in the log—lustily and loyally to the North-North-East. . . . It would take him—as soon as he had got those mutinous dogs aboard again—to where he had set out to go; to Cochin-China and Siam and to Mr. Spalding at Bantam.

CHAPTER XX

THE Japan Captain, in conference with him next morning after a night in the bazaar, just failed to see exactly why Adams had not made short work of their illustrious passenger, when the man had so clearly asked for it. It went against the grain of a seaman more haphazard than Adams to see a tide or a chance wind wasted. But when wasted it had been, it was gone and done with. . . . "An-jin Sama," he said, "what he said of the King—although the speaker was the stowaway-pirate Shobei—is true." They did not refrain any more from naming him openly. The Captain continued: "The house wherein I was entertained last night is no place for politics. And though it is our Shobei himself who started the tale among these islanders, the tale is freely told among them, sober and drunk, how the hair-covered friend of the Lord Ieyasu can sail a sea in a boat, can tread a road with his feet or gauge a distance with his eye and thereafter set down marks with a brush upon paper so that another may cross the sea after him, or follow the road and shoot ordnance over the distance. Such matters are great mysteries to these simpletons. They are very jealous for their castle and for the freedom of their sea to wash up to them any trade it may. They are not considerable men, An-jin, in the sense that we of Japan are considerable. Rather it could be said by a man not scrupulous of the proper laws of hospitality that they are scavengers. A girl of the tavern, knowing nothing of my rank, offered to sell me a Spanish dagger. I bought it so that no other should have it; but you may depend upon it——"

"As to that," said Adams, "let them buy all the arms the island can find for them. When we have paid the crews, and the islanders have fleeced them, they will come on board readily enough. I have thought how to twist the words of Master Shobei so that it is he who shall demand the searching of the passengers. Our haul of weapons, if haul there is, will make a good present for his Majesty."

It worked out less smoothly than this. The crews took their money happily enough after Adams and the Japan Captain had addressed them. They signed a good receipt for it and entered into a fresh bond of loyal service. The Ingari agreed to elect and appoint sailing-officers for Adams, a first and second mate and a boatswain; the Japans accepted responsibility in the finding of a boatswain. Adams had decided to let them go together, and get it over in one burst. In good humour they set off for the bazaar. Some, however, remained. They were ten or a dozen in number, Ingari and Japans, with a weight upon them of some far responsibility or some aim of petty thrift. It was not for the squandering of money, in taverns and brothels, that such as they went to sea to earn or rob it. They pouched it when they had counted it and signed their names or made their marks; and then they sat down on bales and chests to await the cooking of a stingy meal of rations. To them Adams quickly went, bidding them come aboard to jobs of work for extra pay, seeing that their indenture did not operate until the crew was mustered. They came willingly to kill the time and turn a penny; so Adams isolated them from the passengers, as the bazaar's entertainment would isolate the others.

For four good days there was neither solitary musing nor melancholy walking for Adams. The dirty rain had gone and the wind held, gently now but steadily, from the North and North-North-East. A surprising message came from the King, inviting the Pilot to visit the castle and the royal town inland. It was a trap, no doubt, to test the statements of Shobei; and as a trap Adams cannily avoided it. He replied that already he had imposed too far on the hospitality of his Majesty, and that for his own part he had but little spirit for visiting splendid towns and great castles when the urge within him was to be away again at sea. He had need, however, of further friendship from the King. As a mean and quite unworthy present he sent him a fowling-piece and powder-horn and shot, and begged that he might be allowed to purchase, fairly, fresh victuals and rope, a little timber and a bag of nails.

The next day there was rain again, and with the coming of a dirty night the quicker spenders of the crew began to walk

leisurely round the bluff and delicately along the gang-plank to
their roosts aboard.

In the following, murky dawn a litter was lugged aboard
containing one of the swarts with a broken thigh-bone, a cut
scalp and a dislocated shoulder. A Japan was on deck in
the morning with an eye-ball that only a strong stomach
could look upon without retching; and by evening it was
generally felt aboard that there were no more to return
from the bazaar. A Spaniard and one Englishman never did
return.

After a formal muster and the appointment of Hargreaves as
first mate, with a second and a boatswain, and a boatswain of
their own for the Japans, Adams played his trick upon Shobei.

The crews were on board and in proper humour, contemptuous of the passengers and proud enough of themselves
for the way their money had gone. He kept them handy to the
poop with young Sayers and the Japan Captain ready to
dispense cutlasses and pistols from the chests in the deckhouse.
He summoned first the spokesman on board with his minute-
book, and then Shobei. His own scribe stood with them. His
address to the passengers assembled at the side was: "Your
Number One, Shobei Dono the merchant of Nagasaki, has
lodged a complaint with me of an illicit carrying of arms."
There was a suitable murmur and mumbling ashore. "Yes,"
said Adams. "And we know our Shobei. Any man who
disregarded the word of Shobei would be wanting in not only
courtesy but in sense also. Our waiting here is now but a short
matter. Whatever we still lack for our equipment will be made
good as soon as the permission to buy it has come down from
the King. In three days from now—or at most four—I shall
invite you all to come aboard again. As you come, in courtesy
to the honourable Shobei—in compliance with his suggestion—
the person and the belongings of every passenger will be
closely searched." Comment and criticism began to stir in the
crowd, but he managed to quiet it. "Be easy, my friends," he
said, "for I am well aware that the goods carried by any one
merchant travelling among other merchants are a most private
matter. This privacy shall be respected. No merchant shall
see or know what the goods of another contain. I myself will

make the search, attended only by my young countryman here. For his discretion I will myself stand surety to you; and it is known that for fifteen years now my word has been good among you—among soldiers, merchants, craftsmen and seamen. The legal penalty for illicit weapon-carrying is also well known to you." There was no particular ostentation in his gesture; his hands rested on his sword and his dirk.

Shobei stepped forward hurriedly from behind him. But the hubbub that had broken out in the crowd ashore was too much even for Shobei. He left unsaid whatever he had meant to say and went quickly down the gangway and into the crowd where the stir was greatest.

From the deck of the *Sea Adventure* it looked at first like serious trouble, with men being jostled and thrust about, first into the ring that had formed about Shobei and the spokesman and another, and then out of it again. Women chattered and pushed each other and squealed. It all swayed a little in the direction of the boat, so that the Japan Captain quietly drew the gang-plank aboard. Then it settled and moved off, still chattering and ugly, towards the camp. ('Laroms,' Adams logged it, 'and excurciouns.') For the time being it came to no more. Adams and the Captain congratulated themselves on the discomfiture of Shobei; and Adams recorded the mild steadiness of the wind.

The King was anxious enough now that his guests should be on the move. In addition to the profit on the petty deals with Shobei, the pay of a whole crew had been tossed into his bazaar for commodities whereon the royalty was highest. The permit for revictualling and re-equipment was delivered next day with a roll of silk for Adams, and his Majesty's thanks for the kindliness of the fowling-piece.

The cook-boy and scribe brought only the best of information out of their night ashore. Only some, it seemed, of the passengers supported a new suggestion of Shobei's that the disarmament of the ship itself should be demanded to offset this new searching of the passengers. Those who were not apathetic to the arguments of Shobei were violently opposed. Shobei himself, peculiarly, saw reason and justification—if not strict legality—in the Pilot's wish for a search. It was at this point, said the cook, that blood would have spilled itself if Shobei's had not been the only sword in the camp. Talk had been bitter. Shobei said that Ingari seamen with weapons were a menace to peaceful tradesmen, as they were even to one another. A bottle of wine, a harlot, a jeer were enough to make murderers of any of them. He told how only the good luck of his presence had saved the lives of a tavern-keeper, a singing-girl, of Damian and Wickham and possibly of young Sayers also. . . . His opponent scoffed at him: Ingari with weapons were a menace only to one another and to themselves. Their swords, if swords he called them, were so much nonsense. It was well known that any coolie of Japan with his naked hands could snap the thigh-bone or the arm or the neck of an armed Ingari. . . . They were as welcome, so far as he was concerned, to their ironmongery as they were to their whiskers. Nothing would induce him to submit to the indignity of a search. Shobei charged him with having something in his sleeve; and he reviled Shobei for his private dealings and palaver with Adams that had led to this business. . . . The cook had returned to his sleeping-place, leaving them engaged in a speculative research, covering many generations, into their respective ancestries.

Adams and the Japan Captain took the boy's report as good. Some resentment of the threatened search was natural and almost proper, the hucksters were so jealous of the secret of their stocks. At Hirado, before sailing, honest men would have submitted willingly enough: the examiners of their stock and sharers of its secrets would have been left behind. Shobei's willingness for the search, on the other hand, showed how cocksure he still was of his own secret armoury in the hold—which could be slid quietly overboard as soon as they were out at sea again.

They wondered a little that he had, so easily, abandoned his preposterous demand for disarmament. He had an opportunity for pressing it as they passed through the camp at noon on their way to the township; but he let them go unchallenged. It was not till they had arrived at the bazaar that an unease came upon them of the sort that was always produced by the bodily presence of Shobei, though Shobei himself was nowhere in evidence. Ropespinners had not a strand of rope to sell them. They studied their King's permit to the Pilot to buy. Though they realised that it was an injunction to themselves to sell, the bland rascals shook their heads: their stocks were gone and they could, for the time being, spin no more—none, that was to say, of the only quality suitable to the respected Pilot and illustrious Captain—for rats and rot had made havoc of their stores of fibre. With the chandlers it was the same. A few mean bushels of dried and mouldy yams was the most that any man could offer them. Every bag and bin that Adams tapped with his hand or indicated with his thumb may have been full; but the contents were sold and coolies were already, no doubt, on their way from the purchasers to collect them. If the Pilot would deign to wait and eat a sweetmeat and drink a cup of wine—but the Pilot waited for no such thing. He stumped off from the bazaar to the house of the Justice.

Adams was pleased at cornering him neatly in his garden, flying a kite; but he saw that the dog would still have some time to think, since no man of the least breeding—however hurried and indignant some casual misfortune might have made him—would thrust his presence upon another whose thread had at that very moment engaged the thread of an adversary. The engagement was fought out while Adams waited; and the scribe and the Japan Captain discussed the strategy and technique of the duellists. The Justice of the Peace appreciated the Pilot's courtesy; his wrist and thumb plied their nimble art while the detached part of him did its nimble thinking.

The fight ended. The Justice's derelict kite lurched away towards the host of scavengers ready in the bazaar to scramble for loot so good, and his boy with the spool reeled in whatever salvage of thread should be left unsnatched by the loafers waiting for it to fall. The Justice was now all smiles for his guests. He apologised for the discourtesy of his preoccupation and for the poorness of his display. The Pilot himself, he ventured to swear, was as fine a kitesman as any that Japan, the land of illustrious kitesmen, could show. Adams admitted that he had at times found diversion in the flying of a kite; it was the Japan Captain who told that the Pilot was said to have severed the thread, once, of Shongo the old Admiral and twice of his son, Shongo the younger. The Justice was delighted by this, and begged Adams to allow him one day to test his own poor skill against so great an exponent of the art.

Adams took this good opening. Regrettably there would be no time for an honour that would have been exceeded only by the pleasure it offered: he was pressed by affairs to leave the charming island of Lu-Chu and the seductive hospitality of its people as soon as ever he could get his ship to sea again. It was, indeed, for this very purpose that he had sought to encumber the Justice's leisure with his boorish presence. He had with him the licence of the King—franked, no doubt, and sealed by the Justice himself—to purchase his immediate requirements ashore. Despite this august document some corruption had taken the merchants and hucksters so that they would sell him neither stick nor stitch nor seed.

This was beyond the comprehension of the Justice. He stared aghast. Nothing in the world could have caused such outrage—except, possibly, the reasonable accident that all the goods in the bazaar should have been already sold and delivered or bespoke.

That, Adams had to admit, was what the shopkeepers alleged. In that case, said the Justice, time would mend it—also giving him, happily, that opportunity for which he lusted, to fly a kite against Adams.

Adams ventured to doubt his being able to get so much as a kite and line and spool in a bazaar so stripped of merchandise.

Then he asked brusquely if the Justice would deign to help him by virtue of his office, to an execution of the King's order. The function of his office, said the official, was to enforce the law and not to alter it. If goods were sold, they were sold; and it was beyond the power of himself or any other man to unsell them. Only the King himself could enact the confiscation to make such a thing possible.

Very well, said Adams; in that case he would seek out the King in his palace.

In his palace? . . . The Justice smiled. He craved forgiveness for the impertinence of criticising any judgment so clear as that of the Pilot's. Already, he confessed, he had committed it once by secretly applauding his guest's good sense in declining to visit the palace—which was castle and fortress as well; entered only by soldiers, high officials of the island, servants—and sometimes spies.

Adams asked him if it had ever before happened in the history of his island that its bazaar should be sold out of every commodity. The Justice answered that the permutations and combinations of chance and circumstance were a matter beyond his limited comprehension, and outside the scope of his humble office.

Was it gentle words, Adams asked, and the courtesy of a small present that would possibly adjust chances and put circumstances in slightly better order?

The Justice replied that kind words and a present given in the proper spirit seldom failed to produce the same brightness in affairs that they always did produce in the spirit of giver as well as receiver.

The Japan Captain and the scribe drifted away to watch the movements of the victorious kite that still swooped and climbed the sky; and Adams and the Justice went into the house.

Adams's girdle was the lighter when he came out; but within him there was undoubtedly some of the brightness which the Justice had predicted.

"It is undoubtedly Shobei's doing," he said to the Captain as they walked back to the ship. "We are to come again in the evening to the bazaar, when this man has sent some word out. If we cannot then get some satisfaction he will cause an order to be made; and in a few days we will be equipped."

"A few days——" said the Captain, "and in the meanwhile Shobei is at some fresh mischief." He thought of this for some moments and then found comfort. "His quarrel with the man last night, if it is not a farce and a ruse, is a good omen; for the man is amply supported by others so that Shobei does not stand supreme among them all."

When they were half way between the bazaar and the beach they were startled by a shot from the *Sea Adventure's* piece. They hastened.

When there was another report and some spent small-shot buzzed in the air in front of them and plopped into the sand, they trotted; for there would have been no need for small-shot in a mere signal. It was five minutes before they had rounded the bluff; and a rabble was already tumbling out of the bazaar to follow them. At the bluff they walked again, for it looked as though breath might be among urgent requirements. The camp was upside down. The cook-boy sprinted to them and said: "It is well. The shot ended it."

Young Sayers and Hargreaves were on the deck amidships with fowling-pieces. Two or three others of the crew also had firearms, the rest drawn cutlasses. The gunner and his mate were beside the piece; and Wickham lounged, with his sword, against the post of the deckhouse door. It was Shobei and the spokesman and the group of three or four others behind them that kept a limit and a boundary to the hullabaloo and excursions among the rabble of passengers. The two stepped forward from the group as Adams and the Captain neared the junk, and approached them.

In his right hand Shobei carried a dirk in its scabbard; and in his left, by its top-knot, a head.

The spokesman saluted and said, "Shobei Dono would make a deposition." And Shobei said, "I found a man among the passengers improperly and illegally bearing this dirk. I took the liberty of executing justice upon him and of confiscating his weapon. According to the law in the matter I have the honour of presenting to you the malefactor's head, and his dirk. Herewith."

Adams the Samurai, and thus the legal representative of Shobei's own Lord of Nagasaki, took the dirk. He looked down at the head. As he stooped a little to examine it the more closely, Shobei had the natural courtesy to raise it for him. "You handle a sword well for a merchant and a man of peace," Adams observed. A single stroke had done the work.

"It was well deserved," said the other. "And it is said that right and justice will direct a blade truly, notwithstanding the hand holding it have no skill."

Adams turned suddenly on him. "The law, Shobei, directs that you should have reported this man's misconduct. You are no magistrate to be drawing a weapon in punishment."

"It was not in punishment," Shobei said with composure. "It was to avert strife and bloodshed even greater. For the

law also says that the carrier of a sword should draw it unhesitatingly for the keeping of the general peace, so long as he
report his act forthwith and make his deposition to the proper
authority. If it is you yourself who would do all further
disarming, there is still ample work before you. This man was
not alone in his villainous intent."

Adams turned to the crowd to see that a third of it was
armed. Arrows and short bows were flourished. There were
swords, too, among them; and pikes. Adams thought well of
young Sayers standing on deck with his fowling-piece, and of
the saker behind him that had fired its startling shots over the
heads of the mob.

"Who is the man?" he asked, looking down at the head
again.

"A double-faced one," said Shobei. "He who naturally made
the ado when you had proclaimed a search. I remonstrated
with him far into the night; for it is only when persuasion has
failed that a sword may be drawn. There are friends of him
among that spawn of rogues who will be glad, no doubt, to
bury the rubbish of his carcase if your honourable purpose with
it has been fulfilled."

"Lay the head down," said Adams. "Its identity must first
be recorded."

He took his scribe with him, and the spokesman, to the
fringe of the crowd. A dozen of the foremost came scrambling
and babbling to cluster about him. The heaviness of his own
preoccupation soon quieted them, and he said, "Aye, you will
have justice right enough. But first fulfil the law. Who is this
man whose head is now set upon the gang-plank?" A dozen of
them shouted it, and the scribe and spokesman recorded it.

"Now," he said, and he spoke loudly and generally to the
crowd, "Lay down, every man of you, those arms."

For moments there was not a sound in the crowd, nor a
movement. His own eye was naturally alert for the fitting of
any arrow to a bow-string; but he saw none. Then, beginning
nowhere that he could see, a sudden convulsion seized the
crowd. As though released and impelled by his own brief
movement of a hand to his sword-hilt, the whole multitude
reversed and scurried and vanished into the bivouacs and

shelters and behind the stacked bales and bundles of the camp. Adams waved the gunner and his mate away from the reloaded piece; and waved also to young Sayers to lower his blunderbuss. He sent his scribe and the spokesman back to the boat and walked alone, slowly and thoughtfully, into the camp. Right to the middle of it he walked; and then climbed, without looking much about him, to the top of a pile of merchandise.

"Now," he said, "come out and listen."

For minutes there was no movement and he stood still, regarding not the camp and the men hidden in it, but the sky and the wind. From North of North-East it had swung to East of it. But it still held steady, with none of the puffs and minute lulls which an old fisherman of the Islands had once taught him to note with quiet suspicion.

"Come out," he said again, more quietly than before. "Bring your weapons if you will—to brandish them at me, or to shoot me full of arrows if there is a better Pilot hidden among you, ready to sail you to an honourable and profitable trade in Siam, and home again with the changing of the wind. . . . Or do you seek to do me a trivial dishonour in keeping me thus waiting upon you?"

This fetched them, first one man beckoning another who closely followed him; then groups whereof every man was reluctant to be either last or first. When they were gathered uneasily about his rostrum, shuffling their bows and swords and makeshift pikes, he said, "I have to tell you first that the deed of your Shobei has made him my prisoner. It is not for me to say whether he has done well or ill in killing that other. I alone may kill—till we are returned home without question. So, every man of you who carries weapons invites death not once but twice—once at the hands of any enemy, and again at my own. There is an indenture between us whereby I am committed to sail you well and truly to certain destinations. I am committed also to defend you with my life and with my seamen against all hazards of sea and winds and pirates. That is the one side of the bargain: the other party to it is certain merchants of respectable standing and decent repute. But with an armed rabble of brawlers and swashbucklers I have no contract; and I will make none. I cannot by any means compel you to lay down those footpads' tools you have bought or filched from bawdy-houses ashore, and to become merchants again. If you would change your profession, I will show you how you may change it easily and honourably." He paused for an answer, but got neither word nor gesture. "Listen——" he continued, "My colleagues and I will sell you the ship at a fair price. I have consulted them upon it, and indeed we have little heart for going on, with two of them wounded and the King graciously pressing us to accept his hospitality till the new monsoon shall bring other ships from Bantam to take us home again. With the seamen I, for my part, have had some misunderstanding already; so they will be glad, no doubt, to enter into fresh employment with you. The Captain, however, will not go; for in discussing the matter to-day he said how that he, too, would gladly take a few weeks of ease . . ." He could have gone on in this strain quite indefinitely, with his audience gaping at him, hushed and awed. His plan was to tell them next that he was prepared, as an alternative, to refund to them their passage-money to the extent of the journey still unfulfilled and to leave them where they were, clinging to their bows and swords and pikes among any others of their kidney who would have truck with them in the local bazaar.

The plan, however, was checked. One plump merchant, whose weapon was a stout bamboo weighted with lead, dropped this weapon to the ground and split the audience's silence with a peal of laughter. Even Adams, who in fifteen years had had reasons enough for growing accustomed to surprises in the application of laughter to the crises of life, was dismayed by the quality of sheer merriment in this outburst. While he still stared at the laugher the mood was taken up by the rest of the mob, and he found himself standing in their midst as the hugely successful maker of a joke. They cheered him, when they had done quipping each other in breathing-spaces and tumbling off again into paroxysms, as they would have cheered a wrestler or a famous conjurer-swordsman at a fair; and from this they fell again, suddenly, into the utter silence of awe.

"Well?" said he: but the only answer was another round of applause.

"Where is the spokesman?" asked the man who had started the laughter, and was now as solemn as an owl.

"He is with Shobei," said Adams, "for I had no need of a spokesman for the words I have given you. And any man of you may speak in answer. A spokesman is necessary only when the bargain has been made; and as yet we have struck no bargain."

"The joke is yours, An-jin Sama," said the man, "for it is many years now since we first heard the tale of the Pilot who could sail a ship to us from the other corner of the world when the winds of the two monsoons were at variance on the sea—a ship that was timbers scarcely holding together, with sails too scanty to swathe the bottom of an infant, and a score of corpses with half a dozen skeletons for crew. . . . Truly it is rich when this same man offers to sell us a ship for our own sailing." He was ready to laugh again at the richness of it. "It was as though the master-jeweller of Kioto had offered to sell us not his finest jewel but a pair of socks." It was him they applauded now and he, stepping up to the occasion, came to the outside of the throng and made an impressive gesture of taking up his bamboo cudgel and flinging it to the sand. "My bargain holds!" he said magnificently. "Let others send their weapons to join mine there."

Bows were flung out to join it, and arrows and pikes and even swords; for the silence, the speech of Adams and the laughter had removed whatever obstacle usually lies between thought and gesture. One man, however, who even now could not help shrinking from any waste of money, came forward sheepishly with a sword. He said, "What will we do with these, An-jin?" Adams took the sword from him and drew it from the scabbard.

"It is a tolerable blade," he said, and slipped it back again. "A tolerable blade and of our own Japan workmanship . . ." The man would not take it back. "I bought it here," he said, "for the merest nothing. It was filched, no doubt, by some bawd from some merchant; and all blades are alike to me." He shuffled back into the crowd again.

"The bows and pikes and such rubbish you may burn where they lie," Adams continued. "But the swords, even the poorest of them, are too good for burning. By your leave we will give them to the King, or to the Chief Justice, for they would take such a present in kind part."

"But it is to you we give them, An-jin!" came out of the crowd as the words of no particular man but as the sentiment distilled from the spirit of the crowd itself. Before he knew it, as he stepped from his rostrum to the ground, he was holding against his breast an unwieldy sheaf of eight or a dozen blades —swords and dirks, a Malay kris and a Spanish dagger. He was proud and happy that the crew was watching this from the deck—rascals who had had to drink themselves sober before they could decently obey him.

With Master Shobei he dealt forthwith; for the opportunity was good. The wind was still out of that stout merchant's sails when Adams got back to him at the gang-plank, standing glum with the spokesman behind him.

When he had discovered that there was a gang of thugs on board other than his own, and when he had bereft its leader of his head, Shobei had expected that his own wits and the Pilot's simplicity would soon enough make nothing of it. He had been happy enough to see the weapons being surrendered; for Adams, he assumed, must have surrendered something in return. What shook him was the temper in which he now saw the crowd; for the sound coming from it was the happiest of dins—not organised enough to be a cheer, but a working chanty rather—as bows and arrows and pikes were tossed together upon a brazier brought out and overturned on the sand.

"Long life——" they sang, and said, and laughed: "Long life to him, our Pilot."

Nor could Shobei see any sign of reassurance or encouragement from those of his own gang who stood about like stunned pigs among the lively others; and that which gave him the least reassurance of all was something about Adams himself. It was not merely the bunch of swords that the Pilot hugged to his belly; it was the very hug itself, the swagger of the nobleman about to address one who is not considerable.

He addressed him: "Deign to board the ship," he said, "and without delay or hesitation. You spoke of the law which you have been fulfilling during my absence ashore. You will now fulfil it further by becoming my especial guest." The Japan Captain sent a couple of men down the gangway to relieve him of his booty. He gave them the sheaf, leaving his hands free to rest or shift about on his own two hilts. Seeing the direction of Shobei's glances he said, "You may keep your sword—for that also is the law; but you will have no further occasion to draw it. I myself will be at hand to defend you; for if you should have need or the desire to go ashore at any time, it will be my pleasure to accompany you. Understand that. Without the burden of my poor company you may not stir again from the ship. That order will be given to the Taipan and to certain of the Ingari crew who will carry fowling-pieces in particular regard to yourself."

Shobei was eyeing the spokesman, so that Adams was hurried into a guess and a quick decision as to whether those two were better in one basket or apart. "Our spokesman," he said, and stepped between them, "remains with his passengers in the camp." His quickness, the alertness of the waiting crews and the sound from the misbegotten fools around the burning weapons who still mumbled long life to the Pilot, hustled these two into compliance. Shobei slunk to the deck, and the spokesman went back to the camp.

The decision of Adams turned out to be a happy one, for in the night the spokesman's throat was cut. Upon the point, however, there was never any certainty. It was only the cook-boy who reported in the morning that in the space of blackness before the dawn when the moon had gone, there had been a digging and a burying in the sand. He had noted the spot— close to his cookhouse—in case any goods should later be reported missing from the ship or from the landed stores. By evening it was known that the only thing missing was the spokesman.

Shobei tried to make some protest after a day or two, when the last of the ship's victuals and the water were being brought aboard; but Adams and the Captain were both able to smile at him and silence him; for what action could they take in regard to a man who was merely missing from among free men in a free island? If he had deserted, from any base motive, the

King and the Justice of the island would attend to the matter. It would be reported in due form, as they had reported the seamen missing from the crew. Shobei demanded that he himself should be allowed to go freely ashore to investigate among the passengers, since the spokesman was a fellow-wardsman from Nagasaki; but Adams could not countenance so gallant a self-exposure of Shobei to possible vengeance against his recent act of justice. He suggested, rather, that Shobei should withdraw to the cool and shelter of his lodging below the orlop hatch, out of the jostle of seamen. They had given him that place so that he might crawl aft, at his leisure, and quiet himself with the consolation that he and his gang still had, at least, their weapons in the hold.

He mumbled, as he turned to go, of death being allowed to pass unnoticed, murderers unchecked. But Adams begged him not to use words or thoughts of such unhappy omen. There was no death, he said, and there could be no thought of murder regarding the spokesman—this was the law and likewise the truth—till there should be a corpse or a head or sufficient of a limb to prove it. Let Shobei or another produce any of these items and the affair would be fully, and immediately, dealt with. (The cook and the scribe had shifted their pots and sleeping-mats, the brazier and chest of victuals, to pitch their bivouac slightly away from the old spot where the wind had appeared to disturb the fire, on a new one selected by the cook. They now occupied the place where there had been digging and burying.)

Shobei went below. A youth with parents in Wapping, squatting by the hatch with half a yard of pistol on his lap, offered him some unanswered pidgin pleasantry as he went through.

CHAPTER XXI

With Shobei bottled up in the hold and the corpse of his right-hand man under the cookhouse floor, while the crew went lustily about their work and the passengers busied themselves about their goods against the re-shipping of it, it was an easy matter to think only of putting to sea again. Somewhat informally, as befitted the emergency and the temper of the parties, a new spokesman was appointed for the passengers. They chose him who had been the first to laugh and to toss away his cudgel. The Captain and the Japan crew approved the choice, and young Sayers bought his merchandise in the name of the Company to relieve him of the further burden of it, and confirm him in his new office.

Leaving the Captain aboard, Adams took his scribe and went to make certain payments in the bazaar. He found there a certain new liveliness of interest among the merchants, in himself and his plans and the direction of his sailing. He thought at first that it might be due to the events that had been causing the stir on the *Sea Adventure* and among the passengers. But he soon found that the bazaar men, and the officials also, stood in no want of the most detailed information on any such points. It was they, the landsmen, who had some news. The burden of it was obviously causing them an irritation, yet each man was anxious that some other and not he should be the one to give it away. It was, in the end, the scribe who got it, while Adams was in the house of an official, stating that all his stores and tackle and water were aboard and paid for, that none of the men reported missing had as yet reappeared, and that as soon as the passengers and their chattels were aboard, he was ready to put to sea.

That, the official said, made particularly good hearing, for it would save not only himself—which was obviously of no consequence—but the Pilot also, and all his friends, from discomforts and inconvenience beyond calculation. The fact was that intimation had reached him within that very hour that the King would brook no further delay. It had come to his Majesty's ears how certain villainous hucksters had been obstructive to the Pilot till this official's colleague, the Justice himself, had discovered the wrong and together they had adjusted it. The King was one who would not have it said of him that guests to his island found aught but honour and convenience in their going, as in their coming and staying. So he would speed their parting, and their departure must be immediate. "As we welcomed your coming," said the official, "and gave of our poor resources what comfort we could to your staying, so now we speed you. By to-morrow's noon eight skiffs will be manned for towing you out; and beyond that time you may not stay." Adams listened to his humbug and quietly paid his bill for the privilege of filling his breakers with water. If the rascal was trying to imply, with his rigmarole, that only a further gift could make a further stay possible, he was welcome to the illusion; the breakers were filled already, and the passengers would be aboard in three or four hours of the next daylight. The skiffs to tow him out to sea were his normal right: present-making for that service would be as between the Japan Captain and the oarsmen themselves when the work was complete. So the official got no change out of him—not a cash beyond the bare watering-fee. "Understand——" he said, when his careful counting of the money had established this incredible fact as indeed true: "Understand, Master Pilot. Noon to-morrow and no longer."

"It will be a pleasure to obey his Majesty," Adams answered, "and his Majesty's officers. Good-day. And I thank you."

Outside, the scribe came quickly to him from the knot of gossips with whom he had been killing the time.

"Did he say any word of our staying longer in the haven?" he asked.

"Aye," said Adams. "Little else. But we have stayed longer than enough already. We must be clear by noon to-morrow—and a good riddance."

"I have been talking with fishermen," said the scribe. "Many have put in. The bazaar is full of them."

"Good," said Adams. "They will tow us out."

"But it is to the other side of the island that they have

hurried with their boats," said the scribe. "The Eastern side. They have smelled weather."

"Weather?" said Adams, "what is amiss with the weather? The sky is clear and the wind as steady as ever." He stopped and turned his face to it, giving it play at his nostrils and in his beard. "Steady as ever . . ." and then, for an instant, he was not sure. "What is amiss with it?" he repeated.

The scribe shrugged his shoulders. "They have smelled it, they say—out at sea. There is dirt in it. They even say typhoon."

"They say anything," said Adams. "This is no time for typhoon." But he stopped again to give his face to the wind, and to sniff at any secret it might hold.

They saw, as they rounded the bluff, that in the two or three hours of their absence many brown square sails had come into the lagoon-like haven. Some were being furled as oarsmen began to pull the small craft home in the land-locked calm; and more sails were even then rounding the headland that was the outermost rampart of the harbour.

The nose of a fisherman out at sea was the nearest approach that Adams had among his instruments to a barometer. "Go down to the boat," he said to the scribe. "Tell the Captain and Mr. Sayers and Mr. Hargreaves that I will soon return. I go to offer a small present which I omitted in my conversation with the official."

The official was horrified to think that one so illustrious as the Pilot of Yedo in Japan had discommoded himself with a walk back from the beach to the bazaar with a properly forgotten present for one so insignificant as himself. He accepted the two tael with childish gratitude and insisted on his guest's taking a cup of wine; but he made it clear—so that even the sceptical Adams was convinced—that this matter was beyond his control. He did Adams the friendly turn of convincing him—and so of saving him the expenditure of a further unproductive present—that even the Justice of the Peace could not now extend any leave to stay at the island. Their latest orders were explicit; the *Sea Adventure* must be gone by the morrow's noon. Any overstaying of that time would be construed (and dealt with) as the act of an enemy.

Typhoon, in the memory of the King himself—typhoon and calm—had been known to hold ships weather-bound at the island for weeks, till after the change of the monsoon. If that same thing should happen now there was no guarantee in the world that the merchants from China should not come disastrously to meet merchants from Japan. Adams argued that it was as yet far from the time for any talk of the change of the monsoon; and the official, utterly friendly now, said that it was never the time for talk of any sort by a low-born underling like himself when his King had spoken. He must see to it, he and his immediate lord the Justice and certain others, that their guests were speeded on their way by next day's noon.

Adams went back to the ship, recollecting that even the squat noses of fishermen had sometimes lied.

On the *Sea Adventure's* poop his own nose and the nose of the Japan Captain could sniff out no secret in the gentle, steady breeze. The gasps in it—whatever thrust or jerk or caress it had given to the bare limbs or the lungs (or, indeed, to the very spirits) of fishermen out at sea, to set their tillers over and their slabby sails chattering in a scurry for the nearest sheltered bight—these were spent from it when it had traversed land and reached the masthead of craft moored to a jetty, or the noses of seamen standing on the craft's poop. At sea, said the Japan Captain, he would have known whether the fishermen had smelled anything but their women, and the smoke of their braziers to send them scuttling home.

"There's nothing yet," said Adams, looking to the masthead. "The streamer plays as it has done for the past dozen days. To-morrow, if there is need, I will see the King himself."

The smaller fishing boats were being beached and hauled high by the combined crews of all that had already grounded, and by the idlers from the *Sea Adventure's* camp. An old man on the jetty indicated that a riding on a doubled or trebled cable at a good anchor—some distance out, and more under the lea of the Northern cliff—might be a happier situation than the *Sea Adventure's* close mooring on the jetty. They were sheltered enough where they were, it was true, for all ordinary contingencies—but he himself had smelled the dirt in the air at sea.

"The passengers will have got the story now," said Adams morosely to the Captain. "And nothing will get them aboard till the fishermen put out again."

He stood brooding upon this thought till a new idea came to him. He turned again to the Captain: "Take that old fisher," he said, "—since he understands our Japan talk so well. Treat him handsomely with money, so that the skiff's oarsmen will refuse to tow us if the weather thickens. I, in the meantime, will set the passengers to getting their goods aboard."

But ashore he could do nothing. Even as he went towards the camp, passengers came to meet him in a glum knot behind their new spokesman. This man said, "It is surely to bid us stay in the camp that the Pilot comes."

"No," said Adams. "I am ordered by the King to be gone by noon to-morrow. We can stay no longer, except we stay as his enemies; and the way of these islanders with enemies is short. Particularly is it short when the enemies have a good store of merchandise."

"And particularly," said the spokesman, "when the enemies have no arms—having given them all in courtesy—and in confidence—to their lord. We would have fought these rascals, An-jin, and lost our lives fighting them for the right to shelter here from a sea that is said to be brewing a host of demons; but we have given every whit of our strength to the strength of our lord. He alone can fight them now—as it were our father fighting for his strengthless children."

"You are willing to go aboard then?" Adams asked. "With your goods?"

The man considered. "We are not willing to go yet to sea," he answered. "It is that that I came to tell you. If you will give us that word which is said in Japan to be a bond, that you will not put us to sea, we will come aboard. Can you give it?"

Adams said, "You, too, must have heard the order from the King?"

"We have heard it," said the man. "And we have heard more also. A dozen stories are told by these fishers who have spoken with our own fishers and other prowlers out at sea. The battle has been fought. It is said by some that the Prince Hideyori has been killed and burned in the castle of Osaka with his mother. By others that they lost the day and cut their bellies. Some have it that it is our Lord Hidetada that is dead, others that it is his father Ieyasu, while others again that it is both."

"Hidetada dead!" exclaimed Adams, "and Ieyasu?"

The spokesman shrugged. "Fishermen's tales from the sea," he said. "One thing only is perhaps certain from them: the battle has been fought and one of the parties has lost it, and the other has won. Your own friendship for our Ieyasu is well known even here; and here the King, knit somehow to the Lord of Satsuma, is friendly to Ieyasu's enemy. Victorious or beaten, dead or alive, he would honour him, driving you out to a wild sea. I speak only truth, An-jin—openly now, for it is no time for secrets. Such time is past, albeit that it was in such a time that I became aware of a certain treachery and armed myself and two score of other men in another treachery to counter it. Then I saw, from a jest you cracked, that we were safe under the sword and dirk of the Pilot of Yedo, friend of Ieyasu the mighty. If it was meet that Ieyasu himself should give him weapons it was meet that I also should humbly give him what weapons we had—I and the two-score others also— becoming thus his children . . ."

Adams saw that the man could have gone on thus well into the night in the sing-song of a beggar—the perfect spokesman and the inspired suppliant. . . . And the fellow was speaking the full and perfect truth. They were helpless against any rabble that might be sent down from the bazaar to hound them from the shore and to loot their merchandise.

"Do any seem to speak truth?" he asked—"any who bring these tales of Ieyasu and whether he be killed or otherwise?"

"They have but one thought," said the spokesman; "it is of the storm that is coming. For the rest they are simpletons. They have heard with certainty only that the battle is fought, and even that is all one to them."

"It may be," said Adams—and he was talking more to himself than to any spokesman of passengers for all that it was in the spokesman's own language that he spoke—"it may be that the King will have heard some sure intelligence somehow. I will see him to-night. And of the other matter also I will talk to him—of your biding here till the storm is past; or till your minds are easy."

He turned as though to go, but the suppliants were about him and in his way.

"Will you not give us your word, An-jin," the spokesman said for them, "the word of the Needle-watcher of Yedo, that he will not let us be driven to a sea full of demons?"

"Man," said Adams, "I will do what I can."

"You can what you will," said the other.

Adams made due allowance for rhetoric, and quietly asked: "Would you die more gladly at the hands of a thousand islanders who will not harbour you than in a sea?"

The man also spoke quietly now, and conversationally, without any professional intonation. "While you are gone to the King, permit us to go with our goods, aboard. There is no need to search us, wasting time. There are a dozen, or a score of villains among us; but they are marked men, each one of them with three true men standing by, at need, to break his neck or strangle him. They appear to have no arms."

"I have their arms," said Adams quietly, "aboard."

"Very well," said the spokesman. "With us aboard, and the ship put out a little way into the harbour, there is small need for bandying words with any King of this pestilential excretum of coral. Bandy them by all means, in courtesy; but if there is any dying to be done in the matter, let the islanders do it. Your Ingari with their fowling-pieces and the small brass cannon——"

"Begod!" said Adams.

The other, after a pause, said: "You have given your word, then?"

It was all going a little more hastily than Adams would have chosen in such matters, but he said: "Yes. I will not put to sea until we are satisfied of the weather."

CHAPTER XXII

IT was an urgent matter; but he thought it well to follow the official channels. At the house of the Justice he was directed to a tavern where he might, luckily, find that personage; so he and the scribe retraced their steps for half a mile, to the better end of the bazaar. They found him, issuing and accepting challenges in a small coterie of kite-fliers and connoisseurs of singing-girls. Time had to be wasted in courtesies, and Adams wasted an hour of it with as good a grace as he could.

Of the fortunes of Ieyasu's war these Cavaleros had little enough to say; for they cared nothing. The sudden return of the fishermen from the sea was another matter, for in the face of their alarm no immediate and definite fixtures could be made for the flying of kites. The fortunes of these islanders largely depended, moreover, on whatever followed the panics of fishermen and other prognostications of the doings of wind and sea.

Their island, the Great Lu-Chu, was the midmost and the starkest of the coral fangs that grinned between the fury of the Pacific and the dark treachery of the China Sea. There was profit in the scouring of those fangs if craft were plying Southward from Japan or Northward from the Philippines and Moluccas or Eastwards by North from China. It was then, with kite-flying and bazaar chaffering in abeyance, that the islanders were scavengers and ghouls. One in every ten of them could speak Japanese. Three could follow the talk; and the rest were capable of words in Portuguese or Dutch or Spanish.

The Justice, drawn by Adams a little apart from his cronies, was all for postponing the Pilot's business till the morning. But Adams insisted. He had his rights in the matter, and he pressed them. The Justice—or indeed any man on the island, including the King himself—could not prevent a noble sojourner from seeking an audience at any time of night or day on a matter of justice; and Adams now scoffed at the suspicion,

388

which was said to lie upon him, of being a spy. With dusk closing rapidly into night, said he, what could a man spy? He was willing to go blindfold with a proper escort, or in a closely curtained litter. The only point the Justice had to decide, therefore, was whether he himself should turn out to accompany him or whether he should let him go with a minor official, or alone.

Adams paid the score in the tavern and the Justice went with him.

It took an hour and a half of walking at the pace set by the puffing kite-flier; and in the four miles, as they climbed the hill, Adams began to feel a strange kinship with the fishermen who had fled homeward from the sea. He, too, smelled dirt in the weather now, feeling a sudden prickle of warmth and stickiness and then a sudden chill under the tunic and robe upon his breast and shoulders, as the air gasped to an instant's utter vacuum and sprang lightly to a Northern breeze again. He did not concern himself very largely now with the fortunes of Ieyasu and his war. They were, for one thing, no suitable matter for his concern. Ieyasu had managed greater wars and survived greater battles than this; and in addition to these thoughts, he realised that the event was already determined for aught he could do in the matter, walking through the gardens of the King of the Great Lu-Chu where a pallor of blossom was beginning to show in the night upon the plum-trees.

He waited an hour or more, as he had expected to wait, while the Justice of the Peace was closeted with the King. When he was admitted to join them in the King's small chamber and had properly saluted his Majesty, he could not discover what trend their consultation had taken.

The King, whose whole dominion was an island whose length could be walked over by a child in two days and its breadth by a cripple in a forenoon, was flatly ignorant of weather and the sea.

In five minutes of talk Adams became convinced that the only fear in his mind was the honest one that the junk from China would come in time to find the *Sea Adventure* from Japan still there. It was in vain that Adams tried to show him how such a thing could not and would not be: for until the monsoon should change all the ships of China were held fast by the wind from Eastwards and Northwards, against China's coasts. It was upon the consistent steadiness of these same winds that he himself depended for his own direction Westwards and South, and no ship could beat against it.

The King's mind, however, could grasp but one point: as long as the *Sea Adventure* lay at moorings in the haven she clearly would not be gone, and it was only in her being gone that he could feel the safety he desired for his precious relationship with China. China! China! China! . . . thought Adams. There, at Hirado, was little Cocks with his idiot yearning for China, and here was this idiot King with his holy dread of it.

He came calmly to the argument again, emphasising once more the simple and obvious fact that he himself was as hardly pressed as his honourable listener. If he missed his monsoon the whole voyage would be wasted. There were, thus, no two ways about it. He must be clear of the island while the wind still held fast and dead towards China.

But the King waxed dully more apprehensive at this. All he could see was that if the *Sea Adventure* missed her opportunity for making Cochin-China and Siam, there would be no inducement for her to get away at all. Adams could have cuffed him for his tenacity. He undertook, however, patiently and very solemnly to be gone one way or another as soon as the weather should be settled. If he missed his monsoon for China he would return to Japan.

The King's eyes kindled at this; but only with the glint of stupidity in its moment of triumph. He observed, with a sly gloating, that the Pilot himself was admitting the possibility of being weather-bound till the turning of the monsoon.

"No," said Adams, "that I am not. It is more than a month yet to the turning of the monsoon; and no typhoon in the world has been known to last more than a matter of days and nights."

"But," persisted the royal idiot, "have you not been here a month and more already, with no typhoon at all?" After this master-stroke he giggled in the manner of a gamin who has tripped up a portly walker.

It was too much for Adams. He might have gone back again, quietly and patiently, to the beginning of all arguments. But, somehow, at that moment, he could not. This dull and cumbersome idiocy was of a piece with all those other massed stupidities and obstinacies that had always thwarted him. Nothing, so far as he had yet been able to find, could be done by an intelligent man against them.

"Drive us out then!" he exploded upon the King and the Justice of his peace. "Drive us out, I say, and wreck and blast the lot of us! What is it to you if two hundred men are driven to perish in the sea, so long as the rags and sticks of their merchandise are delivered to the jaws of your coasts? What is it to you who have two names among men?—for they call you not only wreckers, hawks and wolves for the sea's garbage, but benevolent and stout men also—good friends and generous hosts."

"Who calls us wreckers and wolves and hawks?" the King demanded, turning the challenge upon his Justice.

"How," answered Adams blandly, "should I say? For what man would be likely to survive with breath enough in his body to say any word at all, turned adrift into a typhoon to fend for himself among the teeth of such rocks as yours? How any such word should have started among men I truly cannot say; but there are merchants, and even seamen, who will never sail for the Lu-Chu. Tales that are told in my Japan are told also in the Philippines and Moluccas; also, it is said, they are told in China."

Stolidly, and now heavily sullen, the King said, "You are to be gone by to-morrow's noon."

Adams could see that 'China' had gone home as nicely as anything could go into a mind like this King's. While he wondered what stroke would be the best with which to follow the success of 'China,' the King showed him that all strokes were equally useless in dealings with such a numskull.

Pouting and swaggering, thumbing the Japan hilts at his Chinese belly, he said, "The law will operate. All strangers still in our territory, when they are no longer our guests, become our enemies. They stand outside the law, for any man to kill or plunder without let or hindrance from me or any other."

Adams said: "Very well."

He was sick in that moment, utterly sick of fools and of all foolishness—the old fools of ancient Rotterdam who had sent him and others slithering over half the world with a bag of broadcloth that was eaten of rats and moths, to be bartered for a bag of gold that was not anywhere. He was sick of the fools that had kept him for a man's whole lifetime in that fantastic country, mooning when he was not wearing out his feet or his backside with that same load of mouldering stuff still upon his shoulders, and the load of gold to answer it still nowhere. . . . He was sick of the fool gaping at him, and gloating in his rogue's security and his idiot's witlessness. But sickest of all was he of Will Adams himself, the arch-fool who had submitted to these others; and had come, when fooleries had seemed fairly spent, on this last and greatest foolery of all in a tub like the *Sea Adventure*, filled with peddlers and their bundled rubbish and a handful of thugs.

So he said, "Very well, have it so, then," and he shrugged his shoulders. "It is of little account to me now whether I die at sea or aland, or in a harbour . . ." He was ready to go, for he had spoken what he knew to be the truth. But he did not at once go, for he had not spoken it all. Sick enough of the fool Will Adams he might have been—sick to the point where the only relief could come from death of one sort or another, somewhere. But Will Adams remained in spite of it. There was a job in hand, unfinished; and although the event of it meant little enough to himself either way, there was no other who could finish it. This meant, simply enough, that he could not leave it; and he had no great heart for the plan of his passengers' spokesman that they should hold their moorings and make a fight for it. They were as thick on their crag of coral as ants in an ant-heap, these Lu-Chuans. They could swim like sharks in their sharkless harbour; and dive like porpoises. The licence of the *Sea Adventure* enjoined upon him that he should observe all laws, as though they were Ieyasu's own, of any land that he might touch, to the glory of the land that was Ieyasu's Japan— if Ieyasu, indeed, still lived. (He had, moreover, caught a glimmer of the snouts of brass cannon as he had come through the castle gates. If there was large ordnance at the castle there was ordnance also on the cliffs; and under floor boards in the bazaar were firearms, beyond doubt or question, for any rascal who could shoulder them against a lawful prize no more than a cable's length away. . . .

So he stayed and said, with his shrug: "Very well. To me it makes no matter. I am but one, with the life I have lived, and but one death to die. But the others whom you would submit to typhoon are many. They are, also, merchants who would haply come again to a good market and good friends." It was only from the expression on the Justice's face that he could gather any response at all; for the Justice smiled and nodded while the King stared on in the angry manner of one whose head has been struck with something flat and heavy.

It seemed to Adams now as though the thing were so nearly done that he might as well do it completely. He said: "But I have already obtruded the trivial bothers of hucksters and seamen for a rudely excessive period upon the patience of a King. It would gratify me, before I go now, to know whether his Majesty has found leisure as yet to test the poor quality of the fowling-piece I made so bold as to send him. He would prefer a lighter weapon perhaps—a chased murthering-piece I happily possess, of Holland workmanship—for use on other occasions. It is not so much a weapon, this other one of which I speak, as a gentleman's toy." It was a rubbishy old blunder-buss lying in the deckhouse rack of the *Sea Adventure*. The cook-boy, Adams had little doubt, could make some show of it with sand and oil and a fistful of seaweed. "Only the pother of a hurried departure," he continued a little sadly, "could deprive me of the pleasure of its unpacking from the hidden place where it is safely stowed, marked by the lord of my country's merchants for a Prince of Siam." If the breach of the old Dutch thunder-gun blew out in the flat face of this poten-tate, it should be the potentate's affair. And the potentate was not over-likely to test his own piece, if it ever should be tested, by firing the maiden shot.

The flat face unflattened for an instant. "If it is indeed true that the wind cannot blow so as to bring a junk from China for at least a full month," said the King, "and if it is also true that whether the wind blow from North or South when this matter of the typhoon is at an end——"

Adams very respectfully interrupted him. "My Lord," he said, "tales are told in Japan of my sojourn of two years on the seas of half the world in all the winds of heaven and hell. Whatever may still be hidden, of the tricks of wind and sky from these poor wits, is an open book to your minister who is wiser to every secret of wind and sky than any other kite-flier on the islands. He also will tell you that what I say is true: There is no magic that can bring the ship-carrying winds from Northwards and East to Southwards and West out of their proper season. Storms there may be, but not steady winds." The Justice gave his assent, and Adams threw out his chest to make his peroration. "As for the second matter, your Majesty, I alone in this room can speak, telling you of other men's sayings in the island of Japan. There is one—a small Lord in that country—of whom it is said, in the manner of bazaar talk, that his heart is as big as his beard. Him the bazaar men heed and obey. When there is trouble among them of the most bitter and dire sort, if he should say a word to them—a few words of counsel and order—they will even bring out their weapons at his bidding, and peaceably burn them." He paused for the Justice to give his assent again; and he gave it with alacrity, for he saw now that this matter could yet be concluded to the satisfaction of all parties in time for his return with the satisfied and open-handed Pilot, to the tavern.

Adams continued: "They heed his words thus because they know them to be sound and true . . ." It was not for nothing that he had listened for fifteen years to talk like Magome Sageyu's. "They are the words and the bond of An-jin, the Pilot of Yedo. If this man should say he will do this thing or that on a certain day and in a certain manner, it is known from among the wild men of Hokkaido to the potters and fishermen of Satsuma that he will do it. He is a nobleman of Japan, this so-called Needle-watcher. There is nought to release him from the bond of his given word—nought in all the world but his own hand's setting his guts adrift with the dirk given to him by his Lord for that purpose and no other. If such a man as this Pilot undertake to depart with a ship from a certain place of his hospitable entertainment before a certain other ship shall have come to it, he assuredly will so depart. It is this, Your Majesty, that I do undertake; and the speaker is such a man."

He had won, clearly enough; for the Justice was making the little unnoticeable movements of preparation for their honourable dismissal.

But Adams himself was aware that it was not himself that had won—he, bragging with the big, windy talk of Magome his father-in-law, smacking his dirk and strutting like an actor. It needed something bigger than postures and a swashbuckler's talk to shift the one idea that had stuck itself in the wooden head of the King of the Great Lu-Chu. It had needed, likewise, some bigger thing than these to make laughter of the suspicion and hate in a rabble, to kindle a bonfire of their weapons and to squash the swaggering gangster, Shobei, till he was now content to slink about the hold and the orlop-deck.

The bigger thing was Japan—and more than all Japan.

It was the fellowship of Japan's nobles; it was the might and majesty and mystery of Ieyasu, friend of the Needle-watcher and mighty Lord of them all.

CHAPTER XXIII

THEY moored the *Sea Adventure* close that same night, with bundled faggots and bales of seaweed for fenders against the jetty. It was a safer way than anchorage, thought Adams, since the cargo of a craft torn from an anchorage and stabbed on a reef might appear, to the strictly legal mind, as fair salvage for the beachcomber; for even the shelter of this very haven could not be guaranteed if a storm should reach any memorable pitch of fury.

For five days and six nights of typhoon she chattered against her fenders, but held.

Shobei the gangster, always the sceptic of any legend that set a man up to be a great one, came somehow to see that the legend of the Pilot of Yedo had something in it. When the guardian crags had ceased their howling and snarl, and men could look again upon the sky with neither hate nor dull suspicion, Shobei craved leave to report to Adams a discovery he had made in the hold: to wit, a case of swords with some pike-heads and bows and arrows.

Adams thanked him.

The crew at the end of those days and nights was a quiet and a good one.

Damian the Spaniard and proud Wickham had again shaken hands.

The old blunderbuss was rubbed up and sent ashore for the King, and the *Adventure* was towed out to sea.

Her cargo was sold handsomely in Siam, and the goods of the huckster-passengers with it. A cargo was shipped to replace it —silks and skins and timber, ivory, coral and ambergris—that yielded Cocks and his precious Company a return of rather more than two for one on their investment.

The experience made of both Wickham and young Sayers competent officers of the Company, wise to the broader tricks of the trade and traffic in those seas; wise also to some of the tricks of their weather.

The adventure gave to Cocks, moreover, a bag of sweet potatoes—an unexpended portion of the victuals shipped on the Great Lu-Chu. With it he stocked his little garden and became, according to one of the proudest statements of his journal, the man who introduced this excellent vegetable into Japan.

It was only for Adams himself that there turned out to be nothing in all of it.

Spalding, Cape Merchant at Bantam, had not fallen short of his letters to the countryman whom he had hoped, for a dozen years and more, to meet. His first handshake was the handshake of an old friend; his hospitality was that of a prince. But he could no more promise any material help towards an adventure of the Passage to the North-West than fly. His hands were tied with the Company's red-tape. Never a ship came out to him at his own disposal, but always under the sealed orders of the Council, signed by Sir Thomas Smyth himself. As for any control of seamen, he could not even have one of the rascals flogged without the order of his ship's master.

From Bantam he sailed the *Adventure* uneventfully back to Hirado—where there might be ships from England.

There were—the *Thomas* and the *Advice*.

To the utter delight of Cocks they were stuffed with pewter-ware—goods whose market the Dutchmen could not cut to ribbons. Of the ship for the North-West adventure the despatches they carried had no word at all. Of Adams himself the only mention was not in the despatches but in the ledger—a debit 'for acco. Capt. Addames' for forty pounds paid to his wife in Gillingham.

There was gossip, however, brought by the master of the *Advice*, and it was enough to explain, to Adams, this silence. Saris had arrived home under a cloud, and the cloud had burst into a storm. For six weeks the returned Captain-General had been a prisoner on board the *Clove* in Plymouth harbour. Surveyors had examined the cargo and Directors of the Company had examined his books.

Saris was likely to be dismissed the Company's service. Certain pictures and carvings were buried in London for their lasciviousness; and Adams wondered how his own gift to their

Lordships had fared—the last work of Kuru before the old man's sight had gone utterly.

Even though it was no greater matter than the squabbling of fools that caused the delay in matters of urgency, Adams saw that there was naught for him to do but wait.

Just before the turn of the monsoon another ship came, the *May Morning*.

She brought a letter for Adams—not from England, however, but from Spalding. She had brought his successor to Bantam, so that Spalding was only waiting now for the *Advice*, homeward-bound. Would not Adams, he asked, go with him to England—to retirement, or to any business he might choose?

Adams, reading the letter, could see no reason why a man should go personally across half the world to explain the self-evident to a group of individuals said to be in possession of their faculties. He therefore wrote to them again, a sheet that lacked some of the expansiveness of the letter of three years before and had in it a note of annoyance at the time that was being wasted. He who expressed annoyance best with a monosyllable and a gesture so that flunkies jumped into a trot, found it less easy with a pen and a sheet of paper addressed to gentlemen in the City of London. He borrowed a pen from Cocks's office and repaired to the house of Zanzeburro for leisure to do the thing out in triplicate—a copy for each of the ships to carry.

He also wrote an answer to the letter from Spalding. Much was in his mind for this good friend of his of a dozen years whom he had seen but once; for much was on his mind concerning another old friend also.

Half the gossips of Hirado and Nagasaki denied the statement of the other half that Ieyasu was indeed dead. There was no evidence either way. Both reports could equally be a political bluff. Adams had sent his scribe to the fisherman of Oita for news that should be more certain than counting-house rumours or the blustering denials of old Ho-in (which were based on the firmest of all the King's convictions, that old soldiers never die.)

The scribe returned with the news that the fisherman and his son were themselves dead, having been pikemen in the battle, and all other news was the same elsewhere as at Hirado or Nagasaki. Some said one thing as certainly as others declared its contrary. The scribe thus established no fact; and he threw no light on the mysteries of friendship and of death.

It was these mysteries that brought immobility to Cocks's borrowed pen in the hand of Adams as he squatted to the letter for Spalding. He set it moving, therefore, and kept it moving, with matters of fact. He wrote a fresh specification of the ship that would best serve for the adventure of the Passage. He enumerated certain desirable stores which he had omitted from the list sent to the Company, and he mentioned by name half-a-dozen seamen who had struck his fancy in the loafing crews of the *Thomas*, the *Advice* and the *May Morning*. They were lusty, cheerful and respectful fellows who would work in well with Japan fishers and deepsea-men. In ending the letter he was faced again with the mysteries—the finding of friends and the losing of them. He bit his pen and found a platitude:

"In this life many troubles and afflixciouns, and in the end death. Therefore it is a blessed thing to die in the Lord, with a faithfull trust in God; for they rest from their labores; etc."

The letters were sealed and stitched into their tarred canvas jackets and handed with the despatches of the House to the masters of the three ships.

The cook-boy packed the Pilot's satchel with his change of garments, his comb, and his bottle of water and they took the road for Yedo.

CHAPTER XXIV

OF the manner of Ieyasu's death no man could give a certain account, nor indeed a statement of the exact day of it. He was dead. That was all that was known. It was known that certain other lesser ones were dead also. Mitsu with no portfolio, physicians, an old mint-master and a groom had seen no particular point in hanging on in a world that now lacked their Lord. They cut their bellies and their throats— all of them save the mintman, who cut his belly only. There was not enough blood, they said, in the withered old body to raise the dirk's weight from nobility's first gesture to its second and last. There was enough to move the lips, however, from an old man's smile to an angry man's curse; for if he had ever before known such disobedience as that of his right hand already drained as pale as wax, he had forgotten it. His best-man saved him from the humiliation of further anger: it was for that very purpose that the ceremonial caused him to kneel behind, alert on one knee, with his sword drawn.

Bikuni wondered whether her Lord also would feel upon himself any constraint of honour in the matter. Old Magome snarled at her that she was a fool, forgetful of the gentle breeding that should have told her how it was only the personal attendants of a dead master that were under any obligation of belly-cutting; else how did she suppose that his own illustrious tripes could still hold food? In any case was not he there for the purpose of expounding etiquette to the Pilot? Had he not so expounded it that the Pilot had never once erred from the conduct of a true nobleman—tradesman and sea-loafer though he also was?

But instruction from Magome or any other pundit of deportment was utterly superfluous to Adams.

It was not of any wildness of belly-cutting that he thought when he knew beyond any question that Ieyasu was dead. Nor indeed did he think of anything specific at all. It was by some process slower and more baffling than thought that he was to learn how a peculiar bleakness entered into the land of Japan with the passing from it of him whose one standard of right and wrong among men was benevolence of conduct only; of him who knew love without the greed of possession; justice without hate, victory without exultation and defeat without rancour; who took fair with fine, rough with smooth, and smiled thereat with the smile of the Buddha whose image he had always carried in his breast.

Of the first of Ieyasu's two predecessors the epigrammatist said in due course:

> "When the cuckoo sings not
> I wring its neck."

Of the second:

> "When the cuckoo sings not,
> I cause it to sing."

Of Ieyasu himself he said:

> "When the cuckoo sings not,
> I wait. And the cuckoo sings."

This, then, was the Ieyasu who was dead. And there departed with him some of the spirit of all laughter from Japan.

Adams, however, was not the man to be immediately or greatly disturbed by so subtle a matter as the departure of a spirit from a land.

Ieyasu was dead; and chuckling Mitsu. But the estate Ieyasu had given him was a living and a lively thing. There was scarcely a villein upon it who had not found, in the nine months of his Lord's voyaging abroad, some grievance against a neighbour. And he had generally nursed it, for his Lord's illustrious father-in-law, as he grew older, was losing the inclination or the faculty for distinguishing very clearly between plaintiff and respondent in any cause. His belief in punishment exceeded his hope of finding justice in the world.

He was anxious, moreover, that the boy Joseph should not become a man before a background of loose and soft ideas. A great hearing of causes therefore awaited the Pilot. The boy Joseph showed a pleasingly alert understanding of the litigants' affairs, dismissing many a liar with half-a-dozen words. Bikuni, too, was able to throw light on the obscure affairs between one neighbour and another. No executions were required in the adjustments. The talk was prodigious; but the confiscations were trifling ones and justice was, on the whole, done. Rancour was quite talked out of the blood, and it was contented and merry men who brought a host of women to the Pilot's house, carrying bundles of new children that their Lord might bestow on each its lucky name.

Andreas this time had had the books and the godown keys; but in dealing with Andreas neither Joseph nor Bikuni was of any practical help to Adams. Nothing was; the only consolation was the vague one that the money was still, in a sense, in the family. But on one point there was not even consolation, but only a dark rage. Andreas had been playing the fool with poor old Cocks, and Cocks was fairly wise to it. In actual figures it amounted to no more than twenty tael; and all Adams could do was make a flat demand for the sum from Andreas. Andreas said he had no such sum in ready money, and Adams said that he himself would lend it to him— on properly drawn documents, at fair interest and with good security.

"What," asked Andreas, "is this great concern of yours for the plump Englishman?"

"I too," said Adams, "am a plump Englishman. . . ." Then he remembered how one single snort from their ancient father-in-law was enough to reduce this sneering rascal to the stature of an orange-pip; and how Magdalena could shut him up with a mere glance containing snobbery. So he said, "What concerns me, my friend, is the keeping of faith by a two-sworded man. Therefore I require twenty tael from you; that they may be given in the morning to my friend Wickham for the Company."

"I will give them myself to Wickham in the morning," said Andreas.

"That would be an unseemly bother," said the cavalero in his best manner. "The only service I shall put upon you is the signing of the documents for the loan and for the payment of interest. The flunkey's work of carrying the money to the far end of Yedo I shall perform myself."

Andreas thanked him. He said also that a penniless and worthless one like himself borrowed better elsewhere than from a brother-in-law whose ideas and ideals were as high in the matter of interest on a loan as they appeared to be in matters of honour.

He sneaked off to get the money, as Adams very well knew, from under the floor of his sleeping room.

In the evening he handed it over; and beyond the weighing of it in Adams's scales and the formalities of thanks, nothing passed between them. Before he went out—for he always spent his evenings out when Adams was at home—he went amiably about the house looking for Adams till he found him in the bath-tub.

He smilingly studied the torso of his brother-in-law and smilingly shook his head. He could be a very pleasant fellow on occasion, a wit and a wag. "Our Needle-watcher," he said, "would still be the old hairy one from the West. So be it. As he is pleased to choose."

"Choose?" said Adams—but he had got the Company's money for fussy old Cocks, so he too was amiable. The bath, moreover, was neither time nor place for any kind of acrimony. "Choose? You, my friend, could go on choosing till your face became darkened; but choosing does not make whiskers grow, or kill them—on chin or chest."

Andreas settled his hands into the sleeves of his elegant going-out jacket. It was a sociable gesture. "It is more of our brother-in-law's heart that I was thinking. It is said that the heart of man is the fruit of his circumstances and of his soul. The soul is, as might be said, the earth from which the whole affair arises. Circumstances are as the seasons. They change; and as with the seasons there comes change in the condition and complexion of all fruit, so with change of circumstances there comes the responsive change in the hearts of men; all men except our An-jin. His heart, it would seem, is more rock than fruit. It does not appear to have changed." He produced a hand from his sleeve and passed a napkin to Adams from the bath-tray.

"What should change it?" asked Adams, and rubbed his chest.

"Japan itself is changed," said the wiseacre. "Native hearts are changing with it. Of old there was nought to change the complexion of Ingari hearts. The Lord of all men, the Mighty Ieyasu who was so good a friend to the Pilot, was the friend and champion of all Ingari. But Ieyasu, most illustrious brother-in-law, is regrettably dead. Dead likewise are his closest friends, and the most gallant of his beneficiaries."

If, thought Adams, the lout was hinting at any belly-cutting nonsense, it would serve him well to be tossed into the bath-tub—going-out jacket, furled umbrella and all. "Speak plainly," he said, eyeing the distance from himself to his communicative brother-in-law, and from him to the steaming water; "for my poor Ingari wits are still too dull to cope with the brilliance of parables."

"My contemptible effort," said the other, "was but to indicate that the most illustrious Hidetada is no champion of Ingari. Nor are his worthy ministers."

"Have no anxiety then, my friend," said Adams, and the assumption of his under-robe gave him suitable dignity, "for a nobleman of Japan."

That, thought he, was one in the fellow's stomach; and the fellow went off.

Adams, too, went out that evening. It was upon Shongo that he called, the ancient Admiral, taking with him the parcel of tobacco that always delighted the old man.

Delight in tobacco, however, was not to hold him away for long from the topic on which Adams had nothing, at the moment, to say to any man. When the trays of sweetmeats, the wine-cup and rinsing bowl and the brazier for their pipe-lighting had been set, and when the girl had drawn the door, the old man said, "Word came to me that ships have again come from your country to Hirado."

"Aye," said Adams, "they have come."

"And yet you have travelled here—on foot?"

"Aye," said Adams. "I've travelled again on foot. The ships are not suitable."

"It is a strange thing, my son. You would think that the great man to whom you wrote would have tried this thing, when he got your letter and your promise——"

"That is the whole matter!" said Adams. "You have said it! They have not had my letter. But I have sent another one. This time it is a friend who carries it."

"The same friend who himself would, you thought, have helped you? The one you went in that junk to see?"

"Aye," said Adams, "and he would have helped me too— but——" The curse of it was that he saw so clearly why poor Spalding had been powerless to help. Yet Shongo would never see it. Even if he had talked with Spalding, and heard him talk, he would never have seen it; for all that Shongo could have seen with his dim eyes was the two good ships that had ridden in the harbour against Spalding's Bantam factory, and the figures of seamen loafing idle on the jetty—even as he himself had seen them; the ships glutted with some fool's cargo waiting for a wind to carry them Westward again, the men waiting for the pay that would set them adrift towards the bazaar. "Aye, he would have helped me—but—but his ships also were not suitable."

"The best ship, An-jin, for the purpose—if not the best ship for any purpose in all the world—was the one we ourselves built. I am convinced that there is no man in your country or any other who is the peer of you and me in shipbuilding." Adams found this easier going than the other ground. Undoubtedly the happiest months of the Admiral's life had been the eighteen of which he had spent every hour of sunshine, sitting in his litter, beside the building slip at Uraga and shouting to Adams to tell him the purpose of every timber that was hoisted to the job. "With such another ship as that," he continued, "such a ship, or one even better, we could start at once to seek the Passage. I am well enough to do it."

"You are as hale," said Adams, "as ever you were." He believed it; for although the Admiral was a cripple now and very nearly blind, he had been a cripple and nearly blind on the day of their first meeting.

"True," said Shongo thoughtfully. "But the time grows shorter with so much waiting. Not many of us are left now. There is your honourable father-in-law, the rascal Magome Sageyu; and old Ho-in of Hirado. It will be a good deed for me to sail over the roof of the world and through its bowels, leaving them to cool their haunches and suck their gums among women and grandchildren. The old dogs. You have not mentioned it to that scoundrel, Ho-in, to set him lusting after coming also?"

"No, indeed," said Adams, "for he is getting a little confused in his mind as to any differences there may be between Hollanders, Englishmen, Spaniards and Portuguese. It was he who told me of the Spanish ship."

"The one that was—by chance—burned, An-jin?"

Adams said very solemnly, "Aye. The one that was burned."

The old man said, "The young Hidetada would no doubt allow us to build another ship."

Adams shrugged his shoulders. "He might," he said. "It would save us but little time, however. Eighteen months we were at the last one—and Kuru was alive then—and there is not another Kuru to take his place. Starting even now the work would take us through the spring and the summer, to the summer after——" He was suddenly startled by the way his thoughts were going; so he startled the old man with his outburst of "Wait! I say, wait! It will be here by then—worthy and victualled and manned. And we shall not be beholden to Hidetada."

"Has he misused you, then?" asked the Admiral.

"Misused me?" said Adams. "Indeed, no. Why should he misuse me? I will serve him as I served his father. But——"

This was another "but" which seemed to end a thought rather than to begin it.

"One man, one Lord," mumbled the old man. "It was truly said." It did not fit in particularly with any thought of Adams'. He was insensible of any feeling as between himself and the young Lord of all Japan. For had he not, in fact and in deed, been Japan's lord already for the space of many years? To a native heart like the Admiral's the loss of a Lord might have had some mystic significance of a lugubrious quality. But to

Adams the loss of Ieyasu stood only in its simplicity, as the loss of a friend.

"If you say the ship will come," Shongo continued, "doubtless it will come; and we will wait a little longer. But how long are we to wait, An-jin? Those old rascals may die before I can show them the life that still holds in Shongo, the son of Shongo and father of Shongo the younger——"

"Two years," said Adams, and he snapped it out. "No more. Less possibly; but very certainly no more. There is still a chance that they may have got the large letter sent them per the young man Saris. Their answer would then come with the next monsoon, short of a year from now. Concerning this Saris, however, I can promise nothing. In his brain there was a twist; all he ever craved was nutmegs and spices from the Moluccas. But Spalding is another matter. He will deliver the letter and he will speak his own words, for he himself sees the urgency of it; and the Company gives good heed to him. The seamen are wise to this voyage now. They are home in one year and out in another. Two years at the utmost. . . ." There was no hesitation as of thought as he made these guesses. What he stated was a habit of mind that had become his creed.

When there was neither sneer nor question from Shongo, but only his amiable, "If you say the ship will come, it will come——" the last doubt vanished from the Pilot's mind and he was, from that moment, insane.

From then onwards, "Two years at the utmost," became the burden of his madness—two years wherein there was nought for him to do but wait for the coming of his own ship, and to stay alert on the shores of Japan lest any other ship creep by him, Northwards, to steal his hidden road. . . .

"They will bring a ship's surgeon, too," he said. (For Verhaegen of the *Liefde* was dead in his bazaar-laboratory before Adams had had any need of him.)

He refused more *saké*.

"Forgive me," said the old man. "In the excitement concerning my friend's plans and his ships, my putrefying old wits lost, for a moment, their anxiety for his stomach. Tell me, An-jin, how is your malady?"

"If malady it is and not a mere distemper," said Adams, "it is better. On the voyage it gave me some trouble, owing to the victual of sweet potatoes, no doubt; and sour wine. But at Bantam, with good flour and fresh meat, it was better. Tea makes easier water than wine; so I drink but little wine these days."

"That is indeed poor news, my son," said the Admiral. "The drinking of good wine stood well among your faculties."

Adams said, a little gloomily, "The occasions for it seem to have grown fewer in the last years. With the men of this country drinking is a matter of leisure. Among my own old countrymen, where I have spent so much time of late, it is a matter of haste."

"And so they swallow air with their liquor," said the Admiral sadly. "I have seen many a good stomach and sweet temper ruined thus; and it is reasonable. Good wine will not stand the pollution of air. Who among us has never cuffed a boy for leaving the bottle uncorked?"

Adams smiled. "Aye," he said. "The first wisdom of the Samurai taught me by my father-in-law was 'Cut a little downwards. Empty the bottle; or cork it.'"

"Very well, then. What is true of the bottle is true of the belly. Therefore you will drink a little with me now, as in the old days; for we will drink with great care and skill, to take no gobbets of air."

Adams could not say no. They drank quietly together and talked far into the night. It was about the past that their thoughts moved—the days and nights when one of the old man's feet could still be set to the ground with his weight full upon it; when Adams had been a gentleman of Yedo with evenings to spare for hospitality and a morning, on occasion, for kite-flying; before Dutchmen came and then the English to make a courier of him, with their fever of wants pursuing him from one place to the other so that he went with the pace of a wolf and the wallet of a beggar along the road that was made for princes.

Of the future they said nothing, for they had said all: it was two years of waiting. Two years at the utmost.

CHAPTER XXV

ADAMS held no office now in any of the departments of Government. Even as to the licensing of sea-going trade-ships he was never consulted now. It was only from hearsay that he knew—when he did indeed know—that there were now no more than a hundred and eighty of these in all Japan.

His private business, in so far as it ran at all, ran smoothly. He did not bother about the rivalry of the hundred or more cheap-jacks that now flourished in the bazaars—rascals with whom Andreas seemed to have some mysterious connection, and who could not have looked upon the light of day a dozen years before. He bothered neither about them nor about Wickham with the petty rivalry of the Company's godown; for he had his old clientele of those who bought only what they knew must be good; and bought therefore from the friend of Ieyasu and son-in-law of Magome Sageyu the swordsman.

Thus he was freer than before; and yet he had no leisure.

Wickham was a blustering, helpless fool. Even his girl, whom he thought he had bought outright, he had legally only hired for two years. He had become very fond of her when she ran home from him to her parents, and the grandparents of Wickham's daughter. Because she understood so much of his English he thought he understood her Japanese.

He had known where to go after the girl, for he himself had chosen her in the bazaar at the sweetmeat shop of her father. He started with fist-shaking and went on to sword-rattling. He ended on his back in the road, with his hand unable to make any further movement with his sword, as his shoulder was out of joint.

Adams adjusted the dispute to the satisfaction of all parties. A fresh deed, this time for the freehold of the girl, was drawn and properly executed. To the purchase money was added a small sum *ex gratia* in compensation to the sweet-seller for the inconvenience to which he had been forced in having to dislocate a man's shoulder before tossing him out of his house.

Every courier with despatches for Wickham from Hirado, with samples and accounts from young Sayers at Nagasaki, or from John Osterwick at Osaka, managed somehow to have a letter for Adams from Cocks. The Cape Merchant wanted a pair of candlesticks matched up by the best lacquer-worker to be found, at a reasonable price. He enclosed a drawing to indicate the kind of thing he meant—and Cocks's drawing of a candlestick could as well have been the design for a piece of artillery. He wanted a pair of the finest screens (to be paid for by himself) and an escritoire (to be debited to the Company), to go per the next ship homeward for the lady of Sir Thomas Smyth. He wanted a dirk for his brother in Northampton-shire, a tobacco-pipe and its furniture for King Ho-in. He had mislaid an address and forgotten a name and trusted to Almyhtie God that Adams could help him: they were of "thould bent man from Langasaque to trym the frute trees"—for his garden was running to a "vild sorie condicioun." He wanted more pigeons for his dovecote, feathers for his hat, a male gold-fish for the garden pond (to replace one which old Ho-in had greatly admired). He was most anxious that the feelings of Wickham should not be hurt in that it was not he who was commissioned for these jobs; and this delicacy he left entirely to the tact of Adams. There was, too, a more urgent call than this upon the same faculty when Eaton ("in his potts as ordenary") gave himself away in a small enterprise of gun-running into Satsuma. In the normal times of three years before it would have been nothing at all. A jocular fine would have met the case; but now, two years after the war, it was not yet certain that the enemy and his prodigious mother were exterminated and not refugees among the still smouldering loyalties of Satsuma. Even old Ho-in, said Cocks, had taken pepper in the nose over the affair.

Adams despatched his own scribe, who had learned from him-self how to travel, with a letter urging Cocks to keep the hearing of the cause, at all costs, at Hirado and away from the depart-mental scaremongers of the Court. It was all quite typical of Cocks; he had got quite out of the scrape before Adams had begun to concern himself with it. For Ho-in soon snorted and sneezed the pepper from his nose: he was easily convinced that the pieces were for sportsmen and not soldiers. Being himself, *par excellence*, a sportsman, he took the weapons into his own armoury, and with them an extra barrel of powder.

Adams, meanwhile, was left with the root of the matter in his mind—the Nagasaki padre who had laid the information against Eaton. For a full dozen years now all padres had been his friends. With the defeat of the first wild fanatic who had wanted him crucified he had defeated them all and done with them as enemies. His ultimate defeat of this one—now a tale so ancient that it was seldom even told—had had a high dramatic value. Cocks wrote home of it: "a frire that wold needs work miracles in these parts to the entent to convert one mr. wm. Adams an Englishman with Certen other duchmen in these parts I say this frire promised to work miracles to convert them to be Roman Catholicks asking them if they pleased to have him to remove a great tree ouer the water, from the top of one mountaine to another, or else yf they would have him to remoue the whole mountaine itselfe or to make the Son to stand still in the fermament as it did in the time of Josua, or yf they would haue him to walk on the water as St. Peter did in fine mr Adames tould hym he did not beleeve he could do either the one or the other not that he stood in doubt but that the power of God was abell to doe them & greater matters too but that he fermly beleeved that all miracles ceased longe since & that those of late tyme were but fictions and nothinge to be respected yet this fryre would needs trie mastries and walke upon the water, and to that entent published it about the towne of Oringou soe that thousands of people came to behold and see the event. Soe the frire being well prouided of a great peece made in forme of a cross which reachgt from aboue his gerdell to his feet and being sufficient to have kept up any reasonable Swymer aboue the water as this man was well knowen to be, and yet for all his Cunynge and holynesse, he had byn drowned had not a duchman Called melchar van Sanfort gone after hym with a boate and saved hym to the utter Scandell of all papistes and other Christians remeanyng amongst these pagons which made a may game of it . . . so this friere got hym packing out of this Contrey for verye shame. . . ."

At the steps from which Santvoort had shoved off to the rescue Adams soon afterwards built his jetty and on the site where the "May-game" had been at its merriest he opened his godown. Between him and padres (Franciscans or Jesuits) from that day there had been no bad blood. He wondered therefore at the prank of antagonism that had set a priest, instead of a rival gun-runner, to expose Eaton. The problem set him visiting and entertaining old friends among the local missionaries.

They could throw no light, but only said, with head-shakings, that things were nowhere quite like the old days. Brothers who wrote, or came, from the towns and villages of the provinces spoke of the ordinary things that are the concern of busy, earnest men; but behind their letters or their speech there was a strain of bewildered and bothered anxiety, a suspicion of unhappiness.

They came to the house of Adams and sat with him trying to explain it and explaining nothing—except that the action of the informer from Nagasaki was obviously the somewhat hysterical outburst of a nervous and overwrought young man. It did not represent a faction—any broad ill-feeling as of Nagasaki priests against Hirado Englishmen. . . .

So they met together in the house of Adams for the purpose of talk that itself had no particular purpose. They had all been young men in that country, strangers to it, and now they were all middle-aged and old in the brotherhood they had found there. In the room of Adams, with the Pilot sitting among them, talking quietly of the small things that might portend great ones or of big ones that might yet be nothing, they were as sailors drifting from the Broad Sea to the Narrow, sniffing the open sky for typhoon.

There was no more particular point in a visit now from Santvoort than there had been at any time. He came as always, and he went. He had nothing specific to say of affairs at Nagasaki except that the curtailment of sailing licences meant surer freights for him whose junk still maintained the red seal without question. When he learned that since the ship had not yet come Adams had another two years to wait for it, he had the same smile for Adams that he

had when Adams told him first that the smear on the horizon
was Japan, and afterwards that it lay false in the chart by
four degrees. . . . Yet the smile was not the same; for Santvoort, too, was a sailor on the same seas; and he, too, was
sniffing the air for typhoon.

CHAPTER XXVI

ADAMS realised, after the visit of Santvoort, that in the midst of all this casual talk about shipping he was himself, for the moment, without a ship or a sailing licence. He discovered a sudden unease in possessing no boat when so many men were being dispossessed of their right to go to sea; and Yedo was never a place for boat-buying. Nagasaki was likely to be the bargain-centre where any man with sense, a building-slip and repair-yard of his own should go, to compete against junk-copers instead of waiting to bargain with them.

Six years before, Adams had picked up the site and the stock of a small yard in Kawachi Roads, a league beyond the ground where he trained Ieyasu's gunners—for even so short a time ago as six years, his mind and his eye had been open to more things than one. There was the purely economic aspect of it. The property was going (as a con-fiscation for murder) at the price of a pair of socks. The Pilot was on one of his visits to the Hollanders newly settled at Hirado. Already he had gratuitously adjusted a dozen quarrels between the Dutch merchant and sail-makers, carpenters and chandlers on jobs that could, in future, be done at his own place four leagues away. He knew, too, that the Spaniards and Portuguese would put work in his way at Kawachi that they could not possibly send to him at Uraga. There was another aspect also which the Adams of six years before had duly considered. On snobbish grounds a small shipyard as far away as Kawachi was better than the same kind of shabby thing as near to a gentleman's home as was the old workshop at Uraga. He closed down the Uraga place, therefore, and transferred his foreman with three or four others to Kawachi as the nucleus for his new staff. The rest came together easily and gladly; for those had been the big days of An-jin of Yedo, friend of Ieyasu and employer of labour along the sea-board of Japan. For two years the yard had flourished, Adams himself bringing business to it on his many visits, making the contracts and designing the detail of the jobs.

After those two years the English had come, and Adams had other fish to fry. The foreman undertook whatever work came his way and the financing was done, on commission, by Zanzeburro at Hirado.

The yard still functioned, after years of personal neglect, in a slipshod, dot-and-carry-one manner; and the sudden feeling of want for the possession of another boat restored to it some of its forgotten importance in the mind of its owner.

He told Bikuni that business called him again to Nagasaki and Hirado.

"But it will soon now be winter," said she. "Travelling is cold."

She knew that he would shrug his shoulders. "Winter or summer," said he, and he shrugged them, "what of it? At one time you are cold, with the wind at your back. At the other you are hot, and the wind is in your face. But it is the same road; and it is all one."

Bikuni looked at him. "The trouble is upon you again," she said. "I thought that you would haply stay at home this winter, keeping dry and warm, eating only such food as I myself prepare for you."

She stood near to him and he laid his hand upon her shoulder. "But I shall be back," he said, "before the winter is done. It is no great business for which I go. Just the buying and the trimming of a boat; and a looking to the work they do at Kawachi."

"A boat?" said she. "Would you be going again in a boat?"

"No," said he. "There is no great reason for me to sail in it."

"Then what need is there to have it?"

"Without a boat a man may not have a licence," Adams explained; for to this extent he had succeeded in explaining the necessity to himself.

"But," said she, "why should my An-jin require either boat or licence if he would not sail?"

Again she was not disappointed in her expectation of a frown that was not for her or for any offence that she had committed. The focus of his eyes was not upon herself, nor upon the screen behind her; for his eyes saw none of these things.

She sighed and turned away from him. "It is as my father said," she said. "The trouble is again upon you."

"I have told you," he said, "that I have had neither pain nor fever nor vomiting since I returned."

"The other trouble," said she, "the trouble of the ship. The black ship that comes not to take you with the mad, illustrious Shongo."

"Who says it comes not?" He first snorted the words, and then laid his palms upon her shoulders that were growing rounded now, with her age advancing to forty years. He shook them, giving to her body the movement of laughter as he had given it, silently, in the darkness of a night when the joke had occurred to him of confronting the old rascal Magome with a pair of sword-hilts as splendid as his own. He laughed now. "Who says it comes not? In two years it will be here— less than two years now. It is upon this matter also that I would go to Nagasaki and Kawachi, and to my friends at Hirado."

She made her contributions to his going. She instructed, for the hundredth time and more, the cook-boy in the preparation of certain foods, enjoining upon him the trust that the Pilot should eat well, and leisurely and regularly.

She set out the small dishes as soon as he was gone, charging them at the proper hours for his spirit with morsels of the same delicate and proper foods that the cook-boy prepared for his jaded stomach.

The spirit of him was so lusty, however, as the scribe and cook trudged behind him along the road, that tavern-keepers forgot, in the first moments of their seeing him, that any change could have come upon him or upon their country.

"Ho! wake up, hog-spawn!" they said to any ostler or scullion dozing in his corner. "It is he again; the Pilot!"

His talk, too, was the old talk of two years before, and five— and ten—and nearly twenty. For he asked of the doings in Nagasaki; of merchants and their merchandise, of the builders and sailers of junks and of gossip that concerned the very junks themselves. If they could tell him nothing, or little, he was untroubled and shrugged his shoulders. This, too, was in the manner of him who of old travelled apace from Yedo—for he himself would soon be at the source of the information he sought, tarrying only for the food and the sleep that were enough to set a man upon his feet again.

The cook and scribe trundled after him, happy to see their lord in such high fettle that flung out his old demon's paces two at a time for every three of theirs. Of any gossip that had been for them alone at the taverns, and not for him, they said nothing. They believed in luck, knowing that so long as a word lies unspoken in a man's heart it is the man's own affair and has no hurt for another; and tavern-keepers' gossip had been of the way in which great men were shrinking to smallness, and small ones were becoming great in the land.

An-jin himself showed but little concern in these matters; for his business was to buy a junk before the copers of Nagasaki had combed the jetties for every likely craft that was going; and to get its fair share of jobs for the yard at Kawachi. It would be well, he now saw, to keep the yard up to a good working pitch, for it was more than likely that much would have to be done to the ship from England.

It was not often, and not for many years, that Adams had been so driven by an urgency that was not some other man's.

The ears of cook and scribe were startled once on the march by a strange sound ahead of them. It was the singing-voice of An-jin engaged upon a song of his native country.

After three weeks of walking they were aboard a pinnace from Osaka to Moji. He had not forced the pace; for it was true that his stomach repaid him handsomely for every rest he gave it after burdening it with food.

Santvoort's junk, the *Rotterdam*, was at anchor in the harbour with the master and his daughter aboard. It was a small boat, of the class to bring her owner in touch with the group of smaller freighters that were likely to be among the first to encounter any kind of trouble. Santvoort, while the cook who was as welcome as his master was preparing a meal, told Adams of the many he knew who had withheld their boats from the market of ravenous copers in the hope that the spring might yet, somehow, produce a licence for them. One of these, he thought, might be induced to sell. After the meal and a smoke they would think of it, and perhaps go ashore and enquire.

But the meal itself was not eaten in leisure. Before they had started it a boat was alongside and a small hamper was handed up to the boy—wine and fish and a pot of Chinese conserve. Before the meal was over there were half a dozen boats, and half a dozen hampers. The tobacco pipe had, therefore, to wait; and when Adams went on deck after the last mouthful of the meal, the boats alongside were a round dozen—Japanese, Chinamen, a Filipino, a Spaniard and a Portuguese.

Adams called to them, "In the name of my host you are welcome to the rough discomfort of his ship." And there was a sombre group before him on the deck.

"And to us," said one of them, "the sight of An-jin among us again is welcome; we are happy that he has accepted our mean gifts."

He gave formula for formula. "Gifts made in friendship he accepts in gratitude. Any trifling service that he may honourably render to the givers will be rendered in friendship."

His fellow-guests on the *Rotterdam* looked at one another in search of a worthy spokesman—the Japs at a Chinaman, the Chinamen at the Spaniard and the Portuguese. Adams had not expected such keen competition among rival junk-sellers. A spokesman detached himself by saying: "The first gift to arrive was, by happy chance, this person's." Surprisingly there was no opposition to the claim, but Adams said, "All the presents are equally first, my friends; for as yet I have had no opportunity to savour the excellence of any. But I detain you unduly with my insignificant chatter. It would be more convenient, no doubt, for me to inspect the obvious merits of your junks in the morning and then to overcome the difficulty of deciding which of boats so excellent I may not buy."

The man to lose all patience at this and to abandon the decorum of ceremonial was neither Spaniard nor surly Portuguese, but an ancient Chinaman. "*Buy!*" he exclaimed, and the word was a snarl that caused the whole group to turn and stare at him as he came to the front of them on his old, bandy legs, and faced up to Adams. "Buy? Think you then that we could not have sold our boats a dozen times, and again a dozen times, to the wolves that have blackened these shores from the moment it was known that honest seamen were to be robbed of the sea? It is not to be rid of our boats that we have come to you, An-jin, but to keep them."

He had quieted himself a little by his talk, and Adams quietly said, "Even though he wear a mask of anger I recognise Shiquan of Tokitsu."

The old man took the rebuke. "The Pilot must forgive this boor," he said. "Many years before the Pilot of Yedo could recognise so humble a person as Shiquan the Chinaman, the poor junk-master recognised a brother-seaman most illustrious. For as many years before that day as lie between that day and this, Shiquan has sailed his junk along these shores and from them to the Islands, to Siam and to China. He was in the harbour of Oita, discharging a cargo when he turned from his coolies to behold the wreck of a ship and the wreck of a man. In the man old Shiquan knew that he beheld a master of their common craft. It was, indeed, a word allowed to fall by the marvelling Shiquan himself that has become a name of so much honour in this land. 'An-jin' is the word men now use when they would speak of one man and no other; the Pilot of Yedo; the lord of Hemi-Mura of Yokosuka; friend of the mighty Emperor."

The others applauded, and Adams very slowly said, "Shiquan, Ieyasu—who was my friend—is dead."

"But the Emperor," said Shiquan, "the mighty Emperor still lives. It is he who has taken our licences from us. And it is only you, An-jin, who can get them back."

It was early yet for Adams to admit that he could do no such thing. From old habit the Pilot of Yedo, the Lord of Hemi, the friend of the mighty Emperor said, "It shall be done, whatever can. You may rest upon it; for I myself am in need of a licence. Also I am in need of a boat. For a good boat a good price, since it is not to sell boats that I buy them, but to sail them."

"As to that," said Shiquan, "I myself could perhaps accommodate you. Not with my own boat, but with another I have recently bought."

"I also," said another; and a third, "And I."

CHAPTER XXVII

WHILE Adams still chaffered with Shiquan at Nagasaki for the junk which the old man offered, a despatch arrived from Cocks begging him for the love of God to go at once to Hirado; his countrymen and the Company needed his services as they had never needed them before.

He could not leave this business of the junk-buying to Santvoort, for Santvoort was as square-headed as ever; he could not see that the junk offered by Shiquan was the only one of the three that was worth a tael. Thus, with the letter from Cocks urging him, he had to hurry the business and pay Shiquan's price instead of the one that lay between it and the figure he himself had named—which could have been achieved by a week's bargaining.

Cocks, he found, had reason enough for his excitement. Successive days had brought him successive couriers—from Wickham at Yedo and from a new man, Hawley, at Osaka. Both had received notice that the agencies in these cities must forthwith close. An edict of Hidetada laid it down that the English might trade now only in Hirado, and also—but only for the time being—in Nagasaki. Godowns must be immediately emptied; stocks returned to Hirado or else cleared to resident Japanese merchants.

Adams was perhaps relieved to find that this was no affair of goldfish or pigeons that had caused him to drop seventy or eighty tael over the junk bargain. But apart from that possible consolation it was all miserable enough.

Old Cocks appeared to get some kind of silly satisfaction out of exclaiming, to anyone who would listen to him, "See the way of it—the villainy! They durst not do it till our Captain Adams was gone from Yedo. But he will soon be back. And then we shall see!" Thus the onus was flung upon Adams, and there was onus enough upon him already—the patiently heard cases of a score of junk owners suddenly dispossessed of their licences. From Shiquan the old Chinaman to

a smooth boy of twenty who had been of the Japan crew on the
Sea Adventure, there was not a rascal among them. They
knew the coasts, and they knew their sullen sky. Humbly and
amiably they were of that great company of "stowte seamen" with whom Adams had felt, for nearly twenty
years now, that he could adventure that passage to the North
and West and—with the willingness of God added to their
straight lustiness—find it. . . . "You will win it back for us,
An-jin," they had said with the voice of old Shiquan that was
peculiarly the voice of all, as the Pilot hurried away from them
to Hirado and Cocks. "You will win it back for us. It is our
livelihood, since we have no craft or trade of landsmen. It is
our right also; for we are deep-sea men. Even as the Pilot of
Yedo has always given justice to lesser men, so it is known that
he has never sought it from the great Lord of us all—whether
for himself or other—without finding it."

It was all very fine for them to talk, thought Adams, they
who had never fenced with Master Hidetada.

"Farewell, then, An-jin," they said. "May a lucky day fall
out for your errand." They then had pressed fruit upon him,
and cakes for his journey to Hirado, and bottles of wine, that
he might win back for them their livelihood and their stolen
right.

And Cocks's bragging became almost a lively snicker if
there was a Dutchman at hand to listen to it (for the Hollanders had never had the right even to open a shop in Yedo):
"It only wants our Captain Adams to return among them. Then
we shall see."

The silly old man even forgot that it cost good money to
run from Yedo to Nagasaki and Hirado and back again; that
official interviews cost money, and that the corridors to the
audience chamber were now paved and carpeted with honourable gifts. He did not know, moreover, that the Dutch were
offering Adams a firm salary to represent their interests in a
merely broad and general way. Adams quietly said to him,
"Will you give me an order on Mr. Wickham for such sums
as I may require?"

Cocks was a business man. "It were better to name the
sum," he said.

"It were best of all," said Adams testily, "to require no sum whatever. But this is no time for talk of betters and bests. What we are dealing with is bad, and could hardly be worse. If I am to go and deal with it I must go soon, and I must have money."

"I will undertake, on behalf of the Company, to refund all that you may reasonably expend for us," said Cocks.

"I can expend nothing," said Adams shortly. "It was to spend most of my own ready money that I came down here; and I have spent it. I have bought me a boat and renewed the stock-in-trade for as handy a little shipyard as any on the coast." His triumph in this statement, and in the next one, was not over little Cocks only, but over himself also. "I have nothing left now for the use of others." It was his own purpose that he had been able, this time, to serve.

That, thought Cocks, would have made ill-hearing if any Dutchman had been there to hear it. None was, however; and he swallowed it.

"For my records," he said, "I would prefer to set a figure."

"Set one, then," snorted Adams. It was one of those cross-grained moods upon him that filled Cocks with what he himself called "Heart's-grief" at the phenomenon of a brother Englishman gone native to the extent of apathy—if not, indeed, antagonism—for the affairs of the Company.

Quite humbly Cocks asked, "What sum shall I set?"

Adams, still in his mood, said, "Whatever you will. It is all one to me." The mood was the mere struggle of that in Adams which would have followed some great or little purpose of its own; or else, having no purpose for the time being, been free to rest in idle content—the struggle of this thing when it was beset by the pother of chance and circumstance that set other men's affairs awry, and made of him their lackey.

But the struggle was already over.

The cook and the scribe heard no song from him as they followed him along the road again. The wind that had touched them in their coming as it were with pats upon the back was now a snarl in their faces, and often it had in it the sting of sleet. Adams was no more carried by the buoyancy of any purpose within him, but thrust and driven by the purposes without; within was only the burden of these other men's bothers, of food that would not always digest and water that would not easily pass.

CHAPTER XXVIII

Bikuni, when she had looked steadily at him, said, "It is illness that has brought you back."

"Nay, little one," said he; "rather it is the hastening back that has brought the illness. We have travelled with the pace of the wind and fed in the manner of wolves. Let the shampooer be sent up, lass, if he has not already heard of my return." For the blind old man who kneaded spent muscles so that they were restored as though by sleep was said by some to be a wizard also. In the kit he carried were certain slender and pliable tubes of bamboo.

Bikuni left him, to send a boy for the shampooer, and returned. "Is your business done so soon?" she asked.

"Aye," said he. "It could be said to be done. I have bought a boat, and set some work on foot at the yard. Has our brother-in-law conducted himself to the satisfaction of your father?"

Bikuni smiled. She had learned from Adams how shoulders may be moved in a shrug. She moved hers so, and looked up at him. "To the illustrious Magome Sageyu," she said, "there is but one son-in-law capable of satisfactory behaviour; and he was away."

"While I bathe and am in the hands of the shampooer," said Adams, "please tell him that I would be glad of his company to-night if he has no appointment less unattractive abroad." This was a private joke between Bikuni and Adams. It was eight years or more since Magome had left the house in the evening; and so avid was he for the company of his son-in-law that Bikuni would often have to spy out the best door for Adams to use in avoiding questions and hindrance from the old man, who prowled in the corridors for any shred of company that offered. After such defeats the old fellow would be satisfied to waylay his grandson and tell him how Magome Sageyu, the Ronin, had taken a nobleman—washed up by the sea from some distant country—and made of him a Samurai of no less a country than Japan.

He was in a dour temper on that night of Adams's return.
"They have been at you again, then," he said, "those hairy
ones! I know it already; for he has been here also, that one
you call Oui-kum or some such, rattling the kitchen-spit in
the metal utensil hanging to his girdle, so that only a swordsman who is also a gentleman of great restraint could refrain
from vomiting. He has been, I say, demanding that I, in the
manner of a juggler at a fair, should produce 'An-jie' for him
from my sleeve. 'An-jie,' mark you, after five years or more
of hearing a speech properly spoken. It took *me* no five years
to teach a man to say 'An-jin' . . . 'Anjie' indeed! Do I call
the fellow 'Oui-kee,' that he should so miscall my son? But
he has said his say out. We shall soon be rid of him and the
cheap-jack shop that has done more harm to a sound business
than even your own running about like a coolie's cub with a
bellyful of raw persimmons. We shall be rid of him, I say; for
already the great seals are upon the locks of his godowns, and
watchmen guard them. Not cripples with staves, either; but
good soldiers—the Emperor's own men. The goods will be
confiscated."

"He will be given ample time to remove them," Adams
quietly suggested. "I have seen a copy of the edict."

The old eyelid below the cleft brow of Magome could still
be lifted a shade, and allowed to fall again. It was not for
nothing that the name which stood for him in the memoranda
of the Company, through a happy fluke of Wickham's, was
'Macchiavelli'. "True, my son," he said, the eyelid completely
at rest again, "most indubitably true. But time alone will not
suffice to move a substantial merchandise from one place to
another so distant as Hirado. Porters would be necessary to
carry it by land, or a boat to take it by sea. I had occasion
lately to confer with a certain father of the brotherhood of
Otokodate, whose profession it is to farm out the coolies
necessary to any large purpose. He assured me that there
would be no coolies in all Yedo for the carrying away of these
excellent goods. Nor, I find, will any reputable boat be available. . . . Thus our Oui-kum will go, and his goods will
remain. In time, luck may rid our city of your brother-in-law

also, and all others of his kidney. On such a lucky day there would be but one importer again of foreign merchandise—a gentleman of the Shogun's own choosing, as of his illustrious father's making. It is a good thought, An-jin."

"Aye," Adams grunted, "a good thought indeed—if there were no other thoughts in a man. But it is no lucky day when seamen are being robbed of the sea. And that is the other business that I have in hand."

"But you would not meddle in this other matter?" Magome said anxiously.

And Adams, staring at him in some amazement, said, "Meddle? I? Meddle? . . ." Any answer was beyond him, against the preposterous suggestion that he had any choice or freedom, when he was seized and driven from one matter to another by the necessity which lay within the matters themselves. As yet he knew only that he must see Hidetada; and it was only so much that he told Magome.

"But him you have never seen," said Magome.

"There has never been occasion," said Adams.

"It will cost money, my son," said Magome.

"It will," said Adams. "But they have given me money for the purpose. Rather they have given me an order on Wickham; he has enough and to spare."

"Ho!" said Magome. "Has he? Yet he called upon this person when you were gone, with a hand as empty as his head. Truly is it said that fortune loves only him whose hand is graceful in its gesture to his friends. You would have thought that a parcel of tobacco—even a kerchief with strange flowers printed upon it—but no doubt there are many such among the goods that are to be confiscated, and will be sold to one who may be aware of the selling. I have had occasions of speech with one who commands the few soldiers guarding the warehouse."

"I myself have brought you tobacco from Nagasaki," Adams casually lied. "A kerchief also. They will arrive in Yedo with the courier for Wickham, to whom I entrusted them on the way." He could pick up the tobacco anywhere in the bazaar for one who now had as much discrimination for tobaccos as a donkey for niceties in carrots. Wickham could give him some sort of handkerchief. . . . "Who is here now," he asked, "of the big ones, to give me access to his Excellency?"

"Oyen is here, the chiefest Secretary," said Magome. "But it were better—easier and cheaper—to see the Mint-Master. It is enough that he is an old pupil of mine."

"On the contrary," said Adams, "Oyen is now perhaps the easiest official in all Japan for me to see. Him I may claim to see in friendship, in his own house."

It was indeed cheering news that the venerable Oyen was now in Yedo. He had been so good a friend to Ieyasu and so sound an adviser that he was appointed Secretary to Hidetada as soon as his own son (who since had cut his belly) was of experience enough to become the Secretary of Ieyasu.

Oyen had stood behind Ieyasu's cushion when Adams and Santvoort were first bundled into the Presence, and Adams had handed over the compass that hung round his neck. He it was who had laughed with his master when Adams had subsequently performed tricks with a pair of compasses and a straight-edge on a piece of paper; and marvelled with him at the feat of a man's doing sums of addition and subtraction —even of division and multiplication—with no frame of coloured beads at his disposal, but only a point of lead in his hairy fist, and a sheet of paper. He it was who had looked, with Ieyasu, upon a fantastic drawing of a ship, and with Ieyasu had stepped, less than two years later, upon the deck of that same ship floating in the Bay of Uraga.

CHAPTER XXIX

THE Chiefest Secretary received Adams with a kindliness that set the Pilot stating his requests without preamble or delay. He spoke openly, as he would have spoken to Ieyasu himself.

At the end of it the old man sadly shook his head. "My son," he said, "for this year at least the edict must stand. No Emperor can make a law in one breath and repeal it in the next. In a year's time, after it has been obeyed by those at whom it is aimed, and forgotten by all others, perhaps. . . . In a year's time, at the next law-making, I can speak of it. But not now."

"But why was it ever made?" asked Adams.

Oyen said, "That, An-jin, is a question you may not ask. Nor I answer. We serve our master."

Adams accepted the rebuke. "Of the action of others, however, he said, "I may properly ask. These Englishmen—have they done a wrong, calling for this retribution? The punishment is a great one; it is ruin."

"It is no punishment," Oyen insisted. "But policy. And it is not ruin. They may appoint a Yedo merchant to hold and sell their goods."

Adams smiled. "My Lord," he said, "is there a Japan merchant in Yedo—or elsewhere—to whom you would entrust goods to the value of some thousands of tael? Goods that must be kept long and sold slowly if they are to be sold at all. Is there?"

It was Oyen now who smiled. "There was a merchant in Yedo," he said slowly, "to whom Ieyasu himself would have entrusted such goods."

And Adams said, "B'God!"

Then thoughtfully, "I would tell him also of the junk-masters of Nagasaki."

"An-jin," said the old man, "why will you not let matters rest?"

"Matters do not rest," said Adams. "The livelihood of those

428

men is going, and I know them to be good men. It may be that
Hidetada is ill-advised. You will remember that I myself for
three years supervised the Department of Licences. I know the
good from the bad among the junk-owners."

"We know them also," said Oyen. "But it is not now a
question of good and bad, but of numbers. More I cannot say.
Hidetada alone could tell you more."

"Therefore," said Adams, "it is necessary that I see him. I
have presents to give to those who will find me an audience;
but of late I have neglected all matters of the court and I do
not know which men——"

"There is no need of presents," said the old man. "The
unworthy Oyen himself is proud to find an audience with the
son for one who found his own audiences with the father by
rapping upon a door and saying 'It is An-jin.'"

The greatness of Oyen, the warmth of his aged benevolence
eased even the digestion of food that had lain like brick-
rubble in the stomach of Adams.

He departed from him proud and satisfied.

For eighteen years he had been a nobleman, but it was not
till now, when an old man had smiled and greatly praised him,
that his nobility was without some trace of a peculiar freakish-
ness. For the old man had called him not Needle-watcher or
Pilot of Yedo but a merchant of the land. And so he was knit
closer still to the stout seamen of Nagasaki; yoked more
firmly to the burden of their cause.

Oyen the Benevolent saw to it that he himself was present
when Adams was admitted to Hidetada.

The young Emperor looked upon the Pilot not arrogantly or
with any particular hostility, but with cool, quiet circum-
spection.

"You would speak with me, An-jin," he said, as one measuring a blade against a blade.

Adams fell into position with words of fitting ceremonial that
would have been foolery if he had offered them to Ieyasu:
"Since my Lord's condescension in deigning to give ear is
equal to this person's presumption . . ."

"Speak then."

But ceremonial was an easier matter than statement of facts to Hidetada; fencing was more desirable than the handling of a real blade.

"I have heard that the privileges granted to my countrymen by your Excellency's most revered father have been curtailed."

This was the first slip.

"You are misinformed," said Hidetada—"Or else you have forgotten. For it was by me that the privileges were granted to your countrymen. They have, in part, been curtailed."

Of such a man it would have been idiocy to ask "Why?"

Adams said, "I am greatly concerned in the affairs of these men."

"Naturally, An-jin," said Hidetada, "and laudably. For are they not your countrymen?"

Adams was not to be caught napping again. "They were my countrymen," he said; "——many years ago, before great friendship and hospitality made your Excellency's country my own also." He was conscious that old Oyen was pleased by this; and went on with somewhat steadier assurance. "Although these men can no longer call me 'countryman,' they have in many matters made me their friend. In return for their friendship I would willingly render them any small service that I may."

"So much has this always been the case, since their coming to this country," said Hidetada with a curious smile, "that when my father once offered you a considerable post with ourselves, your service of these others held you unable to accept it."

"My Lord," said Adams, and he said it slowly, mindful that quick words are apt to become quicker till, indeed, they run away with the speaker, "at the time of which you speak I was rendering no particular service at all to the English. What the mighty Ieyasu offered me was no service that I was not already gladly and proudly rendering him as I travelled my journeys upon other matters. Thus, what he offered to me was a present greater and more magnificent than the many great and magnificent gifts he had already made to me."

"It was, in fact, I that made the offer," said Hidetada.

"It was yourself also that I had the honour to be serving,"

said Adams. "So trivial a matter may not have come to your notice, but it was on that same journey that some ruffians fell upon us as we left an inn one dawn. They were not robbers, for it is well known that when I travel the road I travel with an empty purse. Good luck directed my blade so that I killed two. Their heads and swords were duly given up at the next barrier, with my deposition and the depositions of my cook and scribe."

"You did well," Hidetada admitted. "But it is nevertheless strange that you should have declined our gift."

The simple truth, told in friendship, had never been abused by Ieyasu. Adams tried it on Hidetada. "I was seeking a service from those Englishmen at that time," he said. "They have but a small understanding of certain matters. It seemed to me that a too great elevation of me in this land might make them the less willing to render this service."

Hidetada had not his father's patience for any of life's more peculiar phenomena, least of all for fools.

"If it is that ship of which you still speak," he said, "build it, man—and go. Our worthy Shongo will go with you. Or is this also a gift you will not accept?"

"If your Excellency takes offence at my refusal of these gifts," said Adams, "I am humbly sorry. For the ship I am content to wait. The men in England know now what kind of ship it is that I require. In twenty months from now it will be here. . . . But it was indeed for no other purpose than to ask a gift—another gift—that I have now come to you."

"It is strange that a man so proud as to decline first a great fief and then a ship should so humble himself . . ."

Adams swallowed this. It did, somehow, seem like a joke although the humour behind it was an ill one.

"I understand well," he said, "that the edict concerning the Englishmen's withdrawal from here must stand."

"That, An-jin, was the object with which the edict was made."

"According to its terms, however, they may leave their goods in the hands of a merchant of the place."

"That is so," said Hidetada.

"The gift I ask," said Adams, "——if no man less unworthy

has been brought to the notice of your Excellency—is that I should be that merchant."

Hidetada was not startled, for the reason that he was a great swordsman. He said, "My edict specifies that the merchant appointed should be a Japan."

Adams took his time in answering. The words themselves were leisurely when he spoke them. "Am I otherwise?" he asked.

Hidetada laughed. "Put your hand to your cheeks and your chin, Needle-watcher!" he said. "Lay it in the grizzled fox-skin upon your chest—and then tell me you are a Japan."

"Nevertheless, my Lord," said Adams, "if I have not become a Japan in all these years, I have become nothing."

Hidetada laughed on, and his laugh was not altogether ungenial. At length he turned, despairingly, to his secretary.

"What are we to say to such a man?" he asked.

Solemnly and very thoughtfully, the friend of Ieyasu answered, "It might be argued, my Lord, that such is indeed the law. For by the law, only he who is truly Japanese may hold property of swords and of land and of men and women. The first gift of your illustrious father to this Pilot was swords. Thereafter he gave him both land and men; and you yourself offered him the Lordship of more lands and more men. It might be argued, then, that holding these properties, and esteemed by your Excellency's most worthy self as able to hold them, the man is legally a Japan."

Hidetada's look narrowed upon Adams. "I would say this to you, An-jin," he said; and Adams was conscious of a challenge, of almost a threat. "See to it that henceforth you are a true Japan. You understand?"

"The words indeed I understand," said Adams, "but not your Excellency's hidden meaning. If I have, at any time, fallen short in the matter of bearing, I am unaware of it."

He was lying; but he was fairly confident that his secret was still undiscovered, so he risked the lie. His secret was the map of Japan that he had laboured for six years, unknown, to make. Three copies of it had gone, in the last dozen years, to England; a fourth was rolled away into a stoppered tube of bamboo under the floor of his private trading room in the house.

Indignantly, before his tongue was easy in the language, he had urged and achieved the expulsion of certain Spanish surveyors who committed what he explained to Ieyasu was an act of war in surveying his harbours and his land; and he had himself set about tramping leagues, and taking bearings from mountain to mountain for the making of his great chart. . . .

"Reports have come to us," said Hidetada, still challenging and a little threatening; but Adams faced him squarely, chancing his arm for some explanation of the spy-discovered map—if such it was. Hidetada went on, "These so-called padres have been found in many cases to be our enemies. They were the friends of our late enemies in the South and are the friends still of whatever dregs are left of them." He paused while Adams breathed freely again: "And now," he went on, "it is said that the most frequent and honoured guests in your house are these same padres."

"My Lord," said Adams, "if these men have ever been the enemies of any man in this country, it is of myself. They would have crucified me out of hand, but that your father was benevolent . . ." this seemed to him a fair start towards a good defence; but Hidetada cut him short with a smile.

"A man may forgive offences committed against himself," he said, "but condoning with the enemies of his Lord is another matter."

"I was not aware that these men were enemies. There was no evidence——"

"Except that they came to you," said Hidetada, "with no purpose but the airing of grievances."

Adams thought a moment, and then saw that this was, in fact, the kind of opening he had been waiting for. He took it leisurely. "Other men also have come to me lately to air a grievance," he said, "and these are among the truest men in all Japan."

"I was unaware," said Hidetada, and there was a twist in his smile as he turned to Oyen, "that our Pilot is esteemed a magistrate."

"Alas, no," said Adams, inclined to swagger a little in the inspiration that was come to him. "I am no magistrate. If I had been, it would perhaps have occurred to my dull wits that in stating a grievance these men were declaring themselves enemies. Foolishly, however, I took their cause to heart."

There was still a twist in Hidetada's smile. "We have heard," said he, "for news continues to come to us. It is reported that you took their presents also."

"Aye," said Adams, "I took their presents. For the refusal of a present is taken—sometimes—amiss. Their wine was acceptable to my boatmen and their fruit to the children in the streets of Hirado. If they also are enemies, I who am a loyal servant may say no more. But——"

"You may plead what you have come to plead," said Hidetada. "You may suggest that their licences be given back to them."

"And will they be given back?"

"Some may," said Hidetada. "Others will not."

"I cannot tell these men, then——" Adams began slowly.

"You can only tell them, An-jin," said Hidetada, "——as you have told me—that you are no magistrate; that these matters are not for your decision, but mine. As for that matter of the Englishmen's goods, since it is lawful for you to hold them, you may hold them."

He was dismissed; and there was none of the warm wine within him, as he went, that Ieyasu had always pressed upon him; but only the weight of ill-digested food. He knew that the eyes of Hidetada would always be the cold eyes he had first seen behind the bars of a mask.

CHAPTER XXX

HE reflected glumly that this fantastic business of belly-cutting was not such nonsense after all.

From the highest point of his land he could see the terraced rice plots in their swarthy nakedness of winter. Among them were the squat roofs that housed the feeding, the resting and the breeding of his clansmen. To his right was the Bay—placid and dark as the blue of a starless midnight. To his left was the rampart of blackly bearded hills, with the Road of Princes among them—the road that had ground more sandals and socks from the feet of Adams than he could number; the road whereon every tavern-keeper along its length of a hundred leagues and every scullion, on seeing him afar in the dust of summer or the sleet of winter, had said, "An-jin travels again . . ." And in front of him, a short journey in the mist of winter twilight, was Yedo. These things that had slowly become his own were now made more peculiarly his own by the quibble of kindly old Oyen and by the sanction of their Lord; and yet the coldness of this same ruler had laid them desolate. Friends he still had in plenty; but they were all lesser men than he—lesser, or very old. Of Hidetada it was said that he had no friends, nor needed any; and so it was that the friends of Hidetada's father lived now in a life that was become bleak, and a trifle meaningless. Or they cut their bellies and died.

Even for his belly itself there was now but little to be said. It was so seldom a pleasure any more that he was content to ask of it only that it perform the simplest work; and this it would not always do. Food could be a cold, wretched burden upon it; and it could be the pains of hell.

But the conviction that there is much to be said for suicide is not itself enough to set men at whipping dirks out of scabbards.

A week was fully occupied by the taking over of Wickham's stock; for Wickham, who had neglected it utterly with all the other opportunities of years, became a stickler in surrendering it. He wanted to list everything and to price everything. To the quite arbitrary price Adams was willing to set upon the whole he would not agree. Adams said at last, exasperated, "Man, I will come to Hirado to settle with Captain Cocks himself . . ."

Thus he was upon the road again; for there was too much involved in this business for him to allow it to be destroyed by the obstructiveness of Wickham.

At Hirado the atmosphere was a new one. The details of the Yedo stock were soon dispensed with, for they had become trivial. The important matter now was politics and the relationship of foreigners to the Emperor and his laws; and of foreigners to one another. Even junks at sea fell to brawling. The old *Sea Adventure*, Siam-bound (commanded by Eaton), had been driven into a Satsuma port. Strolling ashore, Eaton passed some Portuguese from a junk bound for Camboia and omitted to "put affe his hat." They "picked occation" on this, and from "wordes they fell to blowes, but the Portingales were well beaten and driven abord." It was a small enough thing in itself; but it brought up the question of licences. Eaton's, fortunately, was in order, and the *Sea Adventure* sailed on. But the Portuguese were detained in custody because their seal was out of date.

There were stories, moreover, that kept properly licensed vessels from putting to sea at all. Though not a vessel came Northward or Eastward in that season, the stories came somehow against the wind of the Hollanders' doings at sea.

The Dutch *Sun* put out from Hirado, ostensibly homeward, bound; and forthwith a Portuguese and a Spaniard slunk back to their moorings at Nagasaki. The armament of the *Sun* and the reputation of her Captain, Barkhoet, had been enough for them.

But they were not enough for Cocks. The English *Advice* was towed out of Hirado in the very wake of the Dutchman; and she was known to carry, in refined plate alone, ten thousand tael; so it began to be said in Nagasaki that only allies of the pirate Barkhoet would dare such a thing as this. And even while Dutch seamen in the Dutch house's skiff were helping to tow out the Englishman, with Cocks and Brower ashore loosing off "complementall" ordnance, stories came from nowhere that Dutchmen and Englishmen—in the Indies and wherever else they could lay hands upon each other—were at open war.

In this atmosphere Adams addressed his spare time to the fitting of his junk in the yard at Kawachi. As though by growth in accordance with a natural law, she developed gun-ports in her sides, gunwales clad in iron, and a powder magazine amidships. He named her the *Gift of God*.

At Hirado an immediate result of the feeling of strain was an intensive hospitality between the Dutch house and the English. Wine and pork and "dancing-beares" kept the evenings busy for Cocks. The house was overfull now that Wickham and Nealson and Eaton were collected there from their dismantled stations in Yedo, Sakai and Osaka. The menu was beyond the stomach of Adams and there were matters for discussion with his agent Zanzeburro for which there was no time except the evenings; so he set out his flag again from the window in the old man's house, and there spread his sleeping-mat.

Brower did all he could to allay the war scares; and he was very mindful, too, of Adams. There was work enough from the Dutch house alone to keep the Kawachi dockyard busy.

There was no immediate need for Adams to return to Yedo. He rigged and re-rigged the *Gift of God* with stay-sails and a fore-and-aft mizzen of the finest poledavy that the Dutch and English houses could combine to give him, till he could sail her within six points of the wind. Brower would gladly have bought her, asking Adams to name what price he would; but Adams would not sell.

He fitted her with a wheel—and he laid her up. For he had no use for her.

*   *   *   *   *

At the beginning of June Barkhoet swaggered into port again with the *Sun*. The common gossip was that in her five months of cruising she had taken sixteen Chinese junks and burnt one Spaniard off the Philippines. Barkhoet himself denied it, saying at dinner that he had taken no more than six. Statistical details apart, Cocks noted only the broad facts: "Yt is serten that the Hollanders have taken more riches this yeare from the Chinas than they did the last, and each mareener hath his cabben full of silk stuffes and musk. . . . They say that, having taken most parte of goodes out of I junck, and seeing her reddy to sinck, they put 900 Chinas in to her, and bad them shift for themselves, etc. . . . Yt is thought both Portingales, Spaniardes and Chinas will goe to Cort, and cry out with open mouth touching that matter, and the rather because themperour will not suffer his own vassales of Japon to doe the lyke." . . . And then came Chinamen themselves to visit Cocks: "All the Chinas which are set at liberty out of a junck came this day and said they found per experience the English nation were honourable people, and soe would report when they retorned into their own cuntrey and made no doubt but that we should have entrance for trade." It was enough to set him off again, pestering Adams for another expedition towards China. Adams had a boat now to which monsoons were nothing; for he had shown loafers on the beach that she could turn on her beams, shake herself and sail right through a wind. . . . But Adams as yet had no licence; and without a licence, for he was an upholder of all law, he would not sail.

They must go, therefore, to Yedo; Cocks would gird up his loins and go with him. They would beard the young Emperor. They would sue for the renewal of the English privileges; and Adams would get his licence.

But Adams would not go.

He waited for a ship from England; but no ship came.

Even from Bantam or Patani there was none.

Towards the end of June Cocks recorded: "There came news that shiping was entred into the rode of Kawachi, and shott offe ordinance; and Albaro Munos sent his man to me to tell me he heard 3 or 4 greate peeces shot affe. I know not wherefore these people doe this but to mock at us, because we have no shiping come in as the Hollanders have, and urge us to send our boates and our men to look for trifells that they may laugh at us better afterwardes. Truely, I think it is not without instigation of Hollanders, who, although they speak us faire, love us not . . ."

At the middle of July still no ship had come, and Adams was still at Hirado.

The licensing of Adams's boat for that trade into China was all that worried Cocks now; and the apathy of Adams in the matter was more than he could understand, or stomach. He invited him to dinners; he waited for him in his room in the house of Zanzeburro; he posted his linguist to waylay him as he returned along the road from Kawachi. Always it was the same; Adams was too tired to dine, too busy to talk—till on an evening in late July when Cocks did succeed in cornering him, the Pilot burst out, "Yedo! Yedo—enough of this talk, man. I am going to Yedo. There is no need for you to go. In three days from now I start." Cocks immediately was relieved; for he had heard enough of that Yedo journey to make his old bones happy at the prospect of avoiding it.

"Good!" said he; and then he stared at Adams. "But are not the Hollanders setting out in three days?"

"Aye," said Adams. "It is with them that I go."

"With them?" exclaimed Cocks. "You—with them?—to the court?—our enemies?" He was aghast.

"They are no enemies of mine," said Adams quietly.

"But they are enemies to the Worshipful Company."

"I am no servant of the Company," was Adams's cold retort. He sat down and clapped his hands for the boy to bring them tea. There was no chair in the house of Zanzeburro, so Cocks remained upon his feet. He took short paces in front of Adams —towards him; and backwards, away from him.

"Man," he kept on saying, "Man—man——" And then, "You can do no such thing as this."

"I can," said Adams. "I do. For twenty years now the Hollanders have been my friends."

"But they are villains!" shouted Cocks. "They are thieves and bloody pirates; robbers of every ship at sea."

At this Adams merely laughed: "What of that?" he asked. "What is that to you? You have no ships at sea—you and your Worshipful Company."

"But it is they that intercept us and rob us," said Cocks.

"On every hand it is said that they are verily blockading the Indies."

Adams shrugged his shoulders. "Whether your Company's ships do not any longer exist, or whether they do exist and cannot get here—it is all one."

"If you prefer their enemies above your own brothers and countrymen——" Cocks began disdainfully.

Adams cut him short. "I prefer ships that sail," he said, "to ships that do not. Honour me now by drinking a dish of this savourless and worthless tea."

Cocks felt that it would choke him, but he swallowed it.

CHAPTER XXXI

ADAMS and the Dutch emissaries to the Court of Yedo had not been gone (to the tune of sixteen pieces of ordnance shot off by the Dutch *Galleas* and the *Sun*) for much over a week when a Dutchman towed in—as large as life, for all the world to see—a disabled Englishman as a prize. Staring at first from the jetty and then glumly from the verandah of the English house, the English colony could not believe its eyes.

Cocks was still speechless when a letter was handed to him from the Dutch Cape Merchant inviting him and his colleagues to dine. As to the ship, the Hollander explained, the Dutch Captain who had towed it in had had no alternative at sea but to capture it; and he himself now had no alternative but to hold it. This much, he said, was demanded by the bare formality of war. In personal friendship, however, he offered that Cocks should go aboard at his pleasure and take over what he pleased of the cargo.

Speechless Cocks might have been; but he still had pen and ink and paper. The moment was the climax of many days wherein reports had been coming to him of things that were commonly said in the Dutch house. "Soe," says Cocks, "being tuched soe neare by this prating Duchman, I took occasion to write him a letter in Spanish, the coppie whereof I have extant, in which I advized that I marveld much he medled in my household affares, bragging that nothing could be done in the english howse but he knew it within xxiiij howrs after, esteeming me a hasty, furious, and he might as well have said, a madd man, doing all things on spleene without councell. Unto which I answered that I desired to knoww my accusers which yf he did not manifest, and that yf any man went upon spleene or ill-will to geve out or speke such ill and false reportes of me, that he or they lied in their throtes. And whereas he said that he sat still in his howse and said nothing tuching thenglish nation, my answer was, they had not geven hym nor them any occation hereto, nether in taking of shipping,

killing of men, and robing them of their goodes. And, yf I spoke
ill of their generall, I did it uppon good ground, holding hym as
an enemy to my soverign lord the Kinges matie. of England and
his estate in taking of shipping, killing his Matis. subjectes and
bereving them of their goodes. And as tuching his thretnyng
speeches I did not well understand his meanyng, but gave him
to understand I did not fear his wordes nor his weapons. As to
the ship: they had pocession, and therefore might make their
benefite, for I was assured to have satisfaction in England.
They might show themselves frendes to thenglish, if they
pleased, ether now or hereafter, but for my parte I did not care
a halfe penny whether they did or noe."

The first thing, following the immense relief of writing this
letter, was to let Adams know of the outrage. Two couriers
were at once sent off—one by water and the other overland—to
catch up with him. These despatches contained the further
information that Cocks himself was starting for Yedo as soon as
the party could be fitted out.

So Cocks set out upon the journey which he had successfully
avoided for so long, accompanied by William Nealson.

The party was told by the Company's agent at Shimonoseki
that Adams had received and read Cocks's letter and that certain
natives had told him quite independently that the Hollanders
had taken no less than five English ships. Cocks expected,
therefore, to fall in with him presently; but at Kioto was only
Cocks's own messenger waiting for him with "such an un-
sezonable and unreasonable letter" as Cocks "would not have
suspected he would have done, saying he was none of the
Companies' servant, and is, as it seemeth, altogether Holland-
ized, persuading me not to goe up about this matter."

It became a wretched journey.

At Osaka he set out presents for the Governor and his
secretary, and dressed himself up to deliver them. But the
castle door was shut in his face: the Governor slept and the
secretary "was bidden out to a banket." With the petty
affront rankling in his touchy breast the Cape Merchant
recorded, "I am of opinion our host Grubstreet doth play the
gemeny, per instigation of Captain Adames, both taking the
Hollanders partes for lucar. If it be proved soe, God reward

them according to their deservinges, and God deliver us from frendly secret fowes." For that was the way of him who muddled peaceably along for ten years with his dream of 'trade into China.' Through the years that all Japan doors were open to him and his gifts were taken in 'kinde parte' or 'frendly sort' he saw in it the mystic greatness of the 'Worfull. Companie' or the 'Kinges Matie. of thenglish nation.' But when doors were shut and presents 'taken in snuffe' he saw only the double heart of Adams.

While 'Mr. Jehan the Scribe was awork to write out an information in Japons against the Hollanders, to deliver up to the Emperour' Cocks went 'to viset the antient monuments of Japon.' It was the only fun in the whole journey. There were two shocks of earthquake. Floods were up at the fords, bridges had been carried away, tavern-keepers were casual and insolent, coolies mutinous. A friendly party of Portuguese, headed for Nagasaki, told them that Adams and the Dutchmen had presented their gifts and obtained their audience ten days before.

They plodded on; and two days' march short of Yedo they saw, coming towards them, headed for home again, the Hollanders themselves.

Any tavern-keeper or scullion of the road could have told them, from the pace of the group when it was still a mile away, whether the Pilot was there or no.

Neither party checked its pace. They met.

"There was small greeting betwixt us; and soe they passed."

Adams was not there.

CHAPTER XXXII

HE met them in the way at the next dawn, ten leagues from Yedo; and God only knew what was in the heart of him. For with him were his son and daughter—the man of fifteen, shaven at his crown, with a brown-black top-knot; sworded at his belly; small and lissom for an Englishman but big already for a natural. Susannah was ten, the quaint little old creature for whom Cocks, in the first five minutes he had to himself, found a picture of Christ and a sash in his own chest, and oranges in the mess-box.

Behind them was the Lordling's half-section of ceremonial pikemen.

"No," was immediately impossible and unconsidered. The invitation of the whole entourage to the house of the Pilot was accepted as it was given—in the manner of one of the pleasanter natural laws.

Cocks's confidence was at once restored in the might of the Worshipful Company whose head office was in Limehouse, and in the King's Majesty of the English nation.

Stepping out beside Adams, Nealson and he and the boy and the child (whose hand Cocks held) turned aside from the Princes' Way, for Yokosuka and the Pilot's home.

The climb left him little breath for the asking of questions, and there was no need to have things out with Adams, so strong was the feeling of confidence, so good the cheer of hospitality. Seeing old Magome in the flesh—or rather in parchment wrinkled to a scar and a toothless smile—he thrilled to see, coming to life, the figure that had been so dramatic in his mind, of Macchiavelli the wily Cavalero. He got a fleeting glimpse of Adams' brother-in-law, the 'craftie knave' Andreas; and that, too, thrilled him—for though he was an ageing and a portly man at the fag-end of a wretched journey, he had, in the right company and before a show of the right sort, the resiliency of a boy. For Magdalena, the sister-in-law, he was ready to weep when he thought of the hastily departed tout, Andreas. With

Mistress Adams he was charmed when she spoke her few sentences 'complemental' in English.

Great was the power of the Worshipful Company, immense the Majesty of England when pikemen preceded them over the more level paths of the estate and when the Pilot's serfs made obeisance.

A garnet ring of his own was added to the presents made to the family; a princely tip was weighed out to Magome for the servants; and the party set out for the Court at Yedo. Adams alone among them walked a trifle heavily.

On the road they met some priests, sore and spent with travel. Adams talked with them while the party went on; and when he rejoined it he was graver than before.

"Portingals?" Cocks asked with his usual interest in such matters.

Adams said, "Aye, very likely. But it is not said any more whether such men be Portingals, Spaniards or Naturals. It is enough in Yedo that they be padres."

"In Satsuma also," Cocks gossiped, "there have been confiscations and banishments of them. And crucifixions. It was told to me on the way——"

"Aye," said Adams, a little impatiently, "I know."

"What will become of such men?" Cocks asked.

"Those?" asked Adams, indicating the road behind and the men they had lately passed. "They will stay at my house for rest and refreshing, to await my return."

Cocks saw that there was, at the moment, no pressing him further.

He tried him next as to their own prospects. "Will we, do you think, regain our lost privileges?"

"Presently we shall know," retorted Adams.

"Did the Hollanders gain theirs?" He saw no point in refraining further from leading questions, when even trivialities failed to get an answer.

"The Hollanders sought no further privilege," said Adams drily.

Cocks tried otherwise. "No," he said. "They have all the privilege they want. So long as they are pirates, all they need is a receptacle for their stolen ships and goods, and a base for their operations. They have them at Hirado."

"Therefore they ask for no more," said Adams.

"But it is to put an end to their thieving and murder that I have taken this journey!" said Cocks. He felt a warmth beginning to tingle under his cravat. "I care nothing for the peck of profit and the bushel of worry we have had from these other factories we have had—at Yedo and Osaka. The only good profit we have had in this country—with neither risk nor worry—was from that voyage of the *Sea Adventure*. But if you are now befriending these Holland murtherers——"

"Bring some ships," said Adams, "and you shall see whose friend I am. But what do you expect of me or any man when no ship at all comes? Of what use is such friendship?"

"How can a ship come if the sea is a-swarm with pirates?"

Adams did not answer, for he knew that the only ship that could sail through a pirate-ridden sea must be the pirates' friend.

Quietly, and cunningly, he said, "These old trading privileges are, as you say, of little consequence to you. The matter of consequence is that you, too, should have a base for your trade—into China."

"Yes!" said Cocks, "yes! yes! . . . But what of the pirates?"

"What of them?" said Adams. "On that voyage of the *Sea Adventure*—when you had neither risk nor worry—there were pirates enough. You yourself set nineteen of them aboard, fully armed. I took them with me and brought them peaceably back again—eighteen of them."

"And you have left these men at large!" exclaimed Cocks.

"I have them somewhat in my hands," was the quiet answer.

"But the Hollanders are not thus in your hands! They have taken that ship of ours; and all Japan may go and see the insult of it."

"All Japan," said Adams, "may now go and see them giving it back."

"Per order of his Majesty the Emperor?" the prickle of warmth had pleasurably gone from under the cravat; and Cocks rubbed his hands together.

Adams shrugged his shoulders. "——Or without the

Emperor's order," he said. "But give it back they certainly will."

Cocks could not be happy till he had stated whatever drama he beheld. So he said: "They *are* in your hands, then, Captain Adams; these Hollander pirates no less than the Japans themselves, as we shall see in Yedo."

CHAPTER XXXIII

But what they saw in Yedo was vastly different.

The Pilot, who had once swung through corridors that had been even seen by only the greatest in the land, and had rapped with his bare knuckles upon the door of the land's ruler, was now kept hanging about in courtyards among fishermen, artisans and hucksters who had petty suits to press upon some lesser secretary.

In two days he was down to the level of those who slipped small bribes to door-keepers and messengers of the palace.

In a week he had still seen no official who was any more than a flunkey.

Day was added to day and Adams came back to the lodging each night jaded and thirsty, but unwilling to drink anything that was not the weakest tea. The presents were still in their handsome bundles, the 'Information' against the Dutch was still undelivered.

Cocks champed and swore and grumbled, and finally demanded to have the 'Information' back in his own hands so that he might take it himself and demand an audience. Adams answered him so that he never made the demand again. All he had said was "You fool!" He sank his chin thereafter into his beard, and his beard upon his chest.

For Adams knew now that so far as being a Cavalero of Japan was concerned, his day was done. With his chin in his beard and his beard on his chest, he thought back through the years of Hidetada's slow and steady growing to the stature that now was his; and beyond the explanation of alert, cold eyes behind the bars of a fencing-mask, which was no explanation at all, he could see none. He did not know that with those same cold eyes Hidetada had been watching, for eighteen years, the antics of the hearty, hairy fellow for whom Ieyasu, in his genial love for him, predicted some ultimate greatness; and the greatness, so far as

Hidetada could see, had never materialised. Odd jobs the man certainly had done, but they were nothing to justify the stupendous height of his father's regard. He had bickered with Portuguese, Spaniards and Dutchmen on occasions with the competence that would have been expected of any man of business. He had built a ship or two with the skill of a sound carpenter, and had sailed them. He had kept the peace, cutting down a foot-pad or two—and odd assassins, road-wolves or enemy-agents in wait for him—in the manner of any travelling soldier. He passed muster adequately enough as a general sort of Number One man; But there, for Hidetada, the matter ended. His revered father had loved the fellow in some fantastic way. Hidetada loved him in no way at all; and now that his father and his peculiar dreams were gone from the land, he had his own dreams and his own counsellors.

He had, moreover, his worries. Japan, to him, was a precious matter; and, preciously, it was small. Its limit was the jagged fringe of it that girt it against the sea.

All that the sea had ever brought into it was chatter and tremor as of winds, petty encroachments as of the tide against the shore; and Hidetada, seeing that no particular good came out of all this nonsense, was tired of it. There were quarrels enough in the country already without the almost meaningless quarrels of foreigners over their ships and goods and fantastic gods. Concerning the last he was particularly bitter; he lost no time in clearing the city of priests. The celebration of Mass was prohibited, and immediate crucifixions followed the many defiances of the edict. Priests were hunted out and flung aboard junks sailing to Nagasaki. When they landed again in disguise, they were caught and crucified naked.

Adams went, by night, to his home, lest refugees be found there. He set the spent travellers upon their road with filled satchels and a purse of money; and he was back by morning, to wait in the courtyard of the palace. Already the score of other loungers there were becoming hail-fellow-well-met to the Cavalero who was growing morose beyond even civility.

The last humiliation came.

He was called by a door-keeper to enter. He swaggered

forward with whatever swagger the three weeks of hanging about had left to him, followed by the bearers carrying his own personal gift to the Shogun and the great chest from the Honourable Company. From his girdle he drew out Cocks's precious 'Information' against the Hollanders.

The document was taken from him—not by the hand of Hidetada himself, for he did not get beyond the first corridor. Nor was it taken by any secretary; but by some trivially pompous clerk with no more than the dummy hilt of a single sword at his girdle.

The presents were bundled in, unexamined, to the company of a hundred other unexamined presents, in a lumber-room.

Adams was bidden to wait.

In due course another official came out to him. This man Adams knew. He was no particular friend, but just one of the familiar many who, in the old days, had stood aside for the Needle-watcher to pass.

"The honourable document," this man now said, as pompous as the rest of them, "will have honourable attention. The answer will be duly given. In the meantime, you have sued for a sailing licence and the same has been granted." He handed to him the red seal that should set the little *Gift of God* free of her shackles. "It is renewable in a year from now."

Adams moved to go, but the man said: "You are invited, honourably, to wait. His Excellency would not suffer a gift-bringer to go empty-handed away."

Adams waited.

The present was duly handed to him—by a swordless flunkey; a package, mean and neatly tied, of ten linen jackets that had been purchased thus in their hundreds from some Yedo contractor, for dishing out to honest wardsmen or perhaps a bumkin-laird of a remote province.

Adams took the absurd thing and stared at it, and mumbled some profanity. A flunkey saved him from any such outrage as that he should have taken the bundle to the door and tossed it out to a coolie. The servant who had been the bearer of Adams's gift of an ivory medicine box to Hidetada stepped forward and took the parcel from his master. He carried it through the courtyard with the strut of one who carried not a bundle of

tradesmen's mean coatlets, but an Emperor's gift to a nobleman.

Nothing was said in the courtyard as Adams passed through.
Men nodded in salutation of him. For tradesmen and pro-
vincials did not as yet snicker quite openly in the face of the
Pilot of Yedo.

CHAPTER XXXIV

His Lordship at Hemimura saw little of him thereafter, and Yedo saw nothing at all. His home became the house of Zanzeburro and the English house in Hirado; he lodged at times with Concepcion in Nagasaki; aboard Santvoort's junk; with Shiquan the Chinaman and in the taverns of Osaka—avoiding only such places that were known to be the resorts of the country's greater gentlemen.

Once, indeed, he was the guest of Shobei; for he was engaged in making money now, by hook or crook, and Shobei—bland as ever and more prosperous—was in the market for all the firearms and small ordnance that the English and the Dutch could land or cast.

In the *Gift of God* he carried some coasting freights, and cruised the Inland Sea; heading her, by reason of the sails on her stays and mizzen, contrary to many a wind that held all other craft to their moorings. He spent the winter thus —the winter of 1618—in gun-running and other matters of trade that brought him profit and high repute among the flashy speculators of the seaboard. Among these second-rate Cavaleros, the outsiders whose only weight was the weight of gold in their purses, he remained the big man with the weight of the symbolic swords at his girdle. So it was among them that he stayed more gladly than that he should go and sit with Magome Sageyu and listen to lugubrious, bitter tales of glories that were departed; for Magome Sageyu had a particular gift for extracting the utmost of reflection from the tragedy of broken men.

Their company was pleasanter than prowling through Yedo— by night, so that none might hail him as a crony who before would have saluted him as Ieyasu's friend, or that those who had hailed him before might not now acknowledge his acquaintance as they acknowledged any other creditor.

Nagasaki, Hirado and Osaka with their cheery merchants and robustious seamen were pleasanter then than the solitude of dark Yedo, even though the empty streets led to the company of Shongo the Admiral who was still friend to him, coldly contemptuous of the boorishness of the stripling Hidetada as he was of all the other nonsense in a new-fangled world. But even Shongo himself was beginning to lose confidence or interest or some other quality of warmth regarding the ship that now, for ten years of waiting, had omitted to come.

It was genially that he had said: "When it does come, An-jin—if I am not dead by then—I am with you."

But it was in anger that Adams had left him, in the same dull smoulder of wrath and resentment he had for all who thwarted him with their own scurryings after such fantasies as cloves and nutmegs, silks and pirates and 'trade into China', or even by their idiot prattle of these matters disturbed his dream. Shongo himself was now amongst these; for if Shongo, prattling about that which had departed from women, about the fire that was gone out of wine and the magnificence that was gone from gentlemen—if Shongo did not sneer at his waiting, it was only because the office of friendship laid it down that upon a friend no friend may ever sneer.

So Adams had prowled off from the house of Shongo when night protected him from the sight of eyes that saw him, or else saw him not—him to whom Ieyasu had given swords and a Lordship, and to whom Hidetada had tossed a bundle of pauper's tunics. Unaccompanied by even boy or scribe he took the road to Hemimura, praying Almighty God to muzzle old Magome in sleep so that he, at least, might be held off from chatter.

Bikuni alone, in all the world, knew whither her lord was going, with the cancer that was now in his stomach and the maggot in his brain.

For his stomach she could only instruct the cook-boy how meticulously he must feed and tend his master; for Adams would not be held any longer at home where men obeyed him not as they had obeyed their Lord, but with the obedience given happily to a well-loved child.

He was off again to Nagasaki and Hirado; to his shipyard and its business at Kawachi; to the Spaniards and Portuguese, the Englishmen and the gun-running, friendly Dutch.

CHAPTER XXXV

ADAMS alone now passed freely between the houses of the last two; for they were openly at war. Swaggering Wickham had gone homeward a year ago; his girl and his children were back in the bazaar of Yedo; but there were still broken heads if Englishmen and Hollanders met ashore. The Dutch, Eastwards of the Indies, were masters; and Adams could not afford enmity for any man who held those seas. The Dutch, likewise, found great profit in the friendship of him who could sell and carry pieces and powder and shot for them; and who could buy for them, even in Kioto, anything they pleased.

So Adams kept the hostility of the houses within the limits of their walls, lodging himself under his St. George's flag at the house of Zanzeburro; till one day, when he was by chance at home, matters came to a crisis. Old Cocks himself was jeered at in the street by a Dutch seaman coming out of a tavern, for the Dutch house had set a price of fifty crowns on the Cape Merchant's head. The fellow performed for him a lewd pantomime that set the tavern and the whole street rocking with laughter. He next jostled the Cape Merchant of the Honourable Company into Hirado's foulest gutter; and the fist of the old Northamptonshire grocer snapped the Hollander's jaw-bone.

Cocks was scarcely home, fuming and sucking his knuckles, demanding paper and pen and ink before his hand should have swelled and stiffened, when there was an uproar in the road as the rascals from the Dutch house came roaring towards the English. There were two hundred of them, or two hundred and fifty. The bare half-dozen in the English house were immediately at the powder-flasks, clanking ramrods after balls down the barrels of their fowling-pieces. Cocks looked to the priming of his pistols, and his mind snapped from his anger into the thought that they were not bad odds to die against for the glory of his country and his Company—thirty or forty to one.

"I'll shoot, Captain. They've got no guns that I can see."
It was young Sayers who spoke from the verandah. "It will
stop them; and we can send to Captain Adams . . ."

But Dutchmen had already seen the piece at Sayers's
shoulder. Tumbling out of the house in their heat to be at the
Englishmen they had grabbed up only the handiest of weapons
—cutlasses, cudgels and a few odd pistols. They hesitated and
scrambled for cover; and some scurried away, back to the
house so that they too should have proper firearms.

Word had already got to Adams, and he was coming. By the
time he was at the English house whatever words he had
spoken on the way had produced a hundred natives at his back.
The rough-and-tumble—the very dregs of that waterside
bazaar that was itself all dregs—this riff-raff was openly
armed with swords and pikes and bows.

In half an hour the Dutchmen were at home again, some
cleanly wounded with blades, some clubbed into a docile
stupor and two or three with a dislocated limb. Adams
took a cup of tea with Cocks; and he took another with the
Dutchmen.

He was proud at first, as he drank the tea with Cocks and
young Sayers and Eaton and the others. He was again proud,
and a little pompous, when he was in the Dutch House,
remonstrating with Brower; for habit was showing him to
himself as a nobleman whose presence and whose word had
mustered a host of loyal volunteers—the same nobleman whose
sarcasm had sent Shobei slinking into the hold of the *Sea
Adventure* while a rabble piled and burnt its arms on the beach
of the Great Lu-Chu.

Walking home he was still proud, and he suddenly laughed
aloud at his pride; for he saw that it had been no nobleman who
had mustered those volunteers, but a swashbuckler whose
shout had flung them together—thugs and assassins—drawing
them from their burrows and crannies with contraband
weapons, in that thug-ridden bazaar.

That he was no longer any great nobleman was amply shown
to him, and to others, the next evening. There was a woman in
Hirado of no high repute but of a standing which gave a certain
significance to her sayings and to the doings of her household.

There was another woman also, Matinga. Of this Matinga the only mentions in the Diary of Richard Cocks are a series of entries enumerating some of the gifts and suggesting others that were made to her by the Cape Merchant over a period of eleven years. There was little love lost between the quiet Matinga and the loud trollop; and with the latter Cocks and the English house had recently 'fallen into termes.' It was among the wits at her parties that lampoons had originated, asserting that what the Englishmen lacked in pluck and seafaring skill they made up in certain other qualities. Adams's leadership of the anti-Dutch rabble made of him, too, a butt for these drolleries. The eunuch and other flunkeys from this woman's household set up a song at the Pilot's back as he returned to his lodging from Kawachi, through the waterside street of Hirado.

Adams walked on . . . Noblemen paid no heed to such things.

The gibers and quipsters followed him. Their leader's song became:

> "Ten mean jackets for the Englishmen,
> Ten fingers to the Shogun's hands.
> Ten . . ."

Adams turned and advanced upon them. His lantern, symbol that it was a Samurai who walked abroad by night, was deftly kicked from his hand; and the Pilot had whacked a pate or two and half-a-dozen behinds with his cudgel before the street was quiet again.

It was, once more, the swashbuckler who had triumphed in a rabble. . . . A nobleman would have dealt with the matter otherwise than with a cudgel and curse flung back for obscene curse. . . . But then, for a nobleman, such a matter would never have arisen.

CHAPTER XXXVI

By January of 1619 he had actually fought with stevedores and carpenters in his Kawachi yard. They had jostled him and abused him over some trifle of pay, and one fellow laid his hand upon him. He went down immediately in a whirl of stars and bright lights and abysmal darkness; for the Pilot's fist was now a weapon readier than his sword. Adams sprang aboard the *Gift of God* and the others came on. He kept his back to the mainmast as he laid into them with his stick; for he knew what the rascals could do to a limb over-reached and offered to them. He banged them; the swings and cuts and thrusts of a swordsman directed his footpad's weapon, and they were beaten back and cowed. Even their snarling and their whimpers had been cuffed to a slinking silence when he stepped to the jetty again.

The sweat in his hand and on his brow and chest was cold. Leaning, with some rag of dignity, on a bollard, he furtively pressed upon it the sudden pain that stabbed his vitals.

For an hour he stood thus, frozen beyond even vomiting and nailed fast to the comfort of rough timber forced hard against his accursed belly. And men said, as they peeped from waterside crannies: "He holds his ground . . ." Their discontent and anger turned to ruffians' easy pride in a ruffians' valour as they watched him standing, stock-still, where another would have glibly fled.

The pain held him fast; and the tale of his standing there was told in bazaars, how that even an insult from the mighty Shogun had not broken or even bent the spirit of him who had been called, in other days, Pilot of Yedo.

And Shobei, smuggler and thug and occasional pirate, expressed no particular surprise; for the men who had bested Shobei afloat or ashore were neither slight in quality nor great in number.

The affair had shaken Adams to the extent that he felt little more at home now, kicking his heels at Hirado or Nagasaki, than he would have felt in the chill of Yedo. Cocks, too, was always at him. There was at least this truth now to support Cocks in his anxiety for trade into China—Japan was utterly lost to him and his Worshipful Company. The Cape Merchant's irritation and impatience had acquired for the English house a junk of fifty tons, christened her the *Godspeed*, obtained a licence for her, and fitted her for sea.

Adams undertook a voyage with her to Tonkin.

For Cocks and the Honourable Company the adventure turned out neither a profit nor a loss; but for Adams it was a surprise.

The *Godspeed* sailed openly as a ship of war, armed with every ounce of ordnance—brass or iron, big and small—that she could carry. The crew that manned her wore the same demeanour as their ship. Of the Englishmen John Coaker had a throat that had been partially cut by Dutchmen; young Sayers had a very recently mended head, and three seamen had escaped from the dog's life of a year's captivity in the Moluccas. There were two Spaniards who still waited upon Adams from time to time from the crew whose Captain had been murdered and ship burnt. The nine Japans were nominees of Shobei; and Adams commanded them directly, without any intermediation of Japan Captain or boatswain.

This crew, with each ruffian armed to his taste and to the full capacity of his belt or girdle, made easier handling than the professedly civilian lot on the *Sea Adventure*.

From Tonkin, the business uneventfully done, he coasted down to Malaya. He had despatches from Cocks for Patani and Bantam; and there were certain Dutchmen he himself was anxious to see again. Of English shipping there was no certain news. Ships either came or they came not—as far as Bantam or Patani; but there was little prospect of their venturing further. Of his particular Dutchmen he could see or hear nothing; for no man could say in those days and in those seas where any Dutch seaman was, or what he was at. There was little news that he could find to take back to Cocks; none that he could hug to himself, till a rumour was brought aboard. It came from the nowhere of a brothel or a tavern; but its terms were most exact; in the Indies about Surat, an

English fleet of seventeen sail was being secretly mustered, to come eastward with the monsoon and settle matters, once and for all, with the Dutch. It was enough for Adams. It accounted to him for the newslessness, and for the present shiplessness, of the Archipelago. It accounted for the absence, upon other affairs, of his Dutchmen. It told him that his time was coming and that Hirado was the place in which to wait for it.

So back to Hirado, with the first changing of the wind, he went to do the last of his waiting.

There came to Japan in the whole of that season of 1619—as there had come in the season before it—no English ship at all. There was neither sight nor any further word of the fleet from Surat; and from the Dutchmen also he got nothing. Those whom he had particularly sought at Patani and for whom he particularly waited at Hirado at last came to him. Two of them he had not seen for two years; one he had not seen for four, and the others for three. To all five of them he had given letters, and money enough for the certain carrying of letters from Rotterdam to London. All five now gave their affidavit that the letters had been delivered, as surely as anything could be sure on earth or sea.

And to all of those five letters, and to the many that had gone before them, with years to spare, there was no answer.

No sign of an answer.

Two of the five—the privately-sent—letters had been to Mr. Nicholas Diggins of Limehouse, shipwright; for Nicholas Diggins had always been a wideawake man, alert for any opportunity. They had contained some drawings and a rough specification of the ship that would most handsomely weather the Northern seas. . . . But it could well have been that old Nich. Diggin was, long ago, dead.

One thread of hope, however, still remained.

The last of Adams's letters had been for the Company. It was the kind of letter which, if they were to answer at all, they must answer immediately; for it was not so much a letter as an order for goods from a customer impatient of waiting for delivery. The only news he gave them was that he was considerably older than he had been at the commencement of his correspondence with them—at the time, even, of his indentured service of them which he had scrupulously fulfilled; and that he was ill of a distemper about his bladder and stomach. Thus time was a factor of importance. Of a ship, he said briefly that he had built two already and could therefore, if put to it, build another. Of men he said no more than that if Englishmen were wanting for such an adventure as he pretended, other men were not. He could muster a crew himself from among the 'stowte seamen' of Japan. His demands upon the Honble. Co. were cut down to sailcloth, to three compass-needles, to hemp tackle, a pair of brass globes and a dozen hundredweight or more of biscuit. These were his necessities, and for these he was willing to pay—in plate bars of Japan silver, in rials-of-eight, or in commodity. Let them but mark the goods clearly for him and invoice them—for Captain Will Addames, or for An-jin of Yedo, in Japan—and the goods would get to him; even if the ship carrying them should fall among enemies, which Almighty God forbid, they would so still reach him; and he would pay Cocks on the spot. His letter was his bond to that effect, and his word was as good as any in Japan (for that letter had been written soon after the voyage of the *Sea Adventure*).

And the Honourable Company sent him not a stitch of canvas, nor a single needle, nor a biscuit-crumb. Not even a word.

Barkhoet of the *Sun* was the last Dutch Captain to come thundering into port, tottering with his own salutes and heavy with plunder. His news of English shipping he gave to Adams with a wink; it was a parcel of letters, intact, for Cocks. How he had come by it he did not exactly say. But there was English pewter in his cargo as well as China silks. His own sails were ragged, however; and the cordage was mended not with hemp but with rope from the Manillas. So Adams believed that the holds of rifled ships had held no coils of ropes or fardels of canvas addressed to An-jin of Yedo.

No ship could come from the West after Barkhoet, for Barkhoet could brag that the last puff of the monsoon had just been tumbled from his sails.

CHAPTER XXXVII

It was October when Adams took the road for home.

On the ferry boats of the Inland Sea there was gossip enough of fellow passengers to keep him engaged; for he was not now aloof when merchants or artisans clustered together for business or talk.

At Osaka he lay for three days and four nights in the house of Cuemon, the Company's agent who figured in Cocks's books as Grubstreet; for his stomach was not what it had been for those short passages, and he was anxious to start in good fettle upon the road.

Grubstreet complained of his stock, of his debtors and of the mastery of the Dutchmen; but then, all merchants were complaining of their stock, their debtors and the mastery of the Dutch. Adams moved on from him, refreshed and morose.

In the first day's travelling there fell in with him one who had been on the ferry boats, a listener rather than a talker in the deck coteries. He saluted and apologised for the mischance upon the Pilot and the smile of good luck upon himself that had flung their roads together again. Adams answered him with full courtesy, for his liking was now generally towards those who were silent rather than those who talked.

The man fell in beside him and jocularly remarked: "It will not be for long, however; for the span of the Pilot's pace——"

"I will shorten my pace, then," Adams interrupted him, "I perceive that you are a seaman—and the company of seamen is growing scarce."

"Only at sea, An-jin," the man replied. "On land there are seamen a-plenty; for it is on land that they must stay now that they have a ship and no licence to sail it, as I have; or else a licence and no ship—as you have."

"Where have you been?" asked Adams, "that you should say I have no ship? I thought every sailor in Japan would have heard of my junk at Kawachi that can turn on her beams and sail to windward."

"True," said the man. "But I have heard more than that—
how that the ship you desire is not a small junk, but a great
vessel to compass the roof of the world—like the ship of the
Spaniards that chanced upon a burning, so that its commander
perished. I have heard that your ship has never come. I have
heard also, An-jin—but I know not with what measure of truth
—that it will not."

He watched the Pilot from the tail of his eye; but the Pilot
continued the slow swing of his paces, his head drooped a little
forward, his shoulders a little bent.

"The measure of truth," he said slowly, "is a full one. It will
not come, that ship. So I go now to Yedo—to the Emperor—
for leave to build one."

"You, An-jin!" the man exclaimed, and had it not been that
laughter on such a point was forbidden by the more obvious
laws of decency, he would have laughed. "You—to build a
ship——"

"And why not?" said Adams. "Again where have you been
that you should not know of the ships I have already built?"

"Not only have I heard—as all men have heard," said the
man; "but I saw your ships; and better ships I never have seen."

"Very well, then," said Adams. "Do you think then that I
have forgotten how to build a ship? Or are you among those
who think that it was Kuru the carpenter that built those
ships, or Shongo the Admiral who is now well-nigh blind?"

"I know," said the man, "as all but imbeciles must know,
that the builder of those ships was An-jin of Yedo and no
other. They know also that the Pilot was in those days a
strong man, hale as a lion——"

"And what has a belly-ache to do with the building of a
ship?" Adams demanded. "It is with his head that a man
builds ships, my friend, not with his stomach."

"True," said the traveller—"and with time."

"My time," said Adams grandly, "is my own."

The man glanced at him again, to note a certain pallor in the
cheeks that had been famously red; but he would say no word
of ill or doubtful omen. He slightly shifted the conversation's
course.

"You have doubtless estimated, An-jin," he said, "how many

—or how few—good ships were sent to the bottom of the sea by certain sea-robbers last year. Tales are told. I name no names. You, not I, may know the truth of these tales. I hear only what I hear—and make no comment. But it is said that between Patani and Hirado, between the Philippines and Nagasaki, in the last year twenty good ships went, empty, to the bottom. They were Englishmen, Spaniards and Portuguese—but the ships were equally good. They were robbed, and then burned or sunk. They could have been equally robbed—and then sailed over the roof of the world."

Adams stopped in the road. In the tongue of his own dim country he exclaimed, "God Almighty—you mean steal a ship?"

The man quietly said: "These ears are doubtless choked with the dirt befitting one so mean as the listener. The purport of your last honourable remark did not penetrate to his addled wits."

"I remarked," Adams explained, and the man saw that his humour was good, "that you would have me steal a ship."

"Rather," said the man; "the demon of presumption urged me to suggest that you rescue a good ship from the fate that befalls garbage, and honour it with a sailing over the world's roof. It is even said of your junk lying at Kawachi with her ports grinning with ordnance and her steel-girt gunwales—but there; it is truly said that gossip is for women, shampooers, barbers and cleansers of ears."

"Seamen," Adams encouraged him, "may nevertheless talk of ships."

"Your new junk, An-jin," said the other, "is no matter of ordinary ships. It is one—alone and by itself. There is no other like it. If I had had such a vessel as yours—but on all the seas there was not such a vessel."

"Sir," said Adams with full ceremony, "my poor name is known to you. The honour of knowing yours is as yet withheld from me."

"I am known by none now," said he. "I am a kinsman of Shobei, the merchant of Nagasaki. In the days before the Dutchman peopled the sea in sixes and in sevens and in round dozens of shot-spitting and ball-vomiting hulks—when there was a steady trade of junks in the seas about us, men used to call me Odori; I was never called by my proper name of Shichi, the seventh son of my mother's bearing."

"To me you are Odori then," said Adams, "for it was in trying to bring that Odori to my presence that I spent eight years in employing brave men in the name of Ieyasu."

"And the junk I had then, An-jin, beside your junk at Kawachi, would be not a junk at all but a worthless log."

When Odori (or Shichi) spoke again it was with a voice mild and soft. "Lend me your junk, An-jin, as soon as the azaleas and peonies are next in bloom, lend it to me—and before men are fishing among lotus buds for trout you shall have a ship worthy of your purpose. The rescuing of a proper ship from men who would destroy it will take no more months than the building of one would take years."

They walked in silence. The pace of Adams was loosening to its natural swing when Odori recalled him to his side.

"I would talk with you, even now," he puffed, "about this Passage. For I have had business Northward as well as South and East and West; and these other seas are now as infested with the thunder-guns of Dutchmen as a cat with fleas."

Adams slowed down to him.

He explained the Passage as he had never been able to explain it to any man before; and Odori the pirate, kinsman of Shobei the thug, tramped, silent, some three hundred miles beside him who had once been An-jin of Yedo. He would have given more than the trivial patience of listening to a madman's talk for the placing of his hands within reach of a weapon like the little ship that lay idle at Kawachi.

CHAPTER XXXVIII

ADAMS strode openly and magnificently about Yedo again that winter on his visits to the city from his home. Pompous men who would have looked the other way from him to whom Hidetada had made a gift of ten mean jackets, could find no otherwhere to look from him who roared across a street to them with a conjuror's good humour and the voice of a laughing bull. He hailed them and bore them off with him—dandies, bloods or curmudgeons—to unbend them in a tea-house with his open hand and his robustious humour, to warm them with his prodigious swagger. They took no offence at it; for the secret in him was neither guile nor vulgarity, but only his happiness. He was a free man, knowing secretly that there was not a cavalero in all the land who was now his master. They who laughed and drank with him—good *saké* or Spanish wine to his endless cups of scalding tea—were no hucksters and underlings. And they thought of him as well as ever they had done, now that his head was held high again.

All they said was that if the tales told of his distemper were true, he carried the brunt of it like a soldier.

Old Shongo found immense pleasure in his visit. In its first minute he knew that there was news. Adams told him that there was no need now for him to solicit Hidetada's permission to build a ship; for at last the ship was come, and waiting. He explained that it was not his junk at Kawachi—for that was too small—but another, from the West.

"It is indeed good, An-jin," said the old man. "For although Ho-in of Hirado is now also dead, there is still your honourable old rascal of a father-in-law to see my setting forth. You must give me time, however, to muster nine of my men, to attend my litter properly through the streets of Yedo. I go, in a manner, to war again. It is fitting that I wear my armour; and it is likely that there are trifles of work to be done upon it by the armourer."

It was more than likely. He had last worn it in the Korean

war when dashing Ho-in from Hirado had bound a bundle of napkins to his wounded thigh and carried off the girl to mother Cocks's friend, Sangero.

Adams told him there was no need for haste. And there must be no publicity. The sailing would be in six months—or seven—or eight. He would send secret word when the ship was secretly in a Northern harbour. It was secretly also—and with great speed—that Shongo must join him; for there were many enemies still abroad to hinder their going.

The old man chuckled.

"Enemies have never been of long duration for Shongo in his armour."

"That may well be," said Adams; "but these are not open enemies; for it is not openly that men have thwarted me in this matter for the last eighteen years. It is not the swords of soldiers that we have to fight against, but the thick heads of imbeciles. If they knew we were going, they would thwart us still. With their very presence they would thwart us. So we must go like thieves—shamefully to do this most honourable of deeds. Of no other honourable man in all Japan would I ask this thing—save of myself; and of you who are still left to me as a friend—to go by night, thievishly. . . ." But even to old Shongo he could not tell more. He said, "Without your armour and your retinue of swordsmen—will you still go?"

There was the new brag and challenge about him—the dash that was impressing the tea- and *saké*-drinkers for whom he played the generous and robustious host; for this was the hour of his *hubris* when all was so clear and straight before him. He said, magnificently, "Will you still come, Shongo-the-Unsinkable, or does the hairy Pilot of Yedo go to this adventure alone?"

"Cool your neck, my son," said Shongo. "If you say 'go quietly,' I go quietly; for it is your adventure, not mine. I go only so that no man may sail from here to go further North than I have been. . . . But you say there are still eight months to the time of going? Eight months——"

"What of it?" said Adams. "Eight months—after eighteen years——"

"It is a pity," said Shongo thoughtfully. "Now would

have been a better time."

"Can you not wait eight months more?" Adams spoke in a gentle, cajoling manner.

"To me it is nothing," said Shongo. "One of my legs and both my eyes are so much cargo; but there the matter rests. With you it is different. So long ago as two years it was estimated by certain men of judgment, who saw you in a spasm, that there were not six months of life in you. Men very easily die within eight months; it often takes them no longer to be born. Therefore I say it is a pity we do not start now."

A shadow, for an instant, darkened the Pilot's grey face—from the wing, perhaps, of Nemesis hovering over the brag of him. He said, "But it was two years ago that men made that estimate; and here I still am. And now that the waiting is a matter of the winter only—and the spring and the early summer——"

Shongo diverted him from the ways of speech that lead towards ill luck. "To me it is all one," said he. "I am ready. To-morrow—or in six months or eight—send me the word. Only let the land journey be a short one. And let us by all means take a human cook with us; for I once ate victuals prepared by a hairy man and even now my stomach is torn by demons in combat with a wild cat at the very thought of it."

"Have no fear," said Adams, "my boy comes with us. I have talked with him fully, and he is ready. I shall soon confer upon him a sword, for he is worthy; he has served me well."

CHAPTER XXXIX

THE *Gift of God* sailed late from Kawachi—as late as the end of the first week in May. For, from the swinging independence and the new, not unpleasing swagger about her owner, there had grown an arrogance in him.

Other men (even Santvoort) with junks and cargoes and licences made a great pother of their preparations to get southward in mid-monsoon; but Adams moved expansively in the manner befitting a gentleman with an easy mind.

Cocks fussed about him, seeing that summer was well on its way to them, and that all other ships in the direction of China had already sailed.

"The winds are already shaking, Captain Adams," he wailed. "You will miss your monsoon."

"Wind?" said Adams. "Monsoon?—what are winds, man—and monsoons—to a ship and a crew like mine?"

For the ship was the wonder of the seaboard and the crew was the very breath of many a tale that was now told of other days. It was of the men who had rallied to the token of Odori whenever that token had been presented to them by a traveller. They had rallied now, the full thirty—except that in the stead of seven of them there came their sons; for the seven were infirm or dead. Odori of the road was now Shichi, the Taipan of these hearties—the Japan Captain of hands properly indentured to An-jin of Yedo under his licence for trade Southward and East.

"But there is my money, Captain Adams——" Cocks insisted; for he had handed over five hundred good tael to Adams, adventuring them personally on the vaguest ghost of a possibility of trade into China.

"Have no fear for your money," said Adams. "It has never been safer than now." It was sealed up and lodged in the strong room of Zanzeburro, to be given back to Cocks in December of that same year, 1620—the end of the tenth moon in the seventh year of Genwa.

The long-shore-men of Kawachi debated whether skiffs would be needed to tow the *Gift of God* from the roadstead to the open sea. Wagers were won by the "Noes"; on the sixth of May her spritsail flickered and filled. The mizzen was hoisted and the two were enough, with Adams at his wheel, to slide her—in the wind's teeth, as the long-shore-men said—out to sea.

The cook, with his new sword-hilt at his middle, ran the flag up to the peak—"Ange's cullers" that had so offended Saris, the old rag of a St. George's Cross that he had always put out at the window of his mean lodging in a poor house of the town. . . .

Thus, sailing at the tail-end of the monsoon, they would waste no time under the scrutiny of prying eyes in harbours. Odori agreed with Adams that a crew was best, in any case, kept out of loitering ashore. The time, till the first and fleetest and best of ships should be coming Eastwards and North, was to be spent in drilling the crew to the handling of the strange sails; also, said Odori, in accustoming them to the tricks of fire-arms. . . .

On the fourth day out at sea Adams gave the wheel to Odori, who cared nothing for the little Dutch compass on the binnacle so long as there was sun and moon or star in the sky. Adams went to his deckhouse and sat for an hour, coldly sweating.

When he could, he went back to the poop again and said, "It is time to set them to learning, Odori. . . . We will put her about, against the wind."

"But you said a week or more, An-jin, of straight southward sailing to get quite clear——"

Adams interrupted him by squatting quickly down. Leaning forward, that Odori need not scrutinise his face, he said, "But the wind is good to-day, Odori. Gentle and steady. We have made great way in the last three days. We have made a week's way, I tell you. Pipe up your men to take in the main, as we have showed them——"

The look which Odori glimpsed of the Pilot's lowered face could have been a look of most hideous anger. The man had to be humoured yet awhile—and the sooner he showed them the secrets of his ship, thought Odori, the better.

The square mainsail and the staysails were taken in and the *Gift of God* was put about to windward.

Adams squatted on beside Odori at the wheel—staring, it seemed, at some spot on the deck before him.

"An-jin," Odori said, an hour after the third staysail had been re-set, and he had been holding her so close that the wind was half a gale in his grinning face.

An-jin made no answer; and Odori, looking down at him, saw that the knuckles of his fists clenched on the deck were knobs of ivory—bloodless; for all the blood of his body seemed to be thrusting knots in the veins of his hairy hands. Such hands, Odori estimated, could strangle a bullock, as such a pressure in veins could well be strangling the Pilot himself—and with him the demon's skill that as yet was his alone for handling that lovely weapon, the *Gift of God*.

"An-jin!" he exclaimed. "Pilot most honourable, are you honourably ill?"

Adams, losing none of the grip that whitened his knuckles and blackened his prodigious veins, said only, "Eh—what?"

"I said, are you ill?" and he yelled, frantically, for the Pilot's boy.

Nursing of men so that life might be maintained in them had never provided much entertainment for Odori. The medicines in the handsome case at his girdle were three only: an emetic, a purge and a poison.

"An-jin," he said again, and he spoke simply and honestly and from the very bottom of his heart. "Honourable An-jin—do not, I pray you, die."

Adams said, "No—not die, honourable Odori. Not die. Call—call to that boy."

Odori called again; and at the moment of his calling the boy came up the small companion with a tray of dishes and tea. He—in front of Adams so that he saw not only his knuckles and his hands but his face also—banged down the tray and dropped to his knees and his haunches before his master.

"It is well, boy," Adams ground out to them between his teeth. "The Taipan will honour me by eating my meal presently. For I—as you see—help me——"

"But the ship, An-jin?" Odori besought him. "Let us put the ship about and set the sail again for our proper course, instead of this homeward one."

"The ship is very well," said Adams. "Very well. It were good for some of the crew to learn to hold her against the wind. For we shall need more steersmen. I shall be back—presently. We will put her about then."

A distinct and peculiar, a not ungenial God Almighty had never been altogether absent from Adams. He prayed to Him now, as he crept and tottered with the boy's help to his cuddy. The burden of his prayers was a request for a few more days and nights of life; and that those same nights should be moonless and starless and that the days should be lighted only by a light that came from a sky like a blanket of lead, with neither sun nor ray from the sun to challenge the needle of a compass.

The odds were already good in favour of concession to his prayer—with regard to the nights at any rate; for a bank of cloud had been rising slowly from the horizon for the past three hours.

The boy had been instructed by the wizard-shampooer of Yokosuka with his soft and slender bamboo tubes. In half an hour Adams was easier to the extent that his jaws no longer clamped his teeth together, and that he lay upon his bunk and for a time quietly wept.

He also thought.

When he could speak without the speech being choked or shaken from him, he said: "The other needle which you packed in my chest, boy. Give it to me; and tell the Taipan that I am better and will come to him when I have rested a while. Then go and bring me some nails. Two or three will suffice; but let no man observe you."

The boy gave him the compass in its wooden case, the exact fellow to the one on the binnacle—a single needle glued to a card, swung on a brass pivot.

Adams said, "Put it under my pillow till you are back to keep the door. And leave the door open now, that I may see the clouds."

When the boy was gone he scrambled to his knees and steadied himself with a hand on the lantern-jamb above his bunk, and prayed again to Almighty God.

He thanked Him very heartily for the present relief in his pain and begged that it might be remitted altogether while he dealt with the matter of the compass, and at such other times as any particular action might be needed of him. And he thanked Him—almost congratulated Him—for the steps that had already been taken with the clouds. It could almost be said now with certainty that the night would be starless.

The boy came back. "The Taipan is in a frenzy, my lord," he said. "It is for four hours now that we have been returning to Japan."

"Four hours," mumbled Adams. "Aye—four hours. At half the pace that we had been coming away from it—for eighty."

He drew himself slowly up to sitting.

"Mind the door," he said, and drew the compass box from under his pillow. He withdrew the lid and got slowly upon his knees again, as he had done to address himself to God. He addressed himself now to the compass, aligning the longer edge of the box to the edge of the lantern-jamb running truly forward and aft.

"Remove my swords," he told the boy, "to the far corner; and lay yours with them."

The boy obeyed. "Now," said Adams, as the needle steadied, "give me the lead-point with which I write, so that I may make a mark."

With the pencil he marked, inside the box, the point where the needle had settled to North. He wiped sweat from his forehead and neck, and mumbled a groan or a curse, or another prayer.

"Can you not rest awhile, my lord?" asked the boy, "—till the pain is abated?"

Adams grinned at him. "At other times, boy," he said, "—before this, there has been no pain. . . ."

He closed his eyes to rest in his pain, or remote from it; to meditate; or to look without thought upon some distant, quiet scene of Gillingham in Kent or of Hemi-mura near Yedo.

When he withdrew himself from the torpor he saw that the boy had assumed his sword again and was watchful by the door. He took the compass and lifted the needle and its card from the pivot.

"The writing lead again, lad," he said, "and a bit of paper."

The boy gave him the lead and a page from the end of the log book.

"Fold it, clean and straight down the middle, for my hands shake. . . . Now again, edge to folded edge . . ." and he had as true a right-angle as was given by the wooden protractor on his table—which was too large to go inside the compass-box.

He took the paper and fumbled it into the box, one corner at the brass pivot, another at the mark he had made. Along the other edge of the folded paper, at right angles to the North line, he drew another line on the box's bottom.

"Now, boy," he said, "along this line you must carve, carefully and steadily with my knife, slots that will take the two honourable nails you have brought. We must fix them in —somehow."

"We can hold them in, master"—said the boy—"for whatever purpose you seek, with plugs of honourable rice."

"Good," said Adams, "for my purpose is, as soon as the darkness comes—with neither moon nor star—that North shall become West; and the East, North. You must help me, boy—you must help me . . ." He had but a little way to go now, with the twisting and racking that was in his vitals, to be talking nonsense and taking the boy's mind from the business that was delicate in the dim light within the cuddy, his eyes possibly from the fingers that nimbly plied the knife-blade to gouge and chip the housings for the nails in the slab of old mahogany. He checked himself; he checked the cook's inattention also, when he was saying, "Is there not my vow to my master—and a further vow also to the Lady Bikuni?"

"Tell me," said Adams, "as soon as the nails will lie in flat and flush. Hurry—but see that you work exactly to the lines. . . ."

The pain was easier, in that he could think somewhere behind it and in some way removed from it, instead of himself being the chaos of torture.

He had no illusions. He had thought at other times, once or twice, that he would die. But this time it was different.

He knew.

With his eyes shut and his hands tightly clenched under the coverlet he could see his chart and the course they had been making—for eighty hours South-West by South as straight as any demon could have stretched a kite-thread, with the great mainsail full before the wind. . . . Another day of it, before he had put them about, would have brought them to Formosa . . . and the mumble from him now was neither groan nor prayer, but a whole-hearted curse.

He fumbled again at the medicine case at his girdle and took a morsel of dark paste from a small ivory ladle set in one of the phial-stoppers.

"Go, get your rice now," he said, when the boy showed him that the nails lay snug in the slots he had carved for them. "Tell the Taipan that I will soon be well enough to join him, and to speak with him."

He hid the box again while the boy was gone.

When the nails were bedded in a paste of rice he hung the card and needle on the pivot and set the case on the lantern-jamb. When it had swung and settled, the card's West nuzzling at the mark he had made for the old North, the sound in his throat would have been, at other times, a chuckle.

CHAPTER XL

When it was full dark and he was still squatted beside Odori on the poop, the boy again brought a tray of food and this time set it before Adams. "I have ventured," said he, "to prepare a dish or two for the Taipan also and have set them in the comfort of his own place."

"Good," said Adams. To Odori he said, "Please accept our small courtesy. While you are gone there is scarcely need of another to come. The boy can hold the wheel while I eat."

"You can eat, then?" asked Odori.

"Aye," said Adams. "The spasms do not last long."

When Odori was gone the boy went quickly down to bring Adams a coverlet, and in the coverlet the false compass. Setting the lantern to light the tray before Adams he drew out the pegs on the binnacle and changed the compasses.

He himself then ate the food.

When Odori returned, Adams said, "We will put her over to Westward presently, in accordance with our talk."

The talk had been, for the most part, a rigmarole to Odori.

The crazy Pilot had tottered up from the cuddy, bringing a crazy chart. The talk concerning the points and marks upon it had been so much crackling breath wasted; for that was not the kind of chart that Odori could follow. A thought satisfied him, however; it was as a rag and a wreck of a man that this same Pilot had sailed the wreck of a ship and the rags of a crew to Japan. If he was no better than a corpse now with the writhing mystery of life somehow still left in it, he could sail them where he had said he was going to sail them—for their ship was no wreck and the crew was one which their old leader knew to be already a matter of legend and history. . . . And the Pilot had said he would carry them straightway to the richest seaboard of China.

It was a crazy thought at the first hearing; but while Odori regarded it, it had become a good one. They were already, Adams explained with his broad thumb stabbing the chart, in the neighbourhood of Formosa. Soon, if they held their original course, they would be among prying lands and among seamen who were lusty and armed and loitering for the turn of the monsoon and whatever the tides might bring to them.

It was possible, said he—if it was not indeed likely—that he himself would shortly die. Odori and his honourable crew as yet knew little of the ship, and nothing of its weapons. In peaceful waters, and unobserved, he could teach them enough concerning both with the life that still remained to him. That very night he would begin his teaching. Their course to the rich coast of China was North-West. Odori should see, from chart and compass and hour-glass in the lantern's light, how to steer North and West and North and again West to carry them there. The men, when they had eaten and rested, should learn in darkness to manage the halyards.

Looking at the chart and at the Pilot's thumb so pressed upon it that its nail was the colour of the chart itself, Odori had seen junks afloat off the coast of China—fat and rich and helpless. He surrendered his own poor wits to the judgment of the Pilot.

So he said: "Very well. We will put her where you will. Is it well that I take the wheel now that you may rest awhile?" He was uneasy to be at his learning of the Pilot's last secrets; uneasy for the Pilot to rest himself so that he might have the strength to show them on the morrow how to lade and lay and fire the pieces, as he had shown that art to pikemen and fishers to batter the walls of Osaka for the mighty Ieyasu.

"A seaman of your genius," Adams said as Odori came beside him, "such a man will have perceived, awake or asleep, even under the planking of a deck, how the wind has gently shifted in the last half-hour."

"I had indeed noted it," said Odori.

Adams said, "Good. From North-East, where you left it, condescending to the uneatable meal we had prepared for you, it shifted to a little West of North."

"I had noted it," Odori bragged, and took the wheel. "We hold her Northward now?"

"Aye," said Adams. "Northward till the sand is out. Then Westward for two turnings of the glass. Then North again for one . . ."

Almighty God had answered his prayer better than he could have answered it himself. Nought was visible but the hourglass and the compass-card swaying below the lantern. Thus Odori, dreaming of China, would hold the *Gift of God* North-Eastward for Japan.

"Go below, An-jin," Odori softly coaxed him. "Rest after the pain that has been upon you." For no man twisted into the earlier sweat could instruct men in the use of ordnance or the handling of sails.

"We will make one turning that you may see how sail is shortened for it."

"Now?" asked Odori.

"Presently," said Adams. "Presently, when the sand is out." His eyes were fastened upon the hour-glass, and he was frightened.

For an hour he had squatted still, utterly still—and he had been easy. When the sands were out and the moment was come for him to bring any movement whatever to his middle, God alone knew what torment might come again upon him.

The sand did run out, and Odori turned the glass and piped up his crew. They nimbly took in the staysails in the black darkness, Odori shouting to them the mumblings of Adams, whose haunches were set tight upon his heels. His fists were hard upon the deck, his arms splayed to stay him against the lurch of the *Gift of God* when she should swing over.

The boy was at the wheel, waiting for the Pilot's word.

The swing of the mizzen boom, and the boat's lurch were a swing and a lurch within Adams; no more. They were a fantastic joke. Just the swing and the lurch inside him; a stiffening and then a sudden slackness. No twinge of pain. The mantle of clammy sweat had been assumed for nothing.

At the shock of painlessness he crumpled forward as other men crumple to the stab of a dirk, for he had knelt tightly upon his robe to make a stay of it from his shoulders to his knees. This detail of forethought was recommended in the rite for those who knelt to take up the dirk for the last privilege of their nobility; for it was not seemly that a gentleman should tumble, from any cause, upon his back.

The boy and Odori both turned at the bump of his forehead and the rattle of his sword hilts on the deck.

"He is dead. He is dead. . . . Our Pilot is dead!" Odori growled in his despair.

"Look you to the wheel," said the boy. "Hold her fast and steady to the West as he directed. He has swooned that he may rest."

"Men will carry him below, that you may revive him quickly," said Odori.

"When he honourably swoons," said the boy, "it is I that carry him. A man, however, may carry the lantern till I have made a light in the cabin."

The joke continued. From the swoon of sheer astonishment Adams drifted to a bottomless, splendid sleep.

After the second turning of the hour-glass Odori set a man at the wheel and came wistfully to the cuddy door.

"Does his Excellency still live?" he asked the boy.

"He sleeps," said the boy, "as a kitten. No man may wake him from such ease."

"But the course?" said Odori. "Whither am I to steer now that the two hours have gone?"

"Steer," said the boy, "even as he has commanded—West-ward. It is well; but look to it that you remember the hours of Westward, so that when he wakes he may perform his magic of making an honourable mark upon his chart."

"When you may wake him, tell him that Odori humbly waits upon his word—steering Westward."

"I will tell him," said the boy.

When he had been vigilantly squatting for some time, listening to the happy breathing of Adams, he drew his fine new sword from its scabbard and moved upon his knees to lay it away in the far corner of the cabin; for this thing he had seen that the Pilot always did for any deep and steady watching of the needle.

He quietly took the binnacle compass-case from Adams's chest and laid its longest edge, as accurately as he could, between his knees along a floor-seam.

He sat and watched it—the true needle, while Odori faithfully steered by the false one.

CHAPTER XLI

When Adams awoke, he started and said, "Is the sky still black and starless?"

"As black," said the boy, "as a virtuous woman's tooth. It is for some three hours that you have slept; and we have sailed for that time steadily West by the Taipan's needle; and by ours North. For I presumed to watch my master's needle—my honourable sword properly remote."

Truly had Adams called certain men of Japan "stowte seamen" . . . and this man was a cook.

"What canvas does she carry?" he asked.

"The mizzen only," said the boy.

"Bid Odori set the staysails as they were before, and the spritsail also."

When the boy had gone, Adams wondered why it was that he hurried so—for the spasm had quite passed and he was well again. He moved cautiously in the bunk, as any man would move among scattered explosives; and there was no detonation of pain—not even a spark or a hiss or a crackle. He was well. . . .

He had thought at other times that he would die and had lived; but he knew that this time, thinking he would live he would, in fact, die.

He thought clearly, and peacefully.

There were the many times in the many years when he could have gone back to England, and had not gone. The only reason he had been able to find, sound enough for setting down on paper, was that the one thing he had set out to do in Japan he had not done. He knew now, with the pain gone from him only because the fury of it was utterly spent, that the only thing that there had ever been for him to do in Japan was die there . . . . He had thought of a great sailing, against great odds. . . And they were making the great sailing now, he and the boy, to bring the *Gift of God*—while there was still breath in his body and the Emperor's licence in his breast—to a mooring in a Japanese harbour, where the *Gift of God* should pass from himself to someone other than Odori.

"There remain some three hours of darkness," he said when the boy came back.

"Four," said the boy, "or four and a half to full light."

"That is no matter," said Adams. "For if the first glimmer come not upon the whole sea and sky in the same moment, but from the East——"

"If you would that the Taipan should fall into a good heavy sleep I could prepare another meal for him. He will in any case be sleepy in two hours from now; for he will have steered all night. It is contrary to his habit."

"That," said Adams, "is a good thought. Prepare the meal so that he will begin to sleep for six or eight hours in about two hours from now. When he wakes again, if the sky is clear, we can put the true compass on the binnacle. North and West instead of East and North for a few hours will be no great matter. . . . A pity; but, if we are put to it by a clear sky, no great matter. I can correct it while he sleeps again." He quickly set his teeth upon his tongue to keep it still, but too late; before he had been able to do it, the words had slipped out—"There will be time . . ."

By the wheel again, he who knew where the East and North truly lay, suspected that he could see the direction from which the dawn stole out along the rim where the sea was held to the lid of heavy sky.

Odori slept below; and no seaman of the crew noted, or cared, whether East were North, or even West. For the Pilot of Yedo, with legends old and new of his wizardry, was at the wheel. For them it was enough.

At noon, when Odori stirred and the woman he had brought with him was seen to be engaged with the tray and pots and dishes, Adams considered the sky. It was still a solid, heavy lid, and there was nought but the beads moved on the binnacle, recording the turns of the hour-glass, to tell any man whether it were noon or morning; nought but the needle to say whether they were heading North or West or East or South. There was a chance that the lid might crack or break or melt in a moment, or at a time when the compass could not be changed. It was a chance; but Adams took it. It was a small compensation, but it was the most he could offer to the demons—or whatever they were—that lurked by the throne of Almighty God to tamper with the destiny of man and to make of his achievements greatness or littleness, or nothing. He offered the compensation of this hazard for the fool's challenge in his words—"There will be time;" for the arrogance of the thought that there was no hurry.

The false compass was left upon the binnacle for a dozen hours.

Odori steered by it.

The *Gift of God* made fine headway for Japan.

The luck held.

The boy had slept through the day that he might watch by night if any star should appear to give the lie to the compass. How he should perform the necessary feat of changing the boxes in such a case had not been exactly determined; but Adams had confidence in him who, among his more casual achievements, had lifted two bottles of Spanish wine from under the very noses of Saris and the lusty, jealous cook of the English house. The only provision made against the appearance of such a star was that the cook was to take his trick at the wheel while Odori rested.

Adams saw the tray of morsels set for him under the cuddy's lantern. He said, "Better not, lad." He drank, however, a cup of tea and very slowly sipped another. The sizzle of it against his thirst encouraged him to think that it arrived, as a liquid, nowhere.

They set the compass upon the floor and saw that the needle on the binnacle held true in its treachery.

"Do we sail now upon that finding of the world's roof?" the boy asked. "Is my steering, when I hold and turn the wheel, upon my Lord's great purpose?"

"Aye," said Adams. "It is upon the great purpose."

The boy said, "It is well."

On the chart spread over the table which stood two handsbreadths above the floor, Adams plotted the day's course from his memoranda. He said, "Another six days like this and we shall do it."

"To-morrow perhaps a little rice could be honourably digested," said the boy.

A man could easily live for six such days, thought Adams, without chancing the honourable digestion of the poison that was rice.

He was wrong. By the next day's noon he was chewing dry rice grains; chewing them, and chewing them and chewing them till they were disintegrated and somehow gone, and there was nothing for him to swallow that could be hurtful. He had the cunning now to drink no drop of tea or wine or water, till thirst should parch him to the marrow; for, looking back, he knew that it was in his bladder that the trouble had first begun.

Odori meanwhile slept soundly again after another breakfast prepared by the boy, and the *Gift of God* raced to North and East and North and East, with the boy at the wheel and Adams close beside him.

The sky was lifting. There was still no cleft in it, no straight ray of light, nor shadow. But any man with an eye or a nose like Odori's, with his mind upon the matter, could have told that North was not East.

Adams could not willingly surrender, even for a few hours, his course.

"Boy," he said, "you shall steer this afternoon, while I entertain the Taipan with some practice of firearms and ordnance."

"Will you yourself man a gun and lay it?" asked the boy. "You who have eaten nothing for two days? Were it not better for you to steer while I teach them the firing of a piece?"

"It were better to go ahead while we may," said Adams. "To-day he would perhaps be better engaged by me than by you. This very night there may be stars; and to-morrow there may be sun."

The boy said thoughtfully: "This blade of mine has not been tested yet. Since you gave it to me, a dozen other weapons have always been tried before my arrival at the executions to which I have hurried; for there are many new swords in the land now. There has been nothing left for me. And since this Odori is one to resist our purpose I could easily kill him, on a pretext."

"But we want the crew," said Adams.

"For how long are they to be in ignorance of the design?"

"Four days should do it," said Adams, looking at the chart. "In four days they can go to hell, the lot of them."

"In four days," asked the boy wondering, "shall we have come to the end of the world?"

"Aye," said Adams. "Likely."

The boy said, "It is well. Four days are a small matter; the girl tells me he is a good drinker. I will give her the bottles that are of such small service to yourself—or to me—while this matter is in hand. Whenever he is not asleep for these four days, he can be suitably drunk."

"But there must be one to steer," said Adams.

"There is this speaker," was the boy's answer.

"There is work enough for him," said Adams, "for he and I must not sleep at the same time. . . ." Suddenly he stopped; and cursed in slow phrases of his own country that became, by an easy transition of thought, a prayer again to his Almighty God. Then he said, "Change that compass now, while you can. Give him the true one. We will hold North and Eastward while we ourselves are at the wheel. You or I. And when we cannot help it, the dog must have his North and West. I can still do it, even so. . . . But that foolery of shooting off ordnance I cannot do—for him or any man. It is coming again; and I must be still."

The boy said, "Below—or here?"

"Here," said Adams, for there had been times when the endurance of dumb and solid immobility had been enough to evade an issue.

The boy with a knee upon the wheel had already changed the compass on the binnacle for the one carried against his breast.

"Set it here," said Adams. "I'll pick out those nails, so that I, too, may watch the needle. Hold her East now—to the new and true East you have before you. We will turn North before he comes up. If I should be—below—do not let him set the mainsail on the Westward runs. We must not make too much way."

Odori was distressed by what he saw when he came up—the Pilot fastened again to the deck in the shape of a timberman's sawing-stool, or a great frog. His face was haggard and set too hard for the small courtesy of even a smile. But Odori's temperament was a buoyant and hopeful one, and he had a good conceit of himself. The man had recovered before and would likely recover again. Already he, Odori, could handle the ship. All he needed was sight of a coast. The Pilot's next day of ease would be enough for the handing over of his last secret—the ordnance. In the meantime he was pleased to see that the Pilot had a needle set before him which, well or ill, he could continue to watch. That would bring the coast.

Euphemistically and very amiably he said, "I am happy to see the Pilot in good health."

Adams answered very quietly—for he was still trying the device of utter stillness. "And I to see that the Taipan has slept well. But excuse me from talk. I have some pain. When it is better—or worse—I will tell you of the course."

"Pray do not so concern yourself," said Odori. "So long as the Pilot watches a needle we others are content." He glanced at the compass and at the sails. "I noted, as I slept," he bragged, "that the wind had again shifted."

Adams grunted.

The sounds that came from him from time to time thereafter were not of words. They came from teeth against teeth.

Then he spoke. "Hold her Northward and Northward and Northward, Taipan, till I send word for West. We make the Yellow Sea, where there are harbours friendly to such as you and me. I watch the course below, for I take my needle and my chart."

"The pain is better, then?" Odori asked.

"It is worse," said Adams.

The boy lifted him down the companion; and he crawled to his lair.

He remained on the floor and rested.

The boy took his swords and laid them in the rack above the bunk and accurately set the compass along a floor-seam before his crouching master. Beside it he set the chart, and beside that the dividers and writing lead.

"At every turning of the hour-glass, boy," said Adams, "if I should forget to tell you, you must go above and drop the log as you have seen me drop it. From the moment it reaches the water till the line is fully out you must count; and then you must come down again and count to me at the same pace."

After the first performance of this duty, when Adams had said paternoster and the doggerel verses to the boy's counting, and had so recorded the pace, he said, "Shut the door and come near. I would speak."

"Speak later, master," said the boy; but he swiftly obeyed. "Speak later, when you are easier."

"I speak, you fool, while I can."

He would have moistened his lips with his tongue; but it was dry also, and in the fumbling movements of it he bit it.

He rested.

"It is possible," he said, "that before we make land, I die."

"So," said the boy, "it would honourably appear."

"And, if I die," said Adams, "you must die also."

"It is fitting," said the boy.

"Thrice damned and blasted fool!" Adams snarled—and then checked his thoughts from one of the languages that was theirs to the other. "It is not of your idiot's belly-cutting pranks that I speak. It is a bigger matter. Let me drink, that I may tell you."

"Drink?" asked the boy, "to distend the Pilot's bladder?"

"To burst the world's bladder!" said Adams, "so long as you understand. . . . Give it to me."

The boy gave him the horn of water.

"These men," Adams said, "are murderers and robbers. The Taipan is Odori, the Dancing Shark, whom I hunted for my Lord Ieyasu and never found. I brought them to steal for me a ship and men for our sailing over the world. If I can get us back to land again—to Japan—all will be well. The *Gift of God* will be taken and held for Joseph, my honourable son; the licence to sail it will be his. These rascals will creep away again to the holes and the shops where they have hidden for ten, and a dozen, years. If I should die here, the bloodiest villains of Japan will have the handiest junk that has ever sailed her seas. . . ."

"Odori, the Dancing Shark, would be killed by me," said the boy.

"It is not enough to kill Odori," said Adams. "Every one of his thirty can sail her now, well enough. You must kill the ship also. When you are satisfied that I am dead, you must go below and fire the magazine. Spill a barrel and spread the powder. Take my pistol and hold it sideways to the floor. . . . You need not prime it. Cock it . . ."

"My flint," said the boy, "struck upon my sword's edge would make a better spark. It is fitting that my sword should operate."

"Sword or pistol," said Adams, "see that you make your spark."

"It is well," said the boy.

CHAPTER XLII

In the night, when Adams saw that the writhing of his hands had rent his coverlet of silk and Holland canvas into three twisted clouts, he cursed the thing and pushed it from him.

The boy knelt on the floor before the hour-glass, the lantern and the compass. In his hand was the writing lead; for he was keeping memoranda of his own on a paper napkin.

"Is Odori still at the wheel?" Adams asked.

"No," said the boy. "It is the one-eyed one, the half-wit. Odori retired two hours ago. Since you last reckoned we have made three hours to Westward and two to North."

"I come," said Adams. "I will lie there again, upon the floor."

The boy laid him down from the bunk and dragged him gently to the chart and moved the lantern. Adams could still move the dividers and protractor accurately enough, with his wrists jammed hard upon the edge of the board, to make a point on the chart.

"Go you to the wheel," he told the boy. "If Odori sleeps, get men enough to shorten sail while you put her over from North to East. When you have done it, send the half-wit to watch by my door, in case I have need to call you. But hold her to the East, and note down the running, in case I myself should swoon. Do not try to rouse me from it unless there is need; for it is comfortable."

Whenever the words which he was grinding out slipped or drifted from one language to the other, he saw his error and came back and put the matter right, so that the instructions were quite clear before the boy went up.

At dawn he was back again in the cuddy kneeling beside Adams.

"You sent for me," he said.

The Pilot was a heap of wreckage; and it was like the movement of wind in wreckage that the short breaths entered his body and rattled out again through the foam of beard.

"Aye, I sent for you . . ." The words left him spent. The boy offered him water, and he drank, and the breaths came again, and went, shaking him to life.

"What would you?" the boy asked.

Stupidly, it seemed, his lord again mumbled, "Aye—I sent for you."

The boy stood thoughtfully over him. "Assuredly," he said, "you are dying."

Adams paid no particular heed.

The boy slowly drew his sword that had not yet been tested, and balanced it—the blade's point upon the floor—to find the grip towards the hilt's end that should give the blade a hurtling swing.

"An-jin of Yedo," he said slowly. "Speak. Would you that I strike, and make an end of it?"

This was, perhaps, the errand for which he had summoned the fellow. But he said, "Wait. I consider . . ."

He looked upon the blade that was a gleam of lantern-light; at the taut, bared arm of the man of six or eight-and-twenty— a father of some dozen years' standing who was called "boy" . . . and he considered. One flicker of that gleam that was the sword's untested edge and all the chaos—of muddled plottings on the chart, of hazard, and of the torment in his vitals —would be, as the boy had suggested, ended. Within a minute of that peace the edge of that same true sword would strike the spark from the boy's flint; Odori and the lot of them would be blown to hell and smithereens. . . . But in some consciousness that was remote from the writhings of tortured viscera, remote from a chart with lines upon it that also writhed in their struggle towards straight accuracy, remote from a vow of fealty and of peace-keeping given to a lord of men now dead, remote also from the respite that was offered by the boy's taut arm, there burst in the heart of Adams a guffaw of laughter.

It was old Magome Sageyu that tickled him to it—Magome Sageyu and the land's countless other old posturing cavaleros like him; little dead Ho-in of Hirado with his pompous limp and his giant's thirst, Oyen the secretary of two Shoguns, and even Shongo-the-Unsinkable (and the well-loved) with his old moth-eaten and rust-corroded armour. "They and their boasted belly cutting!" was the guffaw's purport in the heart of Adams.

For belly-cutting was child's play.

A dirk stuck in his vitals would have been as a cool, clean draught of water, where the thing now twisting was a weapon that any man would have disdained to bring to the slaughter of a hog or an ape.

He said to the boy, "No. Sheathe it. It is well." It was not despite only that brought the speech to him—despite of the swaggering and bragging old ruffians.

It was the boy also; for if the boy was not disintegrated in a blast of gunpowder he would return to Hemi-mura. There, in the hut among rice-plots that overhung, on the one hand the Princes' Road and on the other the Bay of Uraga, he would be lorded over by young Joseph and would truly serve Bikuni. . . . Thus it was not only despite holding him, but a link also, that had been forged between a spirit and a land. And Cocks also was of this link, he and whatever other men were at Hirado from the same country that held the small steep hill of Gillingham in Kent.

This whole business was peculiarly Adams's own. It was not for any other man that he was doing it, but for himself only. Even that other large matter, the matter of finding the Passage in a suitable ship, if such a ship had ever been his—even that had been thrust and put upon him without his properly choosing it. Coming upon him, it had claimed and possessed him, and always it had driven him. And now he was rid of that also.

It had seemed a big thing, and now it was grown small.

The big thing now was the only thing remaining. It was the only thing that had ever been his own, utterly: to get Odori and his crew back to the country that could disarm them of his weapon while it was still undrawn upon any improper purpose.

It was not for any Ieyasu that he was doing the thing. Ieyasu was long since dead. It was not for Hidetada. Hidetada had flung in his face a bundle of coolie's jackets. It was not for any prisoner or fantastic "guest." It was not for a husband of women, or a father, or a swaggering cavalero of Japan.

It was for himself only. . . .

He returned to that which was grinding his teeth together and wringing out sweat from a carcase that was as dry as parched millet-seed.

Later he spoke again, while the boy still knelt beside him.

"You may draw your sword, son."

The boy drew it.

"Perhaps—a measure of blood—like the blood-letter of Nagasaki . . ." and the boy bled him of a full measure of blood.

It may have been that testing of the new Lord-given steel that saved him; for something did.

CHAPTER XLIII

At the fourth dawn from the blood-letting the boy came from the poop to stand beside his bunk and say, "Between us and the rising of the sun, there is land."

"It is well," said Adams. "Get me above."

"But Odori is still at the wheel," said the boy.

Again Adams said, "It is well. Indeed it is better so."

Odori was not over-pleased at this reappearance of the Pilot.

For two days he had rested content in the word the boy had brought him that the Pilot deemed it best, since his indisposition had worsened, to bring the ship to Korea instead of China. Odori, as Adams well knew, was not without old friends on that coast; and Odori had little doubt of his own capacity to handle the *Gift of God* till he had found these friends. Of his powers of diplomacy and tact also he had no doubt; but he would have felt easier without the heap behind him as he stood at the wheel—the heap that was a man, cavernous-cheeked and hollow-eyed and hairy, with great talons of hands; with sword hilts—and more now than even sword hilts—the butt of a great pistol at his girdle.

"It was truly said," he remarked, as much to test the vitality of Adams as to indulge the compliment, "that the Pilot of Yedo can cajole a harbour out of any sea."

Adams did not bother. The land was as yet featureless, a smear in the dawn's haze; so he left his eyes closed.

"Perhaps," said Odori next, "—considering the honourable lassitude of the Pilot, it would be as well for him to instruct his cook to give into my hands the sailing-licence and the Emperor's seal from the Pilot's strong-box."

"The seal and the licence," said Adams, "are here within my robe; next to my swords and pistol. And they are very well so."

In an hour it was advisable for Adams to keep his eyes opened, against any shaping in the sky-line. It was too late now for any fussing with the chart and the mangled plottings upon it. A crag would, perhaps, tell him something before it had told Odori. . . .

But it did not.

After another turning of the hour-glass Odori whipped round suddenly and exclaimed, "It is not Korea there, but Japan! Ahead is Goto."

"Stand fast," said Adams.

The great pistol, its hammer of a horse's head rearing up with the flint in its jaws, was in his two hands. "Stand to the wheel, Odori. Steer as I tell you. The boy sits in the powder magazine with a flint and a steel. If I fire, even as the shot enters your body, the ship will rise as a sheet of flame and smoke into the sky. But land us and there is some money for you. For myself, I die shortly; and you may go again into your honourable retirement."

Odori stood to the wheel.

Adams spoke again. "I have kept faith, however. It was only when I had got my big ship for the sailing Northward that I was to be beholden to you. And I have not got it. Therefore this ship is still mine."

* * * * *

It was perhaps a fluke.

But the whole twenty years of his life in Japan, from the first miracle of his getting there at all, had been a fluke.

It was actually in the Kawachi basin, whence he had sailed, that Adams gave the word for letting go his last anchor.

Two days later, in the house of Zanzeburro at Hirado—the "poor house with an old St. George's Cross for cullers"—he died.

His brother-in-law, Andreas from Nagasaki, visited the sick room and lifted from it the sailing-licence and the great seal. With this as his plausibly alleged inheritance from the Pilot, he manned and lifted the *Gift of God* also, before Adams was, in fact, dead; for Odori and his thirty had again vanished, as they had vanished so many times before.

* * * * *

A trifle still remains; a tale of a nobleman of Old Japan

was the tale of his swords. For his swords were said to be his soul.

The Yoshimitsu blades of Adams were borne in the triumphant hands of Richard Cocks from Zanzeburro's to the English house; for, as Cocks records with a gusto that is dulled only by his grief, it was himself that Captain Addames in his last tormented moments had preferred over all "heathen naturals that he held for so long in frenship" as his trustee and executor; himself and the tough William Eaton.

Cocks held the swords at Hirado, while he fought master Andreas for his *léger de main* in the matter of the licence and the junk; and won the fight.

It took him eighteen months, now that Adams was gone, to gird up his loins for that preposterous journey again to Yedo. But when he had girt them, and finally mustered his boatmen and his coolies and covered the road, he noted:

"Dec. 29, 1621. I rec. a letter fron Shongo Dono, with 10 hens for a present. And I delivered the katana and wakizashi of Capt Addames, left per will to his sonne Joseph; where were tears shedd at delivery."

Thus—if there is aught in the estimates of those old Cavaleros, ended the tale of the Pilot's soul on earth.

*   *   *   *   *

As to his body: regulations were as stringent concerning the movements of the dead as they were for the living. Yet two men in the guise of coolies passed, without let or hindrance, along the length of the Princes' Road to Yedo. The two-sworded guardman of the barriers knew them for a cook and a scribe. They made no examination of the bale they carried, slung, for some hundred odd leagues, on a pole between them. The guardsmen stood aside to let it honourably pass, learning that it was the charred bones of him who had been "Pilot of Yedo."

They were finally put to rest at the top of Hemi-Mura which had been his Lordship, with the road on one hand, and on the other the waters of the Bay of Uraga. Over them was erected the small stone that commemorates him, the Englishman who gave to the legs of a young nobleman of Japan, and to a gentle girl, thigh-bones that were overlong and eyes that glinted not black only with the blackness of smoke, but brown also.

Beside the stone to the Pilot was set, fourteen years later, the stone to Bikuni. What became of Joseph, or of the Yoshimitsu blades which were said by the old ones to have become the soul of Joseph's father, no man knows.

THE END

Other TUT BOOKS available:

SHADOWINGS *by Lafcadio Hearn*

A SHORT SYNOPSIS OF THE MOST ESSENTIAL POINTS IN HAWAIIAN GRAMMAR *by W. D. Alexander*

THE STORY BAG: A Collection of Korean Folk Tales *by Kim So-un; translated by Setsu Higashi*

SUMI-E: An Introduction to Ink Painting *by Nanae Momiyama*

SUN-DIALS AND ROSES OF YESTERDAY *by Alice Morse Earle*

THE TEN FOOT SQUARE HUT AND TALES OF THE HEIKE: Being Two Thirteenth-century Japanese classics, the "Hojoki" and selections from the "Heike Monogatari" *translated by A. L. Sadler*

THIS SCORCHING EARTH *by Donald Richie*

TIMES-SQUARE SAMURAI or the Improbable Japanese Occupation of New York *by Robert B. Johnson and Billie Niles Chadbourne*

TO LIVE IN JAPAN *by Mary Lee O'Neal and Virginia Woodruff*

THE TOURIST AND THE REAL JAPAN *by Boye de Mente*

TOURS OF OKINAWA: A Souvenir Guide to Places of Interest *compiled by Gasei Higa, Isamu Fuchaku, and Zenkichi Toyama*

TWO CENTURIES OF COSTUME IN AMERICA *by Alice Morse Earle*

TYPHOON! TYPHOON! An Illustrated Haiku Sequence *by Lucile M. Bogue*

UNBEATEN TRACKS IN JAPAN: An Account of Travels in the Interior Including Visits to the Aborigines of Yezo and the Shrine of Nikko *by Isabella L. Bird*

ZILCH! The Marine Corps' Most Guarded Secret *by Roy Delgado*

Please order from your bookstore or write directly to:

CHARLES E. TUTTLE CO., INC.
Suido 1-chome, 2–6, Bunkyo-ku, Tokyo 112

or:

CHARLES E. TUTTLE CO., INC.
Rutland, Vermont 05701 U.S.A.